DANGEROUS SEXUALITIES

'. . . a cogent, intelligent . . . book . . . the best survey of the medico-moral complex and the politics of the state regulation of sexuality currently available.'

Roy Porter, *Medical History*

'Mort argues persuasively for a rethinking of social and medical attitudes to form a new politics of health and especially sexuality. A fascinating book, well argued, academic . . . it deserves a wide readership.'

British Medical Journal

Dangerous Sexualities investigates how our ideas of health and disease are linked to moral and immoral notions of sex. Beginning in the 1830s, Frank Mort shows how medico-moral systems of knowledge and power have regulated sexuality – targeting sensitive groups, generating networks of resistance, even moulding our pleasures and desires. Sexuality has been formed as a component of the social project of modernity, and Mort relates his historical narratives to the sexual choices and possibilities facing us now.

This long-awaited second edition takes on board recent scholarship, in particular the methods and techniques of cultural history. Consequently, the national and imperial dimensions of sexuality, questions of sexual geography and the continuing challenges posed for historians by the work of Michel Foucault are addressed in a new introduction. With an extended bibliography and illustrations, the second edition thoroughly updates this classic text.

Frank Mort is Professor of Cultural History and Director of the Raphael Samuel Centre for Metropolitan Cultural History at the University of East London. His recent works include *Cultures of Consumption: Masculinities and Social Space in Late Twentieth-Century Britain*, Routledge, 1996, and *Moments of Modernity: Reconstructing Britain 1945–1964*, co-edited with Becky Conekin and Chris Waters, Rivers Oram Press and New York University Press, 1999. He is currently writing a cultural history of London in the post-war period, to be published by Yale University Press.

DANGEROUS SEXUALITIES

Medico-moral politics in England since 1830

Second edition

Frank Mort

London and New York

First published 1987 by Routledge & Kegan Paul Ltd

Second edition published 2000
by Routledge
11 New Fetter Lane, London EC4P 4EE

Simultaneously published in the USA and Canada
by Routledge
29 West 35th Street, New York, NY 10001

Routledge is an imprint of the Taylor & Francis Group

© 1987, 2000 Frank Mort

Typeset in Sabon by RefineCatch Limited, Bungay, Suffolk
Printed and bound in Great Britain by
Biddles Ltd, Guildford and King's Lynn

British Library Cataloguing in Publication Data
A catalogue record for this book is available from the British Library

Library of Congress Cataloging in Publication Data
Mort, Frank.
Dangerous sexualities: medico-moral politics in England since
1830 / Frank Mort. – 2nd ed.
p.   cm.
Includes bibliographical references and index.
1. Sexual ethics–England–History.   2. England–Moral
conditions.   3. Hygiene, Sexual–England–History.   4. Public health–
England–History.   I. Title.
HQ32.M67   2000
306.7′0942–dc21   99-32888

ISBN 0–415–16733–7 (hbk)
ISBN 0–415–16734–5 (pbk)

CONTENTS

CONTENTS

CONTENTS

ILLUSTRATIONS

The illustrations appear between pp. 78–9.

NOTE ON THE SECOND EDITION

The publication of a second edition of *Dangerous Sexualities* has given me the opportunity to do a number of things: to correct minor errors which crept into the first edition, to provide the reader with a fuller original bibliography together with a bibliographical review of works published since 1987, to assess recent developments in the field of research on sexuality in a substantive new introduction and to include a set of illustrations. The text of the book remains unaltered, for it was the product of a specific moment and I have taken the view that any attempt to rewrite its arguments in the light of subsequent work would probably result in its disintegration as a text. I should like to thank Becky Conekin, who helped me to research the new bibliography, the British Library, the Fawcett Library, the Mary Evans Picture Library and the Masters and Fellows of Trinity College, Cambridge, for permission to reproduce visual material from their collections. Staff in the Humanities section of the British Library were extremely patient when I ordered numerous books and pamphlets, in order to check references. Finally, I wish to thank Heather Gibson and Fiona Bailey, my editors at Routledge, for their patience and understanding, and Daniel Virgili for his continuing support.

INTRODUCTION TO THE
SECOND EDITION

[One] scene has always lived in my memory.... It was a spring evening. Vanessa and I were sitting in the drawing room.... Suddenly the door opened and the long sinister figure of Mr Lytton Strachey stood on the threshold. He pointed his finger at a stain on Vanessa's white dress.

'Semen?' he said.

Can one really say it? I thought and we burst out laughing. With that one word all barriers of reticence and reserve went down. A flood of the sacred fluid seemed to overwhelm us. Sex permeated our conversation.... We discussed copulation with the same excitement and openness that we had discussed the nature of good. It is strange to think how reticent, how reserved we had been and for how long.... When all intellectual questions had been debated so freely, sex was ignored. Now a flood of light poured in upon that department too. We had known everything but had never talked. Now we talked nothing else.[1]

Virginia Woolf was always adept at identifying significant moments of cultural change by the use of anecdote or domestic incident. Like her famous remark that human character changed in or about 1910, Woolf's observations here about sexuality and modernity are told as the story of the Bloomsbury group's coming of age. Describing an incident in her family's London drawing-room, she casually marks the end of Victorianism and announces the beginning of sexual modernism. The atmosphere of the event is conveyed as a movement from reticence and restraint to freedom and self-expression: laughter erupts and light floods in. The transformation from one epoch to another is described as a kind of awakening – a coming alive. All of this is predicated on the subject of sex. The new world is symbolised by a shift from a regime of sexual repression to one of freedom and self-awareness. Society and culture break free from the Victorians and open out to the possibilities of modern life.

Woolf was at the forefront of proposing a new modernist chronology of sex in the years before and after the First World War. Her own and Lytton Strachey's interpretation of the end of nineteenth-century morality were part of much broader arguments made by a wide range of public intellectuals after 1900. Aided by reformulated scientific knowledge, encouraged by the gradual dissemination of Freud's own thesis on the mechanisms of repression and influenced by the social impact of the war, Victorianism became constructed as a unified and restrictive phenomenon from which contemporary society was now breaking free. The influence of this teleological narrative of sexual progress was to reverberate throughout the twentieth century. During the 1960s and 1970s, for example, social and academic interest in 'the Victorians' was revived as part of a debate about the modernisation of social life. In Britain, liberal politicians and pressure groups, together with the burgeoning movements for sexual emancipation, cast the repressive Victorians as the foil for contemporary sexual progressivism. The legacy of the nineteenth century was part of the cultural debris which needed sweeping away in the interests of creating a more tolerant and humane society.[2] Social historians of sexuality disseminated a different version of Victorianism, but they followed a similar plot line: bourgeois morality and respectability were the veneer which frequently concealed a seething underworld of sexual guilt and perverse eroticism. Pornography and prostitution were the disruptive reverse images of nineteenth-century public culture.[3]

Dangerous Sexualities first appeared in 1987, at a moment when a number of distinct traditions of scholarship and politics, together with an impending social catastrophe, were forcing a profound re-evaluation of the established scripts of sexual modernism. Michel Foucault's own major reassessment, published a decade earlier as his first volume of *The History of Sexuality*, had of course opened by challenging the whole framework of sexual repression, arguing that it was essentially part of our own mythology as 'the other Victorians'.[4] Foucault persuasively demonstrated that the progressive chronology of moral enlightenment, which cast late twentieth-century cultures in the vanguard of progress, was dependent on a myopic reading of the sexual history of European societies from the French Revolution to the First World War. Foucault's historiographical critique was double-edged: it took issue with the theoretical model which underpinned so much research on sex (the *episteme* in Foucauldian usage), while proposing an alternative method of actually writing about sexuality in history for those who were prepared to listen. At broadly the same moment, in the 1970s and early 1980s, distinctive genres of feminist, gay and lesbian history were assembling their own critiques of sexual modernisation. Linked to the lifestyle politics of the new social movements, and again challenging linear and developmental accounts, this research brought into focus the troubled and profoundly unstable history of twentieth-century sexuality. Highlighting the fact that freedom for some involved coercion and regulation for many others, these new histories revealed how access to knowledge and power about sex was shot through with ideologies of sexual and gender difference. In a much more immediate way, the accelerating impact of the AIDS pandemic was casting its own grotesque shadow over the utopias of science and progress which had underwritten the belief in sexual freedom. The moral crisis precipitated by AIDS forcibly challenged permissive morality, reasserting the historical links between health and disease and moral and immoral notions of sex.

My book registered the impact of all of these agendas. While the introduction and conclusion argued somewhat instrumentally for the need to understand dangerous sexualities in terms of a history and politics of the present, the substance of the book centred on the medico-moral complex of sexuality from the nineteenth to the early twentieth century. This was essentially a narrative about social medicine's complex entanglement with the problems of moral regulation, but the story was expanded to include competing forms of professional authority and more overt challenges to medical power, especially in the form of feminist politics However, a broader set of interpretative issues also shadowed the main action of the text. These had to do with a number of methodological questions which were raised by writing a history of sexuality. In preparing a new edition, it seems to me that it is these general themes which are among the most important raised by the book. If I choose to focus on them, rather than offering a more comprehensive overview of all of the developments in the field since the work first appeared, it is because they are currently at the centre of an unresolved debate about the future of history as an academic discipline and as a distinctive field of research. Many of these questions relate to what has recently been called the 'linguistic turn' in the human sciences. Such discussions have centred on the significance of language and meaning and their part in shaping culture.[5] For the historian the issues have become focused on the project for a new type of cultural history.

Foucault's approach to both the theorisation and the writing of a history of modern sexuality formed the single most important influence on my own research. Given the continuing outpouring of Foucauldian commentaries and critical assessments, it is worth revisiting those aspects of his work which were most significant. In the context of the story of sexual modernity two themes predominated. As important as Foucault's critique of the whiggish narrative of sexual modernism was his problematisation of the very meaning and status of sexuality itself. This denaturalisation of the object of research was at the heart of Foucault's interrogation of all forms of disciplinary power. The central issue was not whether societies say yes or no to sex, whether they permit or prohibit, but that both of these positions were part of the way in which sex was put into discourse. What mattered in consequence was how sexuality was represented: who writes, or speaks, and from what position. This accentuated relativisation of social phenomena paralleled similar research in the sociology of knowledge and in the field of human relations. In the area of sexuality Foucault's insights were anticipated by the post-war, Anglo-American traditions of labelling and role theory, with their emphasis on the constructed nature of sexual acts and values.[6] But in the 1970s and 1980s Foucault's agenda was read in conjunction with the insights derived from post-structuralist linguistics in order to profoundly question the classic terrain of 'the social', which not only shaped modern strategies of government, but which also underpinned many of the procedures of academic disciplines such as sociology and social history.[7] Together with Saussureian and Derridean linguistics, Foucault's approach raised major doubts about established historiographical procedures. Above all, it was the emphasis on language and discourse which destabilised conventional methodologies. After Foucault and the other post-structuralists, the representational quality of all forms of historical knowledge – including that of sexuality – became a key concern.

Foucault's method disturbed commonsense understandings of what a history of sexuality could be about. It uncovered sex in the most unlikely places, as well as in more familiar areas: within sanitary science, household manuals, statistical tables, medical dossiers and census returns. Sex intruded into the circuits of eighteenth- and nineteenth-century social government, in addition to signifying bodily acts, identities and desires. Modern sexuality was a *dispersed and decentred field*, and it was organised around multiple points of reference. Within this framework Foucault identified a number of nodal points which increasingly classified and regulated sex around the principles of reproductive and biological strength and around what he termed the 'perverse implantations'.[8] The significance of these particular mechanisms of power nomination have been much argued over, but Foucault's basic insistence is worth reiterating; that sexuality is plural, rather than articulated around any single point of reference. One of the most significant consequences of this emphasis for research was that it opened up the space for an extremely productive exploration of the representational quality of sexuality, especially from cultural historians working on the construction of sexual knowledges and identities. For example, rather than simply seeing nineteenth-century visual or literary discourses as expressive of a sexuality which was assumed to be 'already there', these practices were now assigned a much more active role in the representation of sexual meanings and experiences.[9] In a related sense, the erotic impact of modern consumer society, with its elaborate scopic and aesthetic rituals, was also reassessed.[10] If one implication of Foucault's analysis has been to suggest that sex is everywhere, the other has been to identify the very particular networks through which it is produced.

The Foucauldian approach is of course limited, partly because of its grandiose intent. There have by now been numerous critiques of Foucault's project, which concentrate on his shortcomings as a historian of the archive, his recourse to the body as an unexplained arbiter of desire and power, his neglect of the realm of the extra-discursive. Some of the most productive reappraisals have come from feminist scholars, who have been dissatisfied with Foucault's gender-blindness, but who have nonetheless recognised the importance of discourse theory in providing a sophisticated account of sexual difference.[11] Rather than simply rehearsing these criticisms, I want to identify a number of post-Foucauldian trajectories on sexuality which intersect with the larger project for a cultural history. These themes can be grouped under separate headings for the sake of analytical convenience, though they frequently overlap. They are: the self in history, the representational quality of desire, the national and colonial dimensions of sexuality, and sexuality and space.

Dangerous Sexualities worked across an interface between power conceived discursively and structurally and a more humanistic understanding of history propelled by social movements and individual actors. When the book was written this historiographical dualism was at the heart of a series of exchanges between a group of social historians, led by Edward Thompson, with their stress on the political resources of human creativity and action, and structuralist and post-structuralist theorists, who insisted on an altogether more decentred account of subjectivity.[12] Over the past decade these debates have intensified, especially in relation to the ways in which classed and gendered subjects operate in the historical arena.[13] My own book steered a pragmatic middle course on the large theoretical question of self versus social structure, and it also argued for the need to explore this issue not at the level of high abstraction but through more medium-range historical frameworks. As Mary Poovey has observed in analysing the ideological work of gender in the mid-nineteenth century, the conceptual tension between viewing individuals as if they really are agents of social change and a perspective which suggests that they are merely points at which competing cultural forces intersect, needs to be worked through in particular life histories, stories and texts.[14] Those sections of *Dangerous Sexualities* which examined the close-knit encounters between first-wave feminism and evangelical religion, emphasised that this dialogue was as much related to the resources of language and feminine culture as it was to questions about the role of leading individuals, or to the history of political and religious movements. In a similar way, the book's account of the 1830s and 1840s drew on other pioneering research into this formative moment of English class relations, which emphasised the part played by culture in the making of bourgeois identities.[15] Increasing concern with the health, hygiene and strength of the population was not only a matter of public policy for many European nation states during this period, these discourses also helped to shape a distinctive sense of selfhood for significant sections of an emergent middle class. Population politics was both a matter of national aggrandisement and part of the mechanisms of individualisation.

In its most evangelical versions the impact of the linguistic turn has tended to dissolve the whole question of human agency into a subjectless structuralism. But the decentring of subjectivity does not necessarily imply abandoning an interest in individuals within history. Rather, it involves the development of a mode of history-writing which refuses traditional guarantees founded on a fixed and stable understanding of subjectivity. One consequence of this refusal is that the linguistic means by which individuals represent and make sense of their world, to themselves and to other social actors, becomes a specific problem requiring explanation, rather than being naturalised, as it so often has been within conventional historical accounts. Part of the historian's task then becomes to explain expressions of culture in terms of historically situated authorial consciousness.[16] Writing about the languages of class in the nineteenth century, Patrick Joyce has pointed to one distinctive resolution of this theoretical difficulty, by insisting on the intimate connection between histories of the self and histories of 'the social'. If the dominant traditions of nineteenth- and twentieth-century historiography have set the 'I' against the social, Joyce has argued that the insights from post-structuralism reveal how in fact the self and the social constitute each other, and how they have been joined in a mutual dependence.[17] This is a productive but nonetheless a partial truth. Its partiality is particularly evident in researching sexuality. For the story of the self is not exhausted by the story of the social. Cultural history, and in particular histories of sexual life, need to preserve a space for those manifestations of selfhood which partly escape the engineering of the social. Emotion and affect, sexuality and the fields of fantasy and memory, demand a transcript and a narrative register which is distinct from the discourse of the public realm. It is in the gap between the social and the psychic that some of the most significant historical insights are to be found. What is needed is the development of an expanded vocabulary capable of grasping the variable and historically contingent manifestations of sexual and emotional life. While Freudian and Kleinian psychoanalysis has provided one framework through which to explore these issues, concepts drawn from literary and visual analysis have provided another productive route.[18] The search should not be for a new master-narrative of sexuality and subjectivity, but for a series of experiments in historical method.

Recent research has proved particularly adept at identifying the highly malleable and shifting dynamics of sexual desire across the nineteenth and twentieth centuries, and the ways in which such experiences were lived at the level of specific relationships, liaisons and encounters. An important consequence of this work is that we now know much more about the texture as well the structure of these sexual scenarios. This has been made possible by new historical treatments of biography and self-dramatisation. One such instance, which my own account addressed very briefly, was the cross-class relationship between the barrister and inveterate social explorer,

Arthur Munby, and Hannah Cullwick, a Shropshire servant. Leonore Davidoff's pioneering identification of the images, games and fetish rituals played out in this long affair, which began with an encounter on a London street in 1854, argued forcibly that individuals live in the midst of their sexual cosmology, down among it, and are energetically manipulating it.[19] Since Davidoff's study, cultural and feminist historians have returned again and again to examine this remarkable double portrait of a sexual relationship which was eroticised by many of the major Victorian anxieties – dirt, disordered hierarchies of social power and matter out of place.[20] Another instance of the way in which specific case-studies repay detailed investigation is the story of the Men and Women's Club. This self-consciously vanguardist, metropolitan coterie, which met in the late 1880s to debate sex and gender, has become a rich source for feminist historians.[21] The conflicting sexual knowledges generated by the men and women from this élite circle – about prostitution, the woman question and contemporary scandal – was symptomatic of new struggles between rationalist male professionalism and a generation of educated women who were also drawn to the emotional dialectics of sex and feminine fantasy. What is particularly compelling about the Club for historians is the way in which discourses and social divisions around heterosexuality were played out in the form of tangled sexual and emotional relationships between individual members of this hothouse group. Researchers have therefore been able to present these different registers of personal and sexual life stereophonically, for the Club was quite literally a living theatre in which the intellect and the emotions co-existed on the same sexual stage.

Working on broadly the same *fin de siècle* moment, but in a different cultural field, Peter Bailey has analysed a number of the characters associated with late Victorian popular culture as personifications of new and creative manifestations of sexual performance. In particular, Bailey's work on the representational strategies of the barmaid and the 'gent' or 'swell' has identified the auratic properties of 'glamour' inherent in late-nineteenth-century urban culture. This more explicitly heterosocial style of sexual stimulation and containment, in which the visual properties of the city were used to full effect, generated what Bailey has termed a form of 'parasexuality'. Barmaids, shop-girls and other women workers in the service sector epitomised this new 'carefully channelled rather than fully discharged' sexual style which was deployed across a range of urban milieus.[22] Taken together, all of these studies are examples of what we might term a new genre of micro-history. They are highly inventive demonstrations of the way in which particular and localised studies can complexify accounts of sexual identity and experience, revealing how subjectivity is lived out according to specific rules of desire.

These historical accounts are important for what they demonstrate about the complexities of nineteenth-century social organisation, but they are also significant reminders of the fluidity of modern forms of sexual conduct. Over the past decade, however, there has been an attempt to produce a much more exclusive interpretative framework for studying sexuality. This has centred on the cultural tropes of transgression and perversion. In the 1990s the eruption of the umbrella term 'queer' – queer theory, queer identities, queer culture and politics – endowed homosexuality both with a revitalised knowledge base and a distinctive agenda for political action. Yet understood as part of a longer historical *durée*, the loose signifier 'queer' has re-focused a cluster of issues which have been incipient within dissident sexual cultures since the late nineteenth century. Two themes have surfaced repeatedly: competing understandings of perversion and normality and the social meanings attached to sexual acts and lifestyles.

It is not accidental that the recent flurry of discourse over queer sexualities has turned around the question of identity. Given the historical yoking together of notions of personhood, biology and sexual object choice within modern systems of sexual organisation, many of the most hard fought battles of sexual politics have been waged on this terrain. There have been many earlier examples of what is now commonly termed identity politics: the reclamation of 'the spinster' within early twentieth-century English feminism, or the possibilities opened up for self-definition by the medicalised categories of the 'invert' and the 'lesbian' in broadly the same period.[23] All of these self-conscious and inventive reappropriations of official labels have worked with the principle of reverse discourse affirmation, turning a vocabulary of regulation into a language of resistance. New sexual personas are never assembled out of thin air, they have to be forged out of the cultural resources which are historically available.

In a more contemporary sense queerness has raised in a particularly acute form the contradictory impulses embedded within identity politics. One strand of queer theory has been organised around a surprisingly fixed and quasi-essentialist version of homosexual selfhood; with queer pitched against 'straight' and perversion pitted against normality in a stark series of oppositions. Elsewhere the vision has been much more plural, projecting queer culture as part of a broad coalition of sexually diverse and relatively fluid lifestyles.[24] At its most expansive, the idea of queerness has constituted an open-ended signifier, an umbrella term under which a range of sexual identities might come together. Used in this broad sense, the implications have been that queer activism has the potential to embrace not just homosexuals, but the many other identities which are outside of normative sexual discourse: bisexuals, single parents, celibates, and so on. Much of this dynamic exchange of knowledge has taken place across the puritan sexual diaspora, linking political and intellectual movements in Britain and northern Europe with similar traditions in North America and Australia. Such associations confirm that the history of modern sexuality can rarely be understood as a purely domestic scenario, securely bounded by national cultures. Current forms of sexual internationalism often follow routes which were laid down at earlier moments of political campaigning, especially in the first great wave of activism running from the 1860s through to the 1930s.

To what extent has the queer project tabled a new agenda for theories and histories of sexuality? Over the past decade the concept of transgression has become increasingly central to a growing body of cultural research. Despite the differing vantage points of such work, what it shares is a common epistemological reading of sexuality. In Britain as in the United States much of this analysis has been broadly literary in its origins and focus. More often than not it has examined the ways in which texts have disturbed, or mediated, traditional patterns of sexual behaviour, via their cultural and representational coding. Eve Kosofsky Sedgwick's account of the complex negotiation of male homosexuality within late nineteenth-century literary culture in the *Epistemology of the Closet*, 1990, has been a classic point of reference. Refusing the familiar minority status awarded to the homosexual theme, Sedgwick's narrative is premised on a much more all-encompassing idea. This is the bold assertion that: 'many of the major modes of thought and knowledge in twentieth century Western culture as a whole are structured . . . by a chronic, now endemic crisis of homo/heterosexual definition, indicatively male, dating from the end of the nineteenth century.'[25] This understanding that perversion is endemic to and constitutive of modern social life was familiar from Foucault's history, and it was also present in a more conventional form in many of the post-war social histories of Victorianism. But in the work of some contemporary literary critics it has been awarded an even greater status, as a quasi-anthropological principle of human culture.

The analysis of this system of cultural taxonomy is proving to be an immensely productive field of inquiry. Peter Stallybrass and Allon White have delivered some of the most valuable insights into its long-term significance in their study of the poetics of transgression, revealing how that which is literally peripheral is frequently symbolically central to the ordering of modern social life.[26] In a related sense queer theory has made visible the hidden connections between normal and pathological constructions of sexuality, insisting that modern ideas of normality have frequently been forged out of anxieties with conduct perceived to be troublesome or dangerous. *Dangerous Sexualities* itself identified the astonishingly complex reciprocal relationships which existed between sexual order and disorder throughout the long nineteenth century. In the 1830s and 1840s the powerful cloacal imagery which yoked together dirt, disease and the moral chaos of proletarian life was generated by an alliance of medics and sanitarians, who were intent on demonstrating to the world their own sense of intellectual power and control. While in the late nineteenth century, feminists and purity campaigners forged their own energetic projects for moral reform around the marginal figure of the prostitute, projecting an idealised version of the 'fallen woman' to challenge the sexually complacent world of the masculine political élite. What is apparent from so many of these examples is the way in which transgression functions to define the norm, shaping and crystallising ideas about the rules of correct moral conduct.

Yet via a series of characteristic slippages, queer theorists have often moved too rapidly from identifying the structures of perversion to much more global pronouncements on the history of sexuality and culture. In the process awkward questions of periodisation, location and verification have been side-stepped. Arguably, the most problematic element of queer theory has been its move to privilege a binary dualism of sex. Sexual dissidence has been foregrounded as *the* epistemology of sexuality, in such a way that the pervert, as against the norm, has become the guiding principle of sexual organisation. What is implicitly performed by this tendency within the queer project is a reductionist sleight of hand familiar from other, quite different, sexual philosophies. Sex is not now grounded in the family, nor in moral law, nor seen as a function of capitalism, but is defined according to the binary principle of sexual otherness as opposed to normality. That such a conception has occurred within the most sophisticated forms of cultural analysis is a testament to the power of binary dualism within the history of nineteenth- and twentieth-century social thought. Sexual theory is littered with reductionisms, they have proved simplistic because they fail to grasp the plurality of sexual systems and force disabling choices around polarised oppositions.

In contrast to these proliferating accounts of sexual dissidence, studies of the relationship between sexuality and national identity and of the colonial and imperial networks which generated recognisably modern sexual regimes remain relatively underdeveloped. Until recently, part of the difficulty here has been the paucity of concepts for thinking both nation and empire in sexual terms, together with the resolutely domestic emphasis of the majority of histories of sexuality. In this respect Benedict Anderson's insistence that nationality, as well as nationalism, is a cultural construct underpinned by recognisably modern institutions of knowledge and power, remains an important starting point for exploring the historical links between sexuality and nationhood. Anderson's riposte to those restricted accounts of the nation state, which have focused almost exclusively on the emergence of a new legal and civic contract between European governments and civil society, has been to foreground the political and cultural forces which projected nations as 'imagined communities' of interest from the late eighteenth century.[27] Yet while extremely suggestive, Anderson's thesis does not recognise either gender or sexuality as significant elements in this process of historically imagining the nation. One important development in recent work has been to draw on Anderson's arguments to prise open the seemingly opaque and natural lines of connection between the idea of

national belonging and sexual attachment. How do these categories intersect with and constitute each other in ways which sustain and transform the
very idea and experience of nationhood?[28] George Mosse's study of the
relationship between emergent forms of European nationalism and projections of 'decent and correct' morality has been pioneering in this respect.[29]
Mosse's attention to the ways in which German nationalisms, in particular,
shaped both normative projections of the disciplined and the aestheticised
body, while at the same time systematically excluding all non-reproductive
sexualities from their remit, provides significant insights into the cultural
and sexual dynamics of nation-building. Mosse's suggestion that modern
nationalist discourses have been underpinned by distinctively homosocial
forms of male bonding (what Anderson innocently refers to as 'deep, hori-
zontal comradeship') has also provided important ways of rethinking the
historical separation between sanctioned forms of masculine solidarity and
those sexualised male relationships which were removed from the prescribed narratives of the nation.[30]

Faced with such recurrent and deeply embedded mechanisms of sexual
inclusion and exclusion, it is tempting to posit a series of trans-historical
ideas about the links between dominant conceptions of normality, nationalism and the eroticised sexual other. But just as there is no nationalism in
general, there is no single version of the relationship between national identity and sexual selfhood which can provide a blueprint for the myriad competing historical forms in which this connection has been expressed.[31]
Moreover, those discourses which have been at the forefront of campaigns
to promote aggressive versions of sexual nationalism have not always been
intellectually hegemonic. The complex permeation of the science of eugenics
into the social values of English society in the forty years after 1880 provides an instructive case-study of this point. It was undoubtedly true that
the idea of scientific breeding, to increase the quality and quantity of
imperial, British stock, was an influential strand of the new collectivist policies for national efficiency in the years before the First World War. Such
ventures coupled the demands of post-Darwinist evolutionary biology with
the new social pathologies of degeneration, which had been generated by
the inquiries into the condition of the urban poor after 1880. Eugenical
theory worked both to crystallise the link between reproductive sexuality
and national puissance and to define a whole range of degenerate sexual
types as dysfunctional for the progressive imperial state. Yet in the British
context eugenics never gained full ascendancy, either as an accepted form of
social policy or as a dominant force in the emerging science of sex. The
reason for this failure related to the ethical and moral reservations of the
professional and scientific élites; eugenics was impeded by long-standing
liberal and individualist beliefs in social amelioration and human progress
which dated back at least as far as the early nineteenth-century reform
movements. This was especially the case with the medical profession, where

after 1913 eugenics spectacularly failed to become more than an influential but minority pressure group. The early twentieth-century campaigns for social hygiene, which carried much of the nascent 'scientific' thinking about sexuality, provide a vivid illustration of the plural ways in which sex was written into the discourse of nationhood.

Studies of the links between nationalism and sexuality have generally been grounded in a European setting. When they have evoked the wider framework of colonial and imperial power they have done so from the perspective of the metropole. What happens to the extant histories of modern sexuality when they are reconfigured in a full-scale imperial setting? Recent research points to the ways in which many of their explanatory frameworks need to be productively rethought in the light of this agenda. Ann Stoler has argued that Foucault's own conception of 'bio-power' – the technology which brought 'life' and the vitality of the population into the calculations of most European governments – ought to be recast as a crucial mechanism of imperial rule.[32] Far from simply reproducing the processes of colonial domination, policies such as these worked across both metropolitan and colonial sites of power, in ways which shaped some of the most significant tropes of so-called European sexual morality. Respectable 'bourgeois' conduct, many of the dualisms of nineteenth-century desire, together with the making of sexually outcast communities, were frequently the product of these reciprocal networks of empire. Conversely, the colonial territories themselves, far from being distant outposts of imperial administration, might be profitably understood as 'laboratories of modernity', in which recognisably modern conceptions of social discipline and culture were initially produced, before being exported to European environments.[33] Seen in this light, the colonial and imperial dimensions of sexuality are brought into view as constitutive of the affinities and dispositions of the modern world.

Dangerous Sexualities took the social geographies produced by these and other sexual regimes entirely for granted. In that sense it operated with the established conventions of most historiography, viewing space and place as a relatively passive backdrop against which 'real' cultural processes were enacted. The urban geographies of Manchester and London, for example, which featured so prominently in the environmental campaigns for nineteenth-century sanitary and philanthropic reform, were simply assumed 'to be there', as were the more localised spaces of the church and the school-room, which were the habitus of so much moral education. Nor was there any understanding that the professional itineraries of those medical men and social explorers who encountered the industrial world of the new manufacturing districts, or the landscape of the East End of London, might be coterminus with masculine traditions of urban *flânerie*, with their assumed right to privileged forms of spectatorship and control. In a rather different sense, the mental environments and psychic spaces which were the focus of moral reform also remained unexplored, despite the growing impact of Freud's topography of the mind by the early twentieth century. This neglect of social and symbolic geography remains a characteristic feature of research on sexuality. While recent cultural histories have amply demonstrated the significance of language in generating sexual meanings, they have continued to underestimate the spatial dimensions of these codes. Such issues have now been extensively debated outside of history, in the areas of cultural theory and human geography. This research has either focused on the contemporary features of urban space, or else it has pitched discussion at very high levels of abstraction, drawing on marxist and post-structuralist traditions, which extend from Henri Lefebvre through to writers such as Michel de Certeau and David Harvey.[34] In accounts of this type the primary concern has been with theoretical elucidation, in which space as well as time has been cast as a central part of the repertoire of capitalist development, modernity, postmodernity, or other similar global configurations. In contrast, the idea of a cultural history, which evaluates the spatial dimensions of social processes at particular points in time and in more limited settings, remains an underdeveloped project.

How might the idea of a historical geography of sexuality be conceived? Two recent books have pioneered studies of sexuality in the modern city, revealing how distinctive metropolitan environments have both regulated sexual subjects and provided the space for human creativity and action. Judith Walkowitz' *City of Dreadful Delight*, 1992, traced the interrelationships between the politics and poetics of space and the multiple scripts of sexuality in late Victorian London. Reflecting the narrative challenges posed by the new agendas of cultural and literary history, Walkowitz explored the metropolis as a contested terrain, in which diverse groups of social actors were drawn into a series of overlapping narratives of sexual danger. One of the most significant aspects of her analysis was the insight that these socio-sexual relationships were not only embedded in the physical geography of London, but were also present in a series of imaginary urban landscapes, which were shaped by the social scripts of melodrama, science, and masculine and feminine versions of cosmopolitanism. Walkowitz' book is a landmark in the study of urban culture in history. George Chauncey's account of the making of the gay male world in New York in the first part of the twentieth century pioneered a different trajectory of sexuality in the city, centring on the social networks of homosociability created in the streets, private apartments, bathhouses and saloons of Greenwich Village, Harlem and Times Square.[35] Chauncey's history did not simply recover evidence about the extent of the early homosexual city, which was erased by a combination of cultural policing and political neglect, it also mapped an astonishingly plural sexual geography at the heart of America's pre-eminent metropole. More often than not, this gay world existed in the same environments as African-American, Irish and Italian immigrant neighbourhoods. These were plural networks and liminal spaces, which were not structured according to the hetero–homosexual binarism which became the hegemonic sexual regime within the United States during the post-war years. Chauncey's analysis points to the extremely porous nature of modern sexual identities, which are fluid and contingent partly because of their spatial proximity to other cultures and ways of life.

Two different projects emerge out of this research, which address space as a constitutive part of the cultural formation of the metropolis. First, a concern with regulative space and with the spaces of regulation develops further Foucault's project of discipline and sexuality. Official maps of immorality have repeatedly worked to impose strategic order, viewing urban sexuality as a major site of cultural disturbance. This bureaucratic and administrative geography has been pivotal in all forms of social policing. It would be instantly recognisable to the magistrate and the sanitary engineer, as well as to the cartographer. Operating from on high, it mobilises a panoptic vision of the city and its subjects, who are viewed as part of a landscape and an aesthetics of discipline. The panoramic eye which maps the city in this way invariably offers the viewer mastery of its spaces through sight. The weakness of this version of the urban landscape is that it refuses any invitation to come 'down below' to the level of the street and its pedestrians. In that sense it remains a history of the city from above. In contrast, the project advanced by the cultural geographer de Certeau has been one of anti-discipline. In de Certeau's version of urban society, individuals and social groups in space resist the functionalist rationality of the city's grid-plan, drawn up by bureaucrats and administrators. Here we are introduced to different types of spatial practices: the pedestrian rhetorics, the local networks and the wandering activities which produce a subtle logic of place as the site for individual and collective endeavours. De Certeau is not unique in defining space as part of the resistant practices of everyday life. In many respects his approach parallels the recent work of Anglo-American cultural studies, which has sought to rescue the urban cultures of subaltern groups from their banal and degraded status.[36] Like some of that writing, de Certeau's efforts to define space as resistance at times traps him in a sentimental utopianism, whereby local environments and small acts by their very definition constitute places of defiance to official geographies.[37] What is undoubtedly important about de Certeau's project is his emphasis on tracking subjects *in motion* as they move through the urban landscape.

Taken together, these insights provide an expanded vocabulary for the historical treatment of the spectacle, performance and regulation of sexuality in the city. Yet the emphasis should not be on urban sexualities in general, but on particular metropolitan environments and specific cities. To take the milieu which features most prominently, though implicitly, in *Dangerous Sexualities* – London. London's own distinctive moral geography has contributed to particular regimes of sexuality. London's development has not been that of Paris, Berlin or New York. The Danish architect and humanist, Steen Eiler Rasmussen, celebrated the cultural diversity of the English metropolis, as against the continental, planned city, in his influential history, *London, the Unique City*, 1937.[38] The capital's characteristic administrative ad hocery, which was visible in the mid-nineteenth-century approaches to public health and sanitation, generated its own recognisable sexual atmosphere. The capital never experienced a *police des moeurs*, or moral police, on the Parisian or Prussian models, nor were its zones of respectable and disreputable behaviour as strategically zoned as in some other European or American cities. Yet since the eighteenth century London has been shaped by a series of ongoing moral and environmental initiatives, in which fears over disorder and disease have been linked to the sexual practices of its recalcitrant populations.[39] Moreover, the capital's importance as the centre of empire, and latterly of post-colonial migration, has thrown up a series of extraordinarily complex cultures of sexual otherness, which have repeatedly hybridised the city's existing populations. And unlike many Western metropoles in the twentieth century, London has continued in its traditional role as the site of royalty, the court and aristocratic society, with their own elaborate displays of sexual ritual. The project for a spatial history of sexuality needs to address the making of these diverse sexual cultures as part of the fabric of modern metropolitan life.

Dangerous Sexualities ended with a political conclusion, arguing for the significance of its history of sexuality in terms of contemporary dilemmas and demands. This emphasis was in part derived from Foucault's conception of a history of the present, which cast the contemporary situation as the product of particular genealogies of modernity. But the stress on politics was also the product of a more sentimental utopianism, prevalent in many intellectual circles across the spectrum in the 1980s, which assumed that discussion of present-day society and politics provided a satisfactory narrative closure to many historical accounts. The majority of the issues raised in the conclusion are as significant now as they were when the book first appeared, though they have obviously taken on new inflections: the ongoing crisis over AIDS and HIV infection, the issue of medical authority and power and the difficulties involved in promoting a new social settlement around sexuality, which both respects individual freedoms and works towards a sense of shared moral purpose. These remain key concerns. However, I would now propose a quieter though no less ambitious ending, which centres not on the social challenges posed by sexuality but on a new agenda for research. This returns to the idea of a cultural history which I signalled at the outset. Foucault's studies, together with the subsequent work they have inspired, reveal that the domain of the sexual is not simply an interesting but insignificant byway in the grander histories of modern life. Since the eighteenth century this field has been constituted as a component of the social project of modernity itself. Mapping the ways in which sexuality enters 'the social' forces the historian to confront a more general series of questions – about language and the gendered representation of the self, about emotion, affect and fantasy and about the local and the international dimensions of place and environment – which are a formative part of the experience of becoming and of being modern. Writing these things into history, in a way which conceives of them as more than simply epiphenomenal, demands not only a different set of historical narratives but a new language of the historical itself.

ACKNOWLEDGEMENTS TO THE FIRST EDITION

This book took many years to write, years in which its arguments were discussed with friends and colleagues and presented at countless conferences and seminars. These collective contributions are evident on every page. The Social Science Research Council funded the first three years of the project as a doctoral thesis at the Centre for Contemporary Cultural Studies, University of Birmingham. Thereafter, research at the Open University and teaching at Bristol Polytechnic and West Midlands College of Higher Education provided me with the income to finish it. Students at those institutions were remarkably patient when I used them as a sounding board for my ideas. Libraries and librarians loomed large in the research, especially the staff at the British Library, the Public Record Office and the Fawcett Library. David Doughan, the Fawcett's Assistant Librarian, has been a mine of information and a source of encouragement and I owe him a special thanks.

Many of my early ideas came out of discussions with past members of the Centre for Contemporary Cultural Studies, and in particular the state group. Jane Beckett, Deborah Cherry, Philip Derbyshire, Stuart Hall, Rachel Harrison, Sheila Henderson, Stuart Marshall, Lynda Nead, Roy Peters, Adrian Rifkin, Bill Schwarz, Simon Watney, Christine Weedon, Jeffrey Weeks and Bruce Wood also commented at various stages on my ideas or on sections of the manuscript and I am grateful for their help. Nikolas Rose and Maureen McNeil were sympathetic examiners when the material was presented as a thesis and I have acted on much of their good advice. My parents, Lilian and James Mort, were generous with financial support and encouragement, and Gwenllian Rhys was meticulous in typing the manuscript.

Finally, I owe a special debt to three friends. Richard Johnson provided me with much of the initial impetus for the book, sustained me with help and advice, and taught me how to be a historian. Lucy Bland discussed almost every stage of the research with me in joint articles and projects. Her critique and intellectual stimulation has added a major dimension to my approach. Nicholas Green has lived with the book (and with me) almost as long as I have. Without his intellectual support and practical help it might never have seen the light of day.

INTRODUCTION
Narratives of sex

To begin at the end of our story. In May 1982 the medical journal the *Lancet* front-paged an article called 'Risk Factors for Kaposi's Sarcoma in Homosexual Men'.[1] The piece reported on an American study of twenty gay men in New York and California with a particularly rare form of skin cancer. Symptoms included sores, coupled with weight loss and low fever. Pointing to significant links between the spread of the disease and promiscuity, the article drew medics' attention to alarming differences between the sex life of the infected homosexuals and a control group of non-infected heterosexuals. Fifty per cent of the gay patients admitted to having sex with ten or more partners in an average month. The most promiscuous 'confessed' he had had intercourse with ninety different partners in the weeks before succumbing to the virus. Conclusions were tentative, but an initial hypothesis was clearly spelt out – 'deviant' sex was an important factor in spreading this potentially killer disease.

The previous December studies published in the prestigious *New England Journal of Medicine* had signalled the appearance of even more drastic symptoms, again among American gay men.[2] Medics were at a loss in the face of an unidentified virus, which attacked the natural capacity of blood cells to defend themselves against infection. Physical symptoms included respiratory problems, glandular fever, a virulent form of pneumonia (*pneumocystis pneumonia*) and Kaposi's sarcoma. Patients had already died from the syndrome. All known broad-spectrum antibiotics proved useless in checking its career. Research teams concluded that they had identified a new form of acquired cellular immunodeficiency, AIDS. Again they made connections between high rates of 'deviant' sex and the rampant growth of the disease. Doctors concluded that given the abnormally high promiscuity of gay men, some form of sexually transmitted virus or exposure to a common lifestyle played a critical role in establishing immunodeficiency.

Cases of AIDS began to be reported in Britain towards the end of 1982. Almost immediately medical journals, television and the popular press fuelled speculation about the link between promiscuity and killer diseases. Positions were staked out. The medical profession warned gay men against

1

sex. In the absence of any known cure, the best means of prevention was to avoid frequent contacts and reconsider their whole lifestyle. Gay men's self-help groups attacked the lurid press coverage of AIDS, and began to mobilise in the face of government lethargy. Fund-raising and health education has been to the fore in their fight back. Since then, mortality rates have risen dramatically. Successive waves of panic have drawn in heterosexuals, without shifting the burden of blame from gay men. Currently, effective treatment is still some way off. Despite the barrage of prestige medical research into the structure of the virus, AIDS represents the front-line of sexual politics.

This book is about unravelling the narratives which link our beliefs about health and disease to moral and immoral notions of sex. AIDS and all that follows from it cannot be contained by official medical explanations. Nor is it simply a conspiracy, fuelled by the moral right and press sensationalism. AIDS is the contemporary moment in a much longer history, the extraordinarily complex interweaving of medicine and morality with the surveillance and regulation – even the very definition – of sex. The disease has produced gay men as its victims and their sexuality as the problem. This is part of the norms, protocols and procedures written into the history of medico-moral discourse.

The book has a double axis. First, a detailed account of the relation between systems of medical knowledge and power. Second, an analysis of the way medical and other discourses have produced a distinct regime of sex, targeting sensitive or dangerous groups and generating forms of resistance. Historically, our main focus is on the nineteenth and early twentieth century, but in conclusion we shall return with some urgency to our own situation now. It is therefore a history of and for the present; an attempt to use history-writing both to understand why our current dilemmas have arisen and to shape future political demands. This means seeing the present as historical, as the product of a particular combination of structural forces.

What perspectives have suggested the most fertile and incisive questions to break open the area? The introduction is not in the business of providing a general theory, either of sexuality, or of professional experts. Indeed, the book as a whole argues that such concepts can only be grasped within historically specific structures, ranging from the detailed and the immediate to problematics pitched at a much higher level of abstraction. Nevertheless, we are concerned with providing a self-conscious account of the politics and theories which have informed the making of our history. Two influences have been paramount. The revival of marxist and marxist-influenced theory and history, and the impact of the feminisms – both as ways of thinking about the world and with their specific injunctions to men over sexual politics. Feminist interventions have meant that in writing about sexuality as a man I have been made very much aware of the gender-specific access to the questions we ask and the knowledge we seek. This, I believe, should not imply that men abandon the field. But without a recognition that sexuality has constructed men and women in terms of difference – a difference shot through with power relations – the very nature of the struggles confronting us remains distorted or obscured. Like all historical accounts, the narrative is deliberately, though thoughtfully, selective in its choice of material; choices which are made on the back of current concerns. All students of social movements stand in a definite relation to the historical developments they describe, not outside them. Hence we have 'taken sides' and have not held back from explicitly arguing for political and intellectual preferences. Wilful exclusion of these criteria from history-writing not only contributes to the discipline's mystique – and confusion! – but also closes off many of the possible associations between historical understanding and progressive politics.

The base-line insistence underpinning our account is the historical construction of sexuality. An emphasis in the broadest sense on sexuality as historically specific and culturally variable still radically challenges those other accounts of sexual definitions which dominate the field. Since the late nineteenth century, anatomy, physiology and psychology, projecting sex as central to our personality and bodily functions, have exerted a powerful influence on official programmes and political positions. Although now under challenge, they still hold sway over commonsense ideas about what we mean by sex. A history of sex raises a number of expectations. We expect it to cover things like the sex act, procreation, the family, birth-control, motherhood, prostitution, homosexuality. At some level or other we also anticipate the personal or experiential – questions of identity more intimate than in other forms of social or cultural history.[3] This account is primarily concerned with neither. It does not start from lived experience, nor from a set of pre-given objects called sexuality. Rather, it explores one particular field of official knowledge: the linked areas of social medicine and moral politics. The book argues that this domain has been instrumental in producing some of the central meanings and power relations around sex.

Why study the official area at all? The personal dimensions of power are now high on the political agenda, and rightly so – the power of men over women in lived relations, sexual authority within the family, attempts to forge new personas and pleasures. So why study public policy? Because official programmes are not neatly sealed off from more intimate forms of social relations. The whole paraphernalia of government reports and professional knowledge does set the broad conditions for the way we experience our sexual identities. Official discourses do have concrete, if complex and often bizarre, effects on the sexuality of constructed men and women. Unless we hold to a spontaneous or libertarian politics, changing sexual relations must involve transforming the institutions and practices which fix our personal life. This is not to imply that there is any direct, one-to-one, relation between dominant social structures and the personal. Nor is it to suggest that as soon as we accept our sexuality as constructed the personal comfortably evaporates – an argument frequently used by socialist men to get their private life off the hook! But any encounter with officialdom does pose the sharp end of awkward questions which won't go away with the hoped-for installation of a new regime of sex. Questions about legislation, about the power of science and medical knowlege – these issues will continue to be high on the agenda. Used self-consciously, a historical encounter with the official can prove a political education in itself.

It may come as something of a surprise to find that many of the accounts which have opened up the area – histories of state policy and the professions, theories of the state – do not deal explicitly with sexuality at all. In large part this is due to the widely held belief, especially among male academics, that sex is not a fit subject for serious study. We will not spend a great deal of time outlining these theories. Instead we will concentrate on saying what has proved most useful or problematic about them for us.

One way into the medico-moral complex is via the official problematic itself; to go straight to the big histories and sociologies of public health, state administration and government, together with more discrete accounts of medicine and its institutions. In the post-war period these have exercised a decisive influence over many areas of what we might term 'the social' – *social* policy, *social* work, even *social* democracy.[4] The main strength of such work is also its most glaring weakness. Written from a standpoint internal to policy making itself, we are ushered into the more obviously generative social processes – government departments, the world of formal politics, etc. Here we encounter the most immediately responsible persons and organisations – politicians, professionals, articulate interest groups. In doing so, terms like 'morality', 'medicine' or 'education' are taken as given. We are not encouraged to analyse their social meanings and frame of reference. Moreover, politics tends to be treated only as a specialist or expert field. Wider movements of popular and feminist protest go unacknowledged, or are seen as constraints on the policy makers. In short, such accounts work hand-in-glove with the professionals, and write out the whole history of contesting forces beyond their focus.

Recent marxist sociologies of the professions and theories of the state, together with marxist informed social history, have provided a more structural and politically engaged approach.[5] Here, policy and expertise have been probed much more critically, not so much for what is said, as for the underlying ideological problematic, which functions as social control or class regulation. In writing this history, marxism has been most useful in its injunctions to think through the big structures organising conjunctures and social formations. Our main quarrel has been with functionalist and reductionist schools of marxism, and their tendency to lose sight of the particular forms of power and resistance which are not directly related to the needs or interests of capital. At certain key moments, of course, major transformations in the economic forces and relations of capitalist production do set the broad parameters for sexual and moral disciplining. Sanitary politics in the 1830s and 1840s, for example, cannot be understood without reference to these conditions. What is at issue is whether a general theory of capital's needs and requirements can adequately come to grips with the internal complexities of professionalism and expertise, the production of scientific knowledge and the gendered power relations which have been at the centre of our study.

Much of the initial impetus for tackling the medico-moral domain came from the work of the French philosopher and historian, Michel Foucault. Foucault's classic area of study has been the historical interrogation of objects so often designated as natural, but which, he argues, are constructed through particular genealogies and systems of knowledge – 'madness', 'medicine' and 'punishment', as well as 'sexuality'.[6] His radical deconstruction of such objects challenges their conceptual unity. In other words, sexuality is not necessarily what we mean by sex; we find it in the most unlikely places, dispersed across a range of sites and institutions. Foucault's discourse theory is based on a method which scans texts to bring to light their discursive coherence. Under specific historical conditions, statements are seen to combine together and despite, even sometimes because of, contradictions, they exhibit a systematic organisation. Intimate forms of power are produced through these particular regimes of knowledge. Foucault's axiom that power is everywhere in modern societies is complemented by detailed attention to its micro-physics and to the complex mechanisms through which it is exercised. His analysis seeks to understand how power is both regulatory and productive; productive of knowledges and institutions and of bodies, pleasures and desires.

Foucault's paradigm has had most impact on those parts of the book which encounter highly specialised forms of professional expertise, with their own codes, protocols and their own written archive. Discourse analysis works best wherever intellectuals have staked out distinctive monopolies on truth. In this respect Foucault's method usefully preserves linguistic and semiotic emphases on the production of meaning, but now understood much more historically. We have used it as a sophisticated tool to probe the formal character of official representations (and the mechanisms of their 'power effect'), and at moments to grasp how languages of resistance are generated.

There have by now been many critiques of the absences and inadequacies of discourse theory. In putting together this history two related problems have come up time and again: questions about agency and political struggle. What to do about those 'heroes' of official narratives – the great civil servants and sanitarians, Edwin Chadwick, James Kay and John Simon – and the 'heroines' of our history – Josephine Butler, Ellice Hopkins and Christabel Pankhurst. There are protagonists agitating here, not voluntaristic individuals who stand at the centre of events, but socially constructed subjects, the men and women who people our account as policy makers and leaders of resistance. Any account of medico-moral discourse must occupy this moment in the cycle of power and politics. Programmes are implemented and resistances fought out through ideologies which constructed men as if they really were at the centre of the world, and many women as leaders or missionaries in the vanguard of moral reform. Foucault has little to say about all this. Simplistic, polarised distinctions between voluntaristic notions of human agency, on the one hand, and the worst excesses of subjectless structuralism on the other, do little to help the historian. We have understood agents not only as bearers of policy and politics, but also as subjects whose particular formation had effects on the campaigns they were involved in. Letters, biographies and memoirs have provided us with ways into the personal dimensions of agency. They need to be approached with caution, though, for they are not neutral and carry very traditional understandings about individuality and personal life.

A more general point follows from the issue of agency. Shifts and transformations in official power are not generated by their own internal momentum, they are always shaped by negotiations with competing political forces. Large-scale movements of organised revolt, along with more localised though no less significant cultural struggles, have had a major impact on sexual regulation and moral reform. Women's struggles have been central here. In the field of sexuality they were in large part spearheaded by outrage against the medical establishment. From the repeal campaign against the Contagious Diseases Acts in the 1870s, through to the purity feminism of the suffrage movement, successive generations of women put together an alternative strategy – and alternative understandings of sex – which at moments routed the power of male experts. Recent feminist historical work has transformed the way we understand these campaigns. Foucault's sexualisation of bodies and subjects singularly fails to get to grips with the way access to knowledge and power was gendered through ideologies of sexual difference. For the opposition between masculine and feminine understandings of sex provided some of the most heavily contested battles in this area. We need accounts of how these resistances were formed just as complex as our work on official discourse. Resistances did not just drop from the sky, nor were they formed by spontaneous eruptions from below. They were dependent on the languages available, which could endow such struggles with meaning. As we shall see, feminine and feminist appropriations of evangelical religious morality proved especially important in providing women with the voice to resist male professionals.

The two sides of our history need to be worked together, in order to bring out the interrelations between official networks of power and forms of resistance. Here we come up against some of the most difficult problems of history-writing. For while official history is uninterested in the whole question of struggle, history from below baulks at grasping the structural relations which bind these two moments together.[7] The problem has been acute for us, because so often those who refused medico-moral authority – especially middle-class women – themselves stood with one foot inside the power bloc. Hence, though women are to the fore in the book as the collective subject of a progressive sexual politics, their role is never unproblematic.

Finally, a word about presentation. To begin with a *narrative* – of AIDS – is no accident. Forms of story-telling loom large in the book, from cholera in the 1830s, through official wrangles at the Home Office, to small-town rivalries over feminism and sex education. This is not to trivialise the seriousness of the political issues involved. Narrative is one very deliberate technique of history-writing. Interspersed with other genres, we have used it as a self-conscious way of presenting empirical material. It helps to draw attention to the constructed nature of historical facts and events. But there is more to it than that. Medico-moral politics lends itself particularly well to dramatic treatment. Gruesome stories of moral decay and lurid metaphors of punishment and pestilence are the stock-in-trade of writing in this area. They carry with them distinctive sexual scripts – at once terrifying and titillating – which organise the reader's emotional and erotic experience and produce their own forms of pleasure. In writing about sexuality, we realise how many of these pleasures are highly gendered. Nevertheless, negotiating the pleasures of the text – juggling them alongside more traditional political priorities – is a major challenge for the cultural historian. *Dangerous Sexualities* is an attempt to make sense of some of these stories of pleasure and danger.

Part One

MORAL ENVIRONMENTALISM 1830–1860

1 CHOLERA

Asiatic cholera, or *cholera morbus*, spread to Britain from India in a series of epidemics which engulfed much of Europe in the 1820s. The symptoms and the rapacity with which the disease struck must have been alarming even to a population used to the sight of typhus, scarlet fever and small-pox. The Central Board of Health issued a vivid description of the symptomatology:

> The attack of the disease in extreme cases is so sudden, that, from a state of apparent good health . . . an individual sustains as rapid a loss of bodily power as if he were suddenly struck down or poisoned; the countenance assuming a death-like appearance, the skin becoming cold. . . . The pulse is either feeble, intermitting, fluttering or lost; a livid circle is observed round the eyelids. . . . Vomiting soon succeeds; first some of the usual contents of the stomach, next a turbid fluid like whey . . . or water gruel. . . . Spasms, beginning at the toes and fingers soon follow. . . . The next severe symptoms are, an intolerable sense of weight, and constriction felt upon the chest . . . a leaden or bluish appearance of the countenance . . . the palms of the hands and soles becoming shrivelled. . . . At length a calm succeeds and death. . . . The powers of the constitution often yield to such an attack at the end of four hours, and seldom sustain longer than eight.[1]

The epidemic broke out in northern England in the autumn of 1831. In Sunderland, where the approaching threat had become serious as early as April, a local board of health had been meeting to discuss preventive measures.[2] It was chaired by Dr Reid Clancy who, as senior physician to the Sunderland Infirmary, was the closest to an official medical officer of health that the town possessed. On the night of Sunday 16 October twelve-year-old Isabella Hazard was taken violently ill with vomiting, cramps and general fever. At four in the morning the local doctor, Mr Cook, was called. He returned later to find the child weakening. By the following afternoon Isabella was dead. The symptoms seemed unmistakable – Isabella's mother asked the doctor, 'What makes the child so black?' But Cook either missed the diagnosis or tried to ignore it. When William Sport died of similar symptoms on the nineteenth it was clear that cholera had arrived. On 1 November official notification of the presence of the disease in England was sent by Dr Clancy in a special report to the newly established Board of Health at

Whitehall. Thereafter the disease spread to Scotland, the north and Manchester and later to the midlands and London. Mortality for the first outbreak was estimated at 23,000.

There was of course no question of cure; the cholera bacillus was not isolated until 1884. The King's parliamentary speech for 1831 directed that 'precautions should be taken against the introduction of so dangerous a malady.'[3] These amounted to recommendations issued by the Board of Health authorising the creation of local boards, which were to be responsible for the monitoring and control of the disease. Beyond that there were a host of popular remedies, prayers and moral homilies administered by the local clergy. In the summer of 1831 special services of intercession were organised to plead for divine mercy:

> O Almighty God, who has visited the nations with the sudden death
> of pestilence, spare, we beseech thee, this thy favoured land, the
> wrath which to our sins is justly due.[4]

The newly founded medical journal, the *Lancet*, along with other leading periodicals, carried numerous articles on the causes of cholera and the steps to be taken for prevention. Evidence was conflicting and contradictory, reflecting current medical divisions on the origins and transmission of disease. But though there was no agreement about causation, medics, clerics and other local officials were all agreed that the *urban poor* were the human agents responsible for spreading the contagion. As more sporadic outbreaks were reported throughout the summer of 1831, medical evidence sent to the hastily constituted Board of Health confirmed that the environment and the physical and moral habits of the poor actively stimulated the disease. In the metropolis it was in Bermondsey, Southwark and among 'those afloat on the river', rather than in stately Hanover Square or semi-rural Kensington, that cholera was seen to be taking the greatest toll.[5]

In July the board had received disturbing accounts of an outbreak at a flax mill in Port Glasgow. Nancy Kitchen, a mill girl, had been living 'very perniciously' with an Irishman named Murray, who habitually spent his 'idle time' with the girl. Both had been struck down by the disease. The local doctor suggested that the couple's irregular conduct, 'living in the closest intimacy', had acted as a stimulus to infection.[6] When Dr Mahony reported from Hull in August that a soldier serving in the Fusiliers had contracted cholera, Dr Dawn at the Central Board wrote back: 'You will be good enough to make most explicit . . . as to the habits of the soldier in question, the circumstances immediately preceding his illness.'[7] Mahony reported that the man had been in the regiment for twenty years as an officer's servant and was generally of sober habits. But three days prior to his death he had been absent from camp for two nights and had returned 'not absolutely drunk, yet not sober'.[8] On visiting Hull, Dawn concluded that the soldier had been 'living in debauchery' and that his dissolute behaviour had contributed to the onset of the illness. The Central Board, many of whose members had by now fled to the purer air of the country, minuted ominously: 'should this disease ever make its appearance in the country (which God forbid) its first appearance will be among the squalid parts of the population.'[9]

When reports from the north east in November forced Whitehall officials to admit to an epidemic, the condensation of immorality, poverty and the spread of disease became even more pronounced. The first case in North Shields involving a 'mendicant of intemperate habits', Dennis McGair, occurred on 10 December. McGair's wife, also intemperate, died a few days later.[10] More alarming still was the discovery that the disease spread from the dissolute to the sober and industrious. At the height of the outbreak in the north, the Mayor of York wrote to Lord Melbourne, the Home Secretary, alerting him to the large numbers of vagrants and other disorderly persons who were bringing cholera into the city. They arrived at common lodging houses and began to commit acts of vagrancy and indecency; thereby infecting the native population.[11] Equally, the *Westminster Review* warned the city fathers of the danger of hundreds of starving paupers who came to London for relief, and were compelled to herd together 'in much less cleanliness and comfort than the lowest orders of Indians'.[12] All this was not just the metaphoric evocation of pestilence at a moment of panic. Nor was it a simple search for a scapegoat in the absence of any cure. The logic which twinned poverty and immorality with contagion was made through a specific language – the discourse of early social medicine – and was circulated at key institutional sites within the central and local state. The intentions were clear; greater surveillance and regulation of the poor.

The proposed solution was twofold: to isolate the human sources of infection, subjecting them to a regime of compulsory inspection and detention, combined with propaganda to educate the poor into a regime of cleanliness and morality. In Sunderland the Board of Health used the by-laws to isolate vagrants and paupers from the community.[13] The *Cholera Gazette*, the weekly bulletin on the disease, stressed a more educative approach. It advised issuing handbills to impress on the poor the importance of clean, temperate and moral habits as the only sure means of prevention.[14] Local residents in London were warned about the dangers of dissipation; they were told to keep regular hours, strict attention to hygiene and a comfortable and nutritious diet.

Yet from the outset the general response to the epidemic was sporadic and revealed how ill-equipped the central and local state were to deal with public health measures. This was not just an effect of rudimentary medical knowledge. The threat of epidemic disease precipitated heated political arguments about the extent of state intervention, which became condensed with wider debates over reform. The new Board of Health had no legislative powers. It was in effect only a consultative committee – one of those peculiarly English bits of nineteenth-century administrative ad hocery, with an unclear relation to Parliament and statutory authority. Designed to avoid accusations of government expansion, and to side-step the full glare of political scrutiny, it was shunted off to the Privy Council.

Almost immediately its members came under fire from the radical wing of the medical profession, keen to extend their status and authority. In the campaigns leading up to the 1832 Reform Act, Thomas Wakley, editor of the *Lancet*, had been polemicising for the wholesale reform of the medical establishment, as part of the more general scheme of parliamentary and social reform to replace the 'tyrannical ruling oligarchy'.[15] The new board, he claimed, was yet another illustration of the way the profession was being led by drones, sycophants and titled imbecility, most of whom had no personal experience of treating disease, nor any understanding of how infection was transmitted.[16] Far from avoiding contention, the new public health machinery was becoming caught fast in the tangled web of professional politics.

Underlying the battle for control of public health was a fundamental argument about the validity of state intervention. The proposals for compulsory local powers and the whole issue of funding were highly contentious. When the disease began to reach epidemic proportions in the winter of 1831, the Central Board was inundated with desperate letters from local officials, demanding clarification of the extent of their powers. Civic dignitaries in Birmingham asked if money from the parish rates could be used to combat the disease. Mine owners in the north east petitioned for increased state intervention, not on humanitarian grounds but to alleviate losses to capital.[17] The Privy Council replied that they could not authorise the reckless outlay of public money but would apply to the Cabinet for further powers. Whereupon they received a piece of cautionary advice from Spring-Rice, Financial Secretary to the Treasury. He emphasised that while the Exchequer would be ready to assist local efforts, money should be given 'with extreme discretion', lest it repress rather than stimulate voluntary exertions.[18]

State intervention not only meant increased financial expenditure, it also contravened implicit assumptions about the role of government shared by both Whigs and Tories. Pressure from the new professional men, especially medics, for the state to take fuller responsibility for public health was severely qualified by dominant political and administrative ideologies. Government was to be kept cheap, and the central state was not to take on statutory powers for issues which were essentially the province of local authorities and voluntary initiatives.

As the epidemic died down, it became increasingly clear that this new system of health administration was a temporary measure only. There was little notion of a permanent public health network. During 1833 the Privy

Council announced that they would not re-apply for the renewal of compulsory powers, advising local medics that henceforward the management of the disease would be left 'to the prudence and good feeling of those communities where it may occasionally show itself'.[19] Voluntary self-help rather than any state-backed public health network remained the watchword.

Britain was again ravaged by cholera epidemics in 1848–1849, 1853–1854 and 1866. The history of the disease is largely preserved within the narrative of the public health and other reform movements in early Victorian Britain. Health, housing, sanitation, the emergence of preventive medicine, the foundations of a national system of education, the reform of industrial conditions – these objects have formed the classic terrain for histories of government and public administration. Official history, whether in its fabian or tory variants, has been written as a celebratory progress from the early nineteenth-century origins of the welfare state, to its full flowering in the post Second World War period. Such narratives have been carried by their own heroes, the dedicated civil servants and administrators, and by an unswerving commitment to the ideology of professional expertise. But there is another history to be written here. Official transformations at the level of the state defined a new field of social intervention and consolidated a particular regime of moral disciplining. Representations of sexual immorality were constructed through institutional programmes which linked the habits and environment of the urban poor with medico-moral concepts of health and disease. It is this specific domain of sexuality – of sensitive social groups targeted by professional experts and their knowledge – which forms the basis of our history.

2 JAMES PHILLIPS KAY

When cholera reached Manchester in the early summer of 1832 James Kay was senior physician at the Ardwick and Ancoats dispensary, an area chiefly inhabited by Irish labourers and textile workers. Kay was typical of the new type of expert who was instrumental in coordinating plans for state intervention. Like many of his contemporaries he came from a strong nonconformist background, with direct links to the industrial bourgeoisie – the family's capital was in cotton, calico, printing and blacking.[20] Trained as a medical practitioner, in 1826 he was appointed assistant at the Edinburgh New Town dispensary and clerk to the fever hospital, Queensferry. His early work was characteristic of the way many early nineteenth-century intellectuals combined theoretical research with a commitment both to evangelical religion and to the politics of state administration. In the late 1820s and early 1830s he published research on diseases of the brain and the circulatory system, but like Wakley he saw no division between medical inquiry and politics. Research into the causes of infection led inexorably to a wider field of action. As Kay put it, the development of a strategy for the 'mitigation of suffering' had to take in fundamental questions of economic, political and moral causation.[21] He was personally motivated by a nascent professionalism *and* by the culture of his own native dissenting religion, which stressed the importance of practical good works for self-validation and eventual salvation. In a typical passage from his autobiography, written in 1877, Kay showed how he moved from the particular concerns of physical health, through mental and moral considerations, to a full conception of social intervention:

> I came to know how almost useless were the resources of my art to contend with the consequences of formidable social evils. It was clearly something outside scientific skill or charity which was needed. . . . Very early therefore, I began to reflect on this complex problem. Were this degradation and suffering inevitable? Could they only be mitigated? Were we always to be working with palliatives? Was there no remedy? Might not this calamity be traced to its source, and all the resource of a Christian nation devoted through whatever time, to the moral and physical regeneration of this wretched population? Parallel therefore with my scientific reading I gradually began to make myself acquainted with the best work on political and social science, and obtained more and more insight into the grave questions affecting the relations of capital and labour and the distribution of wealth, as well as the inseparable connection between the mental and moral condition of the people and their physical well-being.[22]

The sets of relations posed here were recurrent in Kay's work, as they were in the writings of many early social reformers. Physical degeneracy and mental and moral deterioration demanded scientific solutions, but they were also framed in relation to questions of Christian morality, political economy and social science. Moving beyond mere palliatives, Kay became convinced that it was necessary to intervene in the arena of social and political debate – to abandon 'the purely scientific spirit' in favour of a career in public administration.[23] This change of direction was backed by a utilitarian belief that the health and strength of the great mass of the population was the key to good government, and the indispensable basis for preserving social and political order. In 1833 Kay was appointed an assistant commissioner to the new Poor Law Board, and the following year he served as a major witness to the Select Committee on the Education of the Poorer Classes in England and Wales. As secretary to the new Privy Council committee on education from 1839, he was central to implementing the programme for public education.

A number of distinct elements are brought together in Kay's biography. Through his family background he was linked with industrial capital. But in no sense was he a direct representative of its interests, his specific formation was within the field of preventive medicine. It was this professional discourse which provided Kay with the impetus to scrutinise the physical and moral health of the labouring classes. Here was a programme which was simultaneously medical and moral, directed both at the reform of the environment and at the training of the mind. Sexual immorality was integral to these concerns.

Kay's own early contribution to the debate on the immorality of the urban poor was set out in his pamphlet *The Moral and Physical Condition of the Working Classes Employed in the Cotton Manufacture in Manchester*, 1832. Written in direct response to the problems of cholera, it was dedicated to his mentor, the Scottish political economist the Rev Thomas Chalmers. Chalmers, drawing on his work as a Glasgow minister, always stressed the supremacy of the moral over the physical.[24] Kay's plan for the improvement of the population twinned material and moral reform since, as he pointed out, 'the purely physical condition of the people seemed to me to be incapable of permanent improvement without an increase of their intelligence and virtue ... through the influence of education and religion.'[25]

Reform of sexual conduct was an important part of Kay's schema. Sexuality – always referred to by Kay as sexual *immorality* – was constructed in direct relation to the themes of disease, filth and material squalor, depravity, political sedition and the perceived threat of an oppositional culture:

> No event is more painfully calculated to excite the public mind, than the invasion of pestilence ... no other can be so well calculated to unmask the deformity of evils which have preyed upon the energies of the community. He whose duty it is to follow in the steps of this messenger of death, must descend to the abodes of poverty, must frequent the close alleys, the crowded courts, the overpeopled habitations of wretchedness, where pauperism and disease congregate round the source of social discontent and political disorder in the centre of our large towns, and behold with alarm, in the hot-bed of pestilence, ills that fester in secret, at the very heart of society ...[26]

Moral intervention arose in personal terms for experts like Kay from an emotive perception of the distance between their own lived culture and the patterns of working-class life. Many of their confrontations with working people were traumatic and intense. Close personal observation of the habits of the labouring poor simultaneously confirmed the absolute separation of the reformers' culture from the habits and morals of those under their scrutiny. Kay's use of specific forms of knowledge was a means of coming to terms with these perceived realities – quite literally putting them into discourse to gain some control over them:

> There is however a licentiousness capable of corrupting the whole body of society, like an insidious disease, which eludes observation, yet is equally fatal in its effects. Criminal Acts may be statistically classed . . . but the number of those affected with the moral leprosy of vice cannot be exhibited with mathematical precision. Sensuality has no record.[27]

These passages articulate many of the major themes which will concern us in a detailed unpacking of early nineteenth-century social and moral reform. For the moment it is enough to note the particular combination of elements and the heightened, dramatic language. Gothic images of horror, Old Testament style narratives of pestilence and pollution, dramatised through personal encounters and heavily resonating metaphors – all of this was commonplace. The language of moral *frisson*, combined with the methodology of scientific inquiry, constructed sexuality at the heart of its concerns.

3 EIGHTEENTH-CENTURY SOCIAL MEDICINE AND PHILANTHROPY

This medico-moral discourse was not wholly new. Many of the issues fore-grounded in Kay's scrutiny of the labouring classes had their antecedents in earlier theories of social medicine. The 1830s and 1840s marked the crystal-lisation of debates dating back at least half a century over medical and philanthropic perceptions of the poor. In the eighteenth century a system of hygienics, directed at the improvement of specific institutional populations (prisoners, workhouse inmates and hospital patients) was as much a moral as a medical crusade. As early as the 1750s two London physicians, John Pringle and Stephen Hales, had drawn attention to medical and sanitary hygiene as a means of reducing the rising prison mortality rates. Similar medical programmes were drawn up for deployment within other closed populations, such as the workhouse and the navy.[28]

The sustained crisis over the dual problems of criminality and punishment in the 1770s and 1780s not only produced the stark exercise of legal power, but also condensed new technologies of social disciplining. The planned system of incarceration implemented under the new penal regime was simultaneously medical, hygienic and moral. It involved the surveillance and regulation of minds as well as bodies.[29] John Howard, the nonconformist squire turned prison reformer, laid down rules of prison discipline which combined compassion with a rigid system of regulation. Howard was part of an intellectual and scientific circle of dissenting clerics and medics, who sought a hygienist solution to the linked problems of the diseased state of the prisons, the rising tide of crime and wider threats of social and political upheaval. The polluted state of the prison and hospital populations – and by extension of the poor in general – was defined in a direct relation to their mental and moral condition. The absence of any desire for self-improvement was ascribed to the fact that prisoners were 'inured to misery, by the depravity of their minds; and vice rooted in their hearts'. Filth and disease were as natural to them 'as cleanliness and health are to the virtuous and the industrious'.[30] Corrupt institutions were identi-fied as the breeding ground for physical and moral depravity, precisely because closed communities encouraged contamination of 'the healthy, strong, vigorous and decently habited' by 'the infirm, weak, feeble, filthy and naked'.[31] Daniel Layard, one of Howard's philanthropic circle, was alarmed that the clean and decent were preyed on by the immoral and the depraved, producing a situation 'which daily grows more pestilential as the healthy grow more corrupt'.[32]

This early equation between physical deterioration and a depressed moral condition was not just based on the empirical inquiries of doctors and phys-icians. It also had its intellectual foundations in the Hartleian and Lockean forms of materialism prevailing among reforming and philanthropic groups of the period. Mind and body – the domain of mental and moral behaviour and physical functioning – were equally material according to the phil-osopher David Hartley. Disease produced its own moral or immoral sequence.[33] At the same time, immorality was identified as an important factor in the breakdown of the body's resistance and in the subsequent production of contagion.

Hence, in the practical implementation of prison and hospital reform there was a consistent attempt to link physical and mental regulation. The penal regime introduced at Gloucester Penitentiary after 1784 subjected incoming prisoners to a hygienic ritual of bathing, shaving, medical inspec-tion and the donning of prison uniform. It combined explicit humiliation with rituals of symbolic purification, designed to initiate the inmates into a new moral order. But all of this was not a simple case of 'the language of social and moral condemnation veiled as the language of medicine', as one historian has suggested. It was not medicine developing the scientific legit-imacy for a general social and political offensive against the poor, the impetus for which came from 'class fear'.[34] These early medical concepts had an internal dynamic and history which was *not reducible* to economic and political class relations. Social medicine did not merely reflect pre-given class interests. Rather, through its theories of health and disease and systems of prevention, this discourse staked out the claims of a new domain of expertise. It was this specific regime of professional competence which not only validated the claims of an emergent group of experts, but also became critical to forms of social regulation.

Sexual immorality and sexual disease were classic targets for these early medical campaigns. John Coakley Lettsom's collaboration with James Neild, the prison reformer, led to a national survey of English prisons published in the *Gentleman's Magazine* between 1803 and 1813. In these articles the authors frequently singled out sexual immorality as a major problem for prison discipline. Promiscuous mingling of prisoners – men and women, young and old, debtors and felons – was the main anxiety. The answer lay in a system of hospital police and in the enforcement of broad principles of urban hygiene.[35] For Thomas Percival, a medic prominent in these debates, the cleansing virtues of the hospital restored to virtue and religion those votaries whom pleasure had seduced or villainy betrayed. The lock hospital in particular, designed for the treatment of venereal disease, promoted 'benevolent principles consonant to sound policy, and favourable to reformation or to virtue'.[36] Percival's medical code laid down a strict set of rules to be followed by the hospital physician, who was to eliminate filth, encourage personal neatness and monitor standards of sexual decency. Recovery from disease was also seen to exercise a beneficial moral influence, because convalescence prompted patients to review past offences which were the consequence of vice.

In practice of course these crusades remained relatively localised, dependent on the efforts of particular institutions and professional coteries, especially in the metropolis. Nevertheless, they do point to the early formation of a discourse of social medicine with sexual immorality as one of its component concerns. The expansion of medico-moral politics at the time of the first cholera epidemic formed part of a more extensive network of social policing. Here the strategic aim was much broader, namely the regulation of urban working-class culture in the first stages of industrial capitalism.

4 EXPERTS AND THEIR CONCEPTS

The 1830s and 1840s need to be considered as a key moment in the formation of official concerns over morality. In comparison with the late eighteenth century the perception of problems as well as their solutions had radically changed. The official campaign against cholera, though ad hoc and piecemeal, pointed to the way moral strategies were now promoted by the state in response to the social and cultural dislocations of early industrial society. Qualitatively as well as quantitatively, there were quite fundamental transformations in those government structures broadly concerned with 'reform'. These involved the expansion of existing departments and the creation of new apparatuses, together with the crystallisation of the procedures of social inquiry. Central here was the empirically based royal commission, with its blue-book evidence heralding intervention and orchestrating a wide range of professional knowledges. Many of the investigations had their discursive roots in eighteenth-century medicine, evangelical religion and philanthropy. But such inquiries were now articulated on a transformed social field. The rapid development of a distinct urban working-class politics and culture, along with the shifting balance of forces within the state after 1832, set the broad conditions for almost all of the social reforms of the period. Rather than fixing on the localised scrutiny of the poor, or on particular closed populations, they now targeted the habits and morals of the labouring classes.

Blue-book investigations into health and sanitation, reports from the new poor law commissioners and factory inspectors and the abstracts of the Registrar-General, all precipitated a medico-moral debate about the relation between the individual and the environment and between physical and mental processes. Edwin Chadwick, doyen of the sanitary movement, in his circular letter to assistant commissioners in the Poor Law Commission's inquiry into sanitary conditions, 1842, authoritatively spelt out its environmentalist terms of reference: 'The Commissioners wish to observe that the state of the dwellings occupied by the labouring classes exercise an important influence upon their health.'[37] But the state of the urban or industrial environment was always understood to produce moral as well as physical results. Local officials at the Children's Employment Commission, 1842, were ordered to examine the effects of industrial employment on both moral and bodily health.[38]

'Morals' here condensed a plethora of meanings all jostling for attention. The term served as a synonym for culture, or cultural lack, and to impute blame. Under its rubric were subsumed the terrifying catalogue of barbarous habits which Kay had measured: the collapse of family life, drunkenness, prostitution and political sedition. It was through this nexus of concerns that a specific domain of sexuality was produced. The domain constructed a distinctive repertoire of representations of the sexual around the linked themes of ill-health and immorality. It actively shaped and regulated definitions of class and gender by deployment in key institutional programmes. Mapping this field first takes us deeper into the moral discourses of environmentalism, and to the institutions, forms of knowledge and intellectual agents underpinning the particular construction of sexuality.

A major component of this domain was the social medicine typified by Kay. The medical profession was an influential pressure group campaigning for moral reform, providing the intellectual rationale for state intervention into working-class culture. This statist putsch was intimately bound up with medics' own desire for enhanced status and authority. The 1830s witnessed the beginnings of a distinctive professionalisation of medicine, which was enhanced by members' large-scale involvement in the new apparatuses of the state.[39] The exact position of the local doctor, in terms of class and professional status, remained economically and culturally ambiguous until well into the mid-nineteenth century. He was caught between the trade origins of the barber-surgeons and the superior ranking of lawyers and barristers.[40] Many came from relatively humble origins, like Wakley, the son of a west country farmer and William Farr, a central figure at the General Register Office, who was from a family of agricultural labourers.[41]

The period witnessed early attempts by the profession to carve out a distinctive space of expert knowledge within the emergent culture of the bourgeoisie. The appearance of local medical associations from the 1830s, like Charles Hastings' Provincial Medical and Surgical Association (forerunner of the BMA), reflected growing self-recognition of the importance of professional structures, as did campaigns for the reform of qualifications, taken up in Parliament by Wakley.[42] Prominent medics also played a central role in radical bourgeois politics. Thomas Southwood Smith was friend and physician to the founding father of utilitarianism, Jeremy Bentham. Both Smith and Kay forced a passage into formal politics through their contacts with leading Whig and Tory philanthropists in Parliament. But it was in the state institutionalised programme of reform of the labouring classes that medics first secured professional representation. Here they worked to advance their status as commissioners in the new poor law administration, as local medical officers and as part of the Home Office team of factory inspectors.

Yet medics secured their ascendancy not just through institutional politicking. They also claimed intellectual monopoly over key explanations of human affairs and social progress, notably over the rapid cultural transformations taking place within urban society. As a result, medical research rubbed shoulders with moral philosophy and political economy. Nowhere was this clearer than in the early debates over the causes of contagious disease.

The heated arguments over the origins of infection, prompted by the first cholera epidemic, continued unabated until the 1870s. As late as 1853 the *Lancet* comically listed the range of competing explanations: 'Is it a fungus, an insect, a miasma, an electrical disturbance, a deficiency of ozone, a morbid off-scouring from the intestinal canal? We know nothing; we are at sea in a whirlpool of conjecture.'[43] Three rival theories promoted by medical research were seriously considered by early social reformers. Both the germ theory of infection by a living organism (which stressed that disease was relatively independent of the immediate social environment) and the explanation which maintained that cholera was produced by spontaneous chemical combustion within the blood, were generally dismissed as lacking substantial proof.[44] It was the 'atmospheric' or 'miasmatic' approach which was favoured. Members of the profession like Kay and Southwood Smith, along with prominent sanitarians such as Chadwick and Florence Nightingale, established miasma as the orthodoxy within the public health movement. This theory held that under certain unpredictable circumstances the atmosphere became charged with an epidemic influence, which turned malignant when combined with the effluvia of organic decomposition from the earth. The resulting miasma produced disease within the body.

The choice of miasma theory was influenced both by the internal logic of medical discourse and by wider cultural and political considerations. Miasma fitted well with the scientific materialism of early social medicine. At the level of public debate it was graspable – effluvia could be pointed to and graphically illustrated. But like the concepts of the eighteenth-century hygienists, miasma also targeted the *human agents* of infection – now defined as the labouring classes. The theory was elastic and capable of infinite variation; its environmentalist logic ranged from insanitary conditions to immoral practices.

Southwood Smith's early *A Treatise on Fever*, 1830, was typical. He argued for further research into the diffusion and propagation of infection, together with a survey of the material conditions and habits of the life of the poor:

> The room of a fever patient, in a small and heated appartment of London, with no perflation of fresh air, is perfectly analogous to a stagnant pool in Ethiopia full of the bodies of dead locusts. The poison generated in both cases is the same; the difference is merely in the degree of its potency. Nature, with her burning sun, her stilled and pent-up wind, her stagnant and teeming marsh, manufactures plague on a large and fearful scale. Poverty in her hut, covered with her rags, surrounded by her filth, striving with all her might to keep out the pure air and to increase the heat, imitates Nature but too successfully; the process and the product are the same ... penury and ignorance can thus, at any time in any place, create a mortal plague.[45]

The language here constructed the familiar equation between poverty and disease. But the quasi-Gothic images of squalor, personified in the 'small and heated appartment' of the fever patient, introduced a comparison with primitive society which would have been familiar to Southwood Smith's scientific audience. 'Ethiopia', like the culture of the urban poor and especially the Irish, signified precisely the animalism and lack of civilisation which was in danger of pulling the whole of civilised society back into the abyss. This pre-Darwinist understanding of the nature of progress and decline worked with a comparative historical sociology, which consistently juxtaposed representations of the primitive and ancient world with the problems of contemporary society. Like ancient Greece and Rome, modern commercial enterprise was under attack from barbarous forces.

As in Kay's *Manchester* pamphlet, the range of cultural meanings condensed in Smith's account point to the expansive logic of early social medicine. Immoral conduct was the direct result of the filth, squalor and disease of the urban working-class environment. But immorality – conceived as a general lack of self-reliance and improper habits – was also cited as one of the principal causes of disease. It was no accident that Chadwick placed his weight firmly behind miasma theory, despite his contemptuous dismissal of the whole medical controversy over the origins of infection. Although implacably opposed to medics gaining control of the public health movement, he was not averse to drawing on this type of grandiose scientific pronouncement to bolster arguments for his practical programme of reform, precisely because it had an immediate social field of reference. Miasma served the early sanitarians well.

5 SCIENCE AND RELIGION

For Kay, as for many medics, the cholera epidemic demonstrated scientifically that a 'mighty source of moral causation' was at work in society. Epidemic disease was a providential intervention, and the transgression of God's law through immoral acts brought forth dire consequences.[46] We have seen how Kay mobilised Old Testament language to argue that cholera was a messenger of death, which had been sent to punish the corruption of the people and a flawed system of government. At the time of the second outbreak in 1848, the surgeon John Liddle claimed that doctors were as much Christian philanthropists as scientists, and that they had a duty to interpret God's message to his children.[47]

Recurrent images of retribution drew heavily on religious language which informed medical pronouncements on disease. The clergy were the other key intellectual grouping in the public health alliance, particularly at a local level as poor law officers and members of the new health boards. Many of these men were Anglicans, sharing a traditional paternalist concern about the industrial town. But it was evangelicals in the established church, together with Congregationalists, Methodists and Baptists, who provided the strongest input into the sanitary movement. For these religious fundamentalists cholera was part of a divine plan of providential intervention, designed to punish the nation for wickedness and wrongdoing. At the time of the 1832 epidemic the *Evangelical Magazine and Missionary Chronicle* pointed to the multiple evils besetting the country. Trade slump and the reform bill crisis, secularism among the middle classes and infidelism among the poor, all fuelled the conviction that general moral decline precipitated divine vengeance:

> violence hath been rampant in our cities – wasting and destruction have entered into all our borders – the church languishes – its

vintage faileth – fanaticism and speculation like a wrathful bolt from the skies, have scattered some of the Cedars of Lebanon.[48]

In the industrial parishes of the midlands and the north, cholera was a favourite subject for Sunday sermons, when local vicars used lurid metaphors of disease to demonstrate that sickness was God's chastisement for sin. In the mining district of Sedgley in south Staffordshire, Charles Girdlestone, a low church Anglican vicar, preached his *Seven Sermons* on the fixed equation between physical and moral laws:

> Whatsoever evil we see around us, whatsoever evil we feel within us, is, we know, the consequence of sin. By sin came death. And by sin came that which brought the evil on us. It is Satan that first tempted us to sin, and now works on us this miserable consequence.[49]

Girdlestone noted with satisfaction the general improvement in moral habits among his parishioners under threat of God's wrath. More shops were closing on Sunday, there was a decline in bull-baiting and other barbarous pastimes, while marriages were on the increase, along with a general improvement in morals. He was emphatic that ministers of religion – 'they who are most conversant with man and his interests in a spiritual aspect' – needed to take their place beside medics in the battle for moral reform.[50] Within the public health movement there was little antagonism between religious principles of morality and scientific observation. The evangelical commitment of many medics may itself have been linked to their attempts to define a new professional ethic which was at once distinctive and serious.[51] William Cooke, a fellow of the Royal College of Surgeons, noted in 1839 that in earlier periods science and religion had 'seemed mutually to dread approximation', but in recent years 'reciprocal confidence has been growing, and so far from being now ashamed of each other's company we often see them in the most loving harmony'.[52]

This interleaving of medicine and religion was underpinned by the fundamentally deistic conception of early nineteenth-century science. Scientists had a duty to validate the religious and moral order of the universe. God had granted men the power of rational inquiry to explain the harmonious organisation of the world. Archdeacon William Paley's *Natural Theology*, 1802 – subtitled *'Evidences of the existence and attributes of the deity collected from the appearances of nature'* – was still required reading for all students at Oxford and Cambridge in the 1830s. Paley's popular reading of Newtonian science maintained that scientists who studied the natural world were participating in God's creation, because their inquiries always verified the existence of the Designer, thereby combating atheism.[53] Trees, flowers, plants, animal life and the providential organisation of human society all displayed the hand of the great architect of nature.

This was the dominant Anglican conception of scientific inquiry. It partly explains why the ranks of the clergy mustered such a strong contingent of amateur scientists. Local vicars embarked on a wide range of studies and were especially involved in promoting the nascent sciences of geology, botany and biology.[54] Within their conservative framework, scientific arguments could be used to bolster traditional moral and political sermonising on the virtues of a fixed hierarchy of order and authority. Some dissenting ministers challenged such a comfortable integration of science and religion. At least one Congregationalist preacher used the first cholera outbreak to attack the cold and dreary materialism of medics, who, while busily promulgating scientific laws, roundly ignored the principles of God's moral government.[55] Much more characteristic, though, was the call for increased dialogue between the two arms of social reform.

6 MEDICO-MORAL POLITICS IMPLEMENTED?

Practical alliances between scientists, clerics and other political forces were forged through the various pressure groups campaigning for public health in the 1840s. Such coalitions cut right across class and party lines. The Health of Towns Association, formed in 1844, was especially representative of the diverse class and intellectual coteries pushing for moral reform. It was led by the Marquis of Normanby, Whig Home Secretary, while its committee members included Lord Ashley and Robert Slaney (both reforming Tories), and the evangelical Girdlestone, as well as the medics John Simon and Southwood Smith. The aims and objects of the association made the characteristic move from environmental reform – sewage, drainage, water-supply, air and light, building construction – to the inevitable moral reforms confidently predicted to follow in its wake. Decent material conditions would:

> yield increased facilities to the practice of Devotion ... and to attendance on public worship, and ... in promoting health of the body and cleanliness of person ... will thus at the same time clear the way for the Purifying and Healing of the Soul.[56]

The creation of the General Board of Health under the Public Health Act, 1848, marked a high watermark for medico-moral politics. It seemed as if the plans for state-backed hygienics had at last come to fruition. Yet the limited powers of the new board showed just how far removed early public health administration was from the grandiose ambitions of sanitarians like Chadwick. He had campaigned for a nationwide system of sewers, drains and public burial grounds. The new legislation largely left control of public health in the hands of local authorities. It was founded on the voluntary principle, whereby towns were empowered, rather than forced, to establish public health administration. But the act did set up a central commission appointed for five years and composed initially of three active members: Lord Ashley, Chadwick and the First Commissioner of Woods and Forests as President.

Almost immediately there were familiar cries of outrage from medics over what they saw as their wilful exclusion from the new board. It was deeply insulting, they complained, to set up a 'medical board of two noblemen who are perfectly innocent of medical information and a lawyer'.[57] Even at this stage, medical representation within the state was not a foregone conclusion – though Southwood Smith was hastily appointed to stave off further criticism. Organised opposition was also being mounted from other quarters. Anti-statist groupings, bitterly opposed to what they perceived to be 'prussianism' by big landlords and private drainage and water companies, blocked any move into full-blooded sanitary statism and effectively preserved the balance between voluntary effort and central control.[58]

It was Lord Ashley's membership of the new board which consolidated the medico-moral alliance. As a committed evangelical and social reformer he had long attached 'immense and unparalleled importance to the sanitary question, as second only to the religious and in some aspects inseparable from it'.[59] Chadwick himself was quick to see the benefits of securing Ashley's cooperation, bringing with him the religious and moral wing of the public health movement.[60] Ashley's reaction to his appointment was characteristic, trembling at first with the weight of responsibility but then pledging a firm commitment to God's mission in the world. His work for the board between 1848 and 1851 promoted the continuing alliance between science and religion. He fervently believed that rational sanitary measures were the practical enactment of God's law on earth. It was the evangelical message that was paramount in Ashley's sanitary politics; even in the midst of disease and suffering God's work was manifest. The cholera epidemic of 1848 had brought good out of evil, because religion had made 'visible progress among the poorer sort and many of the wealthy are turning their minds to the improvement of society'.[61] Ashley's main worry, as the cholera abated, was that the spirit of physical and moral regeneration would also diminish. Fearful, he wrote to Chadwick in October 1849: 'The cholera thank God has passed – is not the wholesome fear passing also?'[62]

The strong religious and ethical presence in all the reform movements checked any purely mechanistic theorisation of the individual/society equation which was common among secular Benthamites. They were pushing for a full-blown materialism in tackling the social domain. But among all campaigning groups there was a continual dialectic over the precise importance awarded to moral responsibility as against environmental influences. The tension between the two elements resulted in neither a victory for pure environmentalism nor for moral individualism. What occurred was the relative privileging of one element or another in different fields of intervention, according to different political priorities and different visions of social order. While the new poor law placed emphasis firmly on individual self-improvement, public health tended to stress that material advancement would produce beneficial changes in modes of living and beliefs.[63]

It was this tension which fed into the differing conceptions of the moral duties of the new secular state held by the reformers. All groups were agreed that state intervention into public health was necessary to promote personal morality. But though morality was the ether which all of them breathed, it was composed of different elements for different constituencies: utilitarian discipline as opposed to liberal philanthropy, benevolent paternalism as compared with hard-edged professional expertise.

As an improving Tory aristocrat, Lord Ashley fervently hoped that a properly administered state could embody the values of benevolent paternalism and play the role of a faithful and pious parent. Medics and clerics on the other hand favoured a conception of the ethical state. For Kay, morally humane state intervention was necessary to counteract the inadequacies of pure Benthamism and the laissez-faire fallacy. Political economy was not designed to deal with the problems facing the social body, which could not be constructed on abstract principles like a machine, ignoring the promotion of happiness and the cultivation of religion and morality.[64] Kay's offensive here was aimed at the 'immorality' of sections of the big bourgeoisie, who blocked all attempts at intervention into the social as well as the economic sphere.

As a purer Benthamite, Chadwick's understanding of the role of government was much more utilitarian and secular. The state promoted the health and happiness of individuals, while at the same time delivering important moral and economic benefits to capital. Sickness was a costly thing, especially to the nation state, and hence public health administration needed to form a central plank of the art of government. Health reform would secure real commercial and industrial rewards. A clean, healthy and morally ordered workforce increased the efficiency of labour-power, reduced manufacturers' costs and so promoted a general increase in comfort and wealth for all classes of society.[65]

Despite their internal differences, at no time did the reformers mount a direct attack on the manufacturing system itself as the source of physical and moral deterioration. Such a logic was outside their framework and points to the limits of their analysis. Explanations of the underlying causes of depravity frequently worked with an evils extrinsic argument. The national social body, conceived as fundamentally healthy and morally virtuous, had been subjected to invasions from without, or to divine vengeance which followed in the wake of wickedness. Demoralisation from the Irish, or disease as God's punishment, were characteristic forms of

explanation. Kay's pronouncements were typical: 'the evils ... so f
being the necessary consequences of the manufacturing system,
remote and accidental origin, and might by judicious managen
entirely removed.'[66] There was also a characteristic distinction between
types of evil, those that were avoidable and those seen as inevitable. Economic crises were often depicted using imagery drawn from the natural
world. The periodic fluctuations of the business cycle were attributed to
physical causes. The social order itself and the fundamental inequalities
between capital and labour were understood as fixed and immutable.

Preventive medicine, philanthropy and religion advanced a scientific and
moral critique of the effects of nascent industrial capitalism. But these professional and religious principles did not undermine the basic political and
economic assumptions on which capitalist social relations were based.
Ultimately, the majority of reformers identified the commercial system as a
force whose movement was inexorable. Though tensions between the
experts and other political forces were often acute, the product of real fractures and oppositions within the ruling bloc, they were resolved by this
overarching logic.

7 DE-CODING MORALITY: THE DOMAIN OF THE SEXUAL

We have established that moral reform was a key component in the overall
programme aimed at the disciplining of the early industrial working class.
But the loose and expansive use of the term 'moral' often makes it difficult
to deconstruct its fields of reference. This is not merely a problem of historical interpretation, it points to the fact that the concept was subject to a
wide number of connotative meanings, which were continually being condensed and which are incapable of precise differentiation. Morality at once
referenced a series of codes and practices regulating individual conduct and
a range of protocols and procedures about the art of government. Immorality signified all the practices of working-class life leading to ungovernable
and disruptive behaviour: lack of individual self-reliance, ignorance, criminality, the threat of political sedition, and of course sexual impropriety.
The multiple points of reference condensed here point to the grandiose and
all-embracing approach to reform, involving as it did a general onslaught
on the culture of the poor. In a period in which economic crises and
working-class political agitation were an ever-present threat, the majority of
social problems were seen to be interrelated, though later they were to
become differentiated as distinct pathologies. It was these broad conjunc-
tural factors which set the conditions for the strong professional and
intellectual alliances at work within environmentalism.

In what ways did the reformers stake out a particular construction of the sexual as part of their programme? First, the image of sexuality was almost invariably negative – sexuality was always referenced as *sexual immorality*, an integral part of all of the other immoral and ungovernable habits of working-class life. As always, Ashley was explicit about the evil. In a parliamentary speech in 1843 he put before the house a picture of 'an accumulated mass of squalid wretchedness'. Leeds, for example, boasted a

> beer-shop where there are rooms upstairs, and the boys and girls, old people, and married of both sexes, go up two by two, as they can agree, to have connection ... the most revolting feature of juvenile depravity is the early contamination from the association of the sexes. The outskirts of the town are absolutely polluted by this abomination.[67]

Abomination, depravity, pollution – there were no positive representations of sexuality in this discourse. Debauchery and licentiousness stood at the opposite pole to those forms of social and civilised behaviour – cleanliness, sobriety, industriousness, the structures of home and family – which made up the vision of a disciplined working class. Further, given the constant interplay of moral and material factors within early social reform, sexual debauchery was understood both as a product of material squalor and a causal factor in the decline of the urban environment.

These themes were to the fore in all the official inquiries, but they were particularly dominant in the blue books on sanitary reform. The wretchedness of the working-class environment, the state of the dwellings, non-existent sanitation, lack of concern over personal decency and hygiene were seen to encourage irregular sexual conduct. There were constant references to the effects of overcrowding and bad housing on sexual behaviour throughout the official investigations. In the sanitary report it was a sense of horror and ritual denunciation which predominated:

> How they lay down to rest, how they sleep, how they can preserve common decency, how unutterable horrors are avoided, is beyond all conception. . . . It shocks every feeling of propriety to think that ... civilized beings should be herding together without a decent separation of age or sex.[68]

Then the narrative moved to a more precise classification of specific immoral acts:

> In a cellar in Pendleton I recollect there were three beds in the two apartments . . . in one of which a man and his wife slept; in another, a man, his wife and child; and in the third two unmarried females. . . . I have met with upwards of forty persons sleeping in

the same room, married and single, including, of course, children and several young adult persons of either sex. In Manchester . . . I found such promiscuous mixture of the sexes in sleeping-rooms . . . I have met with instances of a man, his wife, and his wife's sister, sleeping in the same bed together. . . . In Hull . . . I found in one room a prostitute, with whom I remonstrated on the course of her life . . . she stated that she had lodged with a married sister, and slept in the same bed with her and her husband; that hence improper intercourse took place, and from that she became more and more depraved.[69]

Incest was the most common source of moral anxiety, precisely because it dramatically disrupted middle-class norms of family propriety.[70] But these representations contained rather more than the perception that sexual immorality resulted from an impoverished and overcrowded environment. Sexual immorality was defined through the significations of dirt, disease, squalor, corruption and the political and cultural threat of an urban working-class populace. When Chadwick pointed out that the habits of labouring families soon became 'of a piece' with the dwellings, he evoked precisely that type of condensation.[71] Filthy habits of life were never separated from the moral filthiness for which they were the type and the representative. Local medical officers and poor law officials compared the factory operatives, sunk 'into sensual sloth', or revelling in even 'more degrading licentiousness', against their idealised vision of the rural poor. Dr Alison of Tranent was reassured by his visits to the cottages of Scottish agricultural labourers:

With very few exceptions, the condition of the interior of the houses of the hind population is excellent, most pleasing to the eye and comfortable. These respectable people, in spite of the defective construction of their cottages, manage to throw an air of comfort, plenty and neatness and order around their homes. I have often been delighted to observe these characteristics, and not less so to mark the co-existence of pure, moral, and religious principles in the inmates, the presence of practical religion and practical morals.[72]

Such descriptions of the more natural, and the more moral, relations of rural society were always intended to evoke their opposite. Urbanisation had produced a cultural miasma; for public health reformers dirt stood as the grand metaphor for all forms of urban disorder. It was this powerful cloacal imagery of pollution, excretion and disease which lay at the heart of the depictions of sexual immorality. It was reinforced by evangelical religion, which possessed an elaborate language for discoursing on bodily pleasures and animal appetites.

In the 1830s and 1840s evangelical religious language, part visionary, part denunciatory, was mobilised by groups right across the political spectrum, from feminists within the Owenite socialist movement through to professionals and religious reformers. Many women reworked evangelical discourse to advance their political demands or to discuss their sexual and emotional experience. But conservative preachers like Girdlestone used the vivid Pauline oppositions of flesh and spirit, God and mammon, as part of their repertoire for morally disciplining the poor:

> we must not pretend, in affectation of humility, not to see, and know, and feel the difference between serving God, and serving mammon, between walking by faith in love, and living selfishly and sensually, between being brethren of Christ, and being children of Belial.[73]

His rhetoric of moral denunciation was not silent on the issue of immorality; he painted a lurid and explicit picture of lewdness and sensual pleasure, framed by the terrors of the final judgment. Girdlestone appealed to children and to parents, his sermons always mounting to a climax of emotional *frisson* and terror:

> The next idol against which I have to warn you is sensual pleasure. . . . Other sensual pleasures will beset your souls hereafter, with snares most alluring, with poison the most deadly. . . . Oh, when we think how many souls are lost by forbidden indulgence.[74]

Yet though medics and clerics were vituperative in their condemnation of the sexuality of the labouring poor, their moralising was not wholly negative and prohibitive. It held out the promise of definite satisfactions to their patients and congregations who observed the dictates of morality. For some evangelicals, satisfaction lay in the knowledge of having fought the battle between flesh and spirit and ultimately won through, but other reformers promised material rewards to those who heeded their warnings: good health, longevity and a prosperous, settled existence. These were comfortable, homely pleasures, but for a working class dependent on the vagaries of an unstable economic system and subject to extreme social dislocations they must have offered a tempting vision of security. The Health of Towns Association promised the weary labourer, returning from his work, an end to the crowded, dirty, damp and cold washed-out cellar shared with other families. Cheerful society in a cheerful place was what the working man was thought to yearn after. Order, beauty, sweetness and health, with women returned to their rightful place as domestic helpmates, would flow logically from sanitary reform.[75]

In the discourse on the urban poor, reformers constructed the sexual through the class-related polarities which were central to their programme:

physical health/non-health, virtue/vice, cleanliness/filth, morality/depravity, civilisation/animality. The binary oppositions were organised in such a way that each polarity functioned to reinforce the other. Bourgeois cleanliness was impossible without the image of proletarian filth, middle-class propriety could not be defined without the corresponding representations of working-class animality, and so on. All this was not wholly new; it had continuities with eighteenth-century social medicine and with earlier religious constructions of sexuality across the spirit/flesh divide. What was new was that these definitions were now incorporated into a variety of official knowledges as part of a broad programme of state intervention into the culture of the industrial labouring classes. This discourse on sexuality now had distinctive *class articulations*. Hence, though these representations did not originate in the economic, political and cultural transformations of early industrial capitalism, in this period they increasingly became annexed to class–cultural relations.

It is also important to be clear in what sense this configuration around sexuality was a discursive construction, a construction within and by very specific sets of power–knowledge relations, and in what sense it was a product of concrete environmental conditions. To speak of its discursive formation is not to deny that this construction of the sexual was grounded in particular historical conditions and social relations. But discourses did not simply reflect these. We are not dealing with practices either rendering a true picture of reality (that is sexuality constructed as filthy and diseased because filth and disease were the realities of the working-class environment), or as neatly representing pre-given forms of class power and knowledge whose origins lay elsewhere. We are dealing with specific social practices – religion, medicine and sanitary science – whose organisation was an active force in the production of the sexual meanings in play. They neither transparently reflected reality nor did they passively represent class relations. They were active in the construction of both.

8 HYGIENICS AND BOURGEOIS HEGEMONY

If the labouring classes were portrayed as possessing an immoral sexuality, then the cultural identity of the bourgeoisie was formed around its opposite, in relation to the linked themes of health, hygiene, procreation and inheritance. It is tempting to follow Foucault and designate this nexus of concerns 'bourgeois sexuality', but within official discourse the sexual was so strongly identified with the urban working class that it is more accurate to describe it as a code of personal hygiene, moral restraints and procreative ethics.[76] The medical profession acted as powerful ideologues for the professional gentry and sections of the industrial bourgeoisie, laying claim to a middle-class monopoly over the issues of health and hygiene. They endowed these groups with a distinctive cultural repertoire, separate both from the perceived debauchery of the aristocracy and the disease-ridden working class. For Kay, health was the 'precious jewel of life', to be guarded against the proverbial 'thief walking in darkness' who might 'rifle the casket' while one slept.[77] The thief was cholera and the working-class threat personified, but it was also an image of self-destruction brought about by sensual indulgence and voluptuousness.

Specific warnings on the dangers of sexual excess figured prominently in numerous tracts and pamphlets on personal and domestic health which appeared from the 1830s. Almost invariably these injunctions were addressed to men. According to one popular writer offering *Twenty Minutes Advice on Diet, Regimen and All Other Matters Connected with Health*, those who followed the downward path of the voluptuary were always 'cut off in their prime'.[78] The *Lancet* spelt out the dangers forcibly: the 'sexual sensualist' pursued a course which led inevitably to moral degradation, mental and bodily infirmity and even madness.[79] One medic claimed he had isolated a specific form of consumption – *Tabes Dorsalis* or *Spermatic Plethora* – which occurred in 'young men of salacious dispositions' who had indulged in an immoderate use of the sexual function.[80] The physical excitation accompanying 'venereal enjoyments' acted like a convulsion, destroying the nerve tissue, sapping the body fibres and thinning the blood. Moderate exercise of the male sexual appetite was the best possible safeguard against ill-health. Behind these arguments lay the teachings of contemporary physiology, which insisted on the ill-effects of all forms of bodily excess. But in the hands of some medics the notion of moderate sexual indulgence was used to justify occasional but necessary lapses by the bachelor or frustrated husband. Total abstinence was as detrimental to health as overindulgence.[81]

Moderation was the keynote in the professional advice offered to the bourgeoisie on all aspects of their personal habits and behaviour. Physicians prescribed a careful physical and moral regimen for patients, encompassing sleep, ventilation of rooms, diet and control of the sexual appetitite:

> The good secret of health is simply this – Regulate your bowels by taking mild aperients when necessary: Be careful not to eat what disagrees with you: Be regular and temperate in your habits: Refrain from the use of Spirituous Liquors: Retire to rest early, and rise betimes in the morning.[82]

Such a self-conscious code of rituals and restraints was designed to display a set of inner moral qualities, as part of a wider middle-class bid for cultural hegemony over key areas of personal and domestic life. According to William Cooke, only among the middle classes were regular and temperate habits strictly observed; it was 'one of the great causes why the middle classes of society have more of real soundness of mind, as well as body, than either the highest or the lowest'.[83]

Regular habits were a real asset in the successful pursuit of a business or professional career. But for middle-class wives and daughters a regime of sobriety and healthy living was essential if they were to reproduce sound offspring and thereby transmit personal reputation, property, legitimacy and life to the next generation. A spate of medical tracts on marriage and childbirth laid down strict guidelines for 'maternal hygiology' and the management of women during pregnancy, parturition and lactation. The medic Michael Ryan gave detailed instructions on the organisation of the labour chamber: the need for absolute cleanliness, the role of the obstetrician and the duties of the midwife, while Cooke, the surgeon-accoucheur, was concerned with the 'moral management of childbirth', especially the correct medical etiquette to be observed by the doctor in treating his female patients.[84]

This scheme of moral hygienics was carried into official discourse through the programme of population assessment, developed by the early statistical societies and the newly created General Register Office. 'Moral statistics', or as they were often termed, 'vital' or 'life statistics', comprising 'population distribution, consumption, divisions of life, health and public or private charity', formed an important sub-domain of the Royal London Statistical Society, founded in 1834.[85] The Manchester Society produced similar studies on *The Relative Proportion of the Male and Female Population*, 1840, on puberty and early marriages and on the physiology of particular racial groups.[86] With the setting up of the General Register Office, under the provisions of the Births, Marriages and Deaths Registration Act, 1836, there was a specific government agency to address the population issue.[87] With the appointment of William Farr as head of the office's statistical branch, the department had acquired one of the chief protagonists of population politics.

Farr had been pressing throughout the 1830s for more detailed knowledge about the health and moral habits of individuals and groups within the population. His French-influenced system of hygiology, outlined in a series of articles in the *Lancet*, argued that the health of individuals (promoted by the medical practitioner) and the vitality of the general population (the domain of public health administration) were interlinked. Both were concerned with increasing the strength and stamina of the nation state, by raising the health of the population to the greatest degree:

> The true object of hygiene . . . is to increase the *sum of vitality* by extending individual life to its full term (averting death); by obviating sickness; and by increasing the energy of all the vital forces, whether nutritive, formative, locomotive, or sensitive and intellectual.[88]

At the Register Office Farr worked to implement his plans through a skilful mixture of bold polemic and detailed statistical evidence. Refuting the overpopulationist panic of the Rev Thomas Malthus, by arguing for the benefits of an expanding mode of production, Farr hoped to see an increase in the marriage rate and the legitimate birth rate. These factors, he asserted, 'ensured the perpetuity of life and nations', in the midst of the antagonistic forces of disease and death.[89] It was the middle classes above all who held the key to the future prosperity of the country. Through his appendices to the annual reports of the Registrar-General – more statements of policy than mere statistical commentaries – Farr called for greater attention to the rules of maternal hygiene and to the medical supervision of childbirth. His main aim was to promote quantitative and qualitative increase among the middle ranks of society. The local medical practitioner could play a central role in disseminating the principles of procreative hygiene to women of the better classes. The well-informed sections of the community, Farr claimed, owed their enlightenment to the teaching of their medical attendants. It was essential that doctors lost no opportunity of 'laying down the rules of health, and enforcing them, by drawing the attention of families to the sad and often striking consequences of neglect'.[90]

Farr's plans were not implemented in any large-scale immediate policy initiatives. Rather, what occurred were piecemeal elements of legislation throughout the century governing the solemnisation of marriage and the divorce laws, which were designed to promote sound and legitimate off-spring.[91] Nevertheless, his arguments were articulate statements about the links between personal moral hygiene, the health of the population and the power and puissance of the middle class.

What is the relation between this hygienist enterprise and the domain of sexuality staked out by the sanitarians and clerics? Foucault has convincingly argued that the regime of sex instituted in this period was not characterised by negative repression. The bourgeoisie were constantly inciting and evoking the sexual through modes of control which were productive of new identities, pleasures and desires.[92] While pointing usefully to the productive nature of regulation, Foucault's account leaves a number of important questions unanswered about the class articulations in play. First, it would be more accurate to say that it was the new professional experts, working in conjunction with clerics, philanthropists and improving employers, who staked out this field of sexuality – not the bourgeoisie in general. What this cadre of male intellectuals continually incited were representations of working-class sexuality. When it came to their own culture, their public polemic (and we shall come to their private fantasies shortly) was concerned with something quite different. Not sexuality but bourgeois hygienics; the health-giving rituals of moderation and ordered living which led to population increase and promised cultural and economic ascendancy.

36

9 WORKING-CLASS FEMALE SEXUALITY AND PROFESSIONAL MASCULINITY

Early social reformers identified the great mass of the urban working class as the major cultural threat. Yet they did mark out specific gender distinctions and divisions as part of their programme. For not only were the polarised representations of health and hygiene, dirt and disease bound up with class assumptions, they were also overlaid by middle-class notions of sexual difference. Working-class men had been brutalised through the state of the workplace environment and through their own inherent lack of morality as men; they were often described as semi-barbarous and close to nature. Official representations of the morals of working women were more complex and contradictory, shifting across the health/disease, morality/immorality oppositions, according to the focus of the male investigators. The moral judgments made by the experts were heavily determined by their own class-specific expectations of femininity. Working-class women were both eroticised and condemned as immoral pollutants, the cause of the decline of whole communities, and at the same time heralded as the agents of moral reform. In the dramatic local incidents, where experts encountered women colliers and factory operatives, we can see this double axis at work.

The factory commissioners believed that women had become depraved under the improper conditions of heavy manual labour and industrial employment in the mines and factories, where they worked in close and indecent proximity to men:

> I have no doubt the debauchery is carried on, for there is every opportunity; for the girls go constantly, when hurrying, to the men. . . . I think it scarcely possible for girls to remain modest who are in pits, regularly mixing with such company, and hearing such language as they do. I dare venture to say that many of the wives who come from pits know nothing of sewing or any household duty, such as women ought to know.[93]

And the 1842 factory report concluded that:

> all classes of witnesses bear testimony to the demoralizing effect of females underground . . . the girls and boys and the young men and even married women and women with child, commonly work almost naked.[94]

The subcommissioners pursued their quest for immoral behaviour with vigour. Young women operatives were summoned to testify to the extent of the problem, and their accounts give important insights into the gendered dimensions of early factory culture. 'Lads and lassies' arrived at the spinning mills and took off their overclothes. It was then that the big boys 'spied' the big lassies taking off their stockings and shouted naughty and pert obscenities.[95] It seems that sexual harassment has not changed all that much over a hundred and fifty years. Women had their clothes pulled up while asleep in the rest periods, together with other forms of ritual humiliation. The lads called it practical jokes, but one seventeen-year-old girl was adamant: 'a lass stands no chance with so many boys.'[96]

Yet it was the perception of female depravity which filled page after page of the subcommissioners' evidence, intruding into all aspects of their inquiries. Questions about the women's physical suffering, or the specific division of factory labour (issues central to the concern with the male workforce) were subordinated to this obsession. In the male-defined culture of these blue-book reports there was space for officials to indulge, *sotto voce*, their own sexual fantasies. Their moralising diatribes on female behaviour carried a heavily sexualised, erotic sub-text. Detailed descriptions of the girls' physical appearance – their clothing, habits and even their jewellery – tell us much about the sexual desire of these professional men.

Take the lawyer, Jelinger Symons. Symons was from the clerical gentry, a subcommissioner in the Yorkshire coalfield and an early educational expert. Prefacing his report with the pompous statement that it was his official duty to 'direct . . . attention to the deplorable outrage of introducing females into the collieries', he went on to concentrate on the depraved, filthy and animal-like appearance of the pit girls:

> One of the most disgusting sights I have ever seen was that of young females, dressed like boys in trowsers, crawling on all fours, with belts round their waists, and chains passing between their legs, at day pits at Hunshelf Bank, and in many small pits near Holmfirth and New Mills.[97]

In his report from one New Mills mine Symons lingered over the fact that 'the chain, passing high up between the legs of two . . . girls, had worn large holes in their trowsers, and any sight more disgustingly indecent or revolting can scarcely be imagined than these girls at work.'[98] His intention may have been to shock but it also drew attention to his own sexual preoccupations. As he put it: 'No brothel can beat it.'[99] Symons interviewed nearly three hundred witnesses, many of them pit girls. His particular fixation was that they dressed in boys' clothes and thereby became 'unsexed'. He described one ten-year-old as a 'nice-looking child, but of course as black as a tinker, and with a little necklace round her throat'.[100] Similarly, Edward Newman, a Barnsley solicitor, salaciously reported that on more than one occasion he had seen pit girls 'washing themselves naked much below the waist as I passed their door'.[101]

Several aspects of this construction of male sexual desire are significant.

First, it worked through the sexualisation of the physical traits of working-class women's appearance. Dirty clothes, tawdry jewellery, nakedness, all functioned as potent emblems, registering the cultural distance between the male investigator and his female object. This process of objectification involved a particular sexualised way of looking which bore close relation to the protocols of official knowledge shaping the public inquiries of these men – the rules of detailed observation and classification central to the empirical method. But when applied to working women, this discourse eroticised the cultural distance between observer and observed. For these professionals, sexual desire was produced at the interface of the class and gender oppositions set up by environmentalism. Here was male sexuality constructed through the erotic mechanism of a voyeuristic gaze and by the fetishisation of cultural difference.

Yet men like Symons also regarded these women as central to the reform of working-class habits. Their innate but dormant moral qualities needed to be cultivated by sanitary science and religion. This could only be achieved by returning them to their proper sphere of influence – the family. Pit women were judged to be moral if they possessed key domestic virtues such as bakery and cookery, needlework and a knowledge of family economy. Instructions sent out from the Central Board of the Children's Employment Commission to the regions noted under the category 'moral condition':

> In regard to female workers, you will inquire how far their employment during Childhood has prevented them from forming the domestic habits usually acquired by women in their station, and has rendered them less fit than those whose early years have not been spent in labour for performing the duties of wives and mothers.[102]

Subcommissioners made frequent comparisons between the manufacturing districts and the mining communities of the north east. The improved moral condition of the colliers of Northumberland and Durham was due to the more feminine, that is the more domestic, habits of the women: 'In their habits they partake of much of those which prevail in the house; cleanliness and sobriety are much more common traits than the reverse. The young are more feminine than females in a manufacturing community.'[103] Similarly, evangelicals painted their picture of hell with images of domestic chaos, filth and by implication female immorality. Christian virtuousness on the other hand was evoked through feminine metaphors of sweeping, cleansing and garnishing. Girdlestone's sermonising employed this language to appeal directly to women in his congregations: 'When the soul of a sinner has been arrested . . . how truly it is described as being swept and garnished. For how like unto filth in habitation is profligacy in a Christian.'[104]

What were the connections between the experts' double-edged perceptions of working-class women and their own personal and professional culture? Of course, intellectuals and administrators were not the source or origin of this sexual iconography in a psychological sense. Their language was always socially produced. But the experts' lived experience of their constructed personal lives did have effects on their public personas and official actions.

The biographies of men like Symons, Kay and Chadwick point to the beginnings of the male career, organised around an increasingly rigid division between the public world of professional life and the private sphere of women, home and domesticity. The formation of professions like medicine and public administration in this period produced a stricter differentiation of gender roles, which was part of the general separation of spheres and duties for men and women within the bourgeoisie. Professional masculinity was a mixture of scientific, hard-edged expertise, unflinching in its attack on all forms of amateurish incompetence, and an ideology of dedication to public service. This male identity was forged through the new intellectual knowledges which endowed the experts with a caste-like mode of cohesion. A number became related through intermarriage, creating an informal cultural network where ideas could be turned over and disagreements aired. Chadwick married Rachel Kennedy, daughter of John Kennedy, Vice-President of the Manchester Statistical Society, while another daughter was married to Samuel Robinson, the brother-in-law of the educationalist and industrialist Benjamin Heywood.

It was of course a male-defined culture, working systematically to marginalise women. Women figured in this world as objects of grace and adornment and as efficient household managers. They were also expected to oil the wheels of their husbands' careers through the extension of kinship and by organising the social round of entertainment. Rachel Chadwick described her husband's soirées as 'sanitary parties', and it is clear that Chadwick himself viewed his private life as secondary and inferior. On marriage at the age of thirty-nine he was amazed and irritated to discover that domestic affairs involved administrative politics quite as complex as public health law. Writing to a friend in 1839, he complained that this 'new experience in household matters' had brought much annoyance from workmen and domestics. His reponse was characteristic: 'I intend to make these experiences of ... indolence and inattention ... the subject of some remarks on popular education.'[105] When his wife was recovering from childbirth, Chadwick apologised for his non-appearance at public meetings with the comment: 'Mrs Chadwick has had a child and I have had a fever and I have recovered first.'[106]

Not all the private lives of these professional men conformed to the Chadwickian pattern. Half a generation younger than the Chadwicks, John and Jane Simon negotiated a more progressive personal relationship, organised around companionship and cemented by 'mutual affection' and

40

respect.[107] This arrangement gave the wife a considerable degree of informal influence over her husband's public career. We know that Jane Simon was intellectually formidable, competing as a relative equal with men like John Ruskin, Charles Darwin and Chadwick at the regular salons and dinner parties the couple organised.[108]

It is difficult to map the structures of personal and sexual experience which these men and women lived out. What is clear is that middle-class men, dependent on the ministrations of their wives for emotional support and domestic management, transferred the same needs on to working men and a disproportionate burden on to working-class women. At the same time, the experts' erotic perceptions of these women were structured in opposition to norms of middle-class femininity. The Kay household provides us with a particularly incisive account of personal relations within the professional middle class, and of what happened when they went wrong.

Kay's marriage to Janet Shuttleworth in 1842 brought him a connection with the established gentry. As an heiress in her own right, his wife's dowry was considerable, including estates in Lancashire and a large personal fortune. The couple's engagement was the subject for celebration. Symons, a personal friend, penned three pages of rhyming doggerel celebrating the joys of companionate marriage. Kay's own experience of early married life seems to have been bound up with the perception of his wife as both an emblem of cultural status and a mute confidante. She was a decorative object, the 'most good pure beauty', the guiding principle of his public deliberations and the most precious adornment of their two beautiful houses.[109] He infantilised Janet, constantly referring to her as 'my sweet little wife', and using her as an audience for his social philosophising – though there was no notion that the relation was reciprocal. For her part, Janet Shuttleworth's understanding of married love, as for so many women of her class and generation, was expressed in quasi-religious terms. She felt herself happy in Kay's 'strong and holy affection', giving thanks to Him who had bound them together in mutual trust and confidence.[110]

But in the early 1850s the Kays' marriage went disastrously wrong. The couple were estranged and the ensuing litigation hinted at sexual difficulties and Lady Shuttleworth's suspected adultery. From then on Kay's perception of his wife altered dramatically. Structurally she was shifted across the polarities demarcating respectable as opposed to unrespectable womanhood. Kay pathologised her, implying that she was mentally unbalanced. The death of his own mother in 1858 occasioned some bitter comparisons between the two women. His mother had been 'an upright prudent matron' with 'remarkable firmness of mind' who had lived a simple, pure, religious life. All this was in contrast to his own wife.[111] When middle-class women disrupted the boundaries policing their personal conduct, the moral opprobrium was as great as that directed at mill girls and colliers' wives.

10 HIERARCHIES OF EXPERTISE: FEMALE PHILANTHROPY AND THE GENDERED POLITICS OF REFORM

There was a reverse side to the gendered dimensions of professionalism. For though the reformers defined all women in terms of the private sphere of the family, these male experts were not without female allies and competitors in the public domain. The early nineteenth century witnessed the growth of the male professions, but the period also saw the emergence of their female counterpart, namely charity and philanthropy as fit work for middle-class women. Sanitarians, medics and clerics were anxious to forge alliances with lady philanthropists, especially at a local level. The growing dialogue between male experts and female social reformers, particularly from the 1850s, is important to our argument. This gendered alliance both cemented the programme of social disciplining and became a major factor in the political struggles over sexuality in the later nineteenth century. Philanthropy was to act as a springboard for the early women's movement, aiding the development of a full-scale feminist critique of male power and expertise. The contradictions which erupted between these two élites over sexual regulation constitute a major strand of our subsequent history. First it is important to outline the specific position occupied by middle-class women within the discourse of environmentalism.

Like early social medicine, philanthropy was deeply influenced by the culture of evangelical and dissenting religion. Between 1790 and 1830 the new evangelicism, with its emphasis on the regeneration of national morality through the purity of domestic manners and an ethic of practical Christianity, was a major factor in the growing participation of women in philanthropic work.[112] Clapham Sect evangelicals like Hannah More and William Wilberforce were early polemicists for the separate spheres ideology, laying down rigid distinctions between the private female domain of the family and the male-defined world of industrial and professional enterprise. But evangelical definitions of women as moral regenerators opened up an area of considerable power and influence for bourgeois women. Philanthropic work was seen as a natural and socially justifiable extension of women's domestic role into the public sphere.

Philanthropic charities grew rapidly in the early years of the nineteenth century. In the metropolis the London City Mission founded in 1835, the Ragged School Union begun by Lord Ashley in 1844 and the Young Men's Christian Association started in the same year were the most prominent examples. Much of their work was organised around personal contact with the poor, often centring on visits to working-class women by charity workers, who brought moral and material relief and sought to bridge the growing political and social divisions between classes. The most striking feature of the expanding charity network was the dramatic rise in the

number of women members. They acted as non-participating financial pat-
ronesses, or more usually as the backbone of the system of district visiting,
as helpers in lying-in hospitals and asylums and as the organisers of clothing
clubs, soup kitchens, village shops and chapels.[113]

From the 1850s medics and clerics began to grasp the potential importance of this network of female philanthropy for the sanitary movement.
Though public health campaigns were male dominated, at a local level it
was women who became reponsible for the day-to-day supervision of
working-class health and morality. Farr saw the possibilities for an alliance
between medics and a reformed nursing profession, which would put working wives and mothers in touch with sanitary science.[114] In 1855 the Rev
Frederick Maurice organised a series of lectures for middle-class women as
part of his scheme to found a college for training charity workers. Maurice,
a leading figure in the Christian socialist movement, had recently set up the
London Working Men's College. The lectures, given by prominent sanitary
reformers, harped on as usual about the dual principles of medico-moral
improvement. But they sounded a new note by arguing that middle-class
women were especially suited for sowing the seeds of sanitary knowledge.
Edward Sieveking, a fellow of the Royal College of Physicians, quoted the
recent shining example of Florence Nightingale in the Crimea to prove that
women's involvement in sanitary reform was a natural extension of their
domestic role: for 'what we claim for the woman in the house we would
also claim for her beyond its walls'.[115] Medical men, he suggested, more
than any other group of social reformers, urgently needed to enlist the
cooperation of lady philanthropists. These women could 'help to elucidate
much that is otherwise enigmatical with regard to the relation of mind and
body', showing that there is a correlation on the one hand between 'temperance, equable temper, and other moral virtues' and on the other between
'intemperance, vice and misery'.[116] Maurice found that the middle-class
lady's presence in the wards of poor law hospitals provided such a 'soften-
ing, humanizing, health-giving influence', teaching all men that 'in whatever
abyss he might be sunk, he is still capable of health and resurrection'.[117]
Lady hospital visitors could supervise and reinforce the medical regime,
administering medicines, scrutinising the nurses, reporting their behaviour
and above all inquiring into the moral habits of poor patients – factors
which were now known to play such a crucial role in the spread of disease.

All the contributors to Maurice's lecture series stressed the social and
political benefits to be gained from female philanthropy. These were
reaffirmed in numerous tracts and handbooks on charity work. Rapid
industrialisation and urbanisation had produced new and chaotic forms of
society, no longer held together by personal ties of paternalism and deference. The better classes were deserting the inner city areas for the healthier
and more exclusive suburbs. Middle-class women could provide the missing
link between classes and help promote social and political stability.

More unusually, Maurice felt the need to anticipate criticisms of lady philanthropists as proto-feminists. He acknowledged that many male professionals were suspicious of these women. Not only were they challenging the monopoly of male experts, but they also seemed to be at the centre of campaigns for female suffrage, women's higher education and entry into the medical profession.[118] Yet Maurice insisted that if men would only recognise the importance of female philanthropy this would stem the growing demand for women's emancipation. The founding of a ladies' college for work among the poor would 'remove the slightest craving for such a state of things, by giving . . . a more healthful direction to the minds which entertain it'.[119] In short, Maurice saw philanthropy as an effective means of constraining middle-class women, by channelling their energy into a minor form of expertise subservient to male professionals.

Maurice's anxieties about the interrelation between philanthropy and feminism anticipated class and gender contradictions which were present in almost all of the charity organisations in the mid-Victorian period. For while middle-class women were active agents in the regulation of working-class behaviour – especially of working-class women – philanthropic work did provide them with an enlarged social role, employment opportunities and the experience to reflect on their position which often fed into feminist campaigns. Many prominent figures in the movement for women's higher education, suffrage and medical reform had a history of involvement in charity work.[120]

Ellen Ranyard embodied many of these contradictions in the 1850s and 1860s. Her story illustrates the cross-class relations between women played out in the personal dialogue of philanthropy. As a young single woman she had begun work in south London as a collector and distributor for the Bible Society. After marriage she had settled in Kent, but in 1857 Ranyard moved to Bloomsbury, living in an area which bordered on the notorious rookeries of St Giles' Parish, Holborn.[121] It was here that she began to recruit poor biblewomen for work in districts considered impenetrable by many male reformers.

In her published tracts and pamphlets Ranyard stressed that it was vital for women to take the lead in missionary work. She had become convinced that female workers were often more successful than clerics and medics in establishing a foothold in working-class areas and gaining an influence over the women. This, she claimed, was because lady philanthropists were capable of 'getting down, down, deeper down into the hearts of the poor':

> Why are they so wretched in their circumstances and in their habits
> in our great metropolis of civilization? Because the middle-class
> which ought to civilize them, has known so little of them. This
> knowledge is now being daily attained *in a womanly way*.
> The women make their homes – and it is these who must be

influenced. . . . The Lord, in this day of mercy and power, is now awakening Christian Women of all classes to a sense of duty to their sisters – erring and outcast – and especially directing them to those measures which shall prove preventive as well as curative.[122]

The stress on knowledge 'gained in a womanly way' represented an implicit challenge to the routine methods of the male social investigators, backed as they often were by statutory coercion and the full panoply of the state. Ranyard's use of the term 'sisters' condensed a range of meanings – sisters in Christ, but also sisters joined together for mutual help and assistance. She felt that religion not only provided a common bond between women of different classes, but could also awaken the consciences of middle-class and aristocratic ladies who had been taught since birth to be 'lovely butterflies who float and glitter in the fairyland of wealth and fashion'.[123] Charity work, she claimed, could provide these women with a religious vocation, extending their sphere of influence beyond the empty world of dinner parties and morning calls. By drawing on a vocabulary of missionary vanguardism, women like Ranyard not only developed cross-class notions of sisterhood, but also established their position as moral leaders among women of their own class.

Injunctions like these came close to arguing for a genuinely public role for middle-class women. But Ranyard was at pains to close off such potentially disruptive implications, insisting that philanthropy did not contravene the separate spheres ideology. Far from it, the charity worker was 'safe under the shadow of the Bible and the Home' and was fully justified in her activities: 'She forsakes no quiet, womanly aim in dealing with individualities, and in seeking to bring souls one by one to Christ.'[124] Man's power and intellect fitted him to deal with generalities and masses, while woman as his helpmate filled in the smaller details.

Ellen Ranyard was instrumental in setting up the London Bible and Domestic Mission in 1857. City missions had played a prominent part in the network of charity and poor relief in London and other urban centres since the 1830s. Ranyard believed that the system lacked 'sisters' who could serve as 'native agents' to the destitute. Her plan for recruiting poor but respectable biblewomen provided the 'missing link' between the lady philanthropist and the urban poor.[125] The mission scheme expanded rapidly in the 1860s, especially in the East End, fielding over two hundred workers by 1868. Ranyard's 'native agents' were selected from local neighbourhoods: 'good women, middle-aged, pious and humble', who had been trained in what she termed the 'school of affliction'.[126] The system needed both a worker and a watcher – the 'link' and the 'rivet' as Ranyard called them. Lady superintendents brought money, food and clothing for distribution by the biblewomen. But they also came to watch and supervise. The main weekly activity was the mothers' meeting, chaired jointly by the superintendent and her assistant, when classes were given in sewing, cookery, elementary domestic hygiene and childcare.

The power structures linking the lady superintendent, her biblewomen and the poor women in the locality reveal that while philanthropic work contributed to the widening of middle-class women's sphere of influence, it was often directly opposed to the interests of women in the classes beneath them. Scrutiny and supervision characterised the relation between the lady and her assistant. Biblewomen were initially taken on for one month's probationary period and were always under the vigilant eye of the superintendent. Ranyard counselled that it was unwise to trust them with the actual purchase of clothing or the management of accounts. Moreover, the programme these assistants were trained to carry out was one of traditional sanitary improvement, for Ranyard firmly believed that the immoral state of the poor lowered their resistance to disease. Teaching the rudiments of domestic management delivered the usual sanitary and moral benefits. Cleaning, sewing and domestic economy sanctified the home and discreetly encouraged respectable womanhood. Like the factory commissioners, city missionaries were alarmed that poor women were losing all semblance of femininity and were leading independent and hence unnatural lives as petty criminals and prostitutes. Ranyard recounted that in the 'unreformed muddy streets' women of the lowest class stood openly on the path, not hiding from the daylight but advertising their trade.[127] Against these manifestations of recklessness and ignorance she posed the subservient domestic ideal: 'instead of finding her at the gin-shop, he [the husband] finds her in prayer, and his meal ready and the place clean, and a tract or chapter in the Bible, waiting for him too.'[128] Religious conversion, conversion to domestic respectability and female dependence on men went hand-in-hand.

Despite the adherence of many male professionals to a separate spheres ideology, they did see the importance of an alliance with lady philanthropists as critical to the success of sanitary politics at a local level. The domestic position of women, the promotion of hierarchies of discipline and authority between husband and wife and parents and children, the relation of the family to wider questions of social order and stability, all of these issues were taken up by women visitors and charity workers. But equally significant was the way in which this system marked the potential entry of middle-class women into the public arena of social reform. It was the political contradictions embedded here, and the hostility women provoked from male professionals, which generated key conditions for the feminist campaigns around sexuality in the later nineteenth century.

11 CONCLUSION

How then do we characterise this early moment of official intervention into sexuality? We have not been concerned here with an inclusive history of ideas about sex, nor with a sanitary ramble through early Victorian social reform, rather with the way in which a particular domain of sexuality was produced. In the period of nascent industrial capitalism it was the systematic forms of knowledge of sanitary science, social medicine, evangelical religion and philanthropy which staked out a specific regime of sexuality. Historians ignore this discursive dimension of cultural analysis at their peril. Statements by sanitarians and social investigators on the sexuality of the labouring classes were not the official reflection of a pre-given social reality. They were the active product of specific regimes of knowledge and their power relations. Sexual meanings were constructed at the interface of the class- and gender-related polarities laid down by moral environmentalism. They marked out distinctive cultural identities for middle-class men and women and crystallised dominant images of the labouring poor.

This domain was not some purely ideational creation, put together through the discursive combination of concepts free-floating in society. It was deployed by specific historical agents and underwritten by a strategic set of political alliances. These were at work both inside the apparatuses of an expanding state and in the newly enfranchised professional groups within civil society.

Much of moral environmentalism had its broad conditions set by the social and political transformations attendant on the economic expansion of capital and the reorganisation of productive forces and relations. But it was not reducible to those structures, nor were its effects. The distinctive formation of masculine professional expertise is crucial here, with its concepts and procedures of inquiry, its particular cultural experience and its self-conscious distance from industrialists and politicians alike. Injunctions by Kay and Chadwick on health, morality, sexual behaviour and the position of women were not mere marginalia in the expansion of industrial capitalism. This repertoire began to emerge in the period as an important site of control and political struggle in its own right. Nevertheless, in the 1830s and 1840s we can still map out remarkably clear lines of convergence between different fields of intervention. By the mid-Victorian period these connections were becoming more difficult to establish, as forms of knowledge and political positions hardened and generated their own momentum. It is this second stage of sexual and sanitary politics which we now need to consider.

Part Two

THE SANITARY PRINCIPLE IN DOMINANCE

Medical hegemony and feminist
response 1860–1880

1 MEDICAL HEGEMONY AND SOCIAL POLICY
1850–1870

The medico-moral strategy was consolidated in the period after the initial reforms of the 1830s and 1840s. Environmental medicine, working in conjunction with religious principles of moral education, formed a dominant response to the problems posed by the working class in the period between 1850 and 1870. But the history of mid-century educational reform or the public health movement shows how partially the sanitary principle was actually enacted. The solutions, across a variety of fields of intervention, were the product of complex compromises between the various political forces in play. The radical programmes drawn up by the experts were severely qualified. Experts were themselves 'educated' into the political realities lying outside their own specialist domains. Central government intervention into public health, sanitation and housing was cautious and piecemeal in comparison with Chadwick's conception of a centralised supervisory network. It is tempting, but completely illegitimate, to slide from analysis of the production of official solutions to their implementation. The two elements need to be understood as distinct and often disjointed moments of state policy.

The Board of Health was disbanded in 1858 amid a welter of political intrigue and orchestrated opposition. Chadwick himself had been forced out of office four years earlier by a powerful lobby of anti-centralisers, private drainage and water authorities and those with a personal antipathy to the 'wizard of Whitehall'.[1] *The Times*, once an ardent supporter of Chadwick, was particularly vicious in its appraisal of his administrative career, chortling that Mr Chadwick would receive his final reward 'when he falls at last a sanitary martyr to a choked two-inch pipe drain and is carried by policemen . . . to an extramural cemetery'.[2] The board was replaced by a Medical Office within the Privy Council – that refuge for unpopular branches of government which needed shielding from the glare of parliamentary scrutiny. Changes in personnel reflected shifts in overall public health strategy. The appointment of John Simon, as first Medical Officer, heralded the replacement of the grandiose principles of sanitary engineering by those of preventive medicine. Chadwick had always insisted that ultimate sanitary authority needed to remain with non-medical administrators. Simon was a medic, with a background in medical research and a proven record against cholera as Medical Officer to the City of London between 1848 and 1855. His approach to public health combined effective administration (involving a team of inspectors, control of the water-supply and the removal of nuisances) with an emphasis on research into the causes of infection. Simon worked for discreet administrative transformations within government, avoiding until late in his career clashes with ministers over contentious issues of policy and principle. Through skilful manoeuvering he was able to build up a research department which concretised the new importance awarded to scientific inquiry in public health campaigns.[3] His annual reports between 1859 and 1871 were exemplary statements of this dual focus on sound administration and pioneering research.

Like Chadwick, Simon saw public health as an important asset for an industrial nation. But the new Medical Officer gave this conception a more ethical and humanitarian gloss. The improvement of the physical and moral health of individuals was one of the prime duties of a Christian country, for the level of national health reflected the degree of civilisation attained by the state.[4] Simon's public health philosophy was informed by his commitment to Christian socialism, a strong current among many social reformers in mid-century. He formed part of a loose network of clerics, philanthropists and intellectuals, including Ruskin, Charles Kingsley, Louisa Twining, campaigner for workhouse improvement, and Octavia Hill, the housing reformer.

Simon's burgeoning career at the Medical Office in the 1860s coincided with the consolidation of the status of the medical profession, both as a privileged domain of expertise and as a distinctive cultural grouping within the middle class. The new Medical Officer, a highly visible public figure, was instrumental in pushing for increased professional status, especially in the campaigns over the Medical Act of 1858, the single most important measure governing medicine. The act established for the first time the statutory definition of a medical practitioner, together with a register and a General Medical Council to watch over conduct and education. The growth of experimental science, with the new technology of the microscope and the more rigid principles of research established in the laboratory, also contributed to medical ascendancy within social policy.[5] Following the recent work of Louis Pasteur and other European scientists on the micro-organic causes of disease, Simon embarked on major programmes of research into the chemistry of morbid processes and the aetiology of contagion. He attached his team's findings to his own reports, as quiet but conclusive proof of the steady advance of scientific progress and its ultimate conquest over infectious disease. On the wider political stage, in the face of continuing opposition to public health legislation, these statements were designed to promote the image of the doctor as a serious and high-minded questor after truth:

> Every step in the physiological sciences, every better knowledge of the origins of the living body, and of their material and functional fluctuations under whatever influences is of actual or potential gain to us; and such knowledge constantly gives more and more success

to the provisional practice which it enlightens. As regards the ana-
tomical studies of late times, with very varied utilization of the
microscope, and the otherwise greatly improved means of minute
structural investigation, I need hardly say that, by them during the
last thirty years, great parts of the science of disease have been
completely transfigured.[6]

This quasi-evolutionary conception of painstaking scientific progress, with
its stress on technical control over human life, proved a powerful input into
the work of Simon's new department.

Administratively, growing medical prestige and authority was visible in
the series of mid-century acts addressing the health, housing and sanitary
conditions of the urban working class.[7] In practice, the net result of these
medically directed reforms was often to exacerbate the housing and sanitary
conditions of the urban poor, especially in London. Local medical officers
were usually committed to a purely professional radicalism, transfixed by
the reduction of their magic figures, the disease and death rates, in local
sanitary areas. All of the parliamentary statutes lacked compulsory clauses
to enforce rebuilding schemes and the temptation was to 'shovel-off' the
poor on to neighbouring districts.[8] Conceptually, the acts continued to be
underpinned by a dual commitment to physical improvement and moral
regulation. Simon, concluding his report for 1870, staked out the familiar
equation between lack of sanitation, immorality and the depressed quality
of working-class life:

> where grievous excess of physical suffering is bred, large parts of the
> same soil yield, side by side with it, evils of another kind . . . in some
> of the regions of insanitary influence, civilization and morals suffer
> almost equally with health . . . education . . . is little likely to
> penetrate, unless with amended sanitary law, nor human life to be
> morally raised while physically it is so degraded and squandered.[9]

It was this sanitary principle which exerted a major structural influence
on the Contagious Diseases Acts of 1864, 1866 and 1869.[10] This was the
single most important legislative intervention addressing sexuality throughout the nineteenth century. Extensive state-backed medical involvement in
the regulation of venereal disease and female prostitution crystallised an
approach which had its origins in the public health programme of thirty
years before. It was these acts, together with the resistance they provoked,
which resulted in the growing specification of the sexual within official
discourse and a marked polarisation of political positions.

2 THE CONTAGIOUS DISEASES ACTS AND MID-VICTORIAN SOCIAL REFORM

In an immediate sense the legislation was a response to growing official pressure among medics and military chiefs for some form of sanitary scrutiny of the armed forces. Military returns had reported a steady increase in venereal infection among the men since the 1820s.[11] A series of government inquiries in the 1850s and 1860s, precipitated by the Crimean War, testified to the seriousness with which the dual problems of venereal disease and sexual immorality among the lower ranks was regarded in official circles.[12] From the 1840s public anxiety had also been focused on prostitution, the 'great social evil', by studies from evangelical clerics and medics, and by rescue and reform societies campaigning for a police crackdown on the London streets.

The jurisdiction of the 1864 Act applied to a number of naval ports and army garrison towns in England and Ireland. Under its schedules, both police personnel and medical practitioners (acting under the direct supervision of the War Office and the Admiralty, rather than the local constabulary) were empowered to notify a justice of the peace if they suspected a woman of being a common prostitute. The woman would then be taken to a certified hospital for medical examination, where she could be detained for up to three months. Infringement of the hospital rules, or quitting without medical consent, carried penalties of up to two months' imprisonment. There were also penalties for brothel keepers. The acts of 1866 and 1869 extended the geographical locations covered by the regulations, while the Admirality and the War Office were now mandated to provide hospital facilities for inspection and treatment. Provision was also made within hospitals for adequate moral and religious instruction of the women and for the regular fortnightly inspection of former detainees, while the period of compulsory detention was extended to six months.

What concerns us is not so much a detailed account of the politics which led to the passing of the acts and to their eventual repeal in the 1880s. These aspects have received sustained analysis from recent feminist and social historians.[13] Rather, the purpose here is to build on that recent research in order to situate the debates on sexuality and disease in the light of the longer-term history of medico-moral regulation. Within this context the acts represented a high point of sanitary interventionism.

From the 1850s the sanitary principle had been used to justify demands for state intervention regulating sexual disease and immorality. As the *Lancet* declaimed, the state interfered in the case of a diseased woman on the same grounds and by the same right that it interfered with the typhus fever or the smallpox patient – to avert the spread of disease.[14] In 1850 the *Westminster Review* urged that the newly created Board of Health should establish a system of periodic inspection of prostitutes, enforceable at law.[15]

Twelve years later, Sir John Liddell, Director-General of the Naval Medical Department, justified arguments for the hygienic control of diseased prostitutes by invoking the general principles of state medicine.[16] Medical authorities on venereology, like William Acton, pointed to the long-standing concern of French medics and social reformers with the health threat posed by prostitution.[17] Much impressed with the continental system of state hygiene, they were determined to implement a similar programme in Britain. Here was a new putsch for compulsory state action on sexual and moral issues, backed by specialist medical expertise.

The medical profession was the most significant group in support of the new legislation. Numerically, medics were dominant on all the parliamentary inquiries into the working of the acts between 1867 and 1881, pushing hard for their extension to a national system of inspection and detention of prostitutes. In 1867 a report of a committee of the Harveian Medical Society of London called for the expansion of the 1866 legislation to London and other large towns.[18] The enthusiasm generated by this investigation led to the formation of the Association for Promoting the Extension of the Contagious Diseases Acts to the Civilian Population. Its membership was drawn from the ranks of the Tory Party, the Anglican clergy and the aristocracy, but it was dominated by the intellectual voice of the medical profession.

The growing hegemony of state medicine written into the new regulations bore witness to a substantial shift in the balance of forces within the sanitary movement. Men like Acton used the twin issues of prostitution and venereal disease to insist that medics, rather than moralists, now had far greater claim to authority on social and environmental issues. At a meeting of the Royal Medical Society in 1860 Acton gave his own gloss on the prostitution debate. Philanthropists and clergymen had to admit that their own reforming schemes had completely failed. The problem needed to be handed over to scientific investigation.[19] Moral intervention was by itself at best a mere palliative unless coordinated by official sanitary regulation. Prayer and lamentation would not arrest the deterioration of national fibre. Schemes of reformatories and maids' protection societies were but 'paltry, peddling scratches on the surface of evil'.[20] Statements such as these reflected growing confidence and optimism among members of the profession; the conviction that state-backed medicine, as opposed to voluntary and charitable effort, provided the ultimate solution to pressing social problems. The *Lancet*, smug from recent public health victories, captured the new mood of medical optimism in 1871 when it claimed success for the recent improvements in working-class habits. Medics were the true friends of the labouring classes, for they knew more about the genesis of poverty and the needs of the working man than any other group in the community.[21] It was a confidence borne of a quarter-of-a-century of growing medical ascendancy, which was to have far-reaching effects on the sanitary alliance.

Supporters of the acts did not see the principles of state hygiene as contradicting the moral emphases of the public health movement. Far from the state sanctioning male vice by providing the men of the armed forces with a clean supply of women, it was claimed that the acts were essentially moral in aim and intention. Campaigners against the regulations were working to undermine the time-honoured alliance between medicine and morality, but the healer who deployed his art 'honourably and fully' could never be in antagonism with divine law.[22] It was believed that the curative functions of medicine provided their own moral guarantee. Medics presented glowing testimonies to successive government inquiries on the marvellous conversion worked by the acts; where before the conduct of prostitutes was miserable in the extreme, now they had common decency and self-respect. The *Report from the Royal Commission on the Administration and Operation of the Contagious Diseases Acts*, 1871, pointed out that the 'decorous and wholesome' improvement in the manners and habits of the people was a direct result of expanded sanitary regulations. In the same way, the contagious diseases legislation would both sanitise and moralise the people, by purging towns and encampments of those 'miserable creatures who were mere masses of rottenness and vehicles of disease'.[23]

Many of the medical supporters of the legislation had a history of involvement in hospital and sanitary work among the poor, as local medical officers and poor law doctors – work which reinforced their commitment to the acts as part of the wider politics of public health. Their biographies provide us with access to the professional and class alliances which fed into the politics of mid-Victorian social reform.

John Brendon Curgenven, joint secretary to the extensionist association, was typical of the newly professionalised medic who spearheaded the regulationist campaign. From a provincial background, outside the ranks of the medical élite, Curgenven characteristically sought increased professional status by a series of official posts rather than through private practice. In 1852 he was appointed Medical Officer to the Royal Free Hospital, Hampstead, where he handled the local offensive against cholera during the 1854 epidemic. Later he served in the Crimea, officially as medical attendant to Lord Ward but also enlisting as a volunteer surgeon with Florence Nightingale. In addition to his work promoting the Contagious Diseases Acts, in the 1860s he also served on the Parliamentary Bills Committee of the British Medical Association, helping to draft legislation on habitual drunkenness, infant mortality and the examination and registration of midwives. A member of the sanitary committee of the Paddington Vestry, he was influential in forming a local section of the Charity Organisation Society in 1869 and was medical representative on a number of philanthropic bodies.

Curgenven represented one type of medical supporter; Matthew Berkeley Hill, his colleague as joint secretary on the extensionist association, came via a different route.[24] Hill was the third generation of a family of prominent educationalists and social reformers, who had their origins in the radical Unitarian culture of eighteenth- and early nineteenth-century Birmingham. It was the same sort of low church dissenting background which had produced many first-generation medics like Kay and Wakley. But by the 1860s Berkeley Hill had become integrated into the culture of London's professional gentry, where experts rubbed shoulders with the leaders of upper middle-class and aristocratic society. Hill was Professor of Surgery and Pathology at University College, London, with strong links to the military hierarchy through his marriage to the daugher of Sir Thomas Howell of the War Office. Rising professional status involved a negotiation of establishment culture, and Hill dropped many of the public trappings of his evangelical background – embracing Anglicanism and sending his son to Eton and Oxford. For him, regulationism meant adherence to the values and ordered hierarchy of the governing élite as much as to sanitary reform. Hill must have been typical of many mid-Victorian medics who reorientated their social and political allegiances as a result of a shift in class and professional status.

The Contagious Diseases Acts not only involved a subtle shift in the balance of forces within moral environmentalism, they also marked a new and more particular specification of sexuality within sanitary discourse. Early nineteenth-century environmentalism had focused on sexuality as part of a general concern with the habits and morals of the urban working class. Legislation on public health, sanitation and industrial conditions did not contain prescriptions for the direct regulation of sexual conduct. We have seen that it was often difficult to isolate the various sub-domains condensed and subsumed under the general categories of morality and immorality. In contrast, the acts implicated the state and medical expertise in a much more precise and extensive discourse on sexuality – inciting and crystallising representations, especially around female sexuality. This was quite new. It involved the coordination of a number of government departments which was extensive by the standards of nineteenth-century administration. But such a phenomenon cannot be explained by recourse to general principles of 'bureaucratisation' or administrative expansion. It was part of the intensified scrutiny of female behaviour and the sexual habits of the urban poor, under the impact of social and political conditions in mid-nineteenth-century Britain.

The process represented a refined and more detailed application of the principles of environmentalism. Environmentalism in its first phase had advanced its hegemony through a grandiose moral and scientific logic. But at the level of implementation such a totalising conception of social disciplining often lacked precision when it came to dealing with specific problems. Simon's shift of approach away from Chadwick's grand sanitary plan was not only an administrative necessity in the face of political opposition, it was also an acknowledgement of this difficulty. From the early 1850s environmentalists began to define social questions and their solutions in much more specific terms. There was a gradual move away from an insistence on the interrelated nature of all social, political and economic problems and a shift towards specialisation. Medical research into the causes of contagion, secular and religious education, charity and philanthropic schemes, moral reclamation of prostitutes, the work of the temperance movement, all signalled this change of direction, as did the growing tendency towards the pathologisation of recalcitrant individuals, such as criminals, prostitutes and the insane.[25] It was facilitated by the transformations within the administrative process itself. Legislation now produced separate apparatuses and spheres of activity, with distinctive forms of knowledge and expertise. Simon himself was a product of the first phase of this process, while reform of the civil service structure, outlined in the Northcote-Trevelyan report of 1854, proposed a new tier of secular administration within the state.[26]

The move towards specialisation was encouraged by changes in the overall economic and political situation from the 1850s. The relative stabilisation of the economy after the wild fluctuations of the business cycle in the previous decade, together with the defeat of Chartism and early militant trade-unionism, assisted social reformers in their attempts to treat issues as discrete and separate, rather than interdependent. The National Association for the Promotion of Social Science, founded in 1865, typified the new problematic. A loose umbrella reform group, whose members in the early years included both regulationists and their opponents, it embraced an ameliorist approach to social problems, shying away from any attempt to see them as structurally related. Patient and painstaking empirical investigation would reveal the optimum measure of reform. It was a belief backed by the conviction that society was essentially a good order, and that there existed a general professional consensus on the treatment of social ills.[27]

Passing through Parliament with little immediate opposition, the contagious diseases legislation was a significant manifestation of this mid-Victorian consensus, marking the application of precision social engineering to the domain of sexuality. The acts were concerned with the regulation of the sexual and moral habits of two particular groups within the urban poor – female prostitutes and the lower ranks of the armed forces. But the tactics used to discipline these two groups were very different. For what lay behind the assumptions of the legislators were the gender-specific, male-defined norms which had been embedded in the reforming programmes of the 1830s and 1840s. These were now crystallised in an expanded discourse on male and female sexuality.

As an intervention into the health of the army and navy the legislation developed a new 'enlightened' approach to the lower ranks, advocated by the 1857 Royal Commission and in part the outcome of the Crimean War debacle.[28] Witnesses to the Select Committee on Venereal Disease, 1867,

testified to the environmental and sanitary improvements which had a
been adopted. Healthy exercise, rational recreation, better living conditi
and temperance campaigns were all designed to morally arm the me
against temptation. On the vexed question of how far soldiers and sailors
should themselves be subjected to compulsory periodic genital inspection,
medics and military chiefs were divided. Some like William Hickman, the
Royal Navy's Secretary and Paymaster, put the case for compulsory
ablution on sanitary and moral grounds. Yet he acknowledged that 'any
thorough examination ... would be an extremely difficult thing to carry
out on account of the prejudice of the men'.[29] Others, like Dr Barclay, a
staff surgeon-major, argued that such a system would destroy the men's
self-respect and counteract the good effects of environmental reforms, a
position upheld in the report of the 1871 Royal Commission.[30]

It was women who were defined as the human agents of infection, threat-
ening national health and security and challenging the social order by their
active and autonomous sexuality. The acts introduced a more coercive form
of medico-legal regulation of prostitutes, together with an intensified system
of police surveillance. When, flushed with success, pro-regulationists
pressed Gladstone's government to extend the statutes in the late 1860s,
many supporters made the traditional connection between the threat of the
prostitute and wider anxieties about public order and the moral habits of
the unrespectable poor. In a paper to the Social Science Association in 1868,
Curgenven insisted that the acts not only promoted the moral reform of
fallen women but also raised the standard of public order on the streets.[31]
The newly established *British Medical Journal* was quick to stress the general benefits to public morality which would follow if the legislation were
imposed on the northern cities.[32]

Prostitution, drunkenness, vagrancy and other unrespectable manifestations of urban popular culture had long been a headache for local borough
councils. Increasingly, local government used its legal powers to separate
out specific groups as targets for police intervention. As early as the 1850s
Plymouth City Council embarked on this new tack, passing a series of by-
laws to promote police control of the streets and common lodging houses,
with explicit reference to prostitutes.[33] In the following decade many local
police forces were given new powers to discipline drunk and disorderly
streetwalkers, powers strengthened under the Licensing Act, 1872. Central
to this coercive policing was a concerted effort to isolate the prostitute from
working-class culture. A new and powerful medical ideology, crystallising
definitions of normal and deviant female sexuality was the cornerstone of
this process.

3 FEMALE SEXUALITY

the acts, prostitutes were relatively integrated into the
ʌnic life of the casual poor in the garrison towns. As
ʌas demonstrated, prostitution was used by many work-
ʌemporary move to supplement the pitifully low wages
ʌlework, dressmaking or domestic service.[34] A move back
ʌatus through marriage was still possible; it was often the
ʌoute taken by many women in mid-career. The medical and clerical inquiries of the 1840s had frequently complained about precisely these difficulties
of identifying 'immoral' women.[35] Medical definitions implemented in the
contagious diseases legislation made visible the perceived threat of the prostitute, by focusing on her sexuality and isolating it as unnatural and deviant.

Acton typified this new medical discourse. Like Curgenven, his own rising professional career was bound up with a commitment to expansionist
sanitary reform. Son of a provincial clergyman, with a background of work
among the poor at the Islington Dispensary, he specialised in venereology as
medical consultant to the London Lock Hospital and as an *externe* to the
Female Venereal Hospital in Paris. A vigorous campaigner in support of
regulationism, and a major witness on all of the parliamentary inquiries, his
studies *Prostitution* and *The Functions and Disorders of the Reproductive
Organs*, both published in 1857, were key contributions to the new medical
discourse on sexuality. The whole tenor of Acton's approach was to insist
on the primacy of medical knowledge – dismissing popular beliefs, especially those put forward by midwives, as dangerous quackery. Sexuality, he
pontificated, was one of 'the areas of social life that are revealed only to
medical men, in the hope that they may be in a position to suggest some
mode of relief'.[36] Drawing heavily on French physiological science, Acton
premised his theory on a belief in the absolute difference between male and
female physiology and their related forms of sexuality. Male sexuality was
defined as an instinctual force which, while needing constant medical
supervision, was an essential attribute of masculinity. It was a power and a
privilege, giving man 'his dignity . . . his character as head and ruler, and . . .
his importance'.[37] Pre-Darwinist concepts of comparative natural history
were used to show certain fundamental connections between man's physical
organisation and that of the lower mammals. The strength of the male
instinct was proof of this biological link.

The other central feature of this early sexology was its stress on the direct
relation between mind and body. Here Acton followed the general material-
ist principles of contemporary physiology, in which ideas and sensations
were conceived as the direct product of physical processes or environmental
influences. Male 'sex passion' was either the result of stimulation from
external sensations, or of involuntary influences coming from the sexual
organs themselves. Sensations were conveyed from the brain through the

nervous system, resulting in erection. Men could only achieve full physical and mental gratification by discharging their semen in the act of copulation.

There was a constant tension in Acton's writing between his assertion that the male sexual instinct was capable of intellectual and moral control and his stress on male sexuality as a powerful, inevitable expression of basic physiological processes. Acton did advise restraint for men, both inside and outside marriage, as a solution to the problems of promiscuity and infection. Restraint was also necessary because of the massive drain on the body which occurred during intercourse. This was especially dangerous for the urban, professional paterfamilias, 'the hardworked, intellectual married man residing in London', whose health was at risk from the cumulative strain of metropolitan life and frenetic mental labour.[38] These formulations were grounded in the early hydraulic model of the circulation of energy derived from fluid mechanics; the body possessed only a fixed quantity of semen, once expended it was lost forever. Implicitly, the emphasis on conserving energy registered the austere virtues of hard work and cultural restraint which were the hallmark of the professional gentry.[39] Control was possible by exerting the power of the intellect and those 'moral capabilities' which distinguished man from the animals.

In the practical application of his theory Acton became much more pragmatic. Here medical theory intersected with wider class and gender assumptions about sexual behaviour. While male continence was *necessary*, it could not be *guaranteed*, because of the strength of the male urge. When this logic was applied to the lower ranks of the armed forces it also carried the gloss that these men were less capable of intellectual control, being more animal and closer to nature.[40]

In contrast, women were defined in terms of the norm of asexuality and the absence of sexual desire. Acton again explained this as a biological phenomenon, present in all forms of the female species. He noted approvingly that 'in a state of nature wild female animals will not allow the approach of the male except when in a state of rut'.[41] Motherhood, marriage and domesticity were basic female instincts which Acton compared to the unnatural sexual desire of the prostitute, the nymphomaniac and the courtesan. Once more the argument was physiological; maternity and suckling made such vital demands on a woman's organs that 'sexual desire is almost annihilated'.[42]

Acton's work is usually represented as the high point of the mid-Victorian distinctions between the asexual bourgeois lady and the sexually depraved working-class prostitute. What is less often recognised is that it was distinctly innovatory, marking important breaks with earlier theories of female sexuality and helping to generate an intellectual climate favourable to regulationism. Acton's polarised oppositions between pure and impure women connected with a whole range of representations regulating female behaviour in the 1850s and 1860s. These were present in literature and art as well as in medicine. The growth of an overtly moralising genre of English painting from the 1840s staked out similar representations of female purity and immorality. Pre-Raphaelite artists like William Holman Hunt and Dante Gabriel Rossetti, whose work was popular with the northern bourgeoisie, juxtaposed images of the middle-class home against a range of social outcasts. Representations of fallen women, or images of women as fatal seductresses, were central to these didactic narratives. Often such paintings pointed to the maxim that prostitution led to death, confirming the prostitute as the member of an outcast group.[43]

The extent of the shift registered by these approaches becomes clear when compared with their antecedents. Earlier accounts of prostitution, by Congregationalist ministers like William Bevan, Ralph Wardlaw and Robert Vaughn, physicians such as Ryan and Tait and the temperance and moral reformers William Logan and James Talbot, had worked to define the prostitute as a distinctly pathological female type. But she was not juxtaposed against an *asexual* image of respectability. Moreover, in the handbooks on marriage, reproduction and bourgeois hygienics of the 1840s the respectable woman was defined through marriage and the family, but female asexuality was not the guiding principle. Rather, what was emphasised was the family as the source of conjugal love, happiness and companionship, within which sexual and emotional relations between husband and wife played a valid part. Procreation was of course the ultimate goal, but sexual satisfaction in marriage was important for both partners.[44]

The importance awarded to sexual fulfilment within marriage owed much to the rationalist dissenting tradition of Quakers, Unitarians and Congregationalists. Bevan, Wardlaw and Vaughn defined marriage as a civil and religious contract – the basis of a stable and well-ordered society in a world disrupted by industrialisation. But for Wardlaw, as for other dissenters, marriage was also the perfect compact between men and women 'by which they engage in mutual love and friendship for the purpose of procreation'. Pleasure and enjoyment were seen as natural, legitimate and God-given, provided they were not excessive and were linked to the desire for procreation. Morality was contravened only when pleasure was sought 'independently of the end which pleasures are only meant to subserve'.[45] Equally for Ryan, a moderate exercise of the sexual function for both marriage partners was essential to good health as well as for conjugal happiness, regulating 'the functions of the brain or nervous system and consequently of the whole body'.[46] He condemned the practice of marital chastity as highly dangerous; leading to infertility in women, impotence in men and even to death. Bourgeois hygienics, at least for these male reformers, had some conception of acceptable pleasure for women.

In the 1860s medical interventions into the contagious diseases debate polarised earlier representations of female sexuality. They marked out clear distinctions between the asexual respectable married woman on the one hand and the depraved prostitute on the other. In Acton's famous phrase 'the majority of women . . . are not very much troubled with sexual feeling of any kind'.[47] Those few women who shocked public feeling with a display of sexual desire were branded either as prostitutes, nymphomaniacs or lunatics. Schemes put forward by regulationists for the reform of prostitutes in the lock hospitals institutionalised the distinction between 'pure' and 'impure' women. Once inside the hospital, prostitutes were subjected to a programme of physical and moral disciplining, which reinforced their distance from respectable women. Lessons in personal hygiene and ablution were combined with a stress on class deference and a belief that 'fallen women' needed to relearn their femininity through moralising domestic labour. Needlework and laundrywork provided an effective class and gender strategy, designed to prepare the prostitute for her correct place in the female labour force and to re-educate her into an approved feminine role.[48]

Medical isolation of the prostitute in the 1860s went hand-in-hand with a range of related social demarcations. These included the respectable/unrespectable divisions made by many philanthropic organisations, distinctions drawn by the newly founded Charity Organisation Society between the deserving and undeserving poor, together with the healthy/diseased oppositions employed by medical officers of health to identify the carriers of contagion.[49] All such pathologies registered the move towards the particularisation of social problems and their solutions. The new medical polarisations clearly worked to regulate the sexuality of *all* women. They visibly sharpened at the end of the decade, as medics were forced on to the defensive by a growing feminist campaign demanding the repeal of the acts – itself part of the wider upsurge of the mid-Victorian women's movement. In his defence of the legislation before the Association of the Medical Officers of Health in 1869, Acton countered opposition by resorting to increased extremism. The public needed to be made aware that prostitutes were not 'soiled doves', but were a class of women who were almost 'unsexed' and had lost all 'womanly feeling', consorting with as many as 'eight to twelve different men in the same night'.[50]

Medics also responded to the feminist challenge by drawing on their new sexual ideology to label the 'shrieking sisterhood' as immoral and impure for daring to speak publicly about sexuality. Acton's *The Functions and Disorders of the Reproductive Organs* carried a diatribe against the revolting and intolerable insubordination now suffered by husbands from their wives.[51] Parliamentary speeches opposing women's emancipation singled out feminist repealers – 'a defiant sect who would have nothing sacred, nothing veiled, nothing hidden' – as the precursors of what was to come if women were to enter the public arena.[52] Similar dirty tactics were employed in other medical debates. The *Lancet*'s sustained opposition to the first women doctors, the 'advance guard of the Amazonian army' as it dubbed them, was argued on the grounds that young ladies would be rendered indelicate, and by implication immoral, by attending lectures and dissections on human anatomy and pathology.[53]

This strategy of imputing impurity to women who challenged medical hegemony had its effects. In the 1870s leaders of the women's movement, particularly teachers working for the extension of educational opportunities, were caught over support for the repeal campaign. Practically all of them felt it was impossible to back the repeal movement publicly for fear that involvement would jeopardise their own campaigns.[54] When Annie Besant was prosecuted with Charles Bradlaugh for publishing *The Fruits of Philosophy*, a book of contraceptive advice, in 1877, she faced public abuse and insinuations about the immorality of her private life, culminating in the successful attempt to deprive her of the custody of her young daughter. As she confessed much later, it was not the thought of failure which made Bradlaugh and herself pause at the outset:

> It was the horrible misconception that we saw might arise; the odious imputations on honour and purity that would follow. . . . To me it meant the loss of the pure reputation I prized, the good name I had guarded – scandal the most terrible a woman could face.[55]

It was no accident that medical misogyny, with its powerful definitions of moral and immoral female behaviour, reached a peak at precisely the moment when middle-class women were beginning to challenge the hegemony of the male professions.

4 MALE DESIRE

If the mid-nineteenth century witnessed the increasingly polarised representations of women around the definitions of asexual purity/immorality, these oppositions also had a profound impact on class-specific forms of male sexuality. We have already noted the erotic fantasies of men like Jelinger Symons over the appearance and behaviour of the pit girls. Turning to the private letters, diaries and pornography of aristocrats and professional men we can see how their sexual desire was structured around notions of private debauchery, lust and licentiousness. Here desire was incited and pleasure produced through transgression of the sanctioned norms of middle-class marriage and domesticity. More often than not, it was the 'depraved', sexualised and socially inferior female prostitute who was seen to condense these aspects of male fantasy.

The most elaborate and highly wrought codes in this area were of course those of contemporary pornography. Here the new physiological theories of the uncontrollable male instinct were incorporated into erotic fantasy. 'Walter's' *My Secret Life*, the fictional narrative of a debauchee, constructed male desire as an illicit but physiologically based animal appetite, which drove men on to fresh excesses. The growing market in visual pornography, with the improvement of photographic techniques, provides the most striking illustration of the way in which male sexuality was being socially shaped. By mid-century, many scientific and professional groups had grasped the value of the new medium as an aid to empirical verification. According to the *Lancet* in 1859, photography was so 'essentially the art of truth – that it would seem to be the essential means of reproducing all forms and structures which science seeks for delineation'.[56] This realist definition of photography as truth and evidence was reworked in pornographic texts to consolidate the notion of male sexual desire as instantly aroused and requiring constant relief. Visual codes, with their deeply embedded resonances of actuality, reinforced the immediacy of the male urge, responding spontaneously to sensory stimuli.

Both written and visual pornography represented women for the male gaze across the virtue/vice, innocence/depravity oppositions. The clearest examples were in the early photographic studies of child prostitutes, dating from the 1860s and 1870s, where childhood innocence was erotically framed against visible signs of immoral sexuality, such as exposed genitalia or the depraved stare. Similarly, in *My Secret Life* sexual pleasure was signified in total opposition to the norms of bourgeois married life and sexual relations with one's wife:

> I tried to love her [my wife]. It was impossible. Hateful in day, she was loathsome to me in bed. Long I strove to do my duty, and be faithful, yet to such a pitch did my disgust at length go, that laying by her side, I had wet dreams nightly, sooner than relieve myself in her.[57]

In such accounts duty, faithfulness and conjugal union were defined as innately unpleasurable. In contrast, the perceived coarseness and animality of working-class women was the focus for male arousal, producing an experience of sex as illicit and furtive, breaking the boundaries of class and gender:

> Never did a woman enjoy a poking more. . . . She'd lost of course all modesty, if she ever had any, but she must have been reared like a pig . . . her language was indescribably common and coarse, and whether eating, drinking, speaking, washing or even pissing, her vulgarity and idiocy were intolerable. She was a magnificent bit of fucking flesh and nothing more.[58]

These male fantasies reduced working women to a series of purely physical functions organised around sex. They had a continuity with the rites of an upper-class masculine culture acted out in the clubs and pleasure haunts of the Haymarket and other areas of the metropolis from the 1840s. When Flora Tristan, the French feminist and socialist, visited London in 1839 she noted not just the extent of prostitution but the complex ritualisation of male debauchery. Luxurious private supper rooms in the West End known as 'the finishes', organised part orgies part entertainments which centred on the erotic degradation of women by male clients. One of these involved plying a woman with drink until she fell reeling to the floor, where glass after glass of liquor was poured over her until she became 'merely a confusion of filth'.[59]

Arthur Munby's diaries from the 1850s through to the 1870s point to further examples of middle-class male desire centred on the physical coarseness of working women. Munby was a cultivated lawyer and civil servant, working for the Ecclesiastical Commission in Whitehall. A social investigator and lecturer, he established a cross-class liaison with Hannah Cullwick, a Shropshire servant, in the 1850s. Central to Munby's experience of the relationship was a form of sexual desire structured around the cultural polarities of class. Here is Munby's description of Hannah when she was working as a servant in a Margate boarding house in the early 1860s:

> I presently see a figure approaching from a hundred yards off, up the middle of the street: a tall young woman, in a close white cap, and a short frock of lilac cotton, and coarse sack-cloth apron, and strong boots. Her hair is blown about by the wind, for it is cropped like a charity girl's: her arms are bare servile arms, touched with redness and roughness: she carries a pail in either hand. She is but a servant maid, and one of the lowest kind: yet look at her face, as the light of recognising love spreads over it.[60]

Munby's codes of observation drew on the protocols of official inquiry, with which he was personally familiar from his studies of Wigan colliery girls. Hannah was a thing to be explored, dissected through detailed empirical investigation. But, like Symons' case-studies, the male gaze was eroticised through the cultural distance between observer and observed, exemplified in Munby's fascination with the emblems of Hannah's working-class physiognomy.

We should be cautious about building too many general conclusions from these specific cases. But they do point to the complex interrelationship between official discourses and the domain of constructed personal experience and pleasure. All examples reveal a link between the growing polarisation of official definitions of female sexuality and the sexualisation of those representations in the fantasies of certain groups of men. It is possible that what we are dealing with here is the experience of sections of the professional gentry, though it was not confined to that group alone. What is clear is that such private desires were not sealed off from the world of public representations. These intimate forms of sexuality were dependent on specific social codes and rituals to give them meaning.

5 THE REPEAL CAMPAIGN AND THE COLLAPSE OF THE MEDICO-MORAL ALLIANCE

The expansionism of preventive medicine was severely checked by the political opposition provoked by the Contagious Diseases Acts, resulting in their suspension in 1883 and their final repeal three years later. Recent feminist historians have insisted that the repeal struggle needs to be seen not just as one of the single-issue campaigns which characterised the reform politics of radical liberalism, but as a landmark in the history of the nineteenth-century women's movement and in the development of a feminist politics of sexuality.[61] In terms of our longer history of medico-moral politics the battle over the legislation certainly marked a watershed in mid-Victorian social reform. The combined forces of opposition ruptured the earlier environmentalist consensus, making opponents out of former allies, staking out a new regime of sexual regulation and defining sexuality as a crucial site for feminist intervention. The consequences for state medicine were far-reaching and profound.

How did the women and men of the repeal movement contest the discourses of medical expertise and military authority which underpinned the acts? What languages did they draw on to fracture the earlier consensus and what historical forces enabled them to orchestrate their campaign as a national protest? Such questions are important because they probe the conditions under which political and cultural resistance is generated. Movements of struggle are rarely spontaneous eruptions from below. Their forms of organisation are partly structured by dominant networks of power and authority and they are dependent on specific languages to endow their protests with meaning.

Medical efforts to extend the acts first provoked organised opposition at the Social Science Congress at Bristol in October 1869. The newly founded National Anti-Contagious Diseases Acts Association excluded women from its first meeting. Though the association was quick to change its policy, women, led by Josephine Butler, broke away to form the separatist Ladies' National Association (LNA).[62] Almost immediately, the Ladies' Association issued a strongly worded protest in the *Daily News*, signed by prominent figures like Harriet Martineau and Florence Nightingale, claiming that the acts were not only an attack on the civil liberties of all women but also implicated the state in sanctioning male vice. This women's protest was received with expressions of outrage and puzzlement by men within the dominant political culture. One MP confided to Butler that her manifesto had shaken the house very badly. Politicians, he confessed, knew how to manage organised opposition, 'but this is very awkward for us – this revolt of the women. It is quite a new thing; what can we do with such an opposition as this?'[63]

The women in the repeal movement encountered not only the power and outright misogyny of medical and military chiefs, but also the restrictive codes of parliamentary politics, which defined the issues touched on by the acts as indecent and immoral. Divorce, prostitution and women's emancipation were designated as outside the parameters of political discourse, and MPs customarily prefaced speeches on these topics by apologising to the house for intruding on parliamentary time. Discussion of immorality was particularly problematic, given the strongly held belief that to name it and put it into discourse was a dangerous incitement to further acts of depravity. As early as the 1836 debate on divorce bills, proceedings had been referred to select committee in order to 'obviate the necessity of painful and disgusting exhibitions at the bar of the House ... calculated to excite feelings of shame and disgust', which were 'grossly indecent in their character'.[64] Repealers were forced to adopt similar tactics. In the Commons' debate on the Contagious Diseases Acts Repeal Bill, 1873, William Fowler, the proposer, prefaced his speech with the usual apology for intruding on members' time with so disgusting a subject.[65]

This parliamentary etiquette was much more than a mere expression of Victorian prurience. The moralisation of public life, under pressure from evangelicals, was producing a new language of politics and an insistence that men holding public office should outwardly subscribe to respectable standards of personal conduct. Prior to the 1830s, personal morality had not been seen as necessary for political eminence. Sexual intrigues were almost part of the culture of high politics, and were commonplace in the eminent Whig and Tory families in the early nineteenth century. Lord Palmerston was a notorious rake, having had a long-standing affair with Lady Cowper, whom he finally married in the late 1830s. The evangelical Lord Ashley viewed the prospect of marrying into such a family with trepidation, particularly as it was rumoured that his bride-to-be was the illegitimate daughter of Palmerston and Lady Cowper.[66]

Already by the 1830s these aristocratic codes of libertinism were beginning to be challenged, both by organised evangelical pressure groups and by the structural shift in the overall balance of power in favour of the middle classes. The result was not so much the realisation of Ashley's vision of national regeneration, but a growing acceptance by those holding high office of the need to subscribe publicly to an upright moral code. At the level of parliamentary discourse the net effect was a gradual transformation of the field of the political. This involved the crystallisation of a grammar of politics which defined a whole range of sexual and moral issues as apocryphal, irregular and outside the codes of gentlemanly conduct and civilised political debate.

Repealers quickly grasped that this parliamentary language surrounding prostitution and venereal disease increased their difficulties in launching an effective campaign. Thomas Biggs, in his address to the Association for the Promotion of Social Science in 1870, complained that such a 'painful . . . topic is not considered a proper theme for discussion . . . by the great majority of the House of Commons'.[67] In their campaign to rupture parliamentary discretion and medical hegemony, the women and men of the repeal movement drew on the only vocabulary able to bear the moral and intellectual weight of their challenge. This was the militant language of radical dissenting religion. Many other languages fed into the movement and made significant contributions: the secular discourse of anti-statism and personal rights, the tactics of pressure group politics, even the heavily patriarchal morality of the newly enfranchised labour aristocrats in the industrial north. But religious language not only provided a link between different political constituencies, it offered a set of concepts, a rhetoric of resistance and a strength of moral certainty powerful enough to take on the weight of the medical and political establishment. Even more importantly, it supplied many mid-Victorian feminists with a critical perspective on existing social relations. If the growing power of the medical profession was in part derived from the certainty and coherence of its discourse, then the success of the repeal opposition was dependent on the mobilisation of an alternative language, capable of challenging professional power and expertise.

Repealers launched a double-edged assault on medics. One strategy involved tackling the profession on its own terms, refuting statistics and medical claims that the acts led to improvements in morality and public order, through a mass of published tracts and pamphlets.[68] The other approach worked with a scathing moral and religious attack on the concepts of hygiene and sanitation embedded in the legislation. For James Stansfeld, a prominent repealer, the critique of regulationism was founded on the belief that 'humanity is governed by a providential law which can only come from one source'.[69] A sanitary code which sought to evade fundamental moral principles could never ultimately succeed. Acts which contravened moral law were 'calculated to degrade and debase the manhood and womanhood of this country', entangling them 'in the meshes of its wide and sweeping net'.[70] At the International Congress of Geneva, 1877, attended by Butler and other women repealers, delegates avowed that the hygienic principles governing sexual conduct needed to be steeped in the highest personal morality. The indispensable basis of the health of individuals and nations was 'self-control in the relations between the sexes'.[71] Public health could not be restricted to the surveillance and prevention of specific maladies. Nor, it was argued, could medics pursue a mere blind materialism, for the absorbing devotion to material progress, without the subordination of that pursuit to the highest interests of humanity, had generated a crisis of the utmost gravity for morality. The medical profession's eagerness for scientific advance had impaled it on the horns of a dilemma, forcing an unnatural choice between science and morality.[72]

Repealers scored a notable success when Simon, in his annual report of 1868, came out against any extension of the acts.[73] As a Christian moralist, Simon could not tolerate the seemingly deliberate flouting of principle by the extensionist lobby. He emphasised that respectable ratepayers would object to contributing to the cost of giving artificial security to their neighbours' looseness of life. Moreover, since venereal disease was contracted by a man at his own risk he could not claim protection from the medical arm of the state. The real priority was a greater stress on moral responsibility in the education of the sons of the upper class. More than anything else, Simon's report put an end to any immediate prospect of the acts being extended to civilian towns.

The pervasive influence of a combative religious morality was evident not only in the repealers' language but in the common culture which bound many of them together. Though the group which dominated the executive board of the National Association tended to be drawn from the secularist, radical circles of the metropolis, the women and men who effectively led the repeal movement came from the same provincial backgrounds which sustained many other mid-century reform groups. Living in the northern cities, they had a deep commitment to the radical wing of the Liberal Party and were overwhelmingly nonconformist in religion. More specifically, it was the radical and fundamentalist sects in the dissenting tradition (Quakers, Unitarians and Congregationalists), with their long-standing opposition to the power of the established church and their vigorous anti-statism, which produced the majority of leaders.

Mary Priestman and Margaret Tanner, prominent in the LNA, were strict Quakers, in touch with reforming politics via their elder sister's marriage to the Quaker politician, John Bright. Butler herself had rather different origins. Aristocratically connected, she came from a Northumberland background of prominent agricultural landowners with strong Liberal and reforming links. Though an Anglican, she was very much an adherent of the evangelical, low church wing of her religion. Many of the men had direct connections with northern industrial capital. Stansfeld, one of the few prominent radicals in Gladstone's cabinet of the early 1870s, was from a Unitarian brewing family. Henry Wilson from Sheffield typified the northern male repealer. A self-made industrialist, with capital in smelting and spinning, both he and his wife Charlotte were Congregationalists, involved in the anti-slavery and temperance movements. Elected to Parliament in 1885, Wilson was able to bring pressure to bear on the Liberal Party, both for repeal and for a wider programme of moral reform and social disciplining.

In their private lives, many of the repealers sought to live out the ideal of companionate marriage. This was seen as an equal union between husband and wife, founded on a strong sense of religious purpose and cemented by the power of human love. Butler described her marriage as 'a perfectly equal union with absolute freedom on both sides for personal initiative in thought and action'. Her husband, the Rev George Butler, understood it as a true reflection of divine love.[74] The Wilsons' daughter, Helen, testified to a similar if more patriarchal version of the same model in her own parents' marriage.[75]

Repealers were at pains to stress the immense cultural distance which separated them from their opponents; they positioned themselves as wholly outside the political and military élite which upheld the acts. For Butler, medics were always 'those terrible aristocratic doctors' who violated women and who were destroying English civil liberties.[76] In fact, the lines of demarcation between the two camps were much less distinct. Many repealers and regulationists shared a common culture and held similar positions on class and social behaviour – itself one of the characteristics of mid-Victorian consensus politics. Throughout the 1860s feminists like Martineau and Elisabeth Wolstenholme worked together with their future antagonists in the Association for the Promotion of Social Science. The repeal campaign effectively heralded a deep split within the medico-moral consensus over the regulation of sexuality, fracturing the earlier discourse of sanitary interventionism. But in class terms it marked a split within the ruling bloc, not the totalising rupture from without that repealers claimed. The growth of the middle-class women's movement was central to this break in ruling alliances.

6 RELIGION, MORALITY AND REPEAL FEMINISM

Butler, in her retrospective account of the repeal campaign, insisted that the movement had been characterised less as 'the revolt of a sex', than by 'the depth and sincerity of the moral and religious convictions of the mass of the population'.[77] Her analysis may have been inflected by the upsurge of a new wave of militant feminism, from which she felt distanced. For in looking back she underplayed the impact of feminist discourses on the repeal struggle.

The use of the term 'feminism' here requires explanation. In a strict linguistic sense the concept is anachronistic, since it was not referenced in England until the 1890s. Yet the majority of women repealers clearly identified, if not with feminism, then with a body of ideas and aspirations variously known as the woman question, the emancipation of women, the rights of women and so on. This points to the existence of a distinctive women's politics and culture prior to the entry of the term 'feminism' into linguistic usage.

But Butler was correct in her insistence that moral and religious conviction was central to the repeal campaign. Moral and feminist discourses were absolutely inseparable. Religious language provided women with a powerful critique of male sexuality, a language of outrage which gave them their means of representation into the male world of public political debate. This was not the first time feminists had mobilised politically around religion, both to mount a searching critique of patriarchal society and to envisage more egalitarian forms of social organisation. Barbara Taylor has shown how women within the Owenite socialist movement in the 1830s and 1840s had struggled to advance a feminist politics through the language of radical religion.[78]

In a related way, the religious morality of repealers was not merely a passive vehicle for feminist politics; it actively empowered women and gave them the confidence to develop critical concepts. As Butler herself pointed out in language resonant with evangelical fervour, men

> had had the opportunity for many years of looking at the question in its material phases, of appreciating its hygienic results. . . . *Now*, for the first time . . . they are asked to look upon it as a question of human nature, of equal interest to men and women, as a question of the heart, the soul, the affections, the whole moral being. As a simple assertion of one woman speaking for tens of thousands of women, those two words *we rebel* are very necessary. . . . The cry of women crushed under the yoke of legalized vice is not the cry of a statistician or a medical expert; it is simply a cry of pain, a cry for justice and for a return to God's laws in place of these brutally impure laws invented and imposed by men. . . . The slave now speaks. The enslaved women have found a voice in one of themselves. . . . It is the voice of a woman who has suffered, a voice calling to holy rebellion and to war.[79]

Here biblical images of 'rebellion' and 'holy war' were fused, with recent experiences of anti-slavery and republican struggle, to forge a discourse of political representation for women – the enslaved women who had found a voice, a point of identification in one of themselves. In passages such as this it is not only the content which is important (the attack on organised vice and male expertise) but the language through which the ideas are expressed. The two are inseparable, the critical concepts are very much a function of the language.

The LNA launched a dual offensive, attacking both the medical profession and the double-standard on which the acts were premised: 'the false idea that there is one code of morality for men and another for women . . . which has more or less coloured and shaped the whole of our social life.'[80] Feminists isolated male sexuality as the target for reforming intervention, in the interests of creating a higher standard of purity among men. According to the Social Purity Alliance, founded in 1873, male vice lay at the heart of the problem of immorality. The 'new and final solution' to this evil was to lay moral responsibility and obligation on men, every other method being 'fatally incomplete'.[81] Many women believed that these reforms involved transforming the whole tenor of English public life and creating an ethical and moral climate founded on the teachings of religion. Here feminists drew heavily on the evangelical stress on marriage and the family as the foundation of upright national government. They foregrounded the importance of women for national regeneration, thus forcing a connection between public and private life and breaking open the separate spheres ideology. Often their attack was tempered by an anti-capitalist critique. As Mary Hume-Rothery put it in her letter to Gladstone's Liberal government in 1870, men and women had to be raised above the grovelling materialism of handsome houses, slothful ease and sensual indulgence.[82] Only by emphasising the sanctity of domestic life and the ultimately spiritual nature of the marriage union would national morality be remade in the image of the Maker.

It was through the use of tactics such as these that the leaders of the LNA sought to shift the representations of sexuality which had been crystallised by the medical profession and their sanitary supporters. Feminists campaigned to disrupt the gender-specific equation of active female sexuality with vice, filth and animality. The prostitute was not the source of contagion and moral corruption, but the upper-class male, backed by 'the medical lust of handling and dominating women'.[83] As a political strategy it was highly effective, successfully confronting the medical discourse which lay behind regulation. But this judicious shift of definitions carried its own problems. Middle-class women consolidated their feminism through a moral politics which implicitly reinforced the polarised representations of male and female sexuality, albeit in a reverse form. Repealers tended to view sex not merely as male defined but *as male*, while women were promoted as the agents regulating immorality – powerful but asexual guardians of the nation's morals. The political and social tensions thrown up by this strategy became visible in the plans for the rescue and reform of prostitutes which feminists put forward as their alternative to regulation. Such tensions had their genesis in the class and gender contradictions of mid-Victorian feminism.

7 WOMEN AND SOCIAL DISCIPLINING

Repeal feminists justified their entry into the political arena on the grounds that the issues raised by the acts touched on all the great trusts of their womanhood – the questions of virtue, purity, decency and social welfare. They insisted that these issues were of paramount importance to all women because they were fundamental to marriage and the family and to its valid extension in female charity work and social reform. In arguing their case the LNA were clearly drawing on those traditions of philanthropy which emphasised the central role of women in the reform of moral conditions. Nowhere more than in the repeal movement was the link between philanthropic work and an emergent feminist discourse more clearly visible.

Many of the women repealers had a history of involvement in the type of philanthropy and social reform which we have already observed in Ellen Ranyard's bible missions. Elizabeth Kell, wife of a Unitarian minister in Southampton, and Mrs Hampson of Plymouth were both extensively concerned with work among the poor.[84] Butler had also thrown herself into similar work in Liverpool in the 1860s, setting up an industrial home for working-class girls. Her account of her first visit to the oakum sheds of the workhouse must have been typical of the experience of many women from her background. Desolate from the death of her infant daughter, with her husband immersed in his career as Principal of Liverpool College, she 'became possessed with an irresistible desire to go forth and find some pain keener than my own':

> It was not difficult to find misery in Liverpool. . . . I went down to the oakum sheds and begged admission. I was taken into an immense gloomy vault filled with women and girls – more than two hundred probably at that time. I sat on the floor among them and picked oakum. They laughed at me and told me my fingers were no use for that work, which was true. But while we laughed we became friends. I recalled that they should learn a few verses to say to me on my next visit. I recollect a tall, dark, handsome girl standing up in our midst, among the damp refuse and the lumps of tarred rope, and repeating without mistake in a not unmusical voice, clear and ringing, the wonderful 14th Chapter of St John's Gospel – the words of Jesus all through . . . she had seated herself and they listened in perfect silence, this audience – wretched, ignorant, criminal some, wild and defiant others. The tall, dark-haired girl had prepared the way for me, and I said 'Now let us all kneel, and cry to that same Jesus who spoke those words,' and down on their knees they fell every one of them, reverently, on that damp stone floor, some saying the words after me, others moaning and weeping. It was a strange sound, that united wail – continuous, pitiful, strong – like a great sigh or murmur of vague desire and hope issuing from the heart of despair, piercing the gloom and murky atmosphere of that vaulted room, and reaching to the heart of God.[85]

This remarkably self-conscious passage captures many of the contradictions present in middle-class women's involvement in rescue work. Here were not only class tensions and antagonisms but also the yearning – 'that united wail' – for a different form of social relations which would link all women. As always, this visionary, prefigurative language was religious in tone and content. For Butler, evangelical religion, working in the world as practical Christianity, was the means of forging a common bond with out-cast women which would transcend class differences. Like Ranyard, she consistently argued that the personal, cross-class, woman-to-woman dia-logue espoused by philanthropy promoted reform where state-centred ini-tiatives had failed.[86] The feminist repeal movement was highly successful in challenging the gendered power relations inscribed within medical inter-ventionism. Its success checked sanitary dominance and set the tone of moral regulation for at least a generation. Many women used the campaign as a means of deepening feminist consciousness and as a platform for launching a wider programme of demands. Mary Hume-Rothery, for example, stressed that the sexual oppression of poor women brought to light by the acts was all the more reason to give women the vote and extend their educational provision, so that they could exercise formal political power.[87]

Nevertheless, much repeal work still displayed the ambiguities which had always marked middle-class women's participation in the domain of social reform. Temperance-style mass meetings, schemes for moral reclamation and placing prostitutes in domestic service, the setting up of rescue homes – these were all part of the feminist alternative to medical regulation. Eliza-beth Kell made it clear in her evidence to the 1871 Royal Commission that she believed only 'moral measures', carried out by 'voluntary effort' rather than by the state, could achieve lasting reform.[88] She countered medical arguments that repealers were not concerned with remedial measures by outlining her own moralising schemes for reclaiming prostitutes in South-ampton. The point was reiterated by F.C. Banks, secretary of the National Association, amid efforts to revive the flagging campaign in Plymouth in 1876. It was a deliberate lie on the part of regulationists to accuse repealers of having no desire to rescue women from prostitution. Since 1870, Banks insisted, the association had had an office in the town devoted exclusively to the rescue of women and children.[89] The following year, Plymouth and Devonport branches produced an enthusiastic review of their reclamation work in the association's national journal, the *Shield*. The glowing survey read like a standard report from a charity organisation:

> Out of the eighty cases, thirty three have been dealt with in the following manner – 23 sent to Homes in Plymouth and London; 1 sent to service in London, where she is doing well, 5 married and doing well; 2 returned to their parents; 1 provided with employ-ment as a machinist and doing well; 1 with children sent to the workhouse.[90]

Male repealers in Plymouth, like Banks, heartily warmed to the growing focus on reclamation within the movement. In the hands of many such men, 'rescue' meant a punitive and puritanical regime which reinforced the status of prostitutes as fallen women, though the ostensible aim was rehabilitation. This traditionalist stress also received strong support at a rank and file level within the feminist LNA. Alice Bewicke, visiting Plymouth for the association in 1881, found reclamation and educational work in full swing at the local branch. Bewicke, like many leading women repealers, found the work disturbing and felt that what was needed was a revival of the repealers' message of anti-statism and personal liberty.[91] Nevertheless, she joined enthusiastically in traditional debates on the moral effects of overcrowding, and on the relation between lack of cleanliness and the growing local trade in child prostitution among the poor.[92]

Feminists' commitment to moral improvement and environmental reform had a direct influence on their image of the prostitute. They tended to stress that these women were the hapless, passive victims of debauched aristocrats and manipulative medics, who were eager to be reformed given the necessary moral intervention from without. Rescue and reclamation could restore the prostitute to her 'pre-fallen' state of virtuous morality and asexual purity. Repealers were particularly intolerant of unreformed and unrepentant women, adopting a punitive attitude towards them and explaining their resistance as a product of the demoralising effects of forced medical inspection. Kell testified that prostitutes in inspected towns were 'vain girls', under no restraint, and lacking any sense of innate morality. They were indolent and addicted to a life of pleasure: 'They get up at any hour they choose, and go out and amuse themselves.'[93] Feminist debates over prostitution contained no positive representations of active female sexuality, either for prostitutes or for women in general. Members of the LNA were themselves caught in the powerful polarisations of female behaviour embodied in official discourse and they lacked a language to articulate alternative representations. It was felt that married women like Butler should lead the movement, because her status as a wife and a mother gave her more authority to speak about the delicate issue of sexuality. Single women – and there were many among the repealers – occupied a more ambiguous position.

Feminists were not opposed to reforming intervention per se. What they contested was the presumption that moral reform could be achieved through a centralised programme of sanitary intervention which reinforced the sexual oppression of women. Their struggle was over precisely how sexuality was to be regulated and who was to coordinate regulation: sanitary surveillance of prostitution through state medicine or moral reform through private philanthropy and rescue work. The campaign over the contagious diseases legislation aggravated and made explicit the tensions between male and female hierarchies of expertise which had been present in the alliance between medics and lady philanthropists from the 1850s.

Butler took up precisely this issue in her introduction to *Women's Work and Women's Culture*, 1869. She argued that contemporary social reform was becoming too institutionalised and bureaucratic; the present tendency was towards 'centralisation of rule, to vast combinations, large institutions and uniformity of system'.[94] What this harsh and regimented scheme urgently needed was the integration of feminine and domestic influences, setting free 'feminine powers into Workhouses, Hospitals, Schools, Orphanages, Lunatic Asylums, Reformatories and even Prisons'.[95] Her insistence on the importance of middle-class women's participation in social disciplining was clearly an attempt to guard against their displacement by the growing authority of state sanctioned professionals in the mid-Victorian period. The struggles over the Contagious Diseases Acts need to be read both as a feminist challenge to male power and as a battle within the power bloc over the disciplining of the working class. It is only by locating repeal feminism in the broader history of moral environmentalism that we can begin to understand the more obvious class and gender contradictions which surfaced in the politics of the social purity movements in the 1880s and 1890s. It is to these struggles that we now turn.

Plate 1
Chart showing the succession, place and mode of origin of the first 200 cases of the cholera in Manchester, in Henry Gaulter, *The Origin and Progress of the Malignant Cholera in Manchester*, London, Longman, 1833. (By permission of the British Library.)

Plate 2

Children's Employment Commission, *First Report of the Commissioners. Mines*, Great Britain Parliamentary Papers, 1842, vols XV–XVI, p. 79. The accompanying text noted: 'The sketch … is intended to represent Ann Ambler and William Dyson … hurriers in Messrs. Ditchforth and Clay's colliery at Elland [Halifax].' The testimony of William Dyson, aged fourteen, to the commissioners recounted: 'We have but one girl working with us, by name Ann Ambler, who goes down with us upon the clatch harness; she wears breeches when she goes down, and while at work, and comes up the pit cross-lapped with us … when she is down she hurries with us in the same way as we do, without shoes or stockings.' (Evidence collected by S.S. Scriven, Yorkshire Coal-Field, *First Report of the Commissioners. Mines*, Great Britain Parliamentary Papers, 1842, vol. XVII, p. 102.)

Plate 3
Children's Employment Commission, *First Report of the Commissioners. Mines,* Great Britain Parliamentary Papers, 1842, vols XV–XVI, p. 84. The accompanying text noted: 'The . . . sketch . . . represents a female drawer in Lancashire', and quoted from the testimony of Betty Harris, aged thirty-seven, drawer in a coal pit at Mr. Knowles', Little Bolton, Lancashire: 'I was married at 23, and went into a colliery when I was married . . . I worked at drawing when I was in the family way . . . I know a woman who has gone home and washed herself, taken to her bed, been delivered of a child, and gone to work again under the week. I have a belt round my waist, and a chain passing between my legs, and I go on my hands and feet. . . . The pit is very wet when I work, and the water comes over our clog tops always, and I have seen it up to my thighs.' (Evidence collected by J.L. Kennedy, Lancashire Coal-Field, *First Report of the Commissioners. Mines,* Great Britain Parliamentary Papers, 1842, vol. XVII, p. 230.)

Plate 4 Children's Employment Commission, *First Report of the Commissioners. Mines*, Great Britain Parliamentary Papers, 1842, vol. XVII, p. 63. The accompanying evidence from S.S. Scriven stated: 'I have often been shocked in contemplating the hideous, and anything but human appearance of these men, who are generally found in a state of bestial nakedness, lying their whole length along the uneven floor, and supporting their heads upon a board or short crutch . . . or sitting upon one heel balancing their persons by extending the other. Black and filthy as they are in their low, dark, heated, and dismal chambers, they look like a race fallen from the common stock.' (*First Report of the Commissioners. Mines*, Great Britain Parliamentary Papers, 1842, vol. XVII, p. 63.)

Plate 5 'A Court for King Cholera', *Punch*, 1852, vol. 23, p. 139.

Plate 6 Photograph of Sir James Kay-Shuttleworth, *c.* 1862, from Frank Smith, *The Life and Times of Sir James Kay-Shuttleworth*, London, John Murray, 1923, frontispiece.

Plate 7 Arthur Munby's encounter with Eliza Hayes, Rose Bridge Pits, Wigan, 1866. Ink and watercolour sketch by Munby. Munby's written comments observed: 'Talk with Eliza Hayes, aged 25, on Rose Bridge. Eliza: "A've niver done nowt else but this work, all t'daas o'mah lahf."' Munby 110 [17] f2. (By permission of the Masters and Fellows of Trinity College, Cambridge.)

Plate 8 Photograph of Hannah Cullwick, dated in Arthur Munby's hand, February 1872, 114 [9b(i)]. (By permission of the Masters and Fellows of Trinity College, Cambridge.) There are several versions of this image in Munby's collection. On the back of another similar photograph Munby wrote: '*Hannah* cleaning the doorstep of her mistresses house, as she does almost daily. Taken in the street and at her own desire, on Friday morning the 2nd February 1872.' Munby 119 [4].

Plate 9 Photograph of Hannah Cullwick dressed as a lady, dated in Arthur Munby's hand, August 1872. Munby 114 [10c]. (By permission of the Masters and Fellows of Trinity College, Cambridge.)

Plate 10 Photograph of Josephine Butler, undated, Josephine Butler Collection, album no. 5, p. 6 (Ref. 95046/2/10). (By permission of the Mary Evans Picture Library/the Fawcett Library, Guildhall University, London.)

Plate 11 Photograph of Ellice Hopkins, from Rosa Barrett, *Ellice Hopkins: A Memoir*, London, Wells Gardiner and Co, 1907, frontispiece.

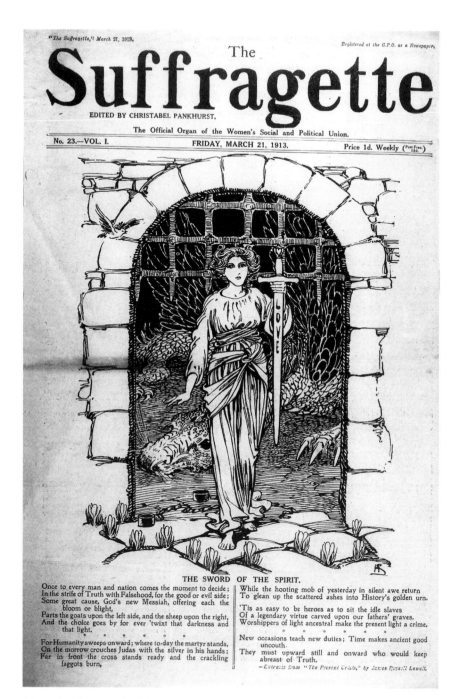

"The Suffragette," March 21, 1913.

Registered at the G.P.O. as a Newspaper.

The

Suffragette

EDITED BY CHRISTABEL PANKHURST.

The Official Organ of the Women's Social and Political Union.

No. 23.—VOL. I.   FRIDAY, MARCH 21, 1913.   Price 1d. Weekly (Post Free. 1½d.)

THE SWORD OF THE SPIRIT.

Once to every man and nation comes the moment to decide;
In the strife of Truth with Falsehood, for the good or evil side;
Some great cause, God's new Messiah, offering each the
    bloom or blight,
Parts the goats upon the left side, and the sheep upon the right,
And the choice goes by for ever 'twixt that darkness and
    that light.

* * * * * *

For Humanity sweeps onward; where to-day the martyr stands,
On the morrow crouches Judas with the silver in his hands;
Far in front the cross stands ready and the crackling
    faggots burn.

While the hooting mob of yesterday in silent awe return
To glean up the scattered ashes into History's golden urn.

'Tis as easy to be heroes as to sit the idle slaves
Of a legendary virtue carved upon our fathers' graves.
Worshippers of light ancestral make the present light a crime.

* * * * *

New occasions teach new duties; Time makes ancient good
    uncouth.
They must upward still and onward who would keep
    abreast of Truth.

—Extracts from "The Present Crisis," by James Russell Lowell.

Plate 12 'The Sword of the Spirit', *Suffragette*, 21 March 1913, vol. 1, no. 23, front
    page.

THE WEEKLY DISPATCH.

TEACHER AND THE · · · GIRLS SHE TOLD.

Miss Outram, the school teacher at the Derbyshire village of Dronfield, whose action in teaching the girls under her the facts of sex, has led to such a storm of protest. Round her are pictures of the girls whom she has so instructed, the one in the centre at the top being the daughter of Mr. and Mrs. Bradwell, who was the first to be taken away from the school by her parents. The matter was referred by the school managers to the Education Committee of the Derbyshire County Council, but Miss Outram was exonerated. The villagers, however, were not satisfied with this, and as a result only eleven of Miss Outram's thirty-six pupils now attend school. A big meeting of the villagers passed a resolution strongly disapproving of Miss Outram's action, and decided to send a petition to Mr. W. E. Harvey, M.P. for the division, asking him to carry the protest to the Minister for Education. Miss Outram says: "I consider this teaching should always be done by teachers who are old and sensible enough if the girls' mothers will not do it for themselves. I always formerly told them to ask their mothers. I suppose I shall have to resort to that way of escape again. Once a girl asked me a most direct question. I shuffled as so many people do with children, and I could see that the child was snubbed and that there could never be the same confidence between us afterwards. It was after that that I decided to explain things simply and naturally."

Plate 13 'Teacher and the Girls She Told', *Weekly Dispatch*, 7 February 1914.

Plate 14 'Should Eugenics Be Taught in Elementary Schools', *Derbyshire Times*, 7 February 1914.

Part Three

FROM STATE MEDICINE TO CRIMINAL LAW

Purity, feminism and the state
1880–1914

1 PROLOGUE

In July 1885 the Salvation Army launched a nationwide purity campaign.[1] In less than three weeks the army gathered nearly four thousand signatures for a petition demanding a new criminal law amendment act, raising the age of consent to eighteen and giving the police increased powers to search and arrest brothel keepers. The monster document, nearly two-and-a-half miles long, was drawn in a wagon to the House of Commons by cadets from the Clapham training home. Over the cart was a white canopy bearing the inscription: 'In the name of the people and the Queen, mother of the country, the Salvation Army demand that iniquity shall cease.' Behind the cadets marched three hundred uniformed women soldiers of the army. The whole line of the route, through the working-class districts of Hackney, Shoreditch and Bishopsgate, was filled with crowds. At Whitehall the petition was unloaded and carried on the shoulders of eight officers into the Commons.

This dramatic demonstration was part of a series of campaigns and rallies which took place in the summer of 1885, as an immediate response to the revelations by the *Pall Mall Gazette* of the horrors of juvenile prostitution. The new popular press played a crucial role in orchestrating public opinion over the affair. In early July W.T. Stead, the paper's editor, had published 'The Maiden Tribute of Modern Babylon'.[2] Drawing on polarised representations of the passive, innocent child-victim and the debauched male client (the stock-in-trade of much popular literature), Stead's articles exposed the underlying depravity in aristocratic and fashionable London society. His sexual script employed the language of moral outrage both to fuel growing demands for law reform and to present a lurid, titillating account of the prostitution trade.

This exposé and the Salvation Army spectacle were symptomatic of a carefully organised campaign by purity workers and feminists to press the Liberal government to pass the Criminal Law Amendment Bill, which had been before Parliament since 1883. After the Maiden Tribute scandal Josephine Butler convened a special meeting with Mrs Bramwell Booth of the Salvation Army and Ellice Hopkins, a prominent member of the new purity movement, to discuss tactics. Protests culminated in a mass rally at St James Hall on 21 August, followed by an open-air meeting next day, which drew over a quarter of a million people. Support came from a broad coalition of clergymen, prominent liberals, purists, feminists, trade-union leaders and some socialists. Stead waxed lyrical, envisaging a new moral order of the 'forces of Democracy and Socialism', which would abolish the 'immolation of the daughters of the people as a sacrifice to the vices of the rich'.[3] The outcome was the formation of the National Vigilance Association (NVA), whose membership included leaders of women's organisations and prominent feminists. The constitution of the association contained a strong commitment to feminist demands for the reform of male sexuality, together with a coercive policy of sexual regulation. The traditional stress on preventive and rescue work was now twinned with an emphasis on legislation to outlaw obscenity, indecency and the foreign traffic in young girls. Intent on winning working-class support, in October the NVA launched a nationwide crusade throughout the industrial centres of England and Scotland.[4]

The purity movement's stress on the criminal law to promote morality marked an important shift away from traditional strategies of environmental reform and private philanthropy. The NVA saw the criminal law as an instrument for improving public morals – positively educative rather than simply repressive, to be used in conjunction with preventive work. William Coote, the association's secretary, believed that the law was 'schoolmaster to the whole community'. Legislation was the best reflex of public opinion, the real moral thermometer of the country.[5] This was a quite new perception of the state's capacity for transforming sexual and moral behaviour. In the thirty years before the First World War purists and feminists consistently argued that criminal law legislation was the key to improving the nation's morals. As Coote himself never tired of pointing out:

> There is a very popular cant phrase that you cannot make men good by Act of Parliament. It is false to say so. . . . You can, and do, keep men sober simply by an Act of Parliament; you can, and do, chain the devil of impurity in a large number of men and women by the fear of the law.[6]

The 1885 Criminal Law Amendment Act signalled a new, more coercive system of state intervention into the domain of sexuality. Subsequent legislation followed the same pattern, extending legal control over familiar areas such as indecency, prostitution and brothel keeping and creating new offences around male homosexuality and incest.[7]

In an immediate sense, purity campaigns for more stringent legislation coincided with the renewed official panic over the urban poor in the 1880s. Worsening economic conditions, the growth of the new socialist and trade-union movements, together with the perceived failure of traditional programmes of philanthropy, all contributed to widespread alarm in official circles about the immorality of the unrespectable poor, or 'the residuum'.[8] As in the 1830s and 1840s, the discourse of social investigation, circulated by novelists and journalists, social scientists and government commissioners, represented working-class immorality as a major source of anxiety.[9]

Lurid semi-fictional accounts by James Greenwood, George Sims and Jack London alluded darkly to acts of debauchery not fit even for the pages of the *Lancet*. *The Bitter Cry of Outcast London*, written in 1883 by Andrew Mearns, Congregationalist minister in Chelsea, exposed a vast mass of moral corruption and absolute godlessness at the centre of the greatest metropolis in the world.[10]

The most extensive moral survey was contained in the *Report of the Royal Commission on the Housing of the Working Classes*, 1884. Incest, as the rector of Christchurch, Spitalfields, bemoaned, was the direct result of overcrowding. The one-room system encouraged children to be sexually precocious, so that they found out everything about physical matters from their home experience.[11] In the familiar language of environmentalism, Mearns demonstrated that overcrowding spread the infection of immorality from the dissolute to honest and upright working-class families.[12] Purity demands for legislation against prostitution, brothel keeping and other acts of immorality often explicitly addressed problems posed by the culture of the urban poor and the difficulties of keeping public order on the streets. Agitation may have been couched in a vocabulary which spoke of *national* morality, but it was clear who were being singled out as the recipients of purity action.

Yet one grouping was conspicuously absent from these campaigns. The medical profession did not contribute to the new crusades, nor was there any resurrection of the medico-moral alliance. The balance of forces around sexuality had definitely shifted. Sanitary science and state medicine were now in partial eclipse.

2 THE ECLIPSE OF STATE MEDICINE

The repeal of the Contagious Diseases Acts marked a severe defeat for the medical profession. It was a defeat which was to have profound and far-reaching consequences for the state medical regulation of sexuality. Though the *Lancet* and the *BMJ* fought a rearguard action right up to the moment of final repeal, it was obvious that the sanitary principle had been success-fully challenged by moralists.[13] By their action, the women and men of the repeal movement had effectively redefined the terms of the debate over sex. This defeat was itself part of the wider eclipse of state medicine in the 1870s and 1880s, which opened the space for purity groups to push for their own conception of sexual reform through the criminal law.

The initial setbacks came as part of the local government reforms of the early 1870s. As Simon himself acknowledged, English public health administration had developed in a piecemeal and ad hoc fashion for much of the early nineteenth century, with national supervision divided between his own Privy Council Medical Office and the Poor Law Board. Under the

Local Government Act, 1871, the two departments were amalgamated to form the new Local Government Board.[14]

But the new act created more political problems than it solved. The old Poor Law Board and the Medical Office had developed highly distinctive forms of administration which were fundamentally conflictual in terms of aims and professional practice. Both departments were heir to the Chadwickian and Benthamite politics of the 1830s, but each had crystallised a specific mode of social intervention. The Medical Office pushed for reform and regulation through the hegemony of state medicine. The Poor Law Office, on the other hand, inheriting the most utilitarian forms of social disciplining, was fundamentally opposed both to medical expertise and to any further large-scale financial outlay in aid of poor relief.

After 1871 the policy of the new Local Government Board was shaped by the poor law tradition, with the ministerial backing of its first president, James Stansfeld. Stansfeld's own personal antipathy to medical involvement in the Contagious Diseases Acts, together with his ignorance of scientific matters – he knew as much of science as a cow does of conic sections, according to one contemporary – may have exacerbated Simon's problems at the new board.[15] What was clear was that the new department was intent on circumscribing medical influence within the state. The battle was fought out as an intense personal rivalry between Simon and the new permanent secretary to the Local Government Board, John Lambert. Lambert was himself a skilled administrator, with a working knowledge of sanitary reform. A member of the 1868 Royal Sanitary Commission and a vigorous promoter of public health as Mayor of Salisbury, he was not fundamentally opposed to state medicine. But he typified a new breed of civil servant. Methodical, precise and administratively cautious, he carried over from his earlier experience as a member of the Poor Law Board a determination to subordinate medical experts to the lay administration. He succeeded in winning Stansfeld's confidence and in stamping his personal authority on all areas of the new department, including Simon's, by intercepting correspondence and seizing responsibility for the smallest details of policy.[16] The result was that though Simon and his staff were retained, the poor law secretariat began to create an inner circle of administration, relegating medics to the peripheries. After a protracted battle, which raised *The Times* and the whole of the medical establishment against Stansfeld and Lambert, Simon resigned as a civil servant in 1876, but the overall situation remained unchanged.

Like the defeat over the Contagious Diseases Acts, Simon's resignation was received as a serious blow by the medical profession.[17] Going beyond the clash of personalities, the *Lancet* probed the underlying causes of this medical decline. It concluded that the Simonian concept of state medicine was far in advance of public opinion and was likely to remain so for some time to come.[18] Such explanations were comforting, if only because they pointed forward to the ultimate vindication of medical science. Yet they obviously failed to grasp the political and administrative realities within which state medicine was increasingly caught in the 1870s and 1880s. The key here lies not with personal rivalries, as administrative historians would have us believe. Much more significant were the conflicting claims of medical expert and lay civil servant over control of social policy, and the shifting relations between politician and bureaucrat in the nineteenth-century state.[19]

Simon outplayed the politicians and Treasury staff with his expansionist policy in the 1860s. However, his action provoked significant comment from Treasury permanent secretaries, committed as they were to a Gladstonian ideology of 'cheap government' and to the subordination of the extravagant missionary zeal of medical reformers. When Simon pressed and won his claim for an assistant inspector to supervise the national vaccination scheme in 1871, the current Permanent Secretary, Ralph Lingen, issued a general warning in the accompanying Treasury minute: 'I do not know who is to check the assertion of experts when the government has once undertaken a class of duties which none but such persons understand.'[20] Lingen typified the new breed of generalist civil servant. Arts-based and classically trained, he was convinced that professional experts of Simon's calibre did not conform to the new conception of the broad-based administrator. For Lingen, state medics represented a clear political force in their own right, rather than the steady, methodical cadre of intellectuals envisaged by the Northcote-Trevelyan reforms of the 1850s. With the growing crystallisation of powers within the state from the 1860s, the reform of the civil service and the abandonment of political appointments, Simon's cunning politicking now seemed out of place. Further, the growth of a discourse of formal political representation and its implementation in the 1867 Reform Act, made politicians uneasy about the political power wielded by civil servants, especially when they operated as statesmen in disguise.

The rise of the purity movement in the 1880s needs to be seen in relation to these medical defeats, for state medicine had lost the initiative not only in the field of sexual regulation but in many other areas of social intervention. Under Simon's successors the medical officership was a much more limited project than previously. Certainly there was no attempt to resurrect the grandiose principles of sexual and sanitary hygiene. On the issue of central health policy the annual medical reports from the Local Government Board were muted in the extreme.[21] Apart from the important field of theoretical research into the causes and treatment of epidemic disease, the influence of the department was severely curtailed. According to Sir George Buchanan, Medical Officer between 1879 and 1892, the current conception of state medicine was but a pale shadow of what it once was.[22]

In the closing decades of the nineteenth century it was moralists and feminists who set the pace in the field of sexual politics. Their campaigns for legal enforcement were backed by a powerful language which identified whole new technologies of sex and forged them into a popular crusade for reform. This broad coalition of forces was central to the enactment of criminal law legislation; organising, investigating, petitioning the state to act. Government itself was rarely the active initiator in the move to criminalise immorality. Hence we now move substantially away from the state and its experts to examine these voluntary movements and popular struggles.

3 PURITY AND SCIENCE

The language of purity demonstrates how popular scientific concepts were reworked to advance a new moralised discourse on sex. It also shows how far state medicine had been checked over sexual regulation. Purity campaigners were not adverse to drawing on science, but for them it was a tool to validate morality. True scientific investigation always revealed the workings of divine law, and the medical profession needed to be kept under constant surveillance, because their narrow commitment to materialistic principles overlooked moral considerations. With the experience of the Contagious Diseases Acts in mind, Ellice Hopkins tartly remarked that there were 'one or two things which the medical profession has yet to grow out of under the influence of an enlightened public opinion'.[23]

Elizabeth Blackwell's career both as a purist and as a medic displayed the new approach to 'Christian physiology'. Blackwell was the first woman doctor, graduating in New York in 1849 and later opening a dispensary on New York's lower East Side. Her origins were similar to those of many leading figures in the repeal movement. She came from a prominent family of nonconformists and industrialists in Bristol, where her father had long been active in the abolitionist movement. Broadly committed to Kingsley's brand of Christian socialism, she established the National Health Society in London in 1871, aimed at improving the health of the working classes. In her writings and lectures Blackwell demonstrated a firm belief in the intimate connection between physical and moral health, addressing women on domestic hygiene and on the relation between health and religion.[24] Her book *The Human Element in Sex*, 1884, was adamant that medicine could not become an end in itself but that it needed to discover the workings of moral law. Sex morality was the area *par excellence* where medics had to be governed by religious responsibility.[25]

This moral appropriation of scientific discourse was common in the 1870s and 1880s. Darwinism had initially shaken the deistic foundations of contemporary science, fuelling the avowed agnosticism and sense of spiritual crisis experienced by a generation of mid-Victorian intellectuals.[26] Many moralists responded to the challenge less by denying evolutionism than by arguing that the new biological theories could be integrated with older moral concerns. In 1872 the Catholic Archbishop, Cardinal Manning, announced that the majority of clerics now believed that there was nothing incompatible between evolutionary science and their own theological system.[27] Darwin's own *The Descent of Man*, published the previous year, also marshalled evidence to show how the growth of moral faculties like self-control, love and altruism were key elements in progressing towards a higher moral culture.[28]

Purity workers developed their own rereading of the Darwinist debate, though they placed less stress on integrating the two systems and more on the subordination of science to the dictates of morality. Mothers were to use stories drawn from plant and animal life to instruct children both about the reproductive cycle and about the evolutionary progress from lower organisms up to man. All this was presided over by an all-seeing God. For though evolution taught that the human race was linked to plants and animals, it also demonstrated that man was separate from other species: 'a spiritual being, incarnate in an animal body.'[29] According to Blackwell, morality involved the evolution of self-consciousness which had developed only in the human species. The moral faculty needed to govern the sexual instinct, organising it on 'broad, well-marked mental foundations'.[30] Chastity, continence and self-control were the highest forms of sexual development because they were regulated by reason and a knowledge of the providential laws of human nature.

Yet evolutionary science also pointed to the precariousness of moral progress – how it could so easily slip back into animal chaos. This was the human dilemma. In their efforts to curb immorality purists carefully distanced themselves from a world-view totally determined by heredity. They were at pains to prove that moral or immoral development was not fixed or inevitable, for all the evolutionary stress on inherited characteristics. The link between sex and morality needed to be *cultivated* and *worked at*, using every resource of civilisation. Animal passion could be refined to become part of the higher stages of evolution, or it could deteriorate into moral evil:

> Sex is capable of great devotion towards good or towards evil. . . . It may grow into a noble sympathy, self-sacrifice . . . and joy. . . . It also allows that perversion and extreme degradation of sex observable in the human race.[31]

Religion coupled with morality could 'alter the evil conditions' and 'cut into the chain which is otherwise endless and circular'.[32] Such insistences provided one important rationale for the criminal law approach to sexual reform. Criminalising legislation was not simply repressive, it was, in Coote's phrase, 'positively educative and improving'.

4 PURITY AND POPULISM

Purity was a self-consciously popular movement in a way that even the repeal campaign had not been. This was evident not only in its mass organisation, but also in the efforts to address working-class audiences and write them into the discourse of moral reform. In that sense purity marks a distinctive break with the earlier sanitary approach to sexual regulation which had been dominated by the élite voice of professional experts. It needs to be seen as part of the renewed offensive launched by militant evangelicalism in the 1880s, which influenced a whole range of single issue campaigns and brought pressure to bear on the Liberal Party hierarchy.

A loose network of campaigning groups formed the base of the new purity movement, with large-scale meetings and the mass publication of tracts and pamphlets. Speeches were often followed by the distribution of membership or pledge cards, when audiences were encouraged to declare their personal adherence to the rules of the movement. Dramatic cases of moral conversion and last-minute rescues from the brink of hell-fire were a particular favourite.[33] In practice, teaching the working class to understand moral law usually meant an Old Testament affirmation of the preordained retribution which followed in the wake of sinfulness. Masturbation was most often used to demonstrate how the transgression of divine law inevitably brought down the wrath of God: 'For he that soweth his flesh, shall of the flesh reap corruption.'[34]

While the working class was the principal target for purists' interventionary zeal they also provided rank-and-file recruits for the new movement. Some organisations laid primary stress on preventive work and moral re-education, especially among working-class girls, for example: the Anglican-run Girls' Friendly Society, founded in 1874, Ellice Hopkins' Ladies' Association for the Care of Friendless Girls, 1876, and the Band of Hope Mission, 1879.[35] Other groups, like the Boys' League of Honour and the Church Lads' Brigade, addressed the leisure activities of working-class boys, setting up night schools and organising sport and mutual improvement societies to counter the idleness which was the first step towards dissipation and self-abuse. Lady visitors were also co-opted in campaigns designed to instruct working-class mothers on practical morality in the home, supervising children's play and paying careful attention to the bathing and sleeping arrangements of sons and daughters.[36]

The populism of the movement foregrounded a specific ideology of nationalism and national culture. Demands for the purification of national life were matters of importance which stood above class differences and the petty divisions of party politics. Practically, purity usually worked by forging alliances between sections of the evangelical middle class, the petty bourgeoisie and the respectable working class against the aristocracy. Attacks on the immorality and decadence of aristocratic culture were the staple diet of purity tracts and speeches. They focused popular discontent over the double-standard and over the complicity of aristocratic men in child prostitution.[37]

The movement also played off representations of *English* morality against the decadence of foreign habits. The French were a favourite target, and the new popular press was instrumental in crystallising xenophobic imagery. When Henry Vizetelly was prosecuted in 1888 under the obscenity laws, for publishing an English translation of Émile Zola's novel *La Terre*, purists seized the opportunity to mount a sustained assault on the morally pernicious influence of French culture. Complaints in the press pointed to the rising tide of juvenile depravity caused by the availability of cheap editions of continental literature.[38] The Oscar Wilde trials of 1895 condensed representations both of aristocratic debauchery and the corrupting effects of foreign morals. Wilde, depicted as the leader of the aesthetic movement, with its unnatural taste for the sensual and the erotic, was pilloried in court as a foreign parasite. He was seen to be attacking the moral, manly roots of English public life with the aid of effeminate, aristocratic tastes.[39] The *Evening News* summed up the affair by calling for greater public vigilance to root out the canker of immorality: 'England has tolerated the man Wilde for too long . . . he was a social pest, a centre of intellectual corruption . . . who attacked all wholesome, manly, simple ideals of English life.'[40]

These new codes of popular journalism – investigative exposé combined with sensationalist melodrama – were part of the repertoire of purity campaigns. Stead's crusade against child harlotry and the press onslaught on Wilde were designed to fuel outrage and to orchestrate the demand for moral action. But their injunctions did not simply denounce immorality. Purity language was transformed through these journalistic codes to produce highly wrought sexual imagery. Rituals of transgression, sensationalist violation and titillating naughtiness became the stock-in-trade of popular news reporting in the late nineteenth century. The success of this language itself needs to be read in the context of purity's growing hegemony.

5 SPEAKING OUT

In all areas of intervention the first step for purists was to speak out about sex. The aim was to confront the conspiracy of silence and shame which surrounded the subject and create a climate where immorality could be tackled seriously. Caution and silence were contrary to God's law. They were dangerous and hypocritical, providing a fertile breeding ground for evil. Here purists were deliberately challenging official arguments which opposed fresh legislation, or greater public discussion, on the grounds that this would only draw attention to sex and incite immorality. In the debates over proposed changes to the criminal law, politicians continued to argue that to speak about sex was to corrupt. In 1903 the Earl of Halsbury, the Lord Chancellor, wrecked legislation criminalising incest with such arguments.[41] In contrast, social purists argued that to speak out was vital. Ignorance was to play into the hands of the enemy, knowledge through education was power:

> It is argued that to speak out on this subject is only to suggest the very evil you want to cure, and to do more harm than good. . . . Let us recognize once and for all that the modest silence . . . has landed England in child harlotry.[42]

Enforced silence was no guarantee of innocence or security. To classify and measure the extent of immorality – to quite literally put it into discourse – was central to getting the problem under control.

The quest for greater knowledge was underpinned by a highly gender-specific discourse on sexuality. Politically this was informed by the demands coming from women's organisations and intellectually by the moralised language of evolutionary science. Representations of male sexuality twinned evangelical images of the struggle between flesh and spirit with an evolutionary stress on the lower and higher impulses of human nature. Campaigners launched a direct offensive against contemporary medical theories, which talked of the inevitability of the male sexual urge, arguing that they failed to take proper account of Darwinist insights. Man's nature was two-sided, only half of it led to wrongdoing, the other half prohibited sin. Purists conceived of masculinity as a never-ending battle, requiring constant watchfulness and careful supervision. The dramatic conflict between good and evil either brought out heroic qualities in boys, or it exposed those who were cowardly and unmanly. In an end-of-term address at Clifton College, Bristol, the Rev J. M. Wilson presented his students with a dramatic choice: 'It has to be settled whether you are to be your own master or slave; whether your body shall be kept under, and you will be strong enough to rule it; or whether your body shall be the target.'[43]

Muscular Christianity was the hoped-for goal, with self-control to be attained through strict mental and physical discipline. The Purity Alliance's rules for daily life advocated cold baths, regular vigorous exercise, moderation in eating and drinking, as well as prayer to guard against moral evil. Those men leading the movement, like Alfred Dyer and Wilson, projected a chivalric vision of masculinity which championed the ideal of asexual, dependent womanhood. Boys were to be taught their knightly duty to serve their mothers and sisters.[44] Many purity leagues drew on emblems from the legends of Christian chivalry, appealing to men and boys by a play on protective and gallant manhood. In the emblem of the White Cross League, founded in 1883, white stood for purity, the league for disciplined strength and the cross for the underlying truth of the fight for Christ.[45]

The language of purity opened a space for women to define their own images of female sexual identity. Speaking out enabled female purity workers to project a vision of moral femininity, which, though problematic, did address the hopes and aspirations of many women. They pressed for a particular rereading of Darwin, to add weight to the older evangelical claim that women had a rightful place in regulating sex.[46] For Hopkins, as for Blackwell, women's moral power lay in their capacity to harness and control male sexual energy by drawing out the spiritual impulses in human nature. This was guaranteed by women's reproductive role, which put them in contact with the great physical and mental powers of the race. Blackwell glossed reproduction in a highly original way, fusing it with claims for an active female sexuality. Countering medical assertions that sex passion was absent from most normal women, she pointed out that because of reproduction the physical aspect of sex weighed more heavily on them than on men:

> Physical sex is a larger factor in the life of the woman, married or unmarried, than in the life of the man. . . . Those who deny sexual feeling to women . . . quite lose sight of . . . [the] immense spiritual force of attraction which exists in so very large a proportion in their nature.[47]

Blackwell insisted that biological reproduction actively contributed to women's higher spiritual self, in contrast to many medics and evolutionary biologists who saw women as closer to nature because of their 'animal' function. In her view, it was bourgeois women who were most oppressed by social definitions of female purity. Taught to believe that sex was shameful, they were denied the spiritual experience of sex passion which involved the transfiguration of the lower by the higher elements.[48] Blackwell's radical ideas point to the beginnings of a discourse on active female sexuality. As recent research is beginning to uncover, the 1880s witnessed the interrogation of current forms of sexual morality by feminist intellectuals – a move which was stimulated by the various public sexual scandals of the decade. Blackwell herself discussed her ideas at the Men and Women's Club, a progressive middle-class coterie whose membership included Olive Schreiner and the social purist Maria Sharpe.[49] For these women, speaking out often led to a wider debate on sexuality and gender. But for the majority it was *purity* which provided the language both to challenge men's immorality and to stake out their own claim to speak about sex.

6 FEMINISM AND SOCIAL PURITY

In the years from the repeal campaign to the suffrage movement women's struggles were a major force in sexual politics. Women's organisations and feminist leaders emerged as a powerful pressure group, whose influence was felt by male politicians and professionals at the level of the state and in public debate. By no means all purists identified with feminism, but the rapid growth of the women's movement in the late nineteenth and early twentieth century cannot be understood without reference to the purity crusades, which drew thousands of women into the political arena for the first time. All of this marked a significant break with the earlier history of medico-moral politics. Women were empowered to speak about sex, challenging the authority of the experts and drawing attention to their gendered power relations. Yet as the tensions inherent in the repeal movement have already shown, this feminist discourse was itself caught in hierarchies of sexual power, retaining strong links with the environmentalist regime of social disciplining. Such contradictions were highlighted in women's growing demands for more coercive criminal law legislation.

In the 1880s and 1890s women like Blackwell, Hopkins, Laura Ormiston-Chant, Millicent Fawcett and Catherine Booth argued that the law was central to implementing feminist demands. Their protests gained renewed impetus in the suffrage struggles immediately before the First World War. They were focused on a massive campaign against the double-standard and its enshrinement in law. The immediate contrast with earlier feminist sexual politics could not have been sharper. For behind the new purity feminism lay the legacy of the anti-statist struggle against the Contagious Diseases Acts. As we have seen, repeal feminists had not been opposed to moral disciplining, but they had promoted it through the more 'feminine' domain of voluntary agencies, attacking the statist solutions of male professionals. Despite this a number of prominent women repealers, among them Butler herself, sat on the first executive council of the NVA and gave support to coercive state legislation. Admittedly, after the initial euphoria following the passing of the 1885 Act, some, like Butler, began to distance themselves from the purity movement.[50] Nevertheless, many feminists did throw themselves wholeheartedly into the purity campaigns. The political and historical problem is how to understand that involvement.

Recent social and feminist historians who have considered the question have bid for explanations on the back of contemporary allegiances. This moment in the history of sexual politics is fast becoming a battleground for voicing current debates and disagreements. Edward Bristow and Jeffrey Weeks fail to see anything specifically feminist in the purity crusades. For Weeks, the purity movement was only significant as a moment of moral panic over sex, condensing wider social and political anxieties.[51] Judith Walkowitz, on the other hand, acknowledges that the latter stages of the repeal struggle were marked by dramatic contradictions within feminist sexual politics. Tensions submerged in the earlier campaign now came to the fore and led more and more to a coercive policy of sexual regulation, especially of working-class prostitutes.[52] By contrast Sheila Jeffreys' account, informed by the politics of revolutionary feminism, stresses that social purity was a landmark in the offensive against male sexuality and downplays the contradictions intrinsic to the movement.[53]

What needs reaffirming, and re-examining, is the complex interrelation between moral languages and the history of nineteenth-century feminism. As we now know, the discourses of practical religion and philanthropy provided women with a means of representation into the male-defined world of public political debate. They also enabled women to challenge male professional power while at the same time implicating them in coercive class regulation. To write the history of late nineteenth-century feminist sexual politics as a 'seduction' by the conservative purity movement, is to ignore this much longer, contradictory history of women's participation in social reform. These tensions were graphically illustrated in the career of Ellice Hopkins.

7 ELLICE HOPKINS

In February 1883 Ellice Hopkins addressed a mass meeting of working men in the mining village of Bishop Auckland, at the invitation of the Bishop of Durham. After prayers and a stirring speech, purity pledge cards were distributed among the men, listing rules for personal conduct:

1   To treat all women with respect, and endeavour to protect them from wrong and degradation.
2   To use every possible means to fulfil the command, 'keep THYSELF pure'.
3   To endeavour to put down all indecent language and coarse jests.
4   To maintain the law of purity as equally binding upon men and women.
5   To endeavour to spread these principles among my companions, and to try and help my younger brothers.[54]

The meeting was an enormous success. Out of an audience of some three hundred miners and clerks, one hundred and thirty came forward to pledge themselves for purity.

Ellice Hopkins was a central figure in the feminist agitation for criminal law regulation in the 1880s. She was an 'organic intellectual' of the new purity movement. Her rise to prominence was the culmination of a career which combined a feminist commitment to challenging male sexual behaviour, with traditional beliefs in moralising philanthropy directed at the poor. The daughter of a distinguished Cambridge mathematics tutor, she began work as a Sunday school teacher in the 1850s. In 1860 she turned her attention to the condition of male agricultural workers in the village of Barnwell, near Cambridge. Through her efforts a mission hall was built, where she started to lecture on moral purity. Hopkins always maintained that work with men was her favourite form of campaigning. It posed a challenge both to her religious motivation and her feminist principles. In *An Englishwoman's Work Among Workingmen*, 1875, she recounted how the dramatic language of evangelical religion enabled her to press her case:

> But how did I try to get this influence over working men? I will try and reply in some detail. In the first place, it was quite useless to preach ready made doctrine to them. My first effort, therefore, was to get them to believe in moral law. . . . And little by little they came to see the great Christian doctrine that eternal sin must be, in the very nature of things, eternal punishment or eternal misery.[55]

As a populist, Hopkins was well aware of the problems facing middle-class reformers in the dialogue with working-class audiences. She warned fellow women workers that it was useless to address working men with 'plain commonplaces', what was needed was vivid and dramatic language: 'the men want strong meat, thoughts as racy as their own expressions; they reject sweet pap fit for children.'[56]

Evangelical religion furnished Hopkins with a powerful rhetoric to arouse mass meetings and personally motivated her to embark on a public career exposing immorality. She represented it quite literally as a call to God's service. On the death of her father in 1866 she suffered physical and mental breakdown, confiding in a letter that it was her religion that held her up. While recuperating in Brighton she plunged into work at the Albion Hill Rescue Home. The job was not easy, and the girls themselves were resistant to her crusading philanthropy. Hopkins saw the need for a revival of the personalised approach to rescue work. Rather than organising mass midnight meetings to confront the evil in working-class areas, she judged it more effective for women to go into the 'dens of infamy' in the morning as friends and advisers. Her efforts sometimes backfired, when she was confronted by a robust culture from the prostitutes themselves.[57]

Her own power and presence as a speaker was perhaps her greatest asset in converting audiences. Many had testified to Josephine Butler's impact on the rostrum. Hopkins had an equally clear awareness of the importance of personal presentation and she worked hard to perfect an appropriate style of public speaking. 'If anyone supposes', she wrote, 'that my power of speaking was a gift that came naturally to me, without any effort on my part, let them once and for all dispossess themselves of any such ideas.'[58] Throughout her career she was subject to a range of nervous disorders. In common with Butler and Florence Nightingale, illness related to the strain experienced by middle-class women who moved into the public sphere. But these women also employed medical definitions of physical and mental weakness as an effective tactical weapon in the battle with men. Hopkins used her frailty, her diminutive size and a 'beautiful speaking voice' as symbols of the power of female purity. She counselled other women to do the same: 'You can make your womanhood a sort of external conscience to them. You can appeal to them never to say or do things which they would be ashamed for you to know.'[59]

All this was done in the face of considerable hostility from her male audiences. On one occasion in the early 1880s she was persuaded to address male students at Edinburgh University medical school. It seems that medics have not changed much over a hundred years. She recalled that many eminent men had declined to give the address because of the expected barracking. Hopkins tamed the students with a characteristic blend of religious fervour and moral conviction:

> Spirit and flesh both quailed before so difficult and rowdy an audience on so difficult and perilous a subject . . . as I sat in the committee room while the order of the meeting was being arranged, and heard my audience shouting, singing, crowing like cocks . . . and keeping up a continuous uproar, I thought to myself, 'I have got to go into that and control it somehow so as to be heard'. . . . The only thing was to push me at once to the front; and almost immediately, after a very few brief words from the distinguished chairman, I found myself face to face with an audience that evidently meant mischief. By some instinct I told them . . . about the lost and degraded womanhood of England, the hosts of young girls slain in body and soul . . . met with at night in our terrible streets. This seemed to strike and sober them . . . a thing which to all of them was so familiar, and to many had been only the subject of coarse jest. They listened to me with profound attention, and I could see that my words went home.[60]

It was not only the antagonism of male audiences that Hopkins was up against. The opposition her career provoked – as a single woman speaking about sexuality – showed that despite the gains made by repeal feminism, women still risked censure and social ostracism when they crossed the boundaries from the private to the public sphere.

Hopkins was clear about the dual strategy of the new purity movement. It needed to focus on the reform of male sexuality *and* the improvement of working-class morals. On both issues she acknowledged the importance of the 'women's movement' in promoting reform, 'the ever increasing activity in all agencies for the elevation of women . . . above all that new sense of a common *esprit de corps* . . . which is now beginning to bind all our efforts together.'[61] For Hopkins as for Blackwell, feminism centrally meant bringing the private sphere of bourgeois womanhood to bear on the public world of social and moral problems. Here again was the connection between feminism and the philanthropic tradition. Women were the 'conscience of the world', social reform concerned women because it touched on all the great trusts of womanhood, the sanctity of the family, the purity of marriage, the sacredness of marriage, the sweet innocence of children'.[62] Both Hopkins and Blackwell argued that women needed to play a decisive role in public debate over the nation's morals, precisely because it was *women* who were centrally concerned with sexuality. Hopkins was militant and uncompromising about the source of moral evil. Male sexuality was the fundamental problem. Prostitution was the direct result of men's immorality, creating an outcast class of women tacitly sanctioned by church and state.[63]

Along with many women in the purity movement, Hopkins increasingly looked to the criminal law to enact feminist demands. This is the key to understanding purity feminists' commitment to coercive legislation in the 1880s. The law could be used to protect women and children, to educate men into self-control and chastity, and to reform working-class morals. Looking back on these campaigns at the end of her life, Hopkins defined the law as the chief agency for enacting God's work and for abolishing the double-standard, which menaced the young and ultimately contributed to the disintegration of the state. Men's immorality not only threatened the stability of the family, in the end it posed a danger to the foundations of good government. It was imperative that the state should intervene to preserve the higher life of the nation:

> When shall we learn that whoever touches the higher life and well-being of the family still more vitally affects the wider family of the State, and threatens its disintegration . . . the State as an organized polity, capable of embodying, preserving and promoting the higher life of the nation.[64]

In forging this connection between familial morality and the strength of the nation state, Hopkins was drawing on a long-established tradition of moral philosophy, dating at least as far back as the late eighteenth century. But the idea that the ethical state had an obligation to protect the weak, to actively promote moral conduct and to encourage human evolution was specific to the late nineteenth century. Purity ideas here resembled philosophic conceptions of the ethical and organic state outlined by Thomas Green, and slightly later by theorists like John Hobson and Leonard Hobhouse.[65] For these new liberal thinkers, society was viewed as a biological organism, with state intervention designed to promote the healthy functioning of the body politic as an integrated totality.

However, in Hopkins' case the aim of reforming intervention remained the overt regulation of working-class behaviour, especially of working-class women. She stressed that middle-class ladies needed to unite with their poorer sisters if men's immorality was to be effectively challenged. 'Feminism' had to be a movement which cut across class barriers.[66] But the dialogue purists envisaged between women of different classes was still the traditional bond of philanthropy, which linked the middle-class donor to her working-class recipient through notions of moral and material charity. Hopkins appealed to working women in the name of 'the common dignity . . . of our womanhood', but moral responsibility was often seen to be precisely what these women lacked and what middle-class women could give. Contradictions such as these were glaringly apparent in her pleas to working women:

> be sure of this . . . no one class can fight this evil alone. We must all combine together. And if I speak a bit plain . . . just think of me as the woman who gave up everything to save you girls from their worst dangers. . . . Dear sisters there is not one of us ladies . . . who won't tell you that we have learnt our most precious lessons of faith . . . and patience, and self-sacrifice and contentedness under trials from you. But on the other hand, our large houses, our separate bedrooms, our greater education, make us . . . more particular in our ways than you – make us feel the importance of little things, little decent ways, little safeguards, and the little constant watchfulnesses in bringing up our children, which the terrible struggle for existence and the pressure of space but too often make you forget and grow careless about.[67]

Many of the women's purity associations were shot through with similar class divisions. Purists could be utterly ruthless about the menace working-class immorality posed to the middle-class home. Hopkins advised against sending reclaimed prostitutes into domestic service because of the danger to middle-class sons: 'better a thousand times that this fearful social evil should be localized in certain spots, which we call dens, than by our hasty and injudicious benevolence it should be struck into the very bosom of our families.'[68] Middle-class ladies needed to vet prospective female servants, they could so easily be morally defective. Purity workers believed they had an obligation to reclaim their 'fallen' sisters, but the problem of prostitution was always tackled by a mixture of benevolent charity and coercive threat.

These disciplinary aspects of Hopkins' work had already become apparent in the later stages of the repeal struggle. They were particularly visible in her campaign over the Industrial Schools Amendment Bill. In 1879 she visited repealers in Plymouth to canvass support for the new bill, which proposed that the courts should remove children living in the society of depraved and disorderly persons and place them in industrial schools. The measures became law the following year. They were explicitly aimed at the unrespectable poor, subjecting their children to the full disciplinary regime of the new training schools. The Vigilance Association for the Defence of Personal Rights, a radical anti-statist grouping whose members included some repealers, launched a counter-attack against the new act, complaining that: 'Miss Hopkins . . . is at present . . . crying for the wholesale kidnapping of little girls who may not have perfect domestic surroundings and their consignment to large prison schools.'[69] But Ellice went a stage further, she began to construct alliances with regulationists – especially with the local police chief, Inspector Aniss, bête noire of the repealers – who warmed to her clear message of rescue, backed by greater control of the streets. Declaring that the local rescue home was far too laxly run, she demanded a stricter system of surveillance. The repeal movement's national leadership, alarmed about Hopkins' activities, wrote warning her against any collusion with the enemy.[70]

At other moments Hopkins, along with many purity feminists, displayed a real awareness of the class contradictions embedded in the new movement. A *Special Report* from the Girls' Friendly Society in 1879 pointed out that middle-class women tended 'to over regulate those women whom we would serve', because they were ignorant of working-class life.[71] Hopkins understood that purity workers needed greater self-awareness of the class power they wielded. Sometimes this consciousness developed into a critique of middle-class morality and economic exploitation. The home happiness, refinement and sheltered grace of middle-class women, she insisted, was bought at the price of other women's toil and suffering. Girls from the upper classes were brought up to believe 'that they were born with a prescriptive right to their social advantages, their graceful culture'.[72]

Hopkins stands very much as representative of the new-style purity feminist. Her biography displays many of the class and gender contradictions which bedevilled women's participation in the purity campaigns of the 1880s. These ambiguities were not merely the result of unfortunate political alliances, but of the much longer history of middle-class women's involvement in the field of social regulation. Once again, it points to the power of particular historical languages in constructing individuals and in shaping their political demands. The moral discourses of purity feminism were neither a reactionary barrier to feminist progress nor were they the simple expression of militant feminist consciousness. They were the battleground on which conflicting aims and intentions struggled for space.

8 PURITY, FEMINISM AND THE RELUCTANT STATE

The tensions in the purity feminist position, and the government's own difficulties in coming to terms with the new movement, surfaced in the debates surrounding the 1885 Criminal Law Amendment Bill. The proposed legislation appeared to mark a stronger move towards direct state regulation of sexuality. But the struggles over the bill bring to the fore much more general questions about how we understand state intervention. They point to the dangers of seeing official action in a unified or monolithic way. The state's approach here fragmented into a number of competing positions: parliamentary and cabinet debate, ministerial and administrative directives, government inquiries and reports. Further, the decision to implement criminal law legislation did not originate with the state in the narrow sense at all, but with purity and feminist groups who were increasingly taking the lead in sexual politics.

The call for fresh legislation was stimulated by the perceived growth in child prostitution and the traffic in girls to the continent – the so-called 'white slave trade' of Stead's *Pall Mall Gazette* revelations. During 1879 and 1880 Alfred Dyer and George Gillet paid several visits to Brussels as representatives of the Society of Friends.[73] Their investigations exposed a well-established trade in English girls, who, Dyer maintained, were being held in tolerated houses in the city. Great publicity was given to their allegations in the British press, with demands for government action. Josephine Butler, together with Stead and Henry Wilson, set up the London Committee for Suppressing the Traffic in British Girls. Butler herself presented a memorial to the Foreign Secretary, signed by a thousand women and calling for changes in the law, so that 'it should be impossible for any young girl to be deprived of her liberty by fraud or force'.[74] The government found itself in a difficult diplomatic position, given the fierce denial of the allegations by the Belgian authorities. Rather than intervening directly, the Home Office appointed an independent commissioner, whose report vindicated Dyer's accusations. A series of prosecutions took place and a number of Belgian officials were dismissed or resigned.

In the face of mounting pressure the British government at last sensed it was incumbent on them to act. Instead of introducing immediate legislation, the Home Office responded with time-honoured delaying tactics. It set up a House of Lords Select Committee in 1881, to examine the extent of juvenile prostitution. The recommendations advocated widespread changes to the criminal law. They proposed raising the age of consent from thirteen to sixteen and extending the provisions of the Industrial Schools Amendment Act. Most controversially, they recommended stronger police powers to search and arrest brothel keepers and make soliciting on the streets illegal.[75] Political pressure for these latter proposals came from the police themselves, who now formed a strong lobby for increased state regulation. Superintendent Dunlap of the Metropolitan Police and Inspector Arnold of the Whitechapel Division argued a convincing case before the Lords' Committee on the advantages of greater state powers. More stringent legislation, they claimed, would lead to improved morality and decency on the streets and bring benefits to public order. They also stressed that prosecutions should be taken up by a state prosecutor, rather than left to the ineffective parish vestry committees.[76]

At the same time women's purity organisations made their move, petitioning the Home Office for a new bill. In February 1884 Sir William Harcourt, Liberal Home Secretary, received petitions from Bath Preventive Mission and Ladies' Association for the Care of Friendless Girls, calling for immediate legislation raising the age of consent to eighteen and giving the police greater powers.[77] In April the London Women's Christian Association appealed directly to Gladstone for better laws to protect children and young girls.[78]

The Home Office's response was cautious. It made public declarations supporting the work done by purity groups, insisting that child prostitution was one of the burning issues of the day. But in private the department held deep reservations about the benefits of fresh legislation and about its purity protagonists. In January 1883 Henry Thring, the Attorney-General, drew up a draft bill which incorporated the main recommendations of the Lords' Committee. The bill was introduced by Lord Rosebery, the Under-Secretary of State at the Home Office. But despite apparent government support a number of ministers objected and the proposals made little headway.

Ministers' main worry was the issue of greater police powers, and with it the question of increased state involvement in regulating sexuality. Lord Hartington, the War Secretary, initially welcomed the proposals as filling the gap created by the recent suspension of the contagious diseases legislation. He was sure that the clauses extending police action would have a beneficial effect on national morality.[79] But Hartington soon became alarmed at the plans to give increased powers to what he termed 'fanatical local authorities', and he wrote to Rosebery asking him to withdraw support for the measures. Like a number of other senior ministers he was ambiguous about the purity campaigners. The discourse of feminists and evangelicals cut against official Home Office ideology, with its deeply embedded male attitudes towards immorality and its implicit stance of toleration. Hartington confided that he did not really believe that prostitution could ever be eliminated. Fresh legislation would only drive it into some more objectionable form. Similarly, the Town Clerk of Hereford, in a letter to the Home Office, claimed that the bill actively discriminated against men by ignoring the innate immorality of many women and girls.[80]

Outside the state public opinion was becoming increasingly polarised over the contentious issue of greater government powers. Opposition from the Vigilance Association for the Defence of Personal Rights and from parliamentary Liberals and trade-union leaders focused on the growing threat to personal liberty. They saw the bill as part of the renewed offensive against the poor, following in the wake of the Contagious Diseases Acts.[81] The repealer James Stuart wrote to Samuel Smith, the purity MP, complaining that the bill had 'far too much of the police in it'.[82] Opponents alleged that police powers had dangerously expanded in recent years while police accountability had diminished. As ever, their remedy for immorality was not a centralised state system of surveillance but a coordinated network of voluntary efforts directed towards moral education and rescue work.

The purity movement was itself divided over the new proposals. There were those like Hopkins, who saw legislation as a growing sign of the improved moral climate in the country and its changing attitude towards women. Others, including Stead, attacked the bill for increasing the arbitrary power of the police on the streets. He believed that public outrage about the prostitution trade could be far more usefully channelled into forming local vigilante groups, as residents in the St Jude's Parish of King's Cross had done.[83] The sticking point for purists was over the balance to be struck between state power and voluntary efforts. Many of them supported the move to recruit the law into their plans for moral reform, but they did not wish to see their own efforts displaced by police powers. Anna Wilkes, who ran a rescue home in Poplar, outlined a form of regulation in which purity workers shared responsibility with the police and the courts, preserving the delicate balance between voluntary bodies and state institutions.[84] It was this solution which was incorporated into the working of the 1885 Act in its final form, when the new Conservative government dropped the contentious clauses extending police powers of search and arrest.

What became enshrined in the new legislation were more stringent penalties for brothel keepers and the raising of the age of consent to sixteen. Along with these measures went the catch-all clause, introduced at the last moment by the Liberal MP Henry Labouchère, outlawing all forms of male homosexual contact.[85] General responses were mixed. *The Times*, which had hitherto kept a dignified silence on such a distasteful subject, pronounced itself well pleased with the modified outcome. But successive editorials warned against 'trusting in showy mechanical remedies', to the exclusion of examining the deeper causes of juvenile misery and vice.[86] Jubilant reaction from the purity camp showed just how central legislation had now become to their programme. When the Salvation Army met on 18 August to hold a thanksgiving service for the passing of the act, William Booth emphasised that the connection between legislation and morality was the keynote of victory.[87] Mrs Booth closed the meeting by announcing that as soon as sufficient numbers of rescue homes had been opened, female 'soldiers' in the army would make a series of daring raids on London's streets to rescue as many fallen women as they could.

9 THE COMPROMISE SOLUTION

In the early years after 1885 purity groups received little or no help from the state in implementing the new act. It soon became disappointingly clear to the NVA that what had been conceived as a two-way process between voluntary bodies and the state, in practice placed the burden of day-to-day regulation on private initiatives. A number of factors influenced this highly cautious approach by central government, local councils, the police and the courts. Some arose from the difficulties of practical implementation, others had to do with the longer term history of state involvement in sexuality. In an immediate sense it was clear that local authorities were ill-equipped to begin the type of prosecutions purity groups were pressing for. In the months after the legislation was passed, the Home Office was inundated with letters from local police chiefs and magistrates, demanding clarification on the extent of the new police powers of prosecution. Police evidence to the Lords' Committee had already shown that parish vestry councils were generally incompetent, badly run and lacked the funds to embark on private prosecutions. The police themselves did not possess the necessary internal organisation to root out specific forms of vice, which often necessitated painstaking investigative work.

It was only late in the 1890s, under pressure from the NVA, that New Scotland Yard established a special department to deal with indecent books and pictures. Until then, police practice involved turning a blind eye to minor breaches of public decency, rather than embarking on lengthy prosecutions. Moreover, as Coote acknowledged, magistrates themselves were initially hostile to the aims and methods of purity groups. They were loath to convict, especially in cases which seemed to contradict common law.[88]

The difficulties in the working of the new act quickly came to a head. In December 1886 the Home Office received a memorial from the Clapham Vigilance Association, complaining that Clapham Common was 'infested' with prostitutes of the lowest type and that actual fornication was shamelessly committed on benches close to the public roadway.[89] Ratepayers who formed this local group grumbled that the police were conspicuous by their absence. Records show the local constabulary to have been remarkably tolerant towards prostitutes and apparently sensitive to the sexual practices of the poor. One suspects that police constables had more in common with local popular culture than with the evangelical vigilantes. The superintendent's report asserted that though prostitutes did ply their calling on the common, they conducted themselves in an orderly manner, as did large numbers of respectable, well-dressed courting couples who 'roamed about the place after dark caressing each other'.[90] As the metropolitan police complained three years later, the whole question of dealing with prostitutes was fraught with problems. While many citizens clamoured for the removal of public women from the streets, any attempt to introduce a continental system of tolerated areas would be rejected immediately because it implicated the state in the immoral recognition of vice.[91] Under these circumstances it was hardly surprising that the police adopted a laissez-faire policy.

But nervousness and vacillation over direct state intervention was more than just a problem of administration. The doubts expressed by ministers and Home Office officials in the 1880s were symptomatic of much deeper structural problems. Central here was the political and ideological legacy of the Contagious Diseases Acts.

Successive Liberal and Conservative governments had lost the battle for the state medical regulation of women largely as a result of sustained feminist opposition. Politicians did not relish a repeat performance of the humiliating defeat they had suffered over the suspension and repeal of the acts. Added to this was the deep suspicion felt by senior ministers, influential judges and lawyers about purists themselves. As an aristocrat, Hartington was not untypical in regarding them as evangelical fanatics who needed restraining. For Sir William Harcourt the issue was even more clear-cut. All the great middle-class moral reforms of the age had been achieved at the expense of pleasure and enjoyment. The English were in danger of becoming a nation dominated by dullness and decorous solemnity.[92] Many senior politicians regarded the purity movement as beyond the pale, an unwelcome intrusion of issues and personnel which had no rightful place in the discourse of parliamentary politics. A number of the purity leaders, like Coote and Alfred Dyer, came from respectable working-class or petty-bourgeois backgrounds. Their strident moralism jarred with both the measured middle-class radicalism of the repealers and the dominant patrician language of high politics. The suspicions of establishment politicians were fuelled by the renewed nonconformist assault on the Liberal Party in the 1880s. Purity MPs like Smith and Wilson mounted a direct challenge to the political and cultural assumptions of men like Hartington and Harcourt. Wilson himself noted enthusiastically that 'the backbone of the Party is more and more teetotal in its sympathies'.[93] When the prominent Liberal Sir Charles Dilke and the Irish nationalist Charles Parnell became involved in divorce scandals, it was Stead and the Methodist leader, Hugh Price-Jones, who were instrumental in destroying them politically.

It was also clear that feminist involvement had much to do with the opposition purity provoked – especially from men within the state apparatuses. Administrators and politicians had been keen to circumscribe the power of scientific experts like Simon. But they were alarmed to discover that sanitarians had been displaced by a new force in sexual politics: the militant voice of articulate, middle-class women who pointed to men as the root cause of immorality. For many men within the power bloc this was a direct challenge to their own masculinist culture, rupturing the ideology of separate spheres and the double-standard. As the women's movement became increasingly central to purity campaigns before the First World War, Home Office officials developed a range of tactics to stifle feminist pressure, from diplomatic stonewalling to outright misogyny.

At a different level a key factor affecting the uneasy dialogue between purists and the state was the partial transformation of political discourse itself. We have already noted how the crystallisation of parliamentary language worked to exclude the issue of sexuality during the repeal struggles. The late nineteenth century witnessed a heightening of this process. Focus on the two-party system, the growing strength of the organised working class and the gradual decline of the big single issue movements which had been such a central feature of the mid-Victorian political scene were visible signs of this transformation. The political itself was redefined. Successive governments from the 1880s hesitated to introduce fresh legislation on immorality partly because the area was seen to lie outside formal politics. Home Secretaries like Reginald McKenna and Herbert Gladstone consistently refused to pledge their government to support a new criminal law amendment bill in Parliament. As Coote himself protested, both men were privately committed to legislation but believed they could not involve the government on the issue.[94]

The highly cautious approach to purity demands undercuts any simple notion of more active state intervention over sexuality in the late nineteenth and early twentieth century. In the fields of economic management, labour relations, political ideologies and educational and welfare programmes the state began to exercise a new and constitutive function in this period. It redefined the nature of social and political problems and their solutions. It altered the relation between dominant and dominated groups by creating new apparatuses with different modes of administrative rationality, and drew in key intellectuals and professional experts. The state was not the originator of all of these transformations but it was implicated in them in quite new ways. Compared with these other fields of intervention, the state itself rarely took the lead in the area of sexuality. There was no expansion of government departments here, no recruitment of intellectuals into the state apparatuses, no equivalent of Hubert Llewellyn Smith at the Board of Trade or Sidney and Beatrice Webb on social policy. The criminal law emerged as more and more significant for sexual regulation before 1914, but the impetus did not come from the state. Government was a relatively junior and often passive partner in the dialogue with purists and feminists. Purity groups remained absolutely central to the enactment of legislation. There was no shift away from these private voluntary initiatives.

Between 1890 and 1910 the dominant strategy of regulation involved a pragmatic compromise between the state and private organisations. In the early years the executive committee of the NVA, angry at the tentative approach of the Home Office, the police and the courts, decided to initiate prosecutions themselves. In a test case of 1887, the Home Office ruled that vigilance associations could not recover their costs for prosecutions from government funds.[95] Out of the NVA's annual income of two thousand pounds, half was spent on legal work. Prosecutions concentrated on indecent advertising, the music halls, prostitution and pornography.

Occasionally the NVA's enthusiasm brought members into direct conflict with state agencies, as, for example, in its campaign against the Rabelais Picture Gallery in the early 1890s. An exhibition of paintings by the French artist Jules Garnier, illustrating the work of Rabelais, was launched amid a blaze of hot publicity. The association complained of obscenity and Coote brought his case to the House of Commons in an effort to persuade Sir Richard Webster, the Attorney-General, to take up the prosecution. Webster's reply demonstrated the government's extreme caution: 'It is utterly impossible. . . . We cannot help you. I am in hearty agreement with you, and privately I am quite prepared to subscribe towards it. But officially the Government cannot be identified with it.'[96] The NVA faced similar problems in its efforts to press successive governments to introduce fresh legislation. As early as 1886 its legal sub-committee had drawn up a whole series of amendments to the criminal law which it wanted to see on the statute book. These included raising the age of consent to eighteen, abolishing the notorious 'escape clause' (allowing male defendants in assault cases to claim they believed the girl to be over sixteen), extending the time limit for prosecutions and criminalising incest and male importuning. It took until 1922 before all these measures had been passed, under continuing pressure from feminist and purity groups.

In the 1890s purists began to make headway at a local level by persuading the police and the courts to support their programme. A number of local police chiefs became members of the NVA, like the Chief Constable of Birmingham and the notorious Inspector Burroughs in Manchester.[97] A two-way system of regulation began to be established, whereby purity groups either presented information to the police or the police referred cases to purists themselves. Cooperation of this kind was most effective in cities with strong nonconformist councils. In Manchester, Sheffield, Leeds, Liverpool and Cardiff the police and the NVA worked in close contact, closing brothels, prosecuting for obscenity and investigating cases of abduction. In Liverpool purity became a hot political issue, when purists succeeded in overturning the lax Tory council sympathetic to publicans and brewers.

Incest was another area which pointed up the growing convergence of opinion between purists, women's groups, the police and the Home Office. The offence was still not covered by any effective punishment under law. By the early 1890s the NVA had begun to pass on evidence of cases to the Home Office, complaining of the difficulties of prosecuting under existing legislation. In 1894 the Ladies' National Association, veterans of the repeal movement, mounted a campaign to amend the 1885 Act to criminalise incest. Though no progress was made when Henry Wilson introduced a bill in 1896, there was growing police backing for legislation. A letter from the NVA to chief constables in 1899 revealed that almost all police chiefs were in favour of a law prohibiting incest.[98] Opposition came mainly from lawyers and magistrates, protesting that prosecutions would increase the number of offences on account of the publicity. Pressure for reform was also mounting from women's organisations. The National Union of Women Workers, NUWW (a philanthropic offshoot of Hopkins' Ladies' Association for the Care of Friendless Girls and formed in 1895), launched a fresh assault on the conspiracy of silence over incest at their annual conference in 1906.[99] When the Incest Act was finally carried in 1908, purity feminists claimed it as a personal triumph.

But it was prostitution which continued to be the major preoccupation for purity workers at a local level. In 1901 many of the newly organised London borough councils appointed their own officials to monitor the trade and liaise with purists.[100] The increased closure of brothels as a result of this drive forced poorer women to solicit in the open, where they were subjected to police harassment. In 1905 the number of women charged with public indecency rose dramatically.[101] This problem was examined in the 1908 Royal Commission on the Metropolitan Police. Allegations by prostitutes of police bribery and unjust and arbitrary exercise of the powers of arrest were discounted in favour of evidence from purity workers. Coote, along with other campaigners, backed the new aggressive police action, testifying to the special relationship which now existed between purists and the police. The Rev Frederick Meyer, minister of Christ Church Westminister, felt that he had been encouraged by the fact that 'Christian men' were backing their efforts.[102] Coote, to his credit, did object to the double-standard enshrined in police practice, and recommended that the existing law should also be used to prosecute male clients.[103] The Royal Commission's report countered this by reasserting the fundamental difference between occasional soliciting by a man ('addressed to a woman who does not resent it') and the prostitute's immoral business, which was offensive to public decency. Besides, it was argued, prosecutions against male clients would not be acceptable to the community at large.[104] Despite this setback, Coote pronounced himself well pleased with the state of the streets in the metropolis. London was now 'an open-air cathedral', whereas forty years earlier 'it was vicious in every particular'.[105] Coote bothered little about the effects of his work on the prostitutes themselves. He was much more intent on maintaining public order. What was needed was more of the same – intensified police action backed by the ever-watchful vigilance of the purity movement.

10 SUFFRAGE AND SEXUALITY: 1908–1914

Sexuality was a major political issue in the suffrage movement. During the years before the First World War the history of sexual politics became intimately bound up with the progress of feminism. Alongside the battle for the vote, women launched a major campaign to transform male sexual behaviour and to protect themselves and their children. Legislation was

106

seen as the key to securing reforms that were in women's interests. It was the language of purity which mobilised many women to develop a trenchant critique of male sexuality. Purity became hegemonic in the early women's movement, though it did not go entirely unchallenged. Other feminists, often from libertarian or utopian socialist backgrounds, rejected purity and worked to forge a new discourse, stressing women's right to active sexual pleasure. The first decade of the twentieth century witnessed the polarisation of these positions under the impact of growing political activism.

The purity language of outrage, like the militant tactics of suffragette politics with which it was linked, continued to provide women with a powerful weapon to challenge men. Feminists perceived that in a world where men and masculinist attitudes had monopolised notions of physical sexual pleasure, the emphasis on chastity and the importance of human love provided a positive alternative. Coupled with this language went a growing stress on the state to enact feminist demands, in the moral as well as the political arena. Many women saw a clear convergence of interests between their own struggle for the vote and purity pressure for legislation.

There was in fact no clear-cut division beween purity associations, suffrage groups and women's oganisations – membership often overlapped. Millicent Fawcett, a moderate suffragist and President of the National Union of Women's Suffrage Societies (NUWSS), was also prominent in the NVA as head of its preventive and rescue sub-committee. Many women in the NUWW also belonged to purity groups. In the period immediately before 1914, the growing political militancy of the Women's Social and Political Union (WSPU), along with the publication of feminist books and pamphlets on sexuality, radicalised the older, more traditional women's organisations. Groups like the British Women's Temperance Association and the NUWW began to define their long-standing crusade for purity and the reform of male sexuality as part of the contemporary feminist struggle. Though the NUWW continued to foreground traditional philanthropy, its annual conferences displayed a growing concern with the problems of male sexual behaviour, informed by current feminist demands.[106] The LNA also became repoliticised under the impact of suffrage politics. Conference delegates at the 1903 Congress of the International Abolitionist Federation insisted that prostitution needed to be opposed because it isolated women as an outcast class. It sanctioned the sexualisation of women by men, making them 'a thing, an instrument devoted to appeasing the sexual passion of the man'.[107] Here was a new wave of feminist militancy, proclaiming that women had the right to a life of their own and should not be the sexual property of men. The memory of Josephine Butler's early struggles acted as a powerful motivating force in this new wave of feminist sexual politics. Following her death in 1906, the *Shield* produced extracts from Butler's speeches and writings, and in 1912 the NUWSS republished a de luxe edition of her *Personal Reminiscences of a Great Crusade*. The *Suffragette* proclaimed: 'the work of this dedicated woman has sown the seeds of a mighty harvest which others are about to reap.'[108]

11 MOBILISING A LANGUAGE

Feminists combined practical demands for criminal law legislation with an effective propaganda campaign. In books, pamphlets and speeches women drew on and reworked the languages of purity, religion, medicine and even mysticism to develop a critical feminist discourse. Representations of female sexuality here were not merely negative, they now offered women positive images of their own autonomy through a stress on celibacy, evolutionary superiority and the power of human love. The vocabulary of social purity was employed to demonstrate that male immorality was the problem to be addressed, not the norm against which women should be defined. Religious and biological concepts of moral and natural law were used to argue that chastity and self-control were essential to personal health and to the future progress of the nation. Feminists were effectively articulating what had been implicit in much of moral purity – an opposition to the idea that the male sexual urge was uncontrollable, and that frequent intercourse was necessary for men's health.

Many feminists insisted that celibacy was a positive step in women's self-advancement. Evidence exists from the period before the First World War to show that some women were choosing not to have sexual relations with men as a political act.[109] Anti-feminist articles in the press noted with alarm the growing trend towards celibacy in women, attributing 'spinsterhood' to degeneracy or an aversion to motherhood.[110] But as Lucy Re-Bartlett asserted, chastity was part of women's revolt against false social conditions.[111] Cicely Hamilton's *Marriage as a Trade*, 1909, was a superb polemic in favour of celibacy, which reasoned that marriage represented a narrowing of women's hopes and ambitions. Through the sex act, men secured women's continuing subordination, by cutting off every avenue of escape from the gratification of their desire, and by denying female sexuality any outlet other than compulsory heterosexuality. Men hated and despised spinsters, Hamilton claimed, because the 'perpetual virgin' proved that the sex act was not 'an absolute necessity for women'.[112]

In polemicising for celibacy and spinsterhood feminists were challenging the growing sexualisation of all women in medicine, psychology and in the work of male sexual radicals like Havelock Ellis and Edward Carpenter.[113] Both Christabel Pankhurst and Hamilton argued that these contemporary theories were deeply linked to male attitudes, which saw women as 'primarily created for the sexual gratification of men'.[114] In the future evolution of society under women's guidance sex would be raised to a higher plane, where physical passion would be transmuted by the power of human love. Quasi-religious languages derived from theosophy or mysticism were used to formulate a new spiritualised conception of sex relations, freed from male control.

Frances Swiney, who began writing in the 1880s, published a large number of books and pamphlets on female sexuality. As president of the Cheltenham branch of the NUWW, she was a prominent lecturer and speaker in the suffrage movement, where her ideas on sexuality were influential. Her own career was remarkable. She was brought up in the colonial culture of India and married to a senior military figure. In her fifties she began developing an elaborate theory – part religious, part mystical – on the natural supremacy of women and on the need to return to a matriarchal society. Her cosmic vision prophesied that as the race evolved intercourse would only be practised for the purpose of reproduction, and then only at carefully spaced intervals under women's direction.[115] Swiney orchestrated a mass of medical, anthropological and religious material to back her arguments. The bible was reinterpreted, even Christ, she argued, had spoken of the eventual disappearance of the male species. For as women delivered the male sex from the sex obsession, men would become more and more like women. This was what Christ really meant when he spoke about the unity of the male with the female in one flesh.[116] These ideas were circulated in Swiney's theosophical society, The League of Isis, which listed rules on chastity and continence, aimed at promoting women's higher self.

Many women were interpellated by this religious and mystical imagery, because potentially it projected a spiritualised fusion of sex and love. Traditions of feminine religious experience, expressing a mystical, quasi-sexual communion with God, had always been a current within Catholicism and in many Protestant sects, and some women drew on its potential. But religion was now twinned with other languages to define pleasure more positively. Evolutionary theory, theosophy, even platonic idealism, all played their part. Bartlett talked extensively of the great evolutionary movement to spirituality through passion: 'Spirituality is, of course, the great counteracting force and ultimate conqueror. But spirituality has to be aroused, and passion is often the medium – the conducting channel.'[117]

12 PETITIONING THE STATE

As the suffrage struggle intensified many feminists began to insist that their campaign for citizenship and demands for legislation to curb men's immorality were interlinked. The vote was perceived as bringing political and *moral* benefits to women. Christabel Pankhurst argued that 'when women are citizens they will have the power to secure the enactment of laws for their protection'.[118] Militant feminists pointed out that sexual antagonism lay at the heart of the suffrage struggle and could never be resolved within the discourse of political liberalism. Bartlett, herself closely associated with the WSPU, claimed that sexuality was the underlying issue in the feminist movement:

> The public roughly seems divided between people who deny the struggle any sexual significance at all, and those who, seeing this significance, attribute it to sexual morbidity and hysteria. The situation with which we are face to face represents indeed a sex war. . . . It is a war which signifies vitality, not decadence.[119]

Purity feminists viewed the state as the tool to circumscribe male power in the moral as well as in the political sphere. Hamilton asserted that in ordinary life it was the strong arm of the law, and not the strong arm of the husband, which protected women from hurt or molestation.[120] The state-orientated approach adopted by many feminists clearly related to their affiliations with social purity. Yet it also had much to do with the overwhelmingly middle-class and aristocratic composition of the suffrage campaigns. Many came to the women's movement from backgrounds where the state was viewed as an instrument for enacting their own class-specific demands. In as much as feminism represented a split within the dominant classes, creating multiple fractures within liberalism, there were many women who carried with them their class perceptions of the ethical and beneficent state.

But feminists rapidly became aware that the state itself was patriarchal and needed profound transformation if they were to be fully represented in the nation's political and moral life. Christabel Pankhurst reasoned that the state was composed of men who not only denied women the vote but who also tacitly condoned male immorality and sexual violence. Men had all the power in the state and therefore made both its laws and its morality.[121] As women escalated their campaign of militant action in 1912 and 1913 they were acutely conscious that male attitudes – deeply embedded in the legal profession, the police and the courts – sustained not just men's political power but also women's sexual oppression. Suffrage papers began to carry reports of cases of sexual harassment and male sexual violence, in an effort to raise consciousness and sustain pressure for law reform. The *Vote* reported one incident of child assault in Surrey, where a man was sentenced to only four months' hard labour. Feminists organised a local protest over the issue at election time, returning a woman to the local council on the specific platform of curbing male immorality.[122] The *Common Cause*, reporting a case of the wrongful arrest of a woman for alleged prostitution, commented that the suspect was 'taken to a man's court, tried and sentenced by men under men's laws for a fault she cannot commit alone'.[123] One suffragette, Rosa Lamartine Yates, recounted that she had witnessed the double-standard in action while standing bail for two women at the west London police court. The preceding case had involved prostitution:

> After, two women filed into the dock, and with a whisper of mock modesty an official suggested that I should leave the court as the case concerned prostitution. 'Are you a respectable woman?' quickly interpolated the magistrate when I said I wished to remain.[124]

As Yates argued, the women's movement was dedicated to abolishing the distinction between respectable and fallen women which was reproduced by the state, upheld in official attitudes and predicated on 'fallen men'.

The NUWW and the LNA had long been campaigning for legislation to raise the age of consent to eighteen and to enforce more stringent penalties against procurers and brothel keepers. The government's attitude, and its relation to feminists and purists, displayed all the hesitations and ambiguities which had characterised similar debates in the 1880s. Male sexual attitudes were deeply entrenched among senior politicians and civil servants, revealing themselves in suspicion of feminist demands and often in outbursts of anti-feminism and misogyny. Behind the doors of the Home Office, feminist pressure for moral reform, combined with the escalation of the suffrage campaign, was confronting the gentlemanly conventions of state administration. Home Office records for the period show how politicians and administrators negotiated feminist pressure by a mixture of amused contempt and double-dealing. While pledging themselves publicly to legislation, they worked privately to block many of the attempts to secure the new acts and statutes.

A new criminal law amendment bill had been drawn up in 1909. This was a result of pressure brought to bear on the Home Secretary by the Jewish Association for the Protection of Girls and Women and the NVA, concerned about fresh revelations in the press over the white slave traffic. When an influential purity deputation petitioned the Home Office, Herbert Samuel, then Under-Secretary of State, expressed himself personally committed to legislation in the interests of national honour, but he refused to pledge the government to introduce proposals in Parliament, or even to support them publicly. Here were familiar ambiguities over state support for purity demands first experienced by Coote twenty years before.

The government kept aloof, if not quite deliberately obstructive. It was true, as successive home secretaries explained to pressure groups, that the government was committed to a mountain of fresh legislation in the new Parliament. What was looming was the protracted constitutional wrangle over Lloyd George's budget and the House of Lords. However, the usual suspicions over purity aims and intentions were now intensified by the militant stance of suffrage feminists, especially the WSPU. Civil servants were keen to discern how widespread public support was for the new measures, though they were aware, as they euphemistically put it, that there would be 'cause for complaint' with the government if the bill were blocked.[125] And official hesitation as to whether legislation on immorality was a proper area for state intervention continued. In response to parliamentary questions, demanding that the government introduce their own bill rather than relying on private members' initiatives, the Home Office made its familiar position clear: 'We strongly support the proposed Bill . . . but do not see how it is possible for the Government to undertake legislation.'[126]

Meanwhile, purity groups and feminist organisations stepped up their pressure with a nationwide campaign. In April 1911 the NUWW convened an emergency meeting in the face of continuing delays: 'expressing the desire that the government will give immediate facilities for the passing of the Criminal Law Amendment Bill.'[127] The LNA acted as the focus for protests, organising a mass rally in June 1912 at Caxton Hall, with deputations from leading feminist and purity groups. A special Pass the Bill Committee was formed and the Home Office was inundated with letters and petitions from suffrage societies. The LNA forwarded to Asquith nearly three hundred resolutions in favour of the bill, with over seventy coming from feminist organisations.[128] Reginald McKenna, the new Home Secretary, again pledged his personal support but insisted that he could not guarantee the bill government time. By this stage even Asquith was worried about government inactivity. He wrote to McKenna, concerned about the continued obstruction and urging that the Home Office should speed up the bill's progress. In the face of mounting political and industrial unrest, Asquith may have been anxious to head off further confrontation with feminists.

The bill became law in December 1912 as the Criminal Law Amendment Act. But in its final committee stages the clauses giving the police greater powers to search and arrest brothel keepers were revised, rendering them almost useless. Though the original clauses were eventually restored, feminists and women's organisations were deeply split on the issue of increased police powers. Just as thirty years before, here again were feminist divisions over using the repressive state to enforce women's demands. There were those in the LNA, the NUWW and the NVA who argued that a more coercive police approach was essential to protect innocent women and children. In a telling exchange at the NUWW annual conference in 1912, one delegate asked if the new police measures would infringe the liberty of prostitutes on the streets. Lady Laura Riding, speaking in support of the proposals, declared that if prostitutes were at times 'liable to be harried', that was the consequence of their own actions. Purity feminist support for these clauses of the bill accepted the traditional polarities of pure and impure women. Lady Laura was insistent: 'though we may feel deep pity for them, their trade is not one of blessing to the nation, to our fathers, sons, husbands; you have to think of that. It is not a trade that should be specially protected.'[129]

The NUWSS on the other hand warned that though the bill deserved general support, the clauses extending police powers needed careful monitoring, 'lest they should lead to further harrying of the unfortunate women'.[130] The *Common Cause* argued that coercive legislation was no substitute for tackling the more fundamental problems of poverty and men's immorality, which stimulated the prostitution trade. These feminist differences surfaced in a more extreme form in the months after the passing of the act. The LNA saw the new measures as only a beginning. The *Shield* insisted that there was enough conviction and enthusiasm among women to carry further legislation, despite the blatant obstructionism from men at the Home Office and in Parliament.[131] The Pankhurst-led WSPU made the twin issues of male immorality and white slavery central to their whole campaign in 1913, as part of a new militant offensive. When Emmeline Pankhurst was tried at the Old Bailey in April she drew attention to the white slavery issue in her speech from the dock. Women, she claimed, believed that the horrible evils now ravaging British civilisation would never be removed until women got the vote.[132]

Not all feminists were so enamoured with such tactics. Teresa Billington-Greig of the Women's Freedom League condemned the strategy of coercion and the sexual ideology implicit in the new act. In an article in the *English Review* in 1913 she argued that the legislation had been carried by hysterical stories circulated by 'neuropaths and prudes' about the entrapment of white women.[133] The government had yielded to sensationalist claims by the three chief agents of irrational emotion – Parliament, the pulpit and the press. Greig's was a rationalist and intellectual critique. She reasoned that the law and the police had long been shown to have little or no educative or preventive power, and that the only way forward was a changed moral outlook and a gradual reorganisation of economic and political conditions. And she went even further. Pointing her finger at the misplaced moral fervour of the WSPU and the LNA, she claimed that these 'dabblers in debauchery' had set middle-class women on the rampage against an evil they knew nothing about. They were 'feeding and flattering' misconceptions which pitted the moral perfection of women against 'the bestiality of men'.[134] Nothing had been done for the women who were exploited by prostitution. All that had been achieved was a more punitive regime, while the cause of sex reform had been set back by the whitewashing of women and the doctrine of the uncleanness of men. Greig's attack was reinforced by Sylvia Pankhurst's *Women's Dreadnought*, paper of the East End Suffrage Federation. Reports pointed out that though the act had been passed for women's protection, it seemed that it was being used almost exclusively to punish poor women.[135]

Other critics developed similar lines of argument. The *Freewoman* (an individualist feminist weekly pledged to a 'new morality' of free sexual unions) strongly criticised the purity lobby and the coercive consequences of women could discover within active heterosexuality. Sex passion was conceived in almost messianic terms, as a form of psychic union with the consciousness of another.[146] New moralists' emphasis on the absolute centrality of heterosexual experience made it impossible for them to see that purity feminism had anything to offer, with the latter's emphasis on celibacy, and its view of sex as male-defined, vicious and depraved. In reality, these increasingly polarised discourses offered women a 'choice' only between celibacy and heterosexual dependence on men. While purity was silent on questions of pleasure and desire, libertarianism sat uneasily with feminist demands and priorities. The problem was quite literally the lack of alternative languages developed by women themselves.

In the inter-war period the growing sexualisation of women and the concerted attack on celibacy in sexology and marriage manuals effectively challenged the credibility of purity feminism. But if purists lost out, so too did those who envisaged greater freedom and equality in sexual relations with men. The optimism and confidence invested in heterosexuality proved to be greatly misplaced.

14 CONCLUSION

The campaigns of the purity movement marked a distinctive moment in the history of medico-moral politics. The growing centrality of the criminal law in the years between 1885 and 1912 represented a sharp break with the earlier sanitary principle governing sexuality. State medicine's defeat over the Contagious Diseases Acts effectively heralded the displacement of the medical profession by a new force in sexual politics, with a different conception of the state's responsibilities in the moral sphere. There was no continuous, uninterrupted growth of scientific expertise or medical control over sex throughout the nineteenth century. What we have encountered is a much more unstable hegemony, which was successfully challenged by competing groups.

This history of the purity movement forces us to reassess accounts of modern sexuality, such as Foucault's, which stress the subordination of legal controls to the growth of more dispersed techniques of discursive power. In legislative terms the reverse occurred in this period. The law dominated the field, but it did not operate through the simple mechanisms of censorship and repression. The law was itself productive: seeking out and redefining forms of dangerous or deviant sexuality, organising the cultural experience of dominated groups and stimulating their political demands. There was no neat distinction between juridical and discursive forms of power.[147]

This transformation in sexual regulation was not the product of some internal dynamic in the technologies of power. The move to a more strongly state-oriented approach was not the result of initiatives taken within government at all. It was the outcome of protracted political struggles taking place outside the state in the narrow sense on the terrain of civil society. Purity campaigns registered not only a shift in modalities of control, but a change in the personnel responsible for sexual regulation and in the sites from which power was exercised. As a significant movement of popular protest over sex, purity marked a successful assault on the authority of male professionals, thereby drawing into the political arena groups hitherto denied access or without a voice.

At the same time the stance of the purity movement was deeply contradictory. For it provided a continuing source of private regulation – and the political will for further coercive measures – in an area where government remained cautious about direct involvement. Feminist purity campaigns were built on this contradiction. Purity provided women with a language which challenged men's sexual power and projected images of their own autonomy. Feminist campaigns around the state effectively unmasked the unofficial masculine culture of politicians, experts and administrators. They exposed the deeply misogynist attitudes which formed the hidden element in policy making. But these positive achievements were enmeshed with the longer history of middle-class women's involvement in social regulation and class disciplining. To reiterate, the purity movement was neither a conservative barrier to women's sexual freedom, nor was it the passive vehicle for an emergent feminist consciousness. It was the battleground on which conflicting aims and intentions struggled for space.

Part Four

FROM PURITY TO SOCIAL HYGIENE
Early twentieth-century campaigns for sex education

1 THE DRONFIELD CASE: THE TEACHER AND THE GIRLS SHE TOLD

In the autumn of 1913 scripture lessons for the pupils of Dronfield Elementary School, Derbyshire, took a radical turn.[1] The girls from standard six were reading the bible with their class teacher and headmistress, Miss Outram. One of the set texts for Advent dealt with the birth of John the Baptist. The verses prompted questions from the children about pregnancy and childbirth. At first Miss Outram told them to ask their mothers, but feeling she might lose the girls' confidence if she blocked their curiosity she took a more direct approach. Telling them to close their bibles, she read them two stories, one about the beginnings of life, the other a warning on the dangers of immorality. Part of the accounts went as follows:

The first story

Shall I tell you a story of how God made things in the beginning, a true story? Well, once upon a time there was no world at all. Doesn't it seem strange to think about it? And everything was dark. But away back in the beginning God was there just the same. And God said, 'Let there be light,' and there was light.

Then God made the wonderful world that we live in. . . . Now, how do you suppose God planned always to have plants on the earth? God said, 'Let them have seed, each after its kind.' He knew that by-and-by, when they were ripe, they would drop down into the ground; there they would keep soft and warm for a while, then they would grow into more plants, with seeds, so there would always be plants on the earth. . . . Then God wanted to have fish in the waters, so He made a mother fish to lay eggs in the water and a father fish to swim about over the eggs and take care of them. . . . 'And God saw that it was good.' . . . Now how do you suppose God planned always to have animals on the earth? Every living thing was to come from a seed or an egg. We saw how it was with the plants and the seeds, and the birds and their eggs but the animals God made could not make nests and lay eggs, because they were so much larger. Such large nests and so many of them would be in the way on the earth. The eggs would get broken if the mother animal tried to keep them warm, as the mother bird does, because she is so heavy. So God did not make the mother animal to lay her eggs. Instead, the eggs stayed safe inside the mother animal's body until they grew

121

into little animals right there. Then, when they were large enough, God brought them out and the mother took care of them until they grew big enough to take care of themselves. 'And God saw that it was good.'

Perhaps some of us knew before of God's plan for the animals. I know of a lovely teacher who told her boys and girls in school about God's plan for the animals and they had a mother bunny in her cage right in the schoolroom. The children knew that the little bunnies were coming and they were so careful of the mother when they fed her with lettuce and cabbage. One morning when they went to school the little bunnies were there in the cage and they were all very happy.

But I must tell you of God's plan for the people. 'In the beginning' there were no people on earth and God said, 'Let us make man in our image,' that is, like ourselves. So he made a man, tall and strong like father, to take care of the plants and animals. And when God saw that the man was lonely He made a beautiful woman like mother to be his wife and to help him. 'And God saw that it was good.' The people were the best of all that God had made, so God planned always to have people on the earth.

Shall I tell you about the very first little baby? Just think, there had never been a little baby on the earth. God knew it would be the most precious of all. He wanted it kept very safe from all harm. So He made a tiny egg, so small that it could not even be seen, and a little room, on purpose for it to grow in, right inside the mother's body. It stayed there and grew for a long time, until it was a real baby. Then when it had grown enough God brought the baby out and the mother took him in her arms. There he was, the very first baby boy. Nobody had ever seen a baby before, and when the mother saw his little body and his little feet and hands, and his little cunning face, she thought 'why he just looks like a little man.' She was very thankful and happy and she said 'I have gotten a man from the Lord.' This is part of God's wonderful plan always to have people on the earth. Once each of you was a tiny egg inside of mother's body. And when father came and took mother for his wife, to live with her and to take care of her, the little egg began to grow and grow into a real little baby. Mother knew you were there and she loved you. She carried you there near her heart a long, long time while you were growing. The food she ate made you grow too, so she was very careful to eat only good food and to take nothing that might harm her little baby. You were really a part of her. The fresh air she breathed made pure blood for you, and often during the day she wondered what you would be like, whether your eyes would be blue or brown, and prayed God to make you a good child. Then when you had grown enough and mother had carried you there nearly a year, God opened a door for you and brought you out into this world.

The second story

'Where is Jack?' asked Mr Rogers, as he came in at six o'clock. 'He was late last night for dinner and he's going to be late again to-night.' 'I saw him with that Jones girl,' answered his sister Dorothy. 'She is a new girl in town, very pretty, but terribly bold. I'm sure she's not nice. I do wish Jack wouldn't go with her.'

Presently the door opened and Jack came in. 'Jack,' said his father, 'I want to show you something.' Relief and interest showed instantly in the boy's face. The dread question was not to be asked after all.

Mr Rogers led the way to his workroom in the attic. There were his carpenter's bench and his tools and his lathe, and in the corner was the dynamo that worked it. Jack had seen them all many times.

'What is it, father?' he asked. Mr Rogers laid his hand upon the dynamo. 'Jack, by means of this, a mysterious power becomes mine. We call it electricity, but no one knows what it is. We only know that if *we treat it in the right way* it will enable us to do wonderful things. It will work our mills, and light our houses and streets, and run our cars. It will enable man to do more than any other power that has been discovered. But at the same time, if you treat it in the wrong way, it will strike you dead.'

'Yes, father, I know that,' said Jack. His father turned toward him with an earnestness that Jack had never before seen in his face. 'There is another power, very like this in its results. There is the mysterious feeling that men have for women and women have for men. Treat that right, and it will bless your life and ennoble it, and make you ten times, yes, a hundred times, the man you could ever be without it. . . . But, treat that feeling wrong, and it will curse you, and blast your life, and *kill your immortal soul*.'

For a moment they looked at each other square in the eye. Then together they went downstairs in silence. In the hall below, Jack put his hand on his father's arm. 'I know what you mean, father, and I'll follow the right,' he whispered.[2]

Miss Outram claimed to have obtained her stories from an American publisher, yet they were typical of early twentieth-century British sex educa-tion teaching. Emotive and negative purity style moral warnings pointed to the twin dangers of promiscuous women and the threat of venereal disease. These were combined with more positive guidance, where the language of evolutionary biology was used to represent sex as responsible parenthood. The natural world, presided over by the image of the benevolent patriarch, was moralised to carry the significations of goodness, health and social harmony, integrated through sound procreation. On the other hand, modern science was used to list a new vocabulary of transgression. This was distanced from the earlier stress on Old Testament religious morality by its rationalism, as in the story's metaphor of electricity, wondrous yet calculable, which demonstrated the inexorable consequences of wrongdoing – disease, death and social degeneracy. The juxtaposition of these polarised accounts of sexuality in the headmistress's teaching was intentional. The girls of standard six, like so many of their contemporaries, were offered the 'choice' between radiant motherhood and unlawful promiscuity.

Outram was not naive in introducing sex education into her teaching. She may also have anticipated trouble with her school managers. Earlier in the year she had discussed circumcision, infertility and basic ante-natal care with her twelve-year-old girls, as part of classes on domestic economy and home management. She was a committed eugenist (involved in a local campaign to get 'race hygiene' on to the syllabus of elementary schools) and an equally strong feminist, having read the children extracts from the *Suffragette*. These two discourses of eugenics and feminism, seemingly distinct yet so often linked in the political language of many early twentieth-century feminists, had clearly influenced Outram's educational thinking. According to the extracted deposition of one pupil, Doris Harrison, Miss Outram had told the older girls about the forced feeding of suffragettes in prison. How: 'One woman went to prison and she would not eat anything so, to open her mouth, they broke her teeth and put something down her throat.'[3] There had already been one heated exchange between herself and the school managers, when Outram had pointedly refused to apologise for introducing controversial subjects. The managers, all men, had been incensed. They were clearly on the lookout for a second opening to pillory their headmistress.

Inevitably, news of Miss Outram's exploits travelled fast in Dronfield. This tightly knit community, lying six miles south of Sheffield on the Derbyshire coalfield, had a population of less than four thousand. Most of the men were employed in the local iron and steel foundries and in metal manufacturing. It was the intellectuals of the skilled, respectable working class, in alliance with the local petty bourgeoisie and small professional men (the grocer, publican, magistrate, two doctors and the Anglican vicar), who set the tone in the village and orchestrated public opinion. A number of children told their parents about the new-style scripture teaching. The publican's daughter told her elder sister, who told her aunt, and so it got back to the girl's parents. One pupil told her grandmother, who was so shocked that she had to be calmed down by her son and daughter-in-law. All the children said that Miss Outram had impressed on them not to 'go home and tell your mothers and make a bother about it'.[4] The parents were outraged; the managers had got the opportunity they had been waiting for.

The contest which followed involved parents, the school managers and their headmistress, and eventually implicated the local and central state. The case typified the competing forces and the class and gender conflicts which surfaced in early sex education campaigns. The first clash occurred at a school managers' meeting the following January. The headmistress was summoned to account for her actions, following a formal complaint by Mr Bradwell of the Victoria Inn. Bradwell was clearly a force to be reckoned with in the village. He used his pub to orchestrate his case as a 'non-conformist conscientious objector'. He condemned Outram's teaching in the language of purity outrage as: 'most disgraceful and disgusting and abominable and I won't have my child taught like what she is teaching.'[5] Bradwell also claimed that the issue highlighted conflicting rights of parents and school over the moral education of the children. The publican's aggressive stance towards the headmistress touched on deeper currents which were becoming condensed in the affair. Outram, the feminist and progressive, was clearly the target of an unrelenting campaign of bigotry and misogyny organised by the local working class and petty bourgeoisie. Parents identified the headmistress as an agent of professional control, setting her knowledge against theirs and condemning their own cultural and moral values. Their anger and frustration may also have been fuelled by Outram's high-handed dismissal of their protests, evident in her exchanges with Bradwell. She consistently refused even to acknowledge his right to protest, let alone answer his questions. As she put it: 'That man is not here to ask me questions. I refuse to answer his questions.' She insisted she would only address herself to the managers.[6] How far Outram's hostility to Bradwell stemmed from a feminist critique of his chauvinist behaviour, how far from the conflicting claims of expert and parent is impossible to say. The two elements were probably interlinked

For the managers the issue was clear-cut. Their headmistress had wilfully departed from the scripture syllabus and her stories had stimulated a prurient interest in sex, thereby corrupting childhood innocence. In her defence, Outram explained that the teaching had led quite naturally out of the children's questions. Right knowledge was a necessary safeguard against the immorality and perversion which stemmed from ignorance. Their exchange illustrated a major bone of contention in the early debates over sex teaching:

MISS OUTRAM: . . . I should not have discussed it at all if I had not been asked the questions.
MANAGERS: Do you mean to tell me that the girls ask you for such stuff as you have been reading? I shall never believe it.
MISS OUTRAM: Well. I was asked questions, and this led out of it.
MANAGERS: . . . The very effect of reading was knowledge to the girls.

MISS OUTRAM: But this was the outcome of their questions.

MANAGERS: That story you have read is not in the syllabus. You have no authority to read stories like that.

MISS OUTRAM: I acknowledge it was a mistake. I shall be careful in the future. It is a lovely little story all the same and there is no harm in it. We all make mistakes. I was not wilfully doing anything wrong. I do not acknowledge that I have done wrong . . .[7]

Moreover, the managers saw a clear link between Outram's feminist politics and her interest in sex education. As one of them sneered, 'I have heard of several ladies in Dronfield having these books and recommending them. There seems to be a movement of that sort amongst a certain class of the people.'[8] They decided to ask the County Education Committee to dismiss Outram at once, though there were disagreements among them over the rights and wrongs of sex education. The local doctors believed that when undertaken by the child's mother it could have positive effects, but fundamentalists like the magistrate insisted that any such teaching was morally wrong.

Unfortunately for the managers their plan misfired. The county council committee refused to comply with the request to remove Outram, pronouncing themselves well pleased with their head teacher. Almost inevitably the issue had become caught up in a tangled web of local education politics. It is unclear whether Derbyshire Education Committee actively endorsed Outram's sex education lessons. But there had been a long-standing dispute between managers, parents and the county over school premises. The county authority claimed that this was the real reason for local hostility to the headmistress. Parents were merely using it as a front to hit back at them over the premises issue.[9]

Dronfield responded with an open public meeting, at which the residents mounted a strong defence of their parental rights – systematically vilifying Outram into the bargain. This time local mothers were to the fore. They protested that the teacher's disgusting and abominable information had undermined the sacredness of the home and the mothers' authority. Many perceived the affair as a struggle between the competing claims of parents and teachers over the education of the child. The fundamental question was, who had the right to initiate children into the laws of sex and with what precise forms of knowledge? Did authority reside in the parents, with their popular language of purity (and one suspects a commonsense discourse about the naturalness and inevitability of procreation and parenthood), or with the power of professionals? Mrs Milnes was clear in her own mind that parental authority was being usurped:

It is too disgusting for the children to know; they have not the same respect for their parents when they know that. (Weeping) There is a proper time and place to tell children. They are old enough when they leave school. . . . I think it is time the thing was put a stop to.[10]

Other parents complained that Outram's action was tantamount to an assault on the moral innocence of childhood. The girls who had been 'initiated' were now corrupting their brothers and sisters and there had been marked signs of mental deterioration in these children. The parents' defence of their own interests was complicated by a vicious attack on Outram as the archetypal spinster. One mother claimed: 'She would not have said such a thing if she had been married. That is what is the matter with her.' Another had told her daughter that *Miss* Outram knew nothing about babies.[11] The managers carefully channelled resentment towards the county council, who, they suggested, were in league with their headmistress. A unanimous resolution, backed by a petition with twelve hundred signatures, demanded Outram's prompt dismissal. This was accompanied by a thinly veiled threat that her retention would cause a serious impediment to the educational efficiency of the school.

By February 1914 the local press had got wind of the affair. If the doctor, the vicar and the local publican represented one major force constructing public opinion in this small community, then the popular press was the other. Articles in the *Weekly Dispatch* and the *Derbyshire Times* presented the case through a familiar blend of factual reportage and lurid sensationalism, designed to titillate local audiences. The *Dispatch* led with the headline: 'Teacher and the Girls She Told', and carried a picture of the wicked Miss Outram surrounded by her innocent young charges, while the *Derbyshire Times* called for the Board of Education to step in to arbitrate.[12]

The board was in fact already informed; its response was superbly bureaucratic. Fearing there might well be a public outcry and an appeal to its authority, the central secretariat had asked one of the inspectors, W.J. Hands, to report on the affair. Hands was thorough. He saw his own role as something between a scientific investigator and a secret agent, and he sent a verbatim report of the managers' meeting back to the board, together with a sheaf of press cuttings. The inspector counselled caution. It seems likely that his real mission was to find an escape route for the board, so that it could steer clear of the incident and avoid involving the central state in any direct decision over sex education. As with contemporary campaigns around the criminal law, the state opted for a neutral course of non-intervention. It was unwillingly propelled into action by the competing forces within civil society.

Hands kept well away from Dronfield, staying at a hotel in Derby, on the grounds that the appearance of an HMI would only implicate the board in Outram's dismissal. His enquiries revealed that the sex teaching had been given in scripture time. Here was the escape clause the board was looking for. The secretariat minuted that under the 1870 Education Act and the existing code the board had no control over the content of religious education. On receiving the petition demanding Outram's resignation they stuck to the principle of laissez-faire. Joseph Pease, the board's President, approved a tactfully worded reply to the Dronfield parents. He explained that the appointment and dismissal of teachers was a matter for the local authority alone and that the board had no authority other than to help supervise the 'educational efficiency' of the school.[13]

But educational efficiency had already been impaired. The *Derbyshire Times* noted that defiant parents were voting with their feet by keeping children away from school. Towards the end of April matters came to a head when parents were threatened with prosecution. They remained firm, if anything their opposition had hardened, particularly against the Education Committee who they believed were pushing them around. According to one parent:

> The Committee had simply patted them on the back like spoilt children and told them, 'Now just send your children back to school.' Were the parents of Dronfield to be treated as naughty boys and girls, or were they to be treated as intelligent working people? Miss Outram was still at school, and the parents' wishes had been ignored in London and Derby.[14]

The protagonists looked to be heading for an all-out clash, but the outbreak of war in August 1914 put an abrupt end to the contest. The local papers turned their attention to the German invasion of Belgium and the problems of recruiting, while the Board of Education closed its file on the case without any apparent resolution.

The Dronfield affair was not an isolated incident. In the first decades of the twentieth century sex education took on great importance within public debate. A broad and often uneasy coalition – of medics, clerics, social purists, eugenists and some feminists – campaigned to raise the question as a matter of vital national and even imperial concern. Books and pamphlets directed at children and parents, conferences and public meetings, together with the formation of influential pressure groups, all testified to the seriousness with which the issue was being treated. The sexual instinct, now redefined as the racial instinct, was to be channelled into healthy and responsible parenthood. In the words of the 1911 *Manifesto* of the National Council of Public Morals, an influential campaigning force, the solution to national immorality lay in educating young men and women into the physiological knowledge and lofty ideals of marriage.[15] Increasingly, sex education was advanced as the alternative to criminal law regulation. There was a growing consensus that sex hygiene teaching held out the best assurance for eliminating vice. Behind this gradual shift of emphasis lay the re-emergence of a broad and powerful alliance around the issue of national health. It was backed by the renewed prominence of the medical profession and medical discourse as a voice within public debate.

2 IN CORPORE SANO

Though state medicine suffered a period of retrenchment in the closing decades of the nineteenth century, *medical research* enlarged its scope and sphere of influence. Despite the restrictions placed on the Medical Department of the Local Government Board, investigations carried out by its research team into the aetiology of the major infectious diseases greatly enhanced its reputation.[16] Medics might bemoan the lack of any broad initiative in public health policy, but they could point to this expanding area of research as a mark of contemporary achievements. When the *BMJ*, in its special commemorative number for the Queen's Diamond Jubilee in 1897, reviewed the development of the profession over the previous sixty years it was this aspect that it chose to trumpet. Discovery of the micro-organic causes of disease and the mode of their transmission had opened up a domain which 'to the minds of our immediate ancestors seemed almost outside of the knowable'.[17]

Major transformations within medical discourse provided the theoretical conditions for this perceived advance. The gradual acceptance of the germ theory of infection, following the research of Pasteur and Robert Koch into viruses and vaccines in the 1870s and 1880s, had resulted in the rapid isolation of the bacilli of all of the major infectious diseases.[18] Medical staff at the Local Government Board impressed the importance of these discoveries on their local health authorities through a constant barrage of memoranda, visitations and staff consultations. Integral to this research was an understanding of how the healthy body provided its own defences against invading bacteria by developing anti-toxins. This medical semiotic produced a new conception of the body as the site of health and disease. It was more and more focused on the internal biochemistry of the individual, as against the older and simpler individual/environment equation. Parallel investigations into cellular pathology worked with the notion that disease had its origins at the level of the cell.[19]

This medicalised scrutiny of the individual, and his/her role as an agent in the maintenance of health or in the transmission of disease, formed a central tenet of medical discourse in the early twentieth century. It was premised on a qualitative shift in the intellectual organisation of medical concepts. As a programme of state medicine it was quite as significant as that which had shaped the environmental reforms seventy years earlier. For Sir George Newman, first Medical Officer to the newly created Ministry of Health in 1919, contemporary medicine was now entering its 'biological setting'. The concept of the environment possessed a new meaning, more personal, intimate and integrated, concerned with the 'life history, heredity, family and domestic life, personal habits and customs' of individuals.[20]

In practice the administrative shift away from environmentalism was much less dramatic than ideologues like Newman were insisting. There was of course no sudden abandonment of the principles of nineteenth-century public health policy. The broad programme of environmental medicine remained intact. Health measures enacted at the Local Government Board between 1871 and 1918 extended and deepened state intervention in familiar areas: sanitation, working-class housing, the industrial environment, nuisances, water-supply, etc.[21] Where the new principles of bodily health posed a direct challenge to environmentalism, as in the eugenics movement, they were opposed by the majority of medics. *In corpore sano* was given its most expansive expression in the broad general pronouncements from the profession. It was put forward in the reports of medical officers such as Newman and his colleague, Arthur Newsholme, and in growing public debate over national health in Parliament and in the press. At the level of policy implementation, impact centred on carefully demarcated areas. Especially important was the growing state medical scrutiny of key individuals within the population – soldiers, mothers and children. In isolating such groups for surveillance and regulation, the profession was drawing on changes within medical discourse. These were themselves deeply implicated in the political and intellectual struggles of the conjuncture before the First World War.

State medicine's involvement in campaigns for improved military efficiency and health regeneration has usually been loosely ascribed to the growing move towards 'collectivism' in the early twentieth century. Medics have been cited as a key example of a modern breed of technical expert, instrumental in extending and deepening state intervention into new and familiar areas.[22] What is absent from these accounts is a structural analysis of the political and administrative conditions which enabled the profession to reassert its position, and to insist on increased representation within the state. This involves grasping the dynamic interrelation between new scientific knowledges and the much broader public debates over national efficiency and imperial survival.

From the late 1860s there had been repeated attempts to obtain greater state aid and recognition for science, in the wake of increased technical competition from Germany. Such efforts had met with little success from Liberal and Tory politicians alike. The *Report of the Royal Commission on Scientific Instruction and the Advancement of Science*, 1875, had polemicised for the importance of a Ministry of Science and Education, but its recommendations were dismissed as utopian. In the same way, attempts by a small but highly articulate pressure group around the journal *Nature*, founded in 1869 to argue for the social utility of scientific research, gained only limited success. Within the state itself, as we have seen, scientific and technical experts were increasingly confronted by a hostile cadre of lay civil servants.

The immediate origins of a greater alliance between the state and science lay in military anxieties over the Anglo-Boer War debacle. Britain's poor military performance sharpened the perceived economic, political and cultural threat to the predominance of the empire from other burgeoning nations, especially Germany and to a lesser extent the USA and Japan. Science now occupied a central place in the ensuing debate over national efficiency. For diverse and often disparate groupings, the language of scientificity stood as a metaphor and a referent, which condensed specific anxieties and signified different solutions to different people. Science in this sense came to stand as a meta-discourse, framed by the broader contours of the conjuncture.

In the late nineteenth and early twentieth century the fabric of mid-Victorian hegemony was shattered by a series of structural contradictions, from economic retardation and industrial unrest, to growing socialist and feminist political militancy and the intensification of anxiety over a whole range of social issues. Each had their own particular history and political trajectory. However, their multiple condensation at the level of the state makes it possible to speak, not just of a set of regional problems, but of a general crisis of hegemony. The swing back to scientific explanations and solutions and the re-entry of the expert into the state apparatuses, needs to be understood both in terms of the internal transformations within scientific knowledge and in the light of these broader economic and political developments. The new cadre of experts were not mere effects of the wider crises and destabilisations. But their professional debates were continually being penetrated by these extra-discursive conditions. At the same time, politicians were increasingly pressed for answers to problems against which the measured, patrician tones of the lay administrator seemed amateur and outdated. Medics in particular capitalised on this state of affairs, mobilising the results of scientific research as part of their broader push for increased representation with the state.

Campaigns to improve the health of the armed forces represented a classic instance of the interrelation between science and politics. Recruitment was a major source of anxiety following the Anglo-Boer War revelations about the high rate of recruits rejected on the grounds of ill-health.[23] More disturbingly, military statistics seemed to confirm the findings on poverty by Charles Booth and Llewellyn Smith. Both sets of inquiries pointed to the existence of a degenerate underclass of the population which formed a residual pool of infection. In 1903 the Director General of the Army Medical Services and the Royal College of Physicians and Surgeons responded to these revelations, by medically verifying the distinction between the healthy and respectable working class and the diseased residuum. Militarily, the demand was for major reforms in army training which took note of new developments in nutrition, hygiene and physiology.[24] Capitalising on the alarm in official circles, the *BMJ* complained that military chiefs had still not learnt the terrible lessons of the South African war. Bacilli were far more deadly than bullets in the battle for imperial survival.[25]

Behind this medical pressure lay the thinly veiled threat that if the government refused to acknowledge its responsibilities towards the armies of the empire, then the result would be destruction. During the Russo-Japanese War of 1904–5, the *BMJ* noted ominously that the Japanese were capable of great feats of endurance on account of their strict attention to the laws of hygiene.[26] Moments of panic in the national efficiency debate – often orchestrated by the new popular press – enabled medics to dramatically represent their scientific concepts in ways that gained them intellectual hegemony and popular credibility.

The model most frequently projected by medics was of a militarised conception of health, which could be extended to key groups within civil society. Though scientists were highly critical of the aristocratic amateurishness of many senior army administrators, they were keenly attracted to the image of a militarily organised society. Their vision was of functionally integrated systems and ordered hierarchies, transcending the atomised, petty divisions of party politics. This sort of militarism made professional sense to many medics because of its connection with their own reformulated medical discourse. Here representations of organicism and physiological integration were pre-eminent, and biology frequently carried an overtly political message. Moreover, as specialised professionals, medics warmed to an ideology of national efficiency precisely because it privileged rational experts over those generalist administrators who had earlier curbed the power of the Simonian specialist.

Pressure for health regeneration was not confined to the army. The medical model of militarised efficiency was carried over into key areas of civil society. Politically sensitive groups, notably the schoolchild and the mother, were specific targets for intervention. The school system of physical training, put forward by the Board of Education in 1902 in close consultation with the War Office, took its impetus directly from military methods. Groups of exercises were designed to strengthen target areas of the body (limbs, trunk, bone structure, the nervous system) in order to promote greater physical efficiency in later life, at work or on the battlefield.[27] This military model of the disciplined body, responding instantly to word of command, remained paramount in the years before the First World War. Though it was aimed most directly at boys, girls were also addressed. The board's medical department insisted that PT was a more effective way of improving national physique than compulsory military service, because army training began too late and excluded women and girls.[28] As always such a system was seen to deliver distinctive *moral* benefits. For the working-class child correct physical development could help eliminate the immoral effects of a dissolute culture or an unhealthy environment, contributing to a gradual improvement of national physique. Medics and educationalists were keenly aware that the best way of inculcating the laws of health was through a stress on the pleasures to be gained from PT. Pleasure was to be produced by the body's obedient and systematic conformity to certain physical norms. As Sir Robert Morant directed in his introduction to the 1909 syllabus:

> The Board desires that all lessons in physical exercise . . . should be *thoroughly enjoyed* by the children. Indeed, freedom of movement and a certain degree of exhilaration are essentials of all true physical education.[29]

The broadly conceived programme of health education not only demonstrated the ideal of militarised efficiency, it also embodied the new scientific concepts derived from physiology and biochemistry. In the panics over the declining birth rate and the continuing high levels of infant mortality, medics campaigned around these new knowledges to shift emphasis away from environmentalism towards close scrutiny of the health of the mother.[30] Scientists like Dr John Ballantyre, Assistant Physician to the Edinburgh Royal Maternity Hospital, together with progressive medical officers like Newman and Newsholme, insisted that recent research into pregnancy and embryonic pathology pointed to new methods of tackling the high infant death rate.[31] The demand was for a state-backed campaign to educate women and girls. They were to be prepared for their maternal duties and given material assistance to maintain a higher standard of motherhood. More often than not the driving force behind this movement was a concern with population politics, a belief that a qualitative as well as a quantitative increase in the birth rate was the key to imperial progress and power. Even Newsholme, who usually avoided the emotive rhetoric of the social imperialists, felt that the choices facing the empire were stark and dramatic:

> It cannot be regarded as a matter of indifference whether the unfilled portions of the world shall be peopled by Eastern races, by negroes, by Slavonic or other Eastern European peoples, by the Latin races, or by the races of Northern Europe.[32]

3 RACIAL HEALTH

An emphasis on the racial component in health maintenance marked a significant development within contemporary medical knowledge. From the 1870s Darwinist theories of racial progress and evolution had worked to transform the way in which physical and moral processes were understood. For social Darwinists like Herbert Spencer, evolutionary theory demonstrated scientifically what earlier social scientists had only grasped in moral terms. The individual and the nation needed to be seen as part of the evolutionary development of the race, through processes which obeyed observable and scientifically predictable laws. The rise of the eugenics movement in the early twentieth century crystallised the intellectual and political imperatives of evolutionary biology. The concept of eugenics was defined by its founder, Francis Galton, in the early 1880s as the 'study of those agencies under social control, which may improve or impair the racial qualities of future generations'.[33] But eugenics only gained theoretical legitimacy and an institutional base in the political and international conjuncture before the First World War. The Eugenics Laboratory, founded in 1907 under the psychologist and social imperialist, Karl Pearson, and the rival Eugenics Education Society, begun in the same year with its journal the *Eugenics Review*, brought together a broad coalition of biologists, medics, clerics and prominent intellectuals and politicians.

At the heart of the eugenist strategy lay a sustained attack on nineteenth-century environmentalism in all its forms – medical, charitable and philanthropic. Environmentalism was unscientific. It was at best a mere palliative and at worst it actively sustained the unfit and degenerate elements of the population in their reckless overbreeding. Medical science mitigated suffering, but by preserving the diseased and degenerate it flew in the face of natural selection and the iron laws of heredity.[34] Eugenists insisted that it was crucial to redefine the terrain of social intervention. The site needed to be shifted back to the regulation of life itself, to the study of sound offspring and to the elimination of all of those racial poisons (alcoholism, venereal disease, feeble-mindedness) which were leading to national degeneration. Havelock Ellis emphasised that the new aim of social reform was to purify conditions at their source.[35] For Caleb Saleeby, concern with race culture stood above politics, cutting across petty divisions of class and self-interest and pointing the way towards national regeneration.[36]

Concern about the relation between national power and the strength of the population was not of course new. There were distinct continuities here between eugenics and the population politics developed in the statistical societies and at the General Register Office from the 1830s. We have seen that this strategy had addressed the relation between certain population habits (what William Farr had defined as the vital statistics of marriage and divorce, fertility and fecundity) and the nation's economic prosperity, health and happiness. What distinguished eugenists from Farr and his colleagues were the laws and theoretical concepts used to assess the population. Earlier statisticians had based population predictions on arithmetical averages, derived from bills of mortality and other statistical tables, and had been primarily concerned with legal and moral intervention into the family. Eugenists argued for a quite different understanding of how norms and averages were to be calculated. Pearson's new science of biometry used calculus rather than arithmetic to conceptualise the population as a bounded space, with individual variation following predictable laws. Increased mathematical precision was deemed to give a new scientificity to biological and evolutionary phenomena. It pointed to man's ability to master his organic environment.[37]

Allied with this theoretical shift went a reconceptualisation of the role played by heredity in individual development. For earlier social reformers, human progress or decline had been seen to depend on the constant interplay of the individual's moral faculties and the state of the environment. This scheme had been modified with the introduction of Darwinist concepts of heredity. But the theories of urban degeneracy put forward by Charles Booth and Llewellyn Smith in the 1880s still followed the principle set by Jean Baptiste Lamarck – that acquired characteristics could be inherited. Eugenists drew on recent research by the German biologist August Weismann to claim that the germ cells which controlled reproduction were distinct and independent of body or somatic cells.[38] Hence inherited characteristics could not be modified by environmental factors. The way lay open for a sustained attack on environmentalism.

The medical profession was deeply divided over eugenics. Pearson acknowledged that the new racial science could do little without the hearty cooperation of medics. Yet his persistent efforts to woo the profession in 1912 only emphasised the distance between the two discourses on the heredity/environment issue. In fact, Pearson's *entente cordiale* involved a scathing outburst against the type of social inquiries undertaken by local medical offices of health. Statistics, he claimed, were incompetently used, while sanitary science still perpetuated the pernicious myth that questions of back-to-back housing, privies and breast-feeding were more important than the hereditary character of the parents.[39]

Proposals by Dr Robert Rentoul for the compulsory sterilisation of the unfit had already been given short shrift by the BMA in 1904, on the grounds that they were contrary to medical ethics.[40] Nevertheless, a number of prominent medics continued to push the eugenic case. At the BMA's annual meeting in 1913, eugenists denounced medics' long-standing but misguided dependence on environmentalism, arguing for amendments to the marriage laws in the interests of eugenically fit unions.[41] The *BMJ* intervened swiftly with a lengthy editorial, bringing the profession out strongly against eugenics. While acknowledging the supreme importance of physical and moral regeneration for national survival, the journal displayed the liberal assumptions of the medical establishment.[42] The BMA could not countenance the challenge eugenics posed to its specific brand of social and physiological individualism, with its stress on the importance of individual initiative and on the value of each and every human life.

Eugenics never achieved the overall hegemonic position that its advocates hoped for. Eugenists gave evidence to the Interdepartmental Committee on Physical Deterioration, 1904, as well as to other government inquiries into feeble-mindedness, alcoholism, marriage and divorce and venereal disease.[43] But eugenists' explanations of the deterioration of national physique in terms of the reckless breeding of the unfit, and their policies of forced segregation of degenerates and the issuing of marriage certificates, were not implemented.

It was hardly surprising that preventive medicine, and state medicine in particular, refused to give unconditional support to eugenics. The ideology of environmentalism was cautiously optimistic about social amelioration and human progress. Such optimism was too firmly embedded in the culture of the profession, and too deeply bound up with medical authority and status, for it to be in any way seriously threatened. Environmentalism remained paramount. What occurred was the expansion and deepening of its concepts to include racial and hereditary factors. At the level of the meta-discourse of the profession, few statements on the future of the nation's health failed to reference the new dimensions of race and evolution. Human biology was now to be studied as a series of stages in the process of evolution. The life history of each and every individual needed to be grasped not merely in the context of his/her immediate environment, but as part of a broader racial history.[44] Newman was aware that when eugenics was deployed in this way – shorn of its critique of environmentalism – it made a valuable contribution to the philosophical underpinnings of the profession. It was useful in raising broad questions about human progress or decline and projecting a grandiose vision of health.

Such a vision was of course racist, patriarchal and anti-democratic. In practice, the philosophy of racial health involved laying down expert injunctions to the working class and to women on the importance of pre-serving imperial stamina and physique. This was posed both against other competing 'civilised' nations and against those black and brown races who threatened to swamp the globe with their animal savagery. Britain would advance to a higher stage of civilisation via favourable environment and sound heredity. In other words, by the harmonious integration of nature and nurture. Racial theories fared best in policy areas already sensitised to the new conceptions of bodily health – motherhood, insanity and poverty, as well as birth-control and venereal disease. Eugenics owes its specific place in our history to its influence on the emergent pedagogy of sex education.

4 SOCIAL AND MORAL HYGIENE

In 1917 the eugenist and social purist, the Rev James Marchant confidently pronounced: 'It is now being fully recognized that all moral reforms for the regeneration of mankind must be brought about by the combination of religion and science.'[45] Under the banner of social hygiene, moralists, clerics, eugenists and some feminists joined forces with medics to resurrect a dialogue between medicine and morality. The new movement condensed a wide range of competing aims and strategies, but two linked concerns remained paramount in the early twentieth century. On the one hand there were the claims of morality and religion, stressing the importance of self-control and discipline for racial progress, and on the other the new medical discourse with its reconceptualisation of the rules of health and hygiene. The resulting interchange of ideas and expertise redefined the terrain of moral problems. It simultaneously produced a renewed moral emphasis within preventive medicine.

The holistic strategy for health forged by the social hygiene campaigns fixed on particular sites of intervention. Along with the problems of adolescence and insanity, sex was singled out by hygienists. The new movement worked vigorously to redefine the domain of sexuality – developing concepts of identity and sexual difference, even a vocabulary of satisfaction and pleasure, which was differentiated from social purity. Training the sexual instinct cut against purity's criminalising strategy, at the moment when purists were achieving their maximum effect in legislation.

Social hygiene took off in the years immediately before the First World War as part of the growing debate over national health and efficiency. Almost immediately the new coalition began to question the criminal law approach to moral problems. In 1911 the inaugural conference of the National Council of Public Morals (NCPM) announced that prevention rather than punishment was to be the keynote in the regeneration of the nation's moral life.[46] According to their rhetoric, public morals were now not merely a job for the criminal law, but for a wide spectrum of social agencies. Repression through fear, combined with rescue work for the fallen, was no longer enough. Positive education, channelling the sexual instinct towards socially approved goals, needed to counter older, negative moralisms.

It would be wrong to over-emphasise the distance between purists and social hygienists, concepts and personnel often overlapped. Those moralists who joined the new coalition were usually motivated by the same structural factors which brought together other groupings: the economic and military threat to empire, alarm over the falling birth rate and over the residuum. But as in the 1830s, their participation involved a reworking of moral discourse. Morality itself now began to be redefined. Its significations were shifted away from the evangelical, nonconformist emphasis of the purity movement. Nowhere was this clearer than in moralists' take-up of scientific logic and a language of rationality.

We have already noted the obstacles preventing any renewed dialogue between medicine and morality in the last decades of the nineteenth century. The eclipse of state medicine, combined with the renewed political clout of nonconformist religion and the stern voice of the purity movement, militated against a revival of the medico-moral alliance. Purists had of course drawn on medical and evolutionary concepts, but always with the proviso that they were subordinate to the dictates of a higher morality.

It was the changed set of political and social conditions in the years before 1914 which paved the way for the re-emergence of an alliance between medics, natural scientists and the established church. Along with this rapprochement went a corresponding attack on the fundamentalist tenets of nonconformist morality. The metaphor of scientific rationality and the figure of the state-sponsored expert were used to attack older voluntary and amateur approaches to social reform. National efficiency campaigners were particularly scathing in their critique of the 'provincial chapel-going radical', who was seen to promote sectional and petty self-interest at a time when national survival was in question.[47] Many historians have commented on the decline of nonconformism as a political force in the early twentieth century. What is less often recognised is the emergence of a new type of moral discourse. Here evolutionary science was fully integrated with moral pronouncements about society's future progress or decline. This religion was more rationalist and ethical, much stronger in defence of the established social order and much less populist in tone and organisation. Old Testament morality, wreaking vengeance on the political establishment, was displaced by imagery of 'the perfect man', as William Inge, Dean of St Pauls, called him, whose overriding concern was with his duties to the state.[48] This gentleman was to be the product not of a 'fallacious biologism', but of true evolutionary progress which preserved the physical and spiritual unity of the organism.

Anglicanism provided the largest number of clerical recruits to national efficiency and social hygiene. Marchant, Inge, Mandel Creighton, Bishop of London, and Canon Edward Lyttleton were all prominent hygienists, equally committed to eugenics. The Church of England may have found it easier to accommodate the cult of hygienics and efficiency. It had a long-standing concern with the problems of authority and discipline, and its stronger philsophical tradition made it more compatible with the intellectual rigour of hygiene theories. Inge was typical of the new type of moralist. From the clerical aristocracy, he had been a leading Anglican theologian as Lady Mary Professor of Divinity at Cambridge before his appointment to the prominent public position of Dean of St Pauls in 1911. Inge was a strong Tory, vigorous in denouncing 'bolshevism'. But he insisted that organised religion needed to meet the challenge of social unrest and moral decay.[49] A member of the Eugenics Education Society, the Clerical and Medical Committee of the BMA, where he campaigned for a stronger moral lead from the profession, and the National Council for Combating Venereal Disease, he moved freely between religious, political and scientific spheres. Inge was important as the type of agent who linked the disparate cultures and intellectual milieus which formed the backbone of the social hygiene movement.

The reverse side of the coin was the renewed visibility of moral concerns within the medical profession. Physiological theories provided the point of entry for a sustained moral logic. Dramatic, popular depictions of cellular processes and biochemical reactions generated a language which was itself implicitly moral in its narrative stress on dynamic causalities, portrayed as inevitable and irreversible. Eugenically based metaphors lent themselves particularly well to this type of moralising treatment. Hygienists spoke of the need to grasp the actual moment when the nerve centres of life were poisoned through hereditary influence or degenerate living. Newman was a master of populist medical rhetoric. In his grandiose overview of the history of medical science published in 1919, he made a powerful case for a totalising conception of preventive medicine. Although disease was now increasingly defined as an internal malfunction of the body, its causes included the whole of the social and moral history of the nation:

> The essentials of disease are thus . . . habit and the powers of resistance of man's body; the seeds or germs or cause of abnormal action . . . lastly, the whole process is profoundly modified by a vast concatenation of variable social, personal, external and even economic factors.[50]

The creation of the Ministry of Health in 1919 registered a self-conscious application of this moralised medical ideology. Under the banner of health education, the Ministry's aim was the creation of an enlightened public opinion. Sanitary legislation could only go so far in monitoring personal health, what was vital was a popular campaign stressing the individual's own responsibility to observe the rules of health.[51] Equally, voluntary initiatives like the People's League of Health, founded in 1917 under royal patronage, with a membership which included medics, moralists and eugenists, pronounced: 'A Nation's Health is a Nation's Wealth.'[52] Popular pamphlets stressed heredity and environment as 'the two determining factors in our lives', and pointed to the inevitable moral consequences for those who broke the laws of health: 'nature knows nothing about "Forgive us our trespasses" . . . she demands payment for every one of her laws which is broken.'[53] Commercial advertising, for Pear's soap, bleach and disinfectant, addressing women as consumers and domestic labourers, intensified the focus on home health and cleanliness in keeping the moral and physical threat of disease at bay.

Like Inge, the careers and culture of leading medical intellectuals displayed distinctive connections between science and morality. As so often in our account, an engagement with official agents pinpoints the way discursive structures were negotiated at the level of personal experience. Both George Newman and Arthur Newsholme combined a commitment to the scientific principles of preventive hygiene with a muscular Christianity. Newman began his career in the 1890s at Edinburgh University and King's College, London, where he was senior demonstrator in bacteriology and lecturer on infectious diseases. He went on to become Medical Officer of Health for Bedfordshire and then for Finsbury, during which time he published research on the bacteriology of milk and on infant mortality. He later became Medical Officer at the Board of Education and then at the Ministry of Health, pioneering school medical inspection and education for motherhood. An active Quaker throughout his life, editing the journal the *Friends Quarterly Examiner* for many years, Newman integrated his duties as medical administrator with more traditional forms of philanthropy and self-help. He worked in the adult school movement in girls' clubs run from the Friends Meeting House in St Martin's Lane, London. His interpretation of preventive medicine was founded on an unswerving faith in the evangelical principles of his own religion and a fervent belief in the duties owed by the citizen to the nation state. It also encompassed a eugenist and imperialist gloss on the importance of domesticity and motherhood. For Newman, homes were the 'vitals of the nation', and the British Empire depended 'not upon dominions and territory alone, but upon men, not upon markets, but upon homes'.[54]

Arthur Newsholme, Newman's older colleague, had his origins in a similar nonconformist background. Medical Officer for Brighton and later to the Local Government Board, where he championed statistical inquiries into infant mortality, Newsholme felt the evangelical revival of the late nineteenth century to have been a potent factor in the social hygiene movement. His participation in the National Council of Public Morals (NCPM) and in the National Council for Combating Venereal Disease (NCCVD) stimulated him to write tracts and pamphlets on sex education and the perils of promiscuity. Like Newman, he frequently used his official status to polemicise for a holistic conception of medicine, which took in moral and social factors as part of the new scientific advances.

The institutional and intellectual alliances illustrated by the careers of leading protagonists formed the backbone of the social hygiene movement in the early years of the twentieth century. As in the 1830s and 1840s, this medico-moral domain specified key concepts of sexuality as part of its concerns. But there was no simple continuity between the two historical moments, no simple development of knowledge about sex. The hygienics of Newman and his colleagues was highly differentiated from the early social medicine of Kay and Southwood Smith – in the organisation of their discourse, their forms of social regulation and in the political and institutional conditions through which they were produced. The field of sexuality was now much more clearly specified and theorised, in comparison with its relatively undifferentiated treatment in the moral repertoire of earlier environmentalists. Newman and Newsholme displayed a high degree of self-consciousness about the place of sex within social relations, which was absent from the work of Kay and Chadwick. A further structural difference was the impact of feminism. As we know, the history of medical politics from the mid-nineteenth century witnessed a growing feminist presence in official debates over sex. It is important to turn again to feminist involvement here. For the hygienist alliance was forced to operate through a series of negotiations with the women's movement.

5 FEMINIST RESPONSES

How did feminists orientate themselves towards the cult of social hygiene? In the early years of this century many women still retained a deep suspicion of medical intervention in the moral arena. The sticking point was the continuing legacy of the Contagious Diseases Acts, and the wider fear that the profession was still sunk in 'blind materialism'.[55] Yet some, particularly purists, believed that the growing *rapprochement* between medics and moralists necessitated a serious rethinking of attitudes towards state medicine. How did this come about?

On the repeal of the acts in 1886 the *Shield* had ended its campaign. But it quickly re-formed in 1897 to challenge fresh regulationism introduced into India, keeping up a constant barrage of propaganda against any return to compulsory medical inspection and detention of prostitutes at home.[56] By the first decade of the twentieth century the majority of medics saw any return to enforced regulation of venereal disease as out of the question. Recent knowledge concerning the disease's diagnosis and treatment, and its redefinition as a primarily civilian rather than a military problem, made the regulationist strategy impracticable.[57] The changed stance on sexual diseases paved the way for a partial reconciliation between purity feminists and medics over the twin issues of morality and health. Tentative articles in the *Shield* from as early as 1905 began to reconsider the role of science in promoting moral reform. Provided medics stressed the absolute necessity for sexual responsibility and self-control then 'the microscope need not be despised'.[58] As one delegate to the International Abolitionist Conference of 1906 argued, science with her austere voice ought to tell man that a higher stage of civilisation depended on the mastery of his instincts.[59] Over the next ten years, the journal recorded an ongoing debate between old-style moralists and younger, often newly professionalised women, who held a more rationalist approach to moral reform. The growing dialogue with medics heightened the moral input into medical discourse. Helen Wilson, daughter of the repeal campaigner and editor of the *Shield*, was herself a trained doctor, as was the purist and eugenist, Mary Scharlieb. When in 1913 Alison Neilans of the Ladies' National Association announced that 'we and our former antagonists can work cordially together', Wilson explained that the olive branch was a result of the change of heart among medics and their new expansive definition of health.[60]

Organisational shifts, alongside changes in the language of purity, reflected this new feminist position. In 1915 the LNA merged with the

British Abolitionist Association to form the Association for Moral and Social Hygiene, with Wilson and Neilans effectively in control. The new name, with its medical inflection, still had the power to evoke old hostilities and suspicions among some purity feminists. The *Shield* tactfully explained the shift. In the past the association had been dedicated to the supreme claims of morality and to the exposure of the error of 'so-called hygiene', which sought to subordinate justice and personal liberty to alleged physical necessities. However, abolitionists who began as moralists had now been 'constrained by the necessities of their struggle' to become hygienists. Purists had recently found that the name 'abolitionist' hindered further progess, implying a problem of 'long ago and far away' and alienating potential allies.[61] Henceforward, members of the new body would be proud to call themselves hygienists, because they had rescued the concept from the degradation into which it had sunk during a 'materialistic age'. They had shown that science must take account of the whole man and not only of his body. To lend weight to the claim, members were reminded of Sir John Simon's own expansive definition of the moral responsibilities of preventive medicine. The readership was offered a vision of the new city of 'Hygeia' – a recurrent image projected by both medics and moralists. The irresistible force of the city was attracting pilgrims from 'widely-sundered starting points'. Like the new Jerusalem, it was planned by God on the foundations of equal justice and morality, but this modern vision of a sanitised cosmopolis was governed by health-giving purity and by the sanctity of family life.[62]

Feminist responses to hygienism were rarely unambiguous, partly because physiological medicine and evolutionary biology were so powerful a mainstay of anti-feminist campaigns. But these concepts did provide some women with categories of self-definition around which to mobilise, negotiate and occasionally disrupt and claim as their own. For many, the issue of national health, like social purity, was used to advance women's influence in the social sphere. It enabled them to hold their own in the face of calls from male experts for a greater professionalisation of the field. The *Shield* alerted its readers to the great possibilities opened up to women by the growing focus on hygiene. The woman of the future would be far more than a nurse or consoler, she would have a positive religion to realise as a high priestess of health.[63] Eugenists like Scharlieb and Alice Ravenhill insisted that biology now conclusively proved that responsibility for safeguarding the nation's morals lay with women. For Scharlieb, it was women's unique position as reproducers which made them so central to the physical and moral training of future generations.[64] Ravenhill saw the revelations of medicine and eugenics pointing to a greater role for women, not only as mothers, but as guardians of those aesthetic qualities which made for physical, intellectual and moral progress.[65]

This alliance of some purists and moderate feminists with the medical profession needs to be contrasted with the ongoing hostility displayed by others. The militant wing of the movement did consciously draw on medical and evolutionary concepts, but to extend and deepen their attacks on men. Both Christabel Pankhurst and Frances Swiney used medical authorities and statistics instrumentally to win specific arguments, while distancing themselves from what they saw as the corrupt power of male professionals. *The Great Scourge* was not only a vigorous purity polemic, it mobilised the evidence of countless medics to insist that up to eighty per cent of the male population was infected with gonorrhea – the race poison of the eugenists.[66] Speaking the language of race and nation, Pankhurst demonstrated that innocent wives were being continually infected by their adulterous husbands, resulting in degeneracy on a scale which heralded race suicide. Her book concluded that continence was both physiologically and morally essential for the fit reproduction of the race.

As always, Swiney's medical polemic was even more extensive, claiming women's innate biological and mental superiority over the rest of creation. In a dazzling subversion of medical and eugenic theories she insisted that women, as the reproducers of life, were not merely central to the perpetuation of the race but were the dominant motivating force behind the human species. They were 'the centre of gravity of the whole biological system', while men were becoming more and more superfluous.[67] Swiney proposed that women's racial superiority was evidenced both by their physical and mental capabilities and in their internal cellular composition. Darwin and Spencer had been wrong to argue that women were in a state of arrested development. Man was the intermediate form. The shape of women's faces were far in advance of men's; in the number of teeth they were leading evolution; they had more grace and more perfect physical beauty. Challenging the biologists Patrick Geddes and John Thomson, Swiney pointed out that 'femaleness' was due to the presence of a chromosome absent in the male. Hence women displayed a more complex cellular composition, which was the positive force behind reproduction, whereas the katabolic male cells led to racial disintegration.[68] Current panics by eugenists and social reformers over national decline were misplaced in blaming the mother. It was *men* who were the cause of racial decay. In language which coupled purity outrage with a conceptual grasp of eugenics and the new biology, Swiney drew together the major social problems – disease, feeble-mindedness, degeneracy and insanity – to expose male vice as the root cause of national decline:

> Well may Dr Rentoul claim that the health of the woman is our greatest natural asset, that the physically and mentally healthy woman has been so ruthlessly, so brutally, so generally mercilessly exploited by the male as women. . . . She stands as the martyr of organized and systematic sexual wrong-doing on the part of the man who should be her mate, and whom alone she has evolved to the human plane. Church and state, religion, law, prejudice,

custom, tradition, greed, lust, hatred, injustice, selfishness, ignorance, and arrogance have all conspired against her under the sexual
rule of the human male. Vices, however, like curses, come back to
roost. In his own enfeebled frame, in his diseased tissue, in his weak
will, his gibbering idiocy, his raving insanity and hideous criminality, he reaps the fruits of a dishonoured motherhood, an outraged
womanhood, an unnatural, abnormal stimulated childbirth and
starved poison-fed infancy.[69]

Swiney's feminist hygienics and Pankhurst's medical polemic were part of
their broader criminal law strategy to halt male vice. But the fact that these
arch-opponents of male professionalism now referenced the concepts of
social hygiene – albeit in subverted form – was a measure of the changing
language of purity feminism. The feminist take-up of hygienics was in part a
skilful form of campaigning, involving an imaginative reworking of dominant knowledges. Yet it also testified to the increasing power of the new
medical strategy and its ability to force a dialogue with competing political
forces. The decline of purity feminism in the 1920s and 1930s needs to be
seen in relation to the overall decline of feminism, and especially to the
unmitigated hostility of male sex reformers. But it was also the result of the
growing hegemony of the social hygiene movement. In the period during
and immediately after the war feminists were confronted by this changing
situation across a whole range of sexual issues: venereal disease, birth-
control and, crucially, sex education.

6 SEX EDUCATION

Our detour has taken us far from Dronfield school and Miss Outram's sex
education teaching. But now we can begin to unravel the complex tangle of
ideologies and political forces which were condensed in the affair. Outram
was very much a bearer of the new social hygiene alliance. She began from a
position of speaking out about sex, in the face of silence and hostility from
managers and parents. But her conception of right knowledge was distanced from the traditional purity approach. It certainly involved negative
proscriptions – especially on the terrible dangers of active female sexuality –
but these were now combined with positive representations. Sex was
defined as procreation, benefiting racial evolution and ultimately contributing to the divine plan for human progress. Outram's political commitment
to the women's movement and to eugenics gave her the power to speak this
new language. Yet as a professional as well as a feminist, she was caught in
contradictions which beset many women members of the purity movement
and the social hygiene alliance. While these discourses gave her a lever of
political representation, they brought her into conflict not just with male

patriarchs on the local school management committee, but also with the mothers and fathers of her pupils, who saw their headmistress as hell-bent on depriving them of their own parental rights. Outram's highhanded dismissal of the parents' protests – her refusal even to acknowledge that they had a right to speak – reveals how her position as expert and educator enmeshed her in some of the power relations of professionalism.

And what of the opposition? The local doctors, vicar, shopkeeper and publican, the parents, together with Mr Hands, the HMI sleuth, and the faceless men at the Board of Education counselling administrative caution – that time-honoured codeword for keeping your hands clean. The headmistress's tactics were a direct challenge to the local clique of male experts, who must have sewn up so many pacts of patriarchal power in the vicarage and the surgery. Their deeply misogynistic response to Outram as a woman provides evidence enough of the way in which these men perceived her as a threat. As for the parents, their own defiance and outrage at the situation took a largely conservative form. They pilloried Outram, mounting a whispering campaign to remove her and asserting traditional, proprietorial rights over their own children. But they did grasp defensively what too many middle-class women failed to understand. The displacement of one form of expertise by another is no substitute for a real shift in the balance of power/ knowledge relations. How could they fail to grasp this essential fact? They felt themselves to be on the receiving end of it! Dronfield parents also had a radical, if again conservative, critique of the growing move to professionalise each and every particle of knowledge about sex. They countered this with a commonsense discourse on the naturalness and inevitability of human sexual relations – what 'every man and woman knows' and does! The board's role in all this, its deliberate and self-conscious fence-sitting, was to set the pattern for the state's response to sex education for the next thirty years.

Many of the issues depicted in the Dronfield affair can be transposed on to the broader canvas of national hygienist politics. The importance awarded to sex education within official debates in the early twentieth century provides a major instance of the way social hygiene transformed the meanings and politics of sexuality. Like Outram, the vast majority of the medico-moral alliance believed that the purity-derived stress on speaking out needed to be maintained. The conspiracy of silence was still perceived as the major obstacle. Right knowledge was the surest protection against polluting influences. Yet as the *Lancet* insisted in 1913, the question of how to dissipate ignorance and with what precise forms of knowledge remained contentious.[70] Most groups agreed that prohibition and moral warnings were not enough. Negative moralising against dirty and indecent practices was an insufficient safeguard because it offered no positive images of sexuality for adolescents and young adults. What was vitally needed was a programme of teaching which acknowledged the importance of sex as a positive force in human life.[71]

This approach signalled a clear departure from the purity strategy and a partial critique of it. Apart from Blackwell's writings, positive images had figured only marginally in purity thinking. With the new knowledge derived from physiology, conceptions of sexuality and sexual difference now became firmly rooted in the biological functions of the human organism. The sexual instinct was potentially a component of every normal citizen. The way lay open for a more affirmatory approach to sex.

What were the features of this sexual model, and how did it differ from earlier conceptions of instinctual behaviour? Mid-nineteenth-century medics like William Acton had theorised the sexual instinct as a mechanical process of evacuation, dependent on environmental stimuli. It was a model which served as an apology for the inevitability of the male urge. Post-Darwinist scientists reclassified the instincts, seeing them located deep in the physical consitution of the organism and operating relatively independently of social influences. Havelock Ellis' third volume in his *Studies in the Psychology of Sex* series, *Analysis of the Sexual Impulse*, 1903, concluded that research into sexual behaviour was becoming more and more a question of physiological chemistry. The whole object of the social ritual of courtship, Ellis argued, was to set in motion processes of sexual tension and release which were instinctually motivated.[72]

In one sense this new understanding tended to reinforce representations of sexuality, and especially male sexuality, as extra-social – a primitive and uncivilised urge, the beast lurking in man. But the powerful voice of moralists and feminists within the social hygiene coalition insisted that men's instincts could and should be educated towards positive goals. Renewed moral stress within contemporary medicine ruled out any return to Acton's notion of uncontrollable male sexuality. As Ellis himself pointed out, crude instinctual theories which remained at the level of biology, refused the whole question of the moral development of the race.[73] It was the mark of man, the only species with true intelligence, that his instincts were plastic and capable of infinite transmutation through education.

All commentators were agreed on the image of sexuality which needed to be put forward for adolescents and young adults. Healthy and responsible parenthood was the ultimate goal. In the years before 1914 every voluntary body concerned with social hygiene (from the NCPM to the Eugenics Education Society) placed the concern with parenthood high on their agenda.[74] A recurrent problem voiced by many social hygienists was one of language. What vocabulary and concepts should they use to represent sexuality as parenthood for the young? According to the purist and eugenist Dr Alfred Schofield, the language of sex education needed to be systematically 'eugenized', shifting the significations away from 'the sexual' to 'the racial'. He counselled teachers: 'Never use the word "sexual" but say racial (propagating the race), and you get a word that is totally free of objection and cannot be resented by parents.'[75] Racial truths looked at the sex organs from the health point of view, while 'the sexual point of view' looked at the same organs selfishly, as self-indulgence and self-gratification. Helen Wilson, speaking at a conference on sex education during the war, argued that sex teaching needed to fuse concepts of sex and parenthood in the minds of the young. Parenthood had to be presented as the *raison d'être* of sex.[76] Purists had been wrong to represent the sex instinct as 'animal and low, a thing as far as possible to be ignored, repressed, treated with silent contempt', positive sex teaching needed to sanctify and hygienise the sexual act. Science alone held out the promise of a rational approach.

In line with political alliances within the social hygiene movement, science was consistently moralised in the tracts and pamphlets on sex education. Like Miss Outram, Elizabeth Sloan Chesser (a prolific writer on sex education material and a lecturer to the Institute of Hygiene and the Women's Imperial Health Association) was confident that elementary botany could be used to introduce young children 'in a perfectly chaste and simple manner' to the great secrets of life, even before their own sexual instincts were awakened.[77] The National Birth-Rate Commission (formerly the NCPM) put out a model syllabus for use in elementary schools in the early 1920s. Simple lessons on personal hygiene (care of hair, nails and teeth, together with 'modesty and reticence in the discharge of bodily functions') could teach habits of personal self-respect. The body, especially its visible orifices and extremities, was to be trained to emblematically display a set of inner moral qualities which prepared the ground for sex hygiene teaching. Then lessons could move to the study of parenthood in the animal world:

> Simple lessons on animal life enable the teacher to inculcate all unconsciously to the child ideas of parenthood, e.g. the life of the bird, loving care and thought in the preparation of the nest, the laying of the eggs, the patient sitting of the mother bird, the father's attention to and care of the mother bird; his finding food and the efforts of both to teach them to get their own living.[78]

Here were Outram's lessons in natural harmony and sound procreation raised to the level of policy directives.

When addressing adults, dramatic polarised imagery was to be used to inculcate moral norms. Health-giving representations of nature were contrasted with the ill-health and disease which followed from immorality. With the aid of government grants the NCCVD fielded an effective propaganda campaign of pamphlets, talks, films and slide-shows, which reached an estimated two-and-a-half million people between 1914 and 1920.[79] The council's film and lecture tours, given to troops at the front, to youth groups and women's organisations, carried lurid titles like 'The Gift of Life', 'Damaged Goods' and 'The End of the Road'. Campaigners were quick to grasp the importance of the visual media in putting across the message. With their powerful ideologies of immediacy, actuality and truth, films and still photographs could translate scientific concepts into a popular language. Sport, sunshine, nature and the animal world were most frequently used to connote health. The sinister temptations of sexual immorality on the other hand were portrayed via images of the city and the 'amateur prostitute' or 'good time girl' – superficially brilliant and attractive but fundamentally unclean and polluting.

Images of health and evolutionary biology not only confirmed the link between sex and parenthood, they also demonstrated that the *power to love* was an important part of all human sexual development. Heterosexual monogamy, cemented by a spiritualised conception of love, was claimed as the high point of species evolution. Such a notion of spiritual bliss was different from the chivalric imagery of purity. It fused the higher emotions with the physical experience of the sex act. Geddes and Thomson noted that zoologists had identified the appearance of 'physical fondness' and 'aesthetic appeal' in lower mammals – tendencies which had become infinitely more beautiful in human relationships.[80] This spiritualised and emotional side of human nature pointed the way forward to further racial progress. In contrast, promiscuous sex, divorced from love and procreation, was not only immoral and unhealthy but was identified as retarded or regressive. Contemporary studies of prostitutes and sexual perverts by the Italian criminologists Caesare Lombroso and William Ferraro and by Havelock Ellis defined them as atavists – primitive throwbacks to an earlier stage of development. The promiscuous sexuality of primitive women studied by early anthropologists was presented as proof of such atavism in the female prostitute.[81]

This essentially Darwinist gloss on the evolution of spiritual and emotional life was also backed up by the work of early social psychologists. It was this approach to mental and instinctual life which tended to be privileged above that of Freudian psychoanalysis in Britain before the war. Professor William McDougall, in his influential *An Introduction to Social Psychology*, 1908, understood all mental life as 'the affective aspect of instinctual processes'.[82] Lower forms of social behaviour, in animals and in primitive races, were the direct product of 'the prompting of the instinct', but the higher stages of social and sexual conduct were always marked by 'voluntary control and regulation of the instinctual impulses'.[83] Hygienists' uncompromising stress on self-control and their clear and direct relation between mind and body fitted more comfortably with the plan for the evolution of 'the perfect man', than did Freud's dream theory of repressed sexual wishes and fantasies. The minimal impact of psychoanalysis in Britain in the early twentieth century needs to be understood in relation to the intellectual and political dominance of social hygiene. Though reviewers in the medical press gave Freud's early work a favourable reception, they were concerned that psychoanalysis gave unconscious life too much autonomy from basic physiological processes. While for moralists like Scharlieb, Freud's challenge to the sexual innocence of childhood was intolerable.[84] When Freudian concepts did begin to enter mainstream British psychology in the inter-war period, it was the biologistic and evolutionary strands, pointing the way forward to correct patterns of psychosexual development, which were appropriated by the mental hygiene movement.[85]

7 THE CONSTRUCTION OF SEXUAL DIFFERENCE: ADVICE TO GIRLS

Hygienists always spoke of the human sexual instinct, but their discourse was highly gender specific. Early sex education was not only dependent on gendered knowledges and assumptions, it actively constructed a new ideology of sexual difference by emphasising the absolute polarisation of male and female sexuality. What was taking place was the transformation of older moral categories of gender difference under the impact of evolutionary biology.

Physiologists and psychologists were agreed that adolescence was the crisis point for girls – a product of linked physical and mental changes within the body, which were highly unstable and bordered on the pathological. It was especially dangerous for girls. Dr Scharlieb argued that puberty was delicately balanced between the normal and the abnormal, when any sudden excitement was 'likely to lead to disaster'.[86] A modicum of knowledge was necessary to guide minds and bodies towards maternity, keeping the love instinct pure in the early years of womanhood, by guarding against any form of promiscuous activity. Carefully prepared talks could monitor dangerous tendencies towards 'unruly behaviour', or to the type of 'unhealthy attachments' to older women which were so prevalent in this unstable period of life. Teachers and youth leaders were told to be on the lookout for a particular type of 'flighty girl' – not always from the poorest home – who dressed over-smartly and was allowed far too much freedom in the evenings. One headmistress, in her evidence to the London County Council inquiry on sex hygiene teaching in 1914, confirmed that London girls were far from ignorant, and that many 'bold girls' had a tendency towards 'sexualism' and were in need of vigorous restraint.[87] Boys were 'at risk', not from the ordinary class of girl, but from the type who had a great deal of knowledge from the wrong source.[88]

This scrutiny of active and dangerous female sexuality paralleled similar anxieties voiced earlier by the purity movement. But what distinguished hygienists' concern was the focus of their disquiet. It was no longer the 'professional prostitute' who was isolated as the source of danger but a new form of threat – the promiscuous girl who gave sex for free. As Lucy Bland has shown, the 'amateur prostitute', as she was christened, was the source of a series of moral panics during the First World War, condensing fears about the rising tide of immorality, illegitimate births and the spread of venereal disease.[89] Though sex teaching was designed to give girls some knowledge for their own protection, there was ambiguity over precisely how much information should be supplied. Educationalists hoped to preserve a delicate balance between innocence and self-knowledge among girls. Such ambiguity reflected continuing confusion over manifestations of female sexuality. It also registered the commonsense assumption that ultimate responsibility for their own moral behaviour – and that of their menfolk – lay with girls themselves. Social hygiene perpetuated the double-standard by insisting that male self-control, though possible, was problematic and that girls should help men to act responsibly by watching their own behaviour:

> you can help the men; they are very largely what women make them, what women expect them to be. It is very specially in the relation of men and women, that women and girls have a great responsibility. . . . A girl cannot be too particular. . . . If a man's friendship is worth having she will not lose it by refusing familiarity, but will make it a better sort of friendship. . . . She will also set a high standard of womanhood and for what women expect of men.[90]

Girls were not told why they needed to be so 'particular', yet the imputed blame for any subsequent wrongdoing was usually laid on them. When girls had already become 'bold and flighty', teachers were advised to isolate them from their friends in order to prevent contamination. Once a girl had 'fallen' there was little to be done other than contain the danger.[91]

The positive pole of girls' early sex education centred on preparation for motherhood. This strategy worked not merely with regulation by ideas and propaganda, but through a regime of pleasure. Girls were promised definite joys and satisfactions if they conformed to their maternal role. In the early years of the twentieth century motherhood not only became central to the construction of women's identity, it also began to be acknowledged as a valid site for their spiritual, sensual and even erotic experience. The sexualisation of motherhood was usually implicit, evoked in the rhetoric of speeches and pamphlets. Though muted, it marked the beginnings of a shift away from the discourse of purity, by sanctioning a positive domain of female sensual or erotic experience.

For Elizabeth Chesser, the desires and pleasures women experienced during pregnancy, childbirth and lactation were essentially spiritual and ethereal. It was a holy and mystical experience for a young woman when she brought a new 'eternal soul' into the world.[92] Chesser believed that most women sought happiness in the sex union, a desire which was felt as an instinctive longing. This sensualised representation – with pleasure produced through conformity to biological and social roles – contrasted sharply with the dominant form of male sexual experience, where satisfaction was gained through notions of transgressive and illicit behaviour.

The debate over female desire was extended by Havelock Ellis in his search for the sexual impulse in women. Drawing on the theory and politics of libertarians and new moralists, Ellis magisterially pronounced that 'true' female sexuality was only expressed in relations with men. But he also noted secondary or subordinate manifestations of women's sexual instinct.[93] A woman experienced definite pleasures when suckling her child, this physical satisfaction was the basis for the emotional bond between mother and offspring. Ellis, like other male experts, sexualised the female body. Women's anatomies were dissected to reveal a hierarchy of erogenous zones, moving from the nipples and clitoris to the vagina. There was, he insisted, a true 'physiological analogy' between heterosexual intercourse and the relation between mother and child during lactation:

> The complete mutual satisfaction, physical and psychic, of mother and child, in the transfer from one to another of a precise organicized fluid, is the one true physiological analogy of the relationship of a man and a woman at the climax of the sexual act.[94]

The most extensive take-up of the joys of intercourse and the cult of maternity was in the writings of the eugenist and birth-control pioneer, Marie Stopes. Stopes was emphatic in denouncing any expression of female sexuality outside marriage as unhealthy and unclean. Yet her celebration of the acceptable forms of women's erotic experience in *Married Love*, 1918, included both marital intercourse and the sensual experiences of motherhood. These two forms of pleasure, she claimed, were inseparable in the experience of most normal women:

> The sensitive inter-relation between a woman's breasts and the rest of her sex life is not only a bodily thrill, but there is a world of poetic beauty in the longing of a loving woman for the child which melts in mists of tenderness towards her lover.[95]

For Stopes, writing as a eugenist, the pleasures and desires of marital sex could be socially sanctioned because they perfected the spiritual side of procreation and led the race onward and upward to a higher completion of its powers.

It is tempting to read these representations of female sexuality solely as ideologies of expertise aimed at the regulation of women's behaviour. Clearly, the choice offered to women and girls between promiscuity and maternity, together with the aggressive stance on heterosexuality, worked as a form of sexual policing. But the opening up of a discourse of desire around motherhood, though highly contradictory, did provide the space for women like Stopes and Chesser to ask questions about female erotic pleasure which were taboo in the purity movement. The privileging of maternity, while socially normative, gave some women the opportunity to think about their own sexual/sensual experience. In the inter-war years the contradictions involved in these representations of femininity became more pronounced. Popular manuals stressed that it was vital for women to experience pleasurable, reproductive heterosexuality within marriage, rendering all other forms of female behaviour inadequate or deviant.

8 MASCULINITY

Sex hygienists also defined puberty as the flashpoint for boys. Here the danger was thought to be more immediate, more the direct product of physiological changes. The boy's organs became sensitive to any stimuli, for the pressure of the sexual instinct was ever-present in the adolescent years. The main approach was still one of deterrence, centred around moral warnings on the crucial importance of self-control and the perils of promiscuity. But as the Rev Edward Lyttleton, Headmaster of Eton, made plain, his experiences had taught him that boys needed to be offered something more than negative prohibitions – they needed positive images of sexual conduct.[96] It was through the idea of mastery and control of the sexual instinct that new militarised and scientificised representations of masculinity were produced, holding out the promise of particular satisfactions and powers.

Purists had projected the young man's fight between conscience and immorality as a fundamentally religious battle, mobilising chivalric images of combat and contest. Hygienists drew on a similar language of conquest, but this was now depicted through biological metaphors as an essential test of masculinity. Instinctual forces needed to be fought, tamed and finally conquered in the progress towards physiological maturity. Boys' ability to master them was conceived as an initiation rite. Success guaranteed lads of all classes their *rite de passage* into adult manhood, with all its privileges; failure was a sign of atavism and effeminacy.

This was the point of entry for militarised conceptions of male sexuality. Obedience to command, rational control over mind and body, technical know-how of physical laws – all this prepared the lad for combat on the battlefield. In 1909 Dr Schofield explained the facts of life to boys using army metaphors. When the embryo was first formed it was simply a mass of cells, but an 'unseen power' detached 'certain patrols' to coordinate the campaign.[97] Sir Robert Baden-Powell, hero of the Anglo-Boer War and founder of the Boy Scouts, presented his own system of masculine hygienics in similarly military style. Boys who were in 'the human rutting season' were to be taken aside by the scoutmaster to have the facts explained.[98] Baden-Powell recommended a frank man-to-man chat, supplemented by selective renderings of popular science. The body was entering a new phase of operations which originated from perfectly natural causes, namely 'the spreading of semen'. At this crucial stage in the battle the boy needed to draw on all his reserves of energy and fighting strength. Otherwise victory would not be his; he would lose his self-respect and risk the consequences of venereal disease. Under pressure from eugenists, teachers and youth leaders also included specific instructions on fatherhood, but this was envisaged less as an introduction to duties and responsibilities than as a male romance. Life was 'a sacred torch', handed down from father to son, which had its beginnings in the first dawn of life on earth.[99] To remain unmarried was not only selfish from the racial point of view, it was also unmanly, because it broke the patriarchal chain which linked countless generations: 'If you marry and hand this life onto children, it does not die out. If you die celibate without marrying then it ends with you.'[100]

At the same time the medical input into sex hygiene produced a different and competing construction of masculinity, with a stronger emphasis on the link between mastery over nature and scientific advance. In the early 1920s Arthur Tansley, University Lecturer in Botany at Cambridge, believed that the romance and intellectual appeal of science was a sure way to hold boys' attention in sex hygiene lessons. The teacher needed to present himself as a fearless questor after truth. He was to be dressed in the 'long white coat of a hospital doctor' and give instruction in a special room, kept scrupulously bright and clean and fitted up like a laboratory. Medicalised imagery carried definite moral benefits:

> The hospital is everywhere associated with beneficent healing ... and purification, based upon sound objective knowledge ... the clean austere atmosphere, both physical and mental ... would probably have exactly the right psychological effect ... on ... boys.[101]

This was not a vision which connoted the masculine culture of the Scouts, nor the public-school ethos of the muscular Christian gentleman. These scientificised representations had most to say to the academic middle-class boy, produced through intellectual competition and a form of 'epistemo-philia' – the pleasure gained through the strenuous search for knowledge.

All these pedagogies derived a large part of their strength by affirming forms of masculine culture which systematically excluded women. The all-male preserves of the Scouts and the Boys' Brigade were the clearest examples, but the images of scientificity were also male-defined. Male teachers were advised that it was better if boys were deliberately kept in the dark about the sexual development of girls. Lyttleton heartily recommended one pamphlet entitled *In Confidence to Boys*, because it dealt with their difficulties frankly but reverently 'without mentioning the female side at all'.[102] Such instruction was often explicitly racist. Initiation into masculinity meant initiation into the echelons of white manhood. Boys were warned that only 'among primitive men' were physical pleasures experienced as animal lusts. Among the white races, control of mind over body had raised the sex act to a sacramental level.[103] Differences of age, rank and class may have separated the scoutmaster from the raw recruit and the science teacher from his pupil, but they were linked together by a bond of élite masculinity which celebrated both misogyny and sexual racism.

9 SCHOOL SEX HYGIENE TEACHING: COMPETING STRATEGIES

The ideology of sex education at first sight appears so coherent and confident, so seamless in its handling of conflicting demands, that we might be tempted to tip over from the moment of ideological production to that of implementation. This error is particularly seductive when dealing with new liberal or state socialist programmes in the early twentieth century. There is a utopianism in these social and political philosophies in the very worst sense, with their projected vision of social order which assumes society to be conflict-free. Most forms of official power are wilfully covert about the tensions in their projects, but many of the initiatives around motherhood and eugenics reproduce the Benthamite mania of the 1830s. Contemporary sex education stands squarely in this totalising tradition. Comparison between Freud's early work and social hygiene is instructive in this respect. While not wanting to privilege Freudianism as a more advanced or sophisticated explanation of sexuality – a common mistake in modernist or evolutionary histories of sex – there is an acknowledgement of complexity in Freud's approach, an awareness that individuals resist official discourses, which throws the buoyant optimism of social hygiene into relief.

The contradictions inherent in sex hygiene only become visible at the point of implementation, the moment of dialogue between competing political forces over the enshrinement of policy in legislation. In the early twentieth century the issue of state-backed sex education teaching in elementary schools was a sharp focus for disagreement among members of the alliance. Most hygienists believed that under ideal conditions the parents, and especially the mother, were the proper agents of instruction. Yet given the continuing perception of working-class family life as immoral, many looked to the state to enact their demands.

Medics were the most vociferous group in support of a full programme of sex teaching in schools. Given the renewed importance of state medicine, the profession was keen to promote its prestige through the education system. Eugenists also provided a powerful lobby for the inclusion of hygiene as a school curriculum subject; as future citizens children had a right to know the laws of life and the state had a duty to impart them.[104] Teachers themselves were divided. Those women teachers, like Outram, who were committed eugenists tended to favour a comprehensive educational programme. Miss T.E. Bonwick, Headmistress of the Girls' Department of Enfield Road School, Hackney, felt it was her responsibility to offer her girls some protection, because she believed that local parents were morally and intellectually bankrupt.[105] The majority of male teachers were more tentative, fearing the destruction of the child's natural reticence and, more to the point, possible subversion of the master's authority in the classroom. The Headmaster of Millwall Central School in London's docklands hinted ominously that if 'precocious boys' were addressed directly then 'the worst features would come out'.[106] In working-class areas fear of disruption and disorder from resistant pupils outweighed any commitment to sexual reform.

For women's organisations and for feminists the issue was clearly more problematic. Professionals like Dr Scharlieb viewed state-sponsored hygienics as a useful extension of philanthropic intervention into the working-class family. It would impart to children 'in a decent way' what they currently grasped 'in a most undesirable way'.[107] Militant feminist sex education material, on the other hand, was largely designed to raise women's consciousness and stimulate public debate about male immorality. On the whole, in the years before the First World War feminists remained lukewarm about introducing sex teaching into schools. This reflected their suspicion that once institutionalised, control would be lost to the power of male experts. Significantly, Helen Wilson was more in favour of privileging sites of female culture, such as mothers' meetings and bible classes, to promote sex education.[108]

There was of course a structural block to the implementation of social hygiene which went deeper than mere internal political differences. This was the purity movement itself. Early sex education campaigns were mounted at precisely the moment that purity was at its high point. There was of course no total division between the two groups. But it became increasingly clear that each projected competing forms of regulation and distinctive representations of sexuality. At its starkest, the contrast was between a commitment to criminalising legislation, mobilised around the old moral/immoral, virtue/vice polarities, as against a broad educational pedagogy, defining sex more positively, under the rubric of national health. If the two strategies were jostling for position before 1914, how was it that hygienists were successful in their bid for hegemony, to such an extent that by the inter-war period a growing consensus held that sex education, not the criminal law, promised the best assurance of regulating sexual behaviour?

The 1920s and 1930s witnessed the increasing marginalisation of purity. After the 1922 Criminal Law Amendment Act the statute book records no further additions to the legal code. The movement which had been spawned by the repeal campaign – a mixture of popular protest and incisive feminist politics, underpinned by a harsh regime of social disciplining – had finally been displaced. When the Home Office moved into this area again in the 1950s and 1960s, it was ostensibly to decriminalise many of the offences created under purity pressure in the late nineteenth and early twentieth century: homosexual practices, obscenity, censorship. What structural factors set the conditions for this shift, sustaining the educational approach to sex so that it has remained of paramount importance through to our own period? These questions take us into the concluding sections of our history. We need to return to the themes which have been central to the project – the role of the state, the entanglement of professional knowledge and voluntary pressure groups and feminist initiatives for the reform of personal relations.

10 THE STATE AND SEX HYGIENE

First the state. The central point here is that the shift away from a criminal-ising to an educational pedagogy was not initiated by the state in the narrow sense. Despite the strong move towards increased government intervention in many areas during the First World War and during the inter-war years, the Home Office, the Ministry of Health and the Board of Education remained highly cautious about introducing sex education into schools. The stance taken over the Dronfield affair was part of a wider laissez-faire policy by government which continued throughout the 1920s and 1930s. At a local level the situation was much the same. Extensive discussion of the issue in London by teachers, school managers and the London County Council led to the setting up of a special LCC inquiry in 1914. Their report came out strongly against formal school instruction, ostensibly on the grounds that the difficult mixture of social classes in London militated against direct class teaching.[109]

The specific conjuncture of the war produced no major rethink by the state. The extensive panic over venereal disease – condensing fears about the amateur prostitute as a threat to military health – did prompt repressive government control of prostitution (via the wartime Defence of the Realm Act, Regulation DORA 40d), along with state funding for medical treat-ment of the disease. But the interventionist approach was more fractured than it appeared. It marked out clear distinctions between the short-term demands of wartime (i.e. the control of infected prostitutes) to be enacted by the state, and long-term educational objectives, to be covered by the voluntary sector. In the *Report of the Royal Commission on Venereal Dis-eases*, 1916, a broad educational offensive was recommended to inculcate the laws of moral hygiene in 'all types and grades of education'.[110] However, it was not in practice government agencies which spearheaded reform. While the commissioners were convinced that a solution to the problem of sexual diseases could be 'accomplished only by the action of Government directed to the solution of a great national problem', they emphasised that private voluntary efforts, notably from the NCCVD, should take the lead.[111]

The 1918 coalition government adopted these proposals, thankful to shift the burden of responsibility on to other shoulders. In fact from 1917 and throughout the 1920s the NCCVD received substantial Treasury grants for its educational and propaganda work. Joint liaison committees were set up between the new Ministry of Health and the National Council. Yet the state was content to be cast as the junior, passive partner in these negotiations, leading to complaints that the ministry was not pulling its weight. In 1920 Viscount Astor restated the government's position on the principle of delegated responsibility:

> The Government can do a certain amount in education and propaganda, but . . . there is a real sphere for voluntary effort. Voluntary bodies conducted by people who understand the subject can do a great deal which a Government Department or a local authority could not do.[112]

The position at the Board of Education was not dissimilar. As inter-war independent surveys showed, many schools and training colleges, supported by progressive local authorities, took advantage of the board's deliberately ambiguous policy in order to introduce their own schemes for sex hygiene, especially for girls. By 1934, for example, Pontypridd in South Wales had a coordinated programme, moving from the usual simple talks on plant and animal life in their infant departments, to specific class instruction on reproduction at upper school level.[113] It was not until 1943, with the publication of the Board of Education's *Sex Education in Schools and Youth Organizations*, that space was provided for sex education within secondary schools. It had taken a campaign of over thirty years, and a quite different conjuncture, before government took action in response to voluntary sector pressure.

11 THE PERSONAL AND THE POLITICAL

Why did the state continue to be so deeply ambiguous about intervening in sexual regulation? What did this register about the wider parameters of state action? These questions return us to the more general issue of the relation between formal political discourse and sexual politics. We have already noted the passive role played by the Home Office in the fierce campaigns to pass fresh criminal law legislation before 1914. Government handling of birth-control in the 1920s displayed a similar timidity. The Ministry of Health initially refused even to commit itself on the question of whether maternity and infant welfare centres could be used for contraceptive counselling. As in the area of sex hygiene, individual authorities could capitalise on this ambiguity to push for birth-control facilities at a local level. It was only when councils and health authorities overstepped the mark that the state moved in negatively to delimit the permitted scope for action.[114]

It is all too tempting to ascribe such non-interventionist policy to financial stringency or to administrative lethargy. But our history of state entanglement in medico-moral politics reveals that much trumpeted economic or administrative constraints were rarely just that. They were almost always enmeshed with broader political and cultural imperatives. More significant than the tight fiscal surveillance of the Treasury during these years were the cultural meanings attached to sexuality within political discourse, in particular the increasing construction of the field of sex as outside politics.

At a number of different moments we have noted how the structures of formal politics excluded discourses on sex. The process of reconceptualising and tightening the political field, begun in the late nineteenth century, was accelerated in the face of the party destabilisations and realignments of the immediate post-war years. This move was institutionalised in the Representation of the People Act, 1918, and through the creation of a new representative state. The Act staked out a new political language, based on the broad categories of citizenship and near universal suffrage. But its discourse also marked out a tighter conception of what politics was and what it was not.[115] At its most banal it signified mere passive participation at the ballot-box, though its scope could also embrace key areas of the social – notably motherhood, health and education – via the linked concerns of nation and citizenship. Sexuality was rarely included in this new political repertoire. Instead, the domain of the sexual was constituted as extra-political. Sex was now defined as an area to be administered by neutral expertise, or it was aligned with the personal, with private domestic life, and hence only tangentially related to formal politics.

This correlation of the sexual with the personal was a key factor in the state's non-interventionary stance. When the National Birth-Rate Commission reviewed sex hygiene teaching in 1920, Christopher Addison, Minister of Health, warned of the problems ahead:

> I think it is obvious that you touch subjects which are more nearly personal than any other class of topic, and in regard to which people as a whole resent, or are apt to resent, outside interference and direction more than any other.[116]

Here was the recognition of the personal life of mass society as outside the politician's orbit. The twinning of sex and the personal had its antecedents in earlier religious and radical liberal traditions. But these had been élite conceptions, confined to sections of the bourgeoisie and the professional classes. The inter-war years witnessed the reformulation of these ideologies in relation to much wider levels of popular experience. A number of economic and cultural changes provided the conditions for this: the decline of family size, increased emphasis on the emotional content of family life by the churches and by popular marriage manuals, together with a rise in real wages for those sections of the respectable working class and petty bourgeoisie in work. The growth of new consumer markets, backed by the expansion of popular journalism, especially women's magazines, was also instrumental in reconstructing domestic life.[117]

Further, the impact of parliamentary feminism had important effects on the way sexuality was handled officially. The entry of women MPs into Parliament after 1918 produced a political discourse which was now implicitly gendered. Specific areas of administration, such as welfare provision, childcare, even health to some extent, were increasingly defined as 'women's issues'. This process of delegation had contradictory effects. While it gave many political women an authoritative voice on certain areas of policy, these were ranked as inferior to masculinist preserves like foreign affairs or the economy. At those rare moments when sexuality crept into political discourse, it was frequently defined as a women's issue, and trivialised. This meant that it was viewed as unimportant for any form of state action. Moreover, the feminisation of sexuality reinforced its associations with private life. For women politicians were still largely perceived as representatives of the private sphere in the public arena. The debate over birth-control was a case in point. Significantly it was Frances Stevenson, Lloyd George's mistress and private secretary, not Lloyd George himself, who handled the prime ministerial dialogue with Marie Stopes.[118] When the Tory feminist Nancy Astor raised the question again in Parliament in 1935, she still felt compelled to apologise for introducing such a 'disruptive issue' into members' 'valuable time'.[119]

These structural factors underpinned the state's nervous dialogue with the social hygiene movement over sex education. Yet the relative absence of state intervention here did not of course mean any abandonment of responsibility for sexual regulation. It was the experts and voluntary bodies who were nominated as the proper agents of control. The inter-war politics of sex points us towards this network of professionalism and to the struggles within civil society.

12 PURITY POLITICS IN DECLINE

The major change in pressure-group politics in the 1920s was the demise of purity. The ongoing decline of nonconformist religion and the reworking of middle-class and popular culture left their mark. But the growing marginalisation of the purity movement was also the result of its own vacillation over sex education.

Characteristically, the NVA perceived sex education more as a threat to morality than as an essential part of preventive work. There was also the underlying, justifiable fear that any full-blooded sex hygiene programme would ultimately displace their own moral discourse by the power of biology and the new preventive medicine. With William Coote at the helm until his death in 1919, the NVA placed its weight very firmly behind traditional struggles against vice, which now embraced the modern dangers posed by the cinema, jazz and dancing.[120]

Early in 1919 Coote had announced his resignation from the hygienist-dominated NCCVD over what were coyly termed 'disagreements over policy'.[121] It was no accident that the bone of contention was sex teaching. Throughout the following decade the NVA continued to distance itself from the educational approach. But ten years later the issue erupted again, this time splitting the purity movement. When the 1928 Biological Education Congress passed a series of resolutions calling for a more enlightened approach to health education, this became the cue for delegates – including some members of the NVA itself – to launch a strong attack on older purity methods. There was still too much emphasis, they claimed, on legislation and prohibition, too little on building the solid foundations of morality through education.[122] Purists were failing to come to terms with the post-war world. Stimulated by the press, the cinema and literature, adolescents were determined to find out the facts of life. No amount of legal control could prohibit immorality. It was this disagreement from within which marked a watershed in purity's decline. The NVA's official response was almost a foregone conclusion. The executive committee ruled that in view of the great difficulty of arriving at any consensus on the subject, it was wiser to leave it alone![123] Although the language of purity continued to exert a powerful influence on public debate, as a campaigning force it now lacked intellectual coherence and popular support.

Shifts within the other strands of the original social hygiene alliance exacerbated the problems facing purity. For the medical profession and the progressive wing of the Anglican church, the most significant factor was the beginnings of a discourse on the importance of sexual fulfilment for both partners within marriage – discussion hitherto largely confined to libertarians and sex reformers. In 1918 the *Lancet* intervened in the debate on celibacy and spinsterhood. It presented research by Sir Arbuthnot Lane, Consulting Surgeon at Guy's Hospital, on the importance of glandular and hormonal secretions for the physical and mental health of women. Drawing on biochemistry, Lane asserted that the production of fluids associated with female sexual desire had a beneficial effect on women's health and vitality. Women who were deprived of these secretions tended to develop 'chronic intestinal stasis, diseases of the breast and a growing feeling of disgust for sexual intercourse'.[124] Despite his scientific caution, Lane had no hesitation in recommending both motherhood and women's active participation in intercourse for their general well-being.

As always, these medical prescriptions were conceived as political interventions, with an implicit attack on purity feminism. Lane claimed to show how the 'poor, thin, static virgin' could be metamorphosised into a 'plump, healthy, happy' individual through intercourse and pregnancy. Subsequent editorials and letters took up the implications of the research with gusto. Sexual fulfilment for married women was hailed as the key both to their happiness and to eliminating those female nuisances (i.e. spinsters) who interfered in all aspects of political and public life with their bizarre demands. According to the *Lancet*, Stopes' *Married Love* was a much more acceptable solution to the problem of female sexuality than the militant politics of purity feminism.[125]

It would be unwise to overstate the scope and impact of these developments. Yet the new emphases did mark a move away from the focus on chastity and marital continence, dominant in medico-moral discourse before the war. Medics further justified their new approach by appealing to contemporary events, which for them pointed to the bankruptcy of purity solutions to sex. Under the impact of the war, followed by new styles of dancing, mixed bathing and the greater freedom granted to women, there was a growing desire for the relaxation of moral standards. Along with the spirit of mere licence and rebellion, such trends contained a valid demand for 'a new moral evolution'. Insights from Freudianism were also showing that 'the barriers of represion were too narrowly set'.[126]

Political and theological ruptures within Anglicanism brought similar changes to the medico-moral alliance. The modernist challenge from inside the church, coming to a head in the 1920s, pushed for a reinterpretation of Christian faith in the light of the upheavals of the war and the renewed expansion of 'scientific materialism'.[127] Theologically, the movement was influenced by pragmatist philosophy. It was a belief that God was only knowable through personal religious expression in prayer and mystical experience, and that the Deity was not only transcendent but immanent in man's highest faculties and creative acts. However, the partial take-up of modernism in the recommendations of the Lambeth Conference of 1930 had as much to do with the church's response to the social and political problems of the post-war world as it did with the niceties of theological debate. The *Encyclical Letter*, produced at the conference, stressed that the growth of a materialistic culture and a socialist politics 'rooted in the denial of God's existence' demanded a new approach to Christian doctrine.[128] The keynote was a humanist emphasis on God working within the world and in men and women at their best.

It was this more personalised religious discourse which informed the church's revised statements on sex and marriage. The conference's recommendations reaffirmed the absolute centrality of Christian marriage and family life, condemning 'illicit intercourse' and remaining cautious on birth-control. But the sex act itself, now partly differentiated from procreation, was viewed as a 'noble and creative function', a potentially God-given factor in the life of mankind.[129] Delegates acknowledged that marriage as an equal partnership now meant emotional and sexual fulfilment for both partners. Marriages, sealed by the 'fullest development of the sex relationship', were part of God's plan for joining two personalities in lifelong union.

Both medical and religious discourse fed into the expanding repertoire of popular marriage manuals and sex education writings in the 1930s. With their dual stress on physical health and spirituality, they projected a vision of sexual fulfilment, especially for women. At the same time, such writing – like Theodoor Van de Velde's *Ideal Marriage*, 1928, or Max Exner's *The Sexual Side of Marriage*, 1932 – continued the unremitting assault on celibacy and purity feminism. Draconian warnings were issued to women who refused to be aroused by their husbands' newly acquired sexual technique.[130]

The combined attack from medicine and religion, together with a popular language of sex reform, contributed substantially to the marginalisation of purity politics in the inter-war years. This was as true for purity feminism as it was for Coote's NVA. In the 1920s many feminists, erstwhile supporters of criminal law legislation, began to shift their allegiance towards sex education. The sea change had much to do with women's experience of the implementation of purity legislation, which proved a political education in itself.

After their successful conclusion of the 1912 campaign, the *Shield* had pronounced that this triumph was merely the beginning. Purity would go from strength to strength, pressing for more stringent legal sanctions to promote feminist demands.[131] The war years provided a fresh impetus for further legislation, but the results proved more contradictory than feminists had envisaged. Above all, there was a growing awareness that the administration of the law was almost invariably directed towards policing *women*. Feminist analysis of the DORA regulations, and of the clauses contained in a number of unsuccessful criminal law amendment bills between 1917 and 1922, provided practical proof of what many had long suspected. Proposals for the criminalisation of the transmission of venereal disease and the coercive reform of young convicted prostitutes, demonstrated that it was women who were usually on the receiving end of punitive purity legislation.[132] Moreover, in line with basic tenets of social hygiene, many feminists now believed that the whole question of sexual promiscuity belonged to the sphere of public health policy rather than to the criminal code. At a Women's Freedom League rally in 1917, one woman doctor made an impassioned plea for a move away from all forms of criminal legislation as the solution to sexual difficulties. Drawing on direct experience of the war, she equated the habit of punishment and coercion with all the old ideas of force and fear which had done so much damage in the world. Repressive legislation was just another example of male law, which politicians fell back on when they had no real answers to social evils.[133] It was a position echoed by many leaders of the women's movement, from the Association for Moral and Social Hygiene to the NUWSS. As the *Common Cause* put it in 1918, 'our great hope is in education'.[134]

The inter-war years witnessed growing feminist participation in sex education, both in moralising writings addressed to children and adolescents and in books and pamphlets stressing the importance of pleasurable heterosexuality within marriage. The biting attack on male sexual behaviour was certainly lost, though the new discourse did provide some women with a language for thinking through questions suppressed within purity feminism. There was no 'glorious unfolding' as Marie Stopes envisaged, for much sex education material was centrally aimed at the regulation of female sexuality. Rather, what occurred were a series of contradictory movements which reflected the more general uncertainties of feminist politics in the inter-war period.

13 CONCLUSION

The white-coated male scientist and the plump, happy mother, these highly gendered representations of sexual responsibility and satisfaction were distinctive motifs of hygiene-based sex education in the early twentieth century. The growing hegemony of social hygiene was secured by an extensive shift in the balance of political forces and intellectual knowledge informing social policy. In the years before the First World War this whole domain underwent substantial transformation, as different forms of expertise responded to a series of domestic and international crises which were seen to be interlinked.

One result of these transformations was that the criminalising approach to sexual regulation was gradually but substantially displaced. The re-emergence of preventive medicine and an imperialist discourse of health and racial survival were the most significant influences here. But sex education cannot simply be understood as the medicalisation of sex. Preventive medicine was one, albeit key, element in the network of political alliances which produced the social hygiene movement. This coalition staked out new representations of sex. It constructed concepts of sexual difference, normality and abnormality, and promised a definitive range of pleasures and satisfactions to those who heeded the message. Government's relationship to these developments was tentative and hesitant – a product of renewed definitions of the sexual as outside the terrain of political intervention. It was the dense network of voluntary and professional bodies which coordinated the move towards sex education in the early twentieth century.

In the context of the longer history of medico-moral politics it is tempting to construct a direct continuity between the sanitary programmes of the early nineteenth century and the hygienics of seventy years later. But there was no direct relation between the two moments, no smooth development of knowledge about sex. Between them lay the sustained challenge of repeal feminism and moral purity. Any examination of the forces which were displaced by social hygiene must record substantial losses. The purity movement – an amalgam of evangelical, patriarchal morality and biting feminist politics – was forced aside by a highly professionalised discourse on sex. Sex education firmly reinstated normalising hierarchies of knowledge, which set teachers above parents, medics over patients and dismissed competing feminist and popular understandings as lunatic, amateur and irregular. Instruction from above was the keynote. There was none of the emphasis on active self-determination which had characterised the positive side of purity feminism. With the renewed expansion of social policy and state provision in the 1940s and 1950s, social hygiene became written into the rubric of the welfare state.

EPILOGUE

It might be wise to end here. But we began by making a strong claim for the importance of history in understanding sexual politics today; how it can be used to grasp our current dilemmas and discontents. What then has been the relevance of all this? What does it really matter that in the 1830s sanitarians blamed cholera on the moral filthiness of the urban poor? Or that eighty years later a local schoolmistress with feminist sympathies confronted her superiors over sex education? To explain how and why means being explicit about the way we understand history-writing. It also means a return to the current state of play around sexual health and disease which opened the book.

Our route into history has been a two-way process. We began with a series of questions about our own situation now. But we were also faced with a number of already constituted historical narratives: an official story, telling of the heroic birth of the modern public health movement, the feminist rediscovery of nineteenth-century women's struggles and a popular melodrama of vice and sexual outrage. Hence the book has worked at the interface between the contemporary milieu and the sexual scripts handed down to us. In the process we have tried to construct the genealogy of particular forms of modernity: starting points for the system of medical authority which we still inhabit, the tension within feminist discourse between disciplining and self-determination, regimes of desire incited through the polarities of purity and danger. Our present is caught up in that past, shaped and moulded by the ongoing resonance of some of these deep structures. There are important lessons here. Some are quite precise and direct, pointing to formations with a very long *durée* indeed. Others are much more fractured and discontinuous. Used self-consciously, a history of the present neither reproduces the faults of evolutionary accounts – a continuous unravelling from past to present – nor should it deliver a blank cheque for every sort of historical analysis. The parameters of where to begin and where to stop are guided by our negotiation with the present. We need to construct modes of history-writing which grasp that past/present relation. Let us develop the argument

165

further by returning to the issue which began this history, the narrative of AIDS:

> It is Saturday night at The Stud Saloon and the shadowy back street bar throbs to a deafening disco beat.
>
> In the crowded dance floor, two young men are locked in a dreamy embrace. Male couples hold hands in quiet corners and a slim-hipped youngster with Boy-George make-up preens coquettishly for an ageing admirer who holds him gently around the waist as he swigs from a long-necked bottle of Budweiser beer. Harassed bartenders can hardly cope with the desperate demand for drinks. It's the same in almost every 'gay' bar in town. 'For Chrissakes, Rick baby, gimme a gin. Better make it a double.'
>
> Looking for love has always been a high risk undertaking for San Francisco's homosexual community. A few stiff drinks often help before you go out in search of sex with a stranger. Now the nights are filled with alcohol and apprehension. For a four-letter word – AIDS – has brought fresh fears into this city by the bay.
>
> 'What the Gay Plague Did to Handsome Kenny',
> *Sunday People*, 24 July 1983

The mythology of AIDS has been constructed through stories like this. These are images, languages, signs of sex which mould and police desire quite as effectively as more overtly coercive regimes of authority. Growing public anxiety in Britain from the autumn of 1982 was the product not just of medical revelations in the *Lancet*, but of a plethora of popular representations. These two genres were not neatly sealed off from each other. Almost despite itself, official medical language has continually been interrupted by the low, rude noises of the popular, while press and television coverage fed off and reworked the discourse of social medicine.

Like other recent panics – drugs, law 'n' order and child abuse – the popular media have played a critical role in shaping opinion over AIDS, setting the parameters for debate, identifying the problem and its potential solutions. This has usually been morality as melodrama, fitting snugly with the long-established tradition of sexual reportage dating back at least as far as Stead's 'Maiden Tribute' scandal of the 1880s. As with many of the journalistic accounts, the *Sunday People*'s 'Handsome Kenny' worked as exposé, mimicking the language of official inquiry. Like Dr Kay's cholera excursion, we, the 'normal' reader, are invited to descend into a gay sexual underworld. Deviant sex is always at the centre of this spiral, whether in the notorious 'hot house', with its 'black leather harnesses', or in Rock Hudson's desperate search for bathhouse lovers.[1] This type of account is of course always framed by moral condemnation, reaffirming the distance between our own sexuality and 'deviant' pleasures. Yet in their voyeuristic fascination with the details of erotica they work to incite sexual desire. The construction of sex as naughty and immoral, but titillating, operates with codes of transgression familiar from our history. Popular sexual pleasures still fixate around moral/immoral opposites. Like the dirty weekend or the proverbial cream cake, sex has to be naughty to be nice. We still need to know more about the genealogy of these structures of desire and their place within the erotica of popular culture.

But the erotic sub-text is always underwritten by the dominant meaning. Promiscuous and 'deviant' sex leads to killer disease. The hyper-realist codes of photographic journalism function as emblems of gay promiscuity. 'Handsome Kenny', his bright eyes showing no hint of the agony to come, as against 'Doomed Kenny', the 'victim', visibly wasting away from AIDS sickness. Rock, 'the hunk who lived a lie', played off against 'the wasted seven-stone shadow'.[2] The very fact that the symptoms can be represented so dramatically, cutting down superstars and handsome young men in their prime, has made AIDS highly accessible to the long-standing protocols of popular investigative journalism. With their sharp polarities between health and disease, good and evil, they set up a direct relation between cause and effect and point to simple, graspable solutions.

By late 1986 this repertoire was being subtly reworked. The second major wave of panic is rooted in the sudden realisation that the whole heterosexual population is potentially at risk. Sex per se is now dangerous. The moral *frisson* has shifted register. No longer is it generated by fascination with deviance – that other sexuality. Danger is everywhere. Like Kay's proverbial thief walking in darkness, AIDS could invade your body, your space.

But tales of sexual outrage have never been told in isolation. Their images of sex and death are read through a wider social and political vocabulary. AIDS has come to occupy a distinctive place in the ideological repertoire of the moral right. Both here and in the United States a fresh generation of ideologues have pushed for a new order of moral absolutes, pointing up links between moral, social and political instabilities. In the wave of panics which have recently swept Britain, the moral lobby has been making all the running, orchestrating a language of polarised opposites. More and more, sexual undesirables have been twinned with the socially undesirable. Drug takers, the homeless, down-and-outs, lesbians and gay men have been run together as outside the healthy body politic.[3]

It is simplistic to see these panics as conspiracies. For public representations to have effects at a popular level they must tap lived experiences. AIDS has done just that. Like the wave of scandals a century ago it focuses genuine fears about current sexual behaviour. Moralists have been quick to exploit the contradictions inherent in 1960s permissiveness and channel them rightwards, demanding a halt to the 'inevitable' by-products of libertarianism: spiralling sexual violence, pornography and disease. At a time of protracted social instability, fundamental truths about right and wrong, good and evil, backed by a socio-biological gloss on our 'true' sexual nature, seem like reassuring certainties.

These popular philosophies of the right do have a history within post-war medico-moral discourse. Since the early 1960s rising rates for venereal diseases, the increase in viral infections, like herpes and resistant sub-strains of gonorrhea, have stimulated renewed scrutiny of sexual disease. Research on the prevention and treatment of infection isolated so-called high risk or target groups. Gay men, black immigrants and young single women were all singled out as potential health hazards.[4] Moreover, it was their lifestyle, psychology and habits (i.e. their promiscuity) which were cited as the root cause of the spread of disease. From the sternest end of social hygiene, moralists like Dr R. Wilcox of St Mary's Hospital, London, argued that sexually transmitted diseases among men 'frequently result from . . . mating with high risk females', women who do not accept 'the responsibilities of marriage' and who suffer 'from a sense of inadequacy, loneliness or rejection with an anxiety to please, or an antagonism to parents or society'.[5]

This is the sharp end of medico-moral discourse. Medics involved in AIDS research have consciously distanced themselves from any such draconian pronouncements. Yet inevitably their concepts, protocols and procedures continue to inhabit the historically produced meanings attached to sexuality, health and disease. In handling AIDS the medical profession have slid through a series of hypotheses, which kaleidoscope different semiologies of disease. When the *Lancet* opened the debate in 1982 knowledge of the syndrome was very much akin to knowledge of cholera in the 1830s. Medics were confronted with an array of symptoms, but knew little about the causal agent or the mode of transmission. Problems were exacerbated because cellular immunodeficiency – the specialism central to AIDS – was relatively underdeveloped as a field of study. At this early stage, the absence of any clearly identifiable virus meant that researchers returned to the 'environmental variables' which were thought to contribute to the syndrome's appearance. When medical hypotheses were twinned with dangerous sex, space was immediately opened up for re-entry of the medico-moral repertoire.

For gay men, as opposed to other high risk groups, the logic pointed irresistibly to a link between the homosexual lifestyle and the spread of AIDS. Was it stimulated by 'poppers', a recreational drug fashionable on the gay scene? Did it only attack those who were genetically disposed – a consequence of some profound defect in immunity? Were levels of promiscuity to blame?[6] The most comprehensive explanation originally advanced was the 'immune overload theory', which suggested that under the impact of a gay lifestyle the body's defences broke down, exhausted by 'overload', a physiological and moral protest against excessive bouts of unnatural sex.

This scenario is preserved in the melodrama of the popular media.

Medical research, however, propelled by its own internal dynamic, has shifted to another register with the eventual isolation of the HIV virus. We are no longer directed to the moral environment of sufferers, but are now deep into the cellular composition of the organism. There we encounter T-helper/suppressor cell ratios and retroviruses which bud at the plasma membrane and interfere with DNA products.[7] Here is a continuity with the cellular biology glossed by Newman and Newsholme in the early years of this century. Yet unlike those early ideologues, current high prestige research associated with AIDS curiously evacuates the social terrain. The ultimate aim may be altruistic, the elimination of suffering, but the path-breaking romance of pure science circumscribes any excursion into the muddy waters of social relations. This is now carried by the public health agencies – health visitors, social workers, the clinics – whose explicit brief is with human management.

Yet when we turn from medicine to those government agencies responsible for public health, we encounter official attitudes to sex laid down in the early years of the century. Still, it seems, where sexual health is concerned the state is cautious and has been slow to intervene. The Communicable Diseases Centre at Colindale, London, has monitored the incidence of AIDS, following the 1982 *Annual Report of the Chief Medical Officer of the DHSS*, which confirmed outbreaks in Britain and admitted significant under-reporting due to lack of knowledge.[8] Gay activists identified such lethargy as the result of Tory government attacks on the National Health Service. But as we know administrative lethargy and fiscal stringency have always been enmeshed with the cultural meanings written into the regulation of sexuality. This is the official designation of sex as extra-political, an unwelcome intrusion into the proper business of politics. When the Department of Health and Social Security finally stirred to mount its first publicity campaign in March 1986, the embarrassment was painful. 'Don't Aid AIDS' coyly avoided naming sexual practices considered unsafe (and unsavoury), like anal sex.[9] At this stage traditional arguments held sway. Releasing explicit information ran the risk of inciting that which was to be restrained. Again it is the threat to heterosexuals, plus spiralling statistics, which has pushed government agencies into more decisive action. In late 1986 we saw a high profile cabinet committee set up under Lord Whitelaw, and a far more sexually explicit media campaign. Leaflets to every household and television and press coverage warned: 'Don't Die of Ignorance.' The upshot of all this is much more public visibility and talk about sex than ever before. Penetration, condoms and alternative forms of pleasure are chewed over on chat shows. Yet levels of funding for research and treatment lag behind the rhetoric and still seem inadequate to meet the needs of sufferers and those at risk.

What broader conclusions are thrown up by this encounter between AIDS and the substance of our history? At the most general level, what the book has charted is the continuing power of medical discourse to define the sexual, setting the parameters for what can and cannot be said, for who can speak and who is spoken to. This is crucial to the hierarchy of power around sex. It is the dominance of expertise in all its forms, marking sharp distinctions of power and privilege between male and female, normal and deviant and having real effects on the identities which individuals live out. But medico-moral discourse is not a conspiracy. It is not a cabal of white-coated men plotting a string of lies in the interests of capital or patriarchy. It is a distinctive regime of power/knowledge relations, rooted in institutions which circulate authoritative representations of sex.

How to combat such dominant discourses? That task has faced all groups targeted by sanitary interventionism since the feminist campaigns against the Contagious Diseases Acts over a hundred years ago. Today the problems thrown up by AIDS are not just ones for the gay community, but for feminists and progressive forces generally. Confronted by the institutional complexity of the professions, it would be naive to think that a simple anti-professionalism was an adequate response. After all, repealers effectively took on the 'terrible power' of the medical oligarchy precisely by drawing on medical concepts to subvert dominant explanations. Since a large part of medico-moral power lies in the coherence of its discourse, any challenge must engage at the level of struggles over representation. To miss the cultural messages surfacing around AIDS is to fail to grasp an important agenda in current health politics.

The question is what languages to mobilise. This needs asking because resistance is rarely a spontaneous eruption from below. Sanitary politics has always depended on specific languages to articulate demands and endow protests with meaning.

Gay medics and community activists, both here and in the United States, have opted for a politics of information, taking issue with media reporting. The Terrence Higgins Trust, the main gay coordinating body in Britain, projects AIDS as essentially a medical issue, distorted by media misrepresentation. Emphasis is laid on empowering individuals to make their own decisions about sex, with the help of adequate medical information which sifts truth from falsity, fact from scaremongering.

These campaigns mark an important educational offensive, not least because they are run by gay men themselves. The problem is, such a programme can remain trapped inside medical discourse. It may criticise the professional treatment of gay men and the lack of state-funded research, but it does not ultimately confront the medical profession's right to colonise the field. When gay groups make the distinction between medical truth and media falsity they continue to reproduce dominant medical hierarchies. What is urgently needed is a much more extensive challenge to the hegemony of preventive medicine.

Moving beyond AIDS, all of this has implications for a future politics of health generally. Who has the right of access to control the body, to define the parameters of sickness and health and to pronounce on sex? These are pivotal issues. Health politics can no longer afford to inhabit narrow campaigns for increased funding and improvement of facilities, which leave institutional structures and their concepts unchallenged. It must work to mobilise positive representations of health – a new Hygeia – which deals in the real discontents of those disenfranchised by present provision and projects a different vision of needs, beyond a mere defence of the NHS settlement. If this is dismissed as mere utopian rhetoric, then it is a testament to the acute impoverishment of initiatives in the field.

That is one conclusion. But AIDS provokes more than a far-reaching critique of medical authority. It also crystallises cultural responses from those communities attacked by the virus and its panic – responses to do with lifestyles, desire and sexual practice. For AIDS is not just of the body, it is about the signs and meanings we attach to bodily functions in the head. The disease condenses and magnifies differences among political groupings loosely linked by their opposition to the moral right and their desire to project alternative regimes of sex. In that sense AIDS does indeed represent the front-line of sexual politics.

Responses within the gay community register more widely held positions. Mirroring the right, there are those who urge repentance and a return to monogamy, under the threat of disease and death. Pragmatic and liberal voices stress the importance of education into 'safer sex' which need not be unpleasurable.[10] The most consciously theorised position – emerging out of sexual radicalism and utopian socialism – argues that though AIDS demands serious attention, gay men should not lose sight of their long-term objectives.[11] What is ultimately envisaged here is a radical pluralism, capable of uniting various disparate tendencies – gay, feminist, socialist, libertarian – in a progressive sexual alliance. Pluralism will stick because it accepts diversity and choice, avoids moral absolutes and underlines the representational quality of sexual desire. Like the fierce charges and counter-charges of seventy years ago, this bid for sexual hegemony is put together as an explicit challenge both to the moral right and to perceived feminist moralisms.

What is wrong with such a vision of our sexual future is that it is ungendered. As this book has shown, discourses of sex have constructed men and women in terms of difference, difference shot through with power relations. That insight must put the issue of male sexuality firmly on the political agenda. Not, let it be clear, men and their desires as the unified, monolithic oppressor, the source of all power, but men as they appear in this history. Men whose constructed sexualities, identities and pleasures have been complexly written into many of the structures of social and political domination. An alliance of pluralist diversity which refuses this insight must ultimately flounder.

Our final question then must be how to put together a new settlement around sexual relations. Within this, male sexuality needs to be prioritised, complexly theorised, though not elevated to the status of a negative obsession. If a hundred and fifty years of sexual politics has taught us nothing else, it should be that a large part of winning the argument about groups' and individuals' need to change involves convincing them that their sexuality is capable of changing. At the risk of repetition, this is germane to the book's whole project; that sex is about representations, in the head as well as in the body. But a strategy for change needs more than biting critique. It needs to project a new vocabulary to speak about masculinity and for men to think about themselves. Such languages do not just drop from the sky, they need to be forged, reassembled from current images and experience. Like the contest over medical professionalism, the debate about masculinity has only just begun.

NOTES

Abbreviations

BMA	British Medical Association
BMJ	*British Medical Journal*
GBPP	Great Britain Parliamentary Papers (roman numerals refer to bound volume numbers, figures refer to page numbers)
HL	House of Lords Sessional Papers (numbering as for Parliamentary Papers)
LNA	Ladies' National Association
NCCVD	National Council for Combating Venereal Disease
NCPM	National Council of Public Morals
NUWSS	National Union of Women's Suffrage Societies
NUWW	National Union of Women Workers
NVA	National Vigilance Association
PRO ADM	Public Record Office, Admiralty Papers, Kew
PRO ED	Public Record Office, Board of Education Papers, Kew
PRO HO	Public Record Office, Home Office Papers, Kew
PRO LGB	Public Record Office, Local Government Board Papers, Kew
PRO MH	Public Record Office, Ministry of Health Papers, Kew
PRO PC	Public Record Office, Privy Council Papers, Kew
PRO T	Public Record Office, Treasury Papers, Kew
PRO WO	Public Record Office, War Office Papers, Kew
WSPU	Women's Social and Political Union

INTRODUCTION TO THE SECOND EDITION

1 Virginia Woolf, *Moments of Being: Unpublished Autobiographical Writings*, ed. Jeanne Schulkind, London, Chatto & Windus for Sussex University Press, 1976, pp. 173–4. For further commentary on this formative moment of sexual modernism see: Frank Mort and Lynda Nead, 'Sexuality, Modernity and the Victorians', *Journal of Victorian Culture*, 1996, vol. 1, no. 1, pp. 118–30; Lucy Bland and Frank Mort, 'Thinking Sex Historically', in Lynne Segal (ed.), *New Sexual Agendas*, Basingstoke, Macmillan, 1997, pp. 17–31.

2 For contemporary accounts see among very many: C.A.R. Crosland, *The Future of Socialism*, London, Jonathan Cape, 1956, chapter XXV, and *The Conservative Enemy: A Programme of Radical Reform for the 1960s*, London, Jonathan Cape, 1962, chapter 16; Roy Jenkins, *The Labour Case*, Harmondsworth, Penguin, 1959, pp. 135–46. For more recent assessments of the impact of Victorianism on twentieth-century intellectual culture in Britain see: Noel

Annan, *Our Age: Portrait of a Generation*, London, Weidenfeld & Nicolson, 1990; Stephan Collini, *Public Moralists: Political Thought and Intellectual Life in Britain, 1850–1930*, Oxford, Clarendon, 1991; Peter Mandler and Susan Pedersen, 'Introduction: The British Intelligentsia After the Victorians', in Peter Mandler and Susan Pedersen (eds), *After the Victorians: Private Conscience and Public Duty in Modern Britain: Essays in Memory of John Clive*, London and New York, Routledge, 1994, pp. 1–28.

3 Ronald Pearsall's *The Worm in the Bud: The World of Victorian Sexuality*, London, Penguin Books, 1969 and Fraser Harrison's *The Dark Angel: Aspects of Victorian Sexuality*, London, Sheldon Press, 1977, were typical examples of this tradition. For more nuanced accounts see: Steven Marcus, *The Other Victorians: A Study of Sexuality and Pornography in Mid-Nineteenth Century England*, London, Weidenfeld & Nicolson, 1966; Peter Cominos, 'Late-Victorian Sexual Respectability and the Social System', *International Review of Social History*, 1963, vol. VIII, pp. 18–48, 216–50.

4 Michel Foucault, *The History of Sexuality*, vol. 1, *An Introduction*, trans. Robert Hurley, New York, Pantheon Books, 1978, Part One. Only this initial volume in Foucault's series on sexuality was available when *Dangerous Sexualities* was being written, and I again focus on it here.

5 For some of the most significant work in this debate see among very many: Hayden White, *Tropics of Discourse: Essays in Cultural Criticism*, Baltimore and London, Johns Hopkins University Press, 1978, and *The Content of Form: Narrative Discourse and Historical Representation*, Baltimore and London, Johns Hopkins University Press, 1987; Gareth Stedman Jones, *Languages of Class: Studies in English Working Class History, 1832–1982*, Cambridge, Cambridge University Press, 1983; Roland Barthes, *The Rustle of Language*, trans. Richard Howard, Oxford, Blackwell, 1986; Mark Cousins, 'The Practice of Historical Investigation', in Derek Attridge, Geoff Bennington and Robert Young (eds), *Post-Structuralism and the Question of History*, Cambridge, Cambridge University Press, 1987, pp. 126–36; Patrick Joyce, 'History and Post-Modernism', *Past and Present*, 1991, no. 131, pp. 204–9; Raphael Samuel, 'Reading the Signs', *History Workshop Journal*, 1991, no. 32, pp. 88–109, and 'Reading the Signs: Part II', *History Workshop Journal*, 1992, no. 33, pp. 220–51; Joan Scott, 'The Evidence of Experience', *Critical Inquiry*, 1991, vol.17, no. 4, pp. 773–97; Anthony Easthope, 'Post-Modernism and the Historians: Romancing the Stone', *Social History*, 1993, vol. 18, no. 2, pp. 235–49; James Vernon, 'Who's Afraid of the "Linguistic Turn"? The Politics of Social History and Its Discontents', *Social History*, 1994, vol. 19, no. 1, pp. 81–97. For opposition to the intrusion of linguistics and post-modernism into history see: Geoffrey Elton, *Return to Essentials: Some Reflections on the Present State of Historical Study*, Cambridge, Cambridge University Press, 1991; Lawrence Stone, 'History and Post-Modernism', *Past and Present*, 1991, no. 131, pp. 217–18; Gertrude Himmelfarb, 'Telling It As You Like: Post-Modernist History and the Flight from Fact', *The Times Literary Supplement*, 16 October 1992, pp. 12–15.

6 Mary McIntosh, 'The Homosexual Role', *Social Problems*, 1968, vol. 16, no. 2, pp. 182–92; John Gagnon and William Simon, *Sexual Conduct: The Social Sources of Human Sexuality*, London, Hutchinson, 1974; Kenneth Plummer, *Sexual Stigma: An Interactionist Account*, London, Routledge & Kegan Paul, 1975.

7 For the interrogation of the social from a perspective influenced by Foucault see: Jacques Donzelot, *The Policing of Families*, trans. Robert Hurley, New York, Pantheon Books, 1979, and his 'The Mobilization of Society', in Graham

Burchell, Colin Gordon and Peter Miller (eds), *The Foucault Effect: Studies in Governmentality with Two Lectures by and an Interview with Michel Foucault*, London, Harvester Wheatsheaf, 1991, pp. 169–79. For the implications for social history see: David Mayfield and Susan Thorne, 'Social History and Its Discontents: Gareth Stedman Jones and the Politics of Language', *Social History*, 1992, vol. 17, no. 1, pp. 165–88; Patrick Joyce, 'The End of Social History?', *Social History*, 1995, vol. 20, no. 1, pp. 73–91. For other interrogations of the social see: Jean Baudrillard, *In the Shadow of the Silent Majorities, or, the End of the Social*, New York, Semiotext(E), 1983; Cornelius Castoriadis, *The Imaginary Institution of Society*, trans. Kathleen Blamey, Cambridge, Polity Press, 1987.

8 Foucault, *The History of Sexuality*, vol. 1, pp. 36–49.

9 For historical work on visual and literary cultures which is influenced by Foucault see: Lynda Nead, *Myths of Sexuality: Representations of Women in Victorian Britain*, Oxford, Blackwell, 1988, and her *The Female Nude: Art, Obscenity, and Sexuality*, London and New York, Routledge, 1992; Ludmilla Jordanova (ed.), *Languages of Nature: Critical Essays on Science and Literature*, London, Free Association Books, 1986, and her *Sexual Visions: Images of Gender in Science and Medicine Between the Eighteenth and Twentieth Centuries*, London and New York, Harvester Wheatsheaf, 1989.

10 There has been a recent expansion of interest in the cultural dimensions of modern consumer societies and their implications for sexuality. See for example: Rachel Bowlby, *Just Looking: Consumer Culture in Dreiser, Gissing and Zola*, London and New York, Methuen, 1985; Elizabeth Wilson, *Adorned in Dreams: Fashion and Modernity*, Berkeley, University of California Press, 1987; Nicholas Green, *The Spectacle of Nature: Landscape and Bourgeois Culture in Nineteenth-Century France*, Manchester, Manchester University Press, 1990; Frank Mort, *Cultures of Consumption: Masculinities and Social Space in Late Twentieth-Century Britain*, London, Routledge, 1996; Sean Nixon, *Hard Looks: Masculinities, Spectatorship and Contemporary Consumption*, London, UCL Press, 1996; Erica Carter, *How German Is She? Postwar West German Reconstruction and the Consuming Woman*, Ann Arbor, University of Michigan Press, 1997; Mica Nava, 'The Cosmopolitanism of Commerce and the Allure of Difference: Selfridges, the Russian Ballet and the Tango 1911–1914', *International Journal of Cultural Studies*, 1998, vol. 1, no. 2, pp. 163–96; Christopher Breward, *The Hidden Consumer*, Manchester, Manchester University Press, 1999.

11 For feminist critiques of Foucault see: Irene Diamond and Lee Quinby (eds), *Feminism & Foucault: Reflections on Resistance*, Boston, Northeastern University Press, 1988; Jana Sawicki, *Disciplining Foucault: Feminism, Power, and the Body*, London and New York, Routledge, 1991; Caroline Ramazanoğlu (ed.), *Up Against Foucault: Explorations of Some Tensions Between Foucault and Feminism*, London and New York, Routledge, 1993; Lois McNay, *Foucault: A Critical Introduction*, New York, The Continuum Publishing Co, 1994.

12 Much of this debate can be traced back to the impact of Althusserian marxism on the British New Left. See: Louis Althusser, *For Marx*, trans. Ben Brewster, Harmondsworth, Penguin, 1969, and *Lenin and Philosophy, and Other Essays*, trans. Ben Brewster, London, New Left Books, 1971; Edward Thompson, *The Poverty of Theory, and Other Essays*, London, Merlin Press, 1978: Richard Johnson, 'Thompson, Genovese, and Socialist-Humanist History', *History Workshop Journal*, 1978, no. 6, pp. 79–100; 'Debates Around *The Poverty of Theory*', in Raphael Samuel (ed.), *People's History and Socialist Theory*,

London, Routledge & Kegan Paul, 1981, pp. 375–408; Richard Johnson, Gregor McLennan, Bill Schwarz and David Sutton (eds), *Making Histories: Studies in History-Writing and Politics*, London, Hutchinson in association with the Centre for Contemporary Cultural Studies, 1982.

13 Stedman Jones, *Languages of Class*; Patrick Joyce, *Visions of the People: Industrial England and the Question of Class 1848–1914*, Cambridge, Cambridge University Press, 1991; James Vernon, *Politics and the People: A Study in English Political Culture, c. 1815–1867*, Cambridge, Cambridge University Press, 1993; Joan Scott, *Gender and the Politics of History*, New York, Columbia University Press, 1988; Joan Scott and Judith Butler (eds), *Feminists Theorize the Political*, London and New York, Routledge, 1992; Joan Scott (ed.), *Feminism and History*, Oxford and New York, Oxford University Press, 1996.

14 Mary Poovey, *Uneven Developments: The Ideological Work of Gender in Mid-Victorian England*, London, Virago, 1988, p. 20.

15 See especially: Leonore Davidoff and Catherine Hall, *Family Fortunes: Men and Women of the English Middle Class*, London, Hutchinson, 1987; Janet Woolf and John Seed (eds), *The Culture of Capital: Art, Power and the Nineteenth-Century Middle Class*, Manchester, Manchester University Press, 1988; Catherine Hall, *White, Male and Middle Class: Explorations in Feminism and History*, Cambridge, Polity, 1992; Robert Gray, *The Factory Question and Industrial England, 1830–1860*, Cambridge, Cambridge University Press, 1996.

16 Judith Walkowitz, *City of Dreadful Delight: Narratives of Sexual Danger in Late-Victorian London*, London, Virago, 1992, p. 9. Walkowitz is quoting from Gabrielle Spiegel, 'History, Historicism, and the Social Logic of the Text', *Speculum*, 1990, vol. 65, no. 1, pp. 59–86.

17 Patrick Joyce, *Democratic Subjects: The Self and the Social in Nineteenth Century England*, Cambridge, Cambridge University Press, 1994, p. 14.

18 For the use of psychoanalytic concepts in historical analyses of gender see for example: Sally Alexander, *Becoming a Woman, and Other Essays in 19th and 20th Century Feminist History*, London, Virago, 1994; Lyndal Roper, *Oedipus and the Devil: Witchcraft, Sexuality and Religion in Early Modern Europe*, London, Routledge, 1994; Michael Roper, *Masculinity and the British Organization Man Since 1945*, Oxford, Oxford University Press, 1994. For accounts which draw on literary devices see: Carolyn Steedman, *Childhood, Culture and Class in Britain, Margaret McMillan, 1860–1931*, London, Virago, 1990; Walkowitz, *City of Dreadful Delight*.

19 Leonore Davidoff, *Worlds Between: Historical Perspectives on Gender and Class*, Cambridge, Polity, 1995, p. 114. Davidoff is quoting here from Mary Douglas, *Implicit Meanings: Essays in Anthropology*, London, Routledge & Kegan Paul, 1975, p. 61.

20 See especially: Liz Stanley (ed.), *The Diaries of Hannah Cullwick*, London, Virago, 1984; Anne McClintock, *Imperial Leather: Race, Gender and Sexuality in the Colonial Contest*, London and New York, Routledge, 1995, chapters 2 and 3. See also Derek Hudson, *Munby: Man of Two Worlds: The Life and Diaries of Arthur J. Munby 1828–1910*, London, Abacus, 1974.

21 For studies of the Men and Women's Club see: Walkowitz, *City of Dreadful Delight*, chapter 5; Lucy Bland, *Banishing the Beast: English Feminism and Sexual Morality 1885–1914*, London, Penguin, 1995, chapter 1; Phyllis Grosskurth, *Havelock Ellis: A Biography*, London, Allen Lane, 1980; Ruth First and Ann Scott, *Olive Schreiner*, New York, Schocken Books, 1980, pp. 144–72; Carol Dyhouse, *Feminism and the Family in England 1880–1939*, Oxford, Blackwell, 1989, pp. 159–66; Ruth Brandon, *The New Women and the Old Men: Love, Sex*

and the Woman Question, London, Secker & Warburg, 1990; Janet Oppenheim, *'Shattered Nerves': Doctors, Patients, and Depression in Victorian England*, New York, Oxford University Press, 1991, pp. 219–22.

22 See especially: Peter Bailey, 'Parasexuality and Glamour: The Victorian Barmaid as Cultural Prototype', *Gender and History*, 1990, vol. 2, no. 2, pp. 148–72, and his 'Champagne Charlie: Performance and Ideology in the Music-Hall Swell Song', in J.S. Bratton (ed.), *Music Hall: Performance and Style*, Milton Keynes, Open University Press, 1986, pp. 49–69. Bailey's collection of essays, *Popular Culture and Performance in the Victorian City*, Cambridge, Cambridge University Press, 1998, contains further studies of these cultural scripts.

23 For the reclamation of the term 'spinster' by early twentieth-century British feminists see: Sheila Jeffreys, *The Spinster and her Enemies: Feminism and Sexuality 1880–1930*, London, Pandora, 1985; Bland, *Banishing the Beast*. For appropriations of the 'invert' and the 'lesbian' see: Lillian Faderman, *Surpassing the Love of Men: Romantic Friendship and Love between Women from the Renaissance to the Present*, London, Women's Press, 1985, and her *Odd Girls and Twilight Lovers*, Harmondsworth, Penguin, 1992.

24 For widely differing interpretations of the queer agenda see: Derek Jarman, *Queer*, Manchester, Manchester City Art Galleries in association with Richard Salmon Ltd, 1992; Pratibha Parmar and Isaac Julien, 'Queer Questions', *Sight and Sound*, September 1992, p. 21; Cherry Smyth, *Lesbians Talk Queer Notions*, London, Scarlet Press, 1992; Martha Gever, Pratibha Parmar and John Greyson (eds), *Queer Looks: Perspectives on Lesbian and Gay Film and Video*, London and New York, Routledge, 1993; Patrick Higgins (ed.), *A Queer Reader*, London, Fourth Estate, 1993; Michelangelo Signorile, *Queer in America: Sex, the Media, and the Closets of Power*, New York, Random House, 1993; Alan Sinfield, *Cultural Politics, Queer Reading*, London, Routledge, 1994; Paul Burston and Colin Richardson (eds), *A Queer Romance: Lesbians, Gay Men, and Popular Culture*, London, Routledge, 1995; Corey Creekmair and Alexander Doty (eds), *Out in Culture: Gay, Lesbian and Queer Essays on Popular Culture*, London, Cassell, 1995; Chris Woods, *State of the Nation: A Critique of Gay and Lesbian Politics in 1990s Britain*, London, Cassell, 1995; Vera Whisman, *Queer By Choice: Lesbians, Gay Men and the Politics of Identity*, London, Routledge, 1995; Simon LeVay, *Queer Science: The Use and Abuse of Research into Homosexuality*, Cambridge, MA, and London, MIT Press, 1996; Steven Seidman (ed.), *Queer Theory/ Sociology*, Cambridge, MA, and Oxford, Blackwell, 1996; Mark Simpson, *It's a Queer World*, London, Vintage, 1996; Martin Duberman (ed.), *Queer Representations: Reading Lives, Reading Cultures: A Center for Lesbian and Gay Studies Book*, New York and London, New York University Press, 1997.

25 Eve Kosofsky Sedgwick, *Epistemology of the Closet*, Berkeley, University of California Press, 1990, p. 1. For other literary accounts which operate within similar frameworks see: Jonathan Dollimore, *Sexual Dissidence: Augustine to Wilde, Freud to Foucault*, Oxford, Oxford University Press, 1991; Joseph Bristow (ed.), *Sexual Sameness: Textual Differences in Lesbian and Gay Writing*, London, Routledge, 1992; Alan Sinfield, *The Wilde Century: Effeminacy, Oscar Wilde and the Queer Moment*, London, Cassell, 1994.

26 Peter Stallybrass and Allon White, *The Politics and Poetics of Transgression*, London, Methuen, 1986.

27 Benedict Anderson, *Imagined Communities: Reflections on the Origin and Spread of Nationalism*, London, Verso, 1983.

28 Andrew Parker, Mary Russo, Doris Sommer and Patricia Yaeger, 'Introduction',

in Andrew Parker *et al.* (eds), *Nationalisms and Sexualities*, New York and London, Routledge, 1992. See also Catherine Hall, Jane Lewis, Keith McClelland and Jane Rendall, 'Introduction', *Gender and History* (special issue on gender, nationalisms and national identities), 1993, vol. 5, no. 2, p. 159–64.

29 George Mosse, *Nationalism and Sexuality: Respectable and Abnormal Sexuality in Modern Europe*, New York, Howard Fertig, 1985, p. 1.

30 Anderson, *Imagined Communities*, p. 16.

31 This point is well made by Etienne Balibar, 'Racism as Universalism', *New Political Science*, 1989, nos 16–17, p. 19. See also Homi Bhabha (ed.), *Nation and Narration*, London, Routledge, 1990.

32 Ann Stoler, *Race and the Education of Desire: Foucault's History of Sexuality and the Colonial Order of Things*, Durham and London, Duke University Press, 1995, chapter IV.

33 ibid., pp. 15–16.

34 Among the classic texts in this tradition are: Henri Lefebvre, *The Production of Space*, trans. D. Nicolson-Smith, Oxford, Blackwell, 1991; Michel de Certeau, *The Practice of Everyday Life*, trans. S. Rendall, Berkeley, University of California Press, 1988; David Harvey, *The Condition of Postmodernity: An Enquiry into the Origins of Cultural Change*, Oxford, Blackwell, 1989.

35 George Chauncey, *Gay New York: The Making of the Gay Male World, 1890–1940*, London, Flamingo, 1995.

36 See for example: Dick Hebdige, *Subculture: The Meaning of Style*, London, Methuen, 1979; Janice Radway, *Reading the Romance: Women, Patriarchy and Popular Literature*, Chapel Hill, University of North Carolina Press, 1984; Rosalind Coward, *Female Desire*, London, Paladin, 1984; David Morley, *Family Television, Cultural Power and Domestic Leisure*, London, Comedia, 1986.

37 For a critique of de Certeau's politics of space see: Kristin Ross, 'Streetwise: The French Invention of Everyday Life', *Parallax*, 1996, no. 2, pp. 67–75; Brian Rigby, *Popular Culture in Modern France*, London, Routledge, 1991.

38 Steen Eiler Rasmussen, *London, the Unique City*, London, Jonathan Cape, 1937.

39 For studies in the sexual and spatial histories of London see the essays in *New Formations: Sexual Geographies*, 1999, no. 37.

INTRODUCTION: NARRATIVES OF SEX

1 Michael Marmoor *et al.*, 'Risk Factors for Kaposi's Sarcoma in Homosexual Men', *Lancet*, 15 May 1982, vol. 1, pp. 1083–6.

2 Michael Gottlieb *et al.*, '*Pneumocystis Carinii* Pneumonia and Mucosal Candidiasis in Previously Healthy Homosexual Men: Evidence of a New Acquired Cellular Immunodeficiency', *New England Journal of Medicine*, 10 December 1981, vol. 305, no. 24, pp. 1425–31.

3 Commonsense, pre-given assumptions about the meaning of sexuality are a recurrent problem in social histories of the family, sex and marriage. See especially: Edward Shorter, *The Making of the Modern Family*, London, Fontana, 1977, and Lawrence Stone, *The Family, Sex and Marriage in England, 1500–1800*, London, Weidenfeld & Nicolson, 1977, where sex is assumed to be a basically physiological phenomenon overlaid by changing historical meanings.

4 The Oxbridge school of official or administrative history has been particularly important here. Influenced by post-war debates about the origins of welfarism, the classic texts focus on the early nineteenth century as the period witnessing the growth of modern government. See especially: Samuel Finer, *The Life and Times of Sir Edwin Chadwick*, London, Methuen, 1952; Oliver MacDonagh, 'The

Nineteenth-Century Revolution in Government: A Reappraisal', *The Historical Journal*, 1958, vol. 1, no. 1, pp. 52–67; Royston Lambert, *Sir John Simon, 1816–1904, and English Social Administration*, London, MacGibbon & Kee, 1963. Differences of interpretation centre on the understanding of factors influencing transformations within government institutions. 'Tory' accounts such as Mac-Donagh's stress the pragmatic nature of state formation, with its often accidental character and effects. Finer's 'Fabian' reading foregrounds the role of Benthamite planning. Both place differing but heavy emphasis on the role of individual experts and civil servants.

5 Social histories which have been particularly influential here include: Richard Johnson, 'Educating the Educators: "Experts" and the State 1833–1839', in A. P. Donajgrodski (ed.), *Social Control in Nineteenth Century Britain*, London, Croom Helm, 1977, pp. 77–107; Michael Ignatieff, *A Just Measure of Pain: The Penitentiary in the Industrial Revolution, 1750–1850*, London, Macmillan, 1978; P. Richards, 'State Formation and Class Struggle, 1832–48', in Philip Corrigan (ed.), *Capitalism, State Formation and Marxist Theory: Historical Investigations*, London, Quartet, 1980, pp. 49–78; Gareth Stedman Jones, *Outcast London: A Study in the Relationship Between Classes in Victorian Society*, Harmondsworth, Penguin, 1984.

6 Michel Foucault, *Madness and Civilization: A History of Insanity in the Age of Reason*, trans. Richard Howard, London, Tavistock, 1971; *The Birth of the Clinic: An Archaeology of Medical Perception*, trans. A. M. Sheridan Smith, London, Tavistock, 1973; *Discipline and Punish: The Birth of the Prison*, trans. Alan Sheridan Smith, London, Allen Lane, 1977; *The History of Sexuality*, vol. 1, *An Introduction*, trans. Robert Hurley, New York, Pantheon Books, 1978.

7 For extended discussion of these polarised positions within cultural history and cultural theory see: Richard Johnson, 'Histories of Culture/Theories of Ideology: Notes on an Impasse', in Michèle Barrett, Philip Corrigan, Annette Kuhn and Janet Wolff (eds), *Ideology and Cultural Production*, 1979, pp. 49–77.

PART ONE MORAL ENVIRONMENTALISM 1830–1860

1 Lords of HM Privy Council, Papers Relating to the Disease called Cholera Spasmodica in India now Prevailing in the North of Europe, 1831, PRO PC1/105. For general accounts of nineteenth-century cholera epidemics see: Margaret Pelling, *Cholera, Fever and English Medicine, 1825–1865*, Oxford, Oxford University Press, 1978; Norman Longmate, *King Cholera: The Biography of a Disease*, London, Hamish Hamilton, 1966. For a detailed account of the 1832 outbreak, attentive to the class-articulated ideology of early social medicine, see R.J. Morris, *Cholera 1832: The Social Response to an Epidemic*, London, Croom Helm, 1976.

2 For the impact of cholera in the north east see Longmate, *King Cholera*, pp. 20–49.

3 King's speech, Lords, *Hansard's Parliamentary Debates*, 21 June 1831, third series, vol. 4, col. 86.

4 Quoted in Longmate, *King Cholera*, p. 15.

5 Central Board of Health, Daily Report of Cholera Cases from Central Board of Health, Council Office, Whitehall. London and Vicinity, 19 April 1832, PRO PC1/4395, Part I.

6 John Marshall to Central Board of Health, 19 July 1831, Minutes of the Central Board of Health, 21 June–17 October 1831, PRO PC1/101.

7 Dr Robert Dawn to Doctor Mahony, undated, Mahony's original letter dated 11 August 1831, Minutes of the Central Board of Health.

8 Mahony to Central Board of Health, 12 August 1831, Minutes of the Central Board of Health.

9 Sir Gilbert Blane to Central Board of Health, 30 September 1831, Minutes of the Central Board of Health.

10 An Extract from the Proceedings of the Central Board of Health, 10 December 1831, case no. 3, PRO PC1/2662.

11 Mayor of York to Lord Melbourne, January 1832, *Copies of Certain Papers Relating to Cholera Together with the Report of the Central Board of Health Thereupon*, 1832, GBPP 1831–32, XXVI, p. 479. See also complaints by Dr W. Haslewood to Central Board of Health, 1 November 1831, Daily Report of Cholera Cases from Central Board of Health, PRO PC1/4395, Part II.

12 'Spasmodica Cholera', *Westminster Review*, 15 October 1831, vol. XV, pp. 485–6.

13 Board of Health, Sunderland, to Central Board of Health, 1 November 1831, Daily Report of Cholera Cases, PRO PC1/4395.

14 *Cholera Gazette*, 28 January 1832, preserved in An Extract from the Proceedings of the Central Board of Health, PRO PC1/2662.

15 'History of the Apothecaries', *Lancet*, 11 December 1830, vol. 1, p. 370.

16 'The Board of Health', *Lancet*, 2 July 1831, vol. 2, pp. 433–4. The new board did draft extensive recommendations for dealing with the epidemic, involving the creation of local boards with at least one medical representative. Almost immediately the *Lancet* intervened again, arguing that medics were being deliberately marginalised at a time of national emergency: 'Conduct of the Board of Health', *Lancet*, 24 September 1831, vol. 2, p. 820.

17 Mr Hubbard, Chairman of the Durham Board of Health, to Central Board of Health, 15 November 1831, Minutes of the Central Board of Health 1831–1832, PRO PC1/105. See also Mr Spooner of Birmingham to the Privy Council, letter not preserved. For the reply to Spooner's request see Charles Grenville to Spooner, 19 November 1831, warning that the Privy Council had no legal authority to sanction use of the parish rate, Daily Report of Cholera Cases, PRO PC1/4395, Part II.

18 T. Spring-Rice to Central Board of Health, 14 November 1831, Minutes of the Central Board of Health 1831–2.

19 Central Board of Health to Dr Walker, 15 August 1833, PRO PC1/96.

20 Frank Smith, *The Life and Times of Sir James Kay-Shuttleworth*, London, John Murray, 1923. See also Barry Bloomfield (ed.), *The Autobiography of Sir James Kay-Shuttleworth*, Education Libraries Bulletin, supplement 7, 1964. The text is from Kay's own autobiographical manuscript of 1877. For a more sophisticated study of Kay as the agent of early educational professionalism see Richard Johnson, 'Educational Policy and Social Control in Early Victorian England', *Past and Present*, 1970, no. 49, pp. 96–119.

21 Bloomfield, *The Autobiography*, p. 5.

22 ibid.

23 ibid., p. 17.

24 See Thomas Chalmers, *The Christian and Civic Economy of Large Towns*, Glasgow, William Collins, 1821–6, 3 vols.

25 Bloomfield, *The Autobiography*, p. 12.

26 James Kay, *The Moral and Physical Condition of the Working Classes Employed in the Cotton Manufacture in Manchester*, London, James Ridgway, 1832, p. 8. There are two editions of the pamphlet which differ significantly. The second edition is used here.

27 ibid., p. 62.

28 See Michael Ignatieff, *A Just Measure of Pain: The Penitentiary in the Industrial Revolution, 1750–1850*, London, Macmillan, 1978, p. 45.

29 Many recent historians, from widely differing intellectual traditions, have stressed the complex technologies of eighteenth-century punishment and incarceration. See especially: Michel Foucault, *Discipline and Punish: The Birth of the Prison*, trans. Alan Sheridan Smith, London, Allen Lane, 1977; Douglas Hay *et al.* (eds), *Albion's Fatal Tree: Crime and Society in Eighteenth-Century England*, Harmondsworth, Penguin, 1977; Ignatieff, *A Just Measure of Pain*.

30 Daniel Layard, *Directions to Prevent the Contagion of the Jail-Distemper, Commonly Called Jail Fever*, London, James Robson, 1772, p. 5.

31 Layard, *Directions*, p. 6.

32 ibid., p. 8.

33 David Hartley, *Observations on Man, his Frame, his Duty and his Expectations*, London, James Leake and William Frederick, 1749.

34 Ignatieff, *A Just Measure of Pain*, p. 60. Ignatieff's understanding of eighteenth-century social medicine is generally complex, but there are points where he falls back into a more conspiratorial explanation of medical ideology.

35 'Dr Lettsom's Third Letter on Prisons', *Gentleman's Magazine*, February 1804, vol. 74, pp. 99–101.

36 Thomas Percival, *Medical Ethics, or a Code of Institutes and Precepts Adapted to the Professional Conduct of Physicians and Surgeons*, Manchester, J. Johnson, 1803, p. 24. See also Jonathan Wathen, *Practical Observations Concerning the Cure of Venereal Disease by Mercurials*, London, J. Rivington, 1765.

37 Circular Letter of Instruction to the Assistant Poor Law Commissioners in England, *Report from the Poor Law Commissioners into the Sanitary Condition of the Labouring Population of Great Britain*, 1842, HL 1842, XXVI, p. xii. See also Instructions from the Central Board of the Children's Employment Commission to the Subcommissioners, Children's Employment Commission, *First Report of the Commissioners. Mines*, 1842, GBPP 1842, XV, pp. 275–81.

38 Children's Employment Commission, *First Report of the Commissioners. Mines*, p. 3.

39 See: M. Jeanne Peterson, *The Medical Profession in Mid-Victorian England*, Berkeley, University of California Press, 1978; I. Inkster, 'Marginal Men: Aspects of the Social Role of the Medical Community in Sheffield 1790–1850', in John Woodward and David Richards (eds), *Health Care and Popular Medicine in Nineteenth Century England: Essays in the Social History of Medicine*, London, Croom Helm, 1977, pp. 128–63; Ruth Hodgkinson, *The Medical Services of the New Poor Law 1834–71*, unpublished Ph.D. dissertation, London University, 1950, 2 vols.

40 As late as 1869 the *BMJ* still felt it necessary to warn medics that gentlemanly codes of conduct were essential for professional success: 'Memoranda for Students', *BMJ*, 11 September 1869, vol. 2, p. 286. Elizabeth Gaskell's *Wives and Daughters*, published in 1866 but looking back to the early nineteenth century, contained an ironic commentary on the ambiguous status of medics and their wives. George Eliot's study of the doctor Lydgate and his wife Rosamund in *Middlemarch*, 1871, was also acute on medical ambition.

41 See: Noel Humphreys (ed.), *Vital Statistics: A Memorial Volume of Selections from the Reports and Writings of William Farr*, London, Sanitary Institute, 1885; Samuel Squire Sprigge, *The Life and Times of Thomas Wakley MD*, London, Longman, 1897.

42 The new association was established in 1832 to provide a national organisation

for provincial doctors, with a journal and regular meetings. Reform of entrance to the profession was taken up by Wakley, who had founded the *Lancet* in 1823. As MP for Finsbury after 1835 he acted as the coordinator for radical medics. A parliamentary select committee, appointed in 1834 to examine the state of medical education, recommended sweeping reforms, but these were systematically blocked until the 1850s. See: Sprigge, *The Life and Times of Thomas Wakley*, pp. 227–34; Paul Vaughan, *Doctor's Commons: A Short History of the British Medical Association*, London, Heinemann, 1959, pp. 13–14.

43 'Government Cholera Commission', *Lancet*, 22 October 1853, vol. 2, p. 393.

44 See Royston Lambert, *Sir John Simon, 1816–1904, and English Social Administration*, London, Macgibbon & Kee, 1963, pp. 48–9. Lambert understands the early dominance of miasma in terms of the internal dynamics of social medicine and its inter-professional rivalries. Wider social and political influences on the formation of medical knowledge are generally ignored.

45 Thomas Southwood Smith, *Treatise on Fever*, London, Longman, 1830, p. 324.

46 Kay, *The Moral and Physical Condition*, p. 5. See also Henry Gaulter, *The Origin and Progress of the Malignant Cholera in Manchester, Considered Chiefly in Their Bearing on Contagiousness and the Secondary Causes of the Disease*, London, Longman, 1833, p. 127.

47 John Liddle, *On the Moral and Physical Evils Resulting from the Neglect of Sanitary Measures. A Lecture*, London, Health of Towns Association, 1847, pp. 5, 27.

48 *Evangelical Magazine and Missionary Chronicle*, 1832, new series, vol. 10, p. 22.

49 Charles Girdlestone, *Seven Sermons Preached During the Prevalence of Cholera in the Parish of Sedgley*, London, J.G. & F. Rivington, 1833, p. 2. See also: Girdlestone's *Farewell Sermons: Preached in the Parish Church of Sedgley*, London, J.G. & F. Rivington, 1837, p. 55; Edward Miller, *Counsel to the Young. The Substance of a Sermon Preached at Putney Chapel*, London, Roake and Varty, 1833, p. 6.

50 Charles Girdlestone, *Letters on the Unhealthy Condition of the Lower Class of Dwellings Especially in Large Towns. Founded on the First Report of the Health of Towns Commission*, London, Longman, 1845, p. vii.

51 See Inkster, 'Marginal Men', p.128.

52 William Cooke, *Mind and the Emotions Considered in Relation to Health and Disease*, London, Longman & Co, 1839, pp. 37–8.

53 Henry Brougham, *Paley's Natural Theology with Illustrative Notes*, London, Charles Knight, 1826, pp. 8–9. See also Brougham's *A Discourse of the Objects, Advantages and Pleasures of Science*, London, Society for the Diffusion of Useful Knowledge, 1827, pp. 6, 47. A number of leading scientists saw their work as intimately linked to their religious faith. Michael Faraday was a devout Sandemanian (a small sect believing that ultimately God was only knowable through faith), who stressed that scientific discoveries allowed man better understanding of the divine plan. See Rollo Appleyard, *A Tribute to Michael Faraday*, London, Constable and Co, 1931, pp. 74–5.

54 See Thomas Heyck, *The Transformation of Intellectual Life in Victorian England*, London, Croom Helm, 1982, p. 56.

55 *Congregational Magazine*, 1832, vol. 15, p. 72.

56 Health of Towns Association, *Address from the Committee of the Health of Towns Association to the Bishop of London and the Rev. the Clergy*, London, Richard Barrett, 1848, p. 32.

57 Edward Tilt, *The Serpentine 'As it is' and 'As it ought to be'. And the Board of Health 'As it is' and 'As it ought to be'*, London, John Churchill, 1848, p. 32. Tilt was physician to the Farringdon General Dispensary and Lying-In Charity.

58 For attacks on the General Board of Health see: Joshua Toulmin Smith, *Centralization or Representation? A Letter to the Metropolitan Sanatory Commissioners*, London, S. Sweet, 1848; T. Hawksley, *A Letter to the Most Hon. The Marquis of Chandos M.P. in Relation to the Extraordinary Powers Assumed by the General Board of Health*, London, Saunders and Stanford, 1853. The board could only initiate public health measures in areas where the death rate had reached twenty three per thousand, elsewhere it had to await a petition signed by local ratepayers. Local authority jurisdiction covered drainage, water-supply and paving, supervised by the Central Board through circulars and a superintending inspectorate, Public Health Act, 11 and 12 Vict., ch. 63.

59 Lord Ashley, 26 September 1848, Shaftesbury Broadlands Manuscript, National Register of Archives, London SHA/PD/5.

60 Chadwick to Ashley, 25 September 1848, Chadwick Manuscript, The Library, University College, London.

61 Ashley to the Duchess of Beaufort, November 1849, Shaftesbury Broadlands Manuscript, SHA/PC/18/1.

62 Ashley to Chadwick, 29 October 1849, Chadwick Manuscript.

63 These differences are discussed in Michael Cullen, *The Statistical Movement in Early Victorian Britain: The Foundations of Empirical Social Research*, Hassocks, Harvester, 1975, p. 62.

64 Kay, *The Moral and Physical Condition*, pp. 63–4.

65 See *Report into the Sanitary Condition of the Labouring Population*, pp. 233–78.

66 Kay, *The Moral and Physical Condition*, p. 15. See also Richard Johnson, 'Educating the Educators: "Experts" and the State 1833–1839', in A.P. Donajgrodski (ed.), *Social Control in Nineteenth Century Britain*, London, Croom Helm, 1977, pp. 77–107.

67 Lord Ashley, *Moral and Religious Education of the Working Classes. The Speech of Lord Ashley M.P. in the House of Commons*, London, John Ollivier, 1843, pp. 10–11.

68 Evidence of Dr Gilly, Canon of Durham, *Report into the Sanitary Condition of the Labouring Population*, p. 124.

69 Evidence of Mr Ridall Wood, ibid., p. 125.

70 See evidence of Mr Baker, Assistant Commissioner for Leeds, ibid., p. 126. For discussion of incest within the working-class family see Anthony Wohl, 'Sex and the Single Room: Incest Among the Victorian Working Classes', in Wohl (ed.), *The Victorian Family: Structures and Stresses*, London, Croom Helm, 1978, pp. 197–216.

71 *Report into the Sanitary Condition of the Labouring Population*, p. 127. For analysis of the sexual dimensions of sanitary reform see: Anthony Wohl, 'Unfit for Human Habitation', in Harold Dyos and Michael Woolf (eds), *The Victorian City: Images and Realities*, London, Routledge & Kegan Paul, 1973, vol. 2, pp. 607–24; Frank Mort, 'The Domain of the Sexual', *Screen Education*, 1980, no. 36, pp. 69–84.

72 Evidence of Dr Scott Alison of Tranent, *Report into the Sanitary Condition of the Labouring Population*, p. 142.

73 Girdlestone, *Farewell Sermons*, p. 55. For feminist appropriations of evangelical discourse see Barbara Taylor, *Eve and the New Jerusalem: Socialism and Feminism in the Nineteenth Century*, London, Virago, 1983. Charlotte Brontë's *Jane Eyre*, 1847, not only contains a lengthy debate on evangelical morality, via the character of St John Rivers, but also employs evangelical language to convey women's sexual and emotional experience.

74 Girdlestone, *Farewell Sermons*, pp. 138–9.
75 Health of Towns Association, *Address*, p. 6.
76 Michel Foucault, *The History of Sexuality*, vol. 1, *An Introduction*, trans. Robert Hurley, New York, Pantheon Books, 1978, pp. 120–7.
77 Kay, *The Moral and Physical Condition*, pp. 7–8.
78 Anon., *Twenty Minutes Advice on Diet, Regimen and All Other Matters Connected with Health*, undated, pp. 8–9.
79 James Smyth, 'Miscellaneous Contributions to the Pathology and Therapeutics of Impotence and Sterility', *Lancet*, 28 August 1841, vol. 2, p. 779.
80 Anon., *Tabes Dorsalis or, the Causes of Consumption in Young Men and Women*, London, J. Bailey, 1832, p. 8.
81 ibid., p. 31.
82 Anon., *Twenty Minutes Advice*, p. 34.
83 Cooke, *Mind and the Emotions*, p. 5.
84 Michael Ryan, *The Philosophy of Marriage, in its Social, Moral and Physical Relations; with an Account of the Diseases of the Genito-Urinary Organs*, London, John Churchill, 1837. See also William Cooke, *An Address to British Females on the Moral Management of Pregnancy and Labour*, London, E. Cox and Co, 1817.
85 H. Macrosty and J. Bonar, *Annals of the Royal Statistical Society 1834–1934*, London, Royal Statistical Society, 1934, pp. 52–5. See also: Cullen, *The Statistical Movement*, pp. 77–133; Thomas Ashton, *Economic and Social Investigations in Manchester, 1833–1933: A Centenary History of the Manchester Statistical Society*, Hassocks, Harvester, 1977.
86 J. Roberton, *The Relative Proportion of the Male and Female Population*, Report of the Manchester Statistical Society, session 1839–40. See also Roberton, *On the Alleged Influence of Climate on Female Puberty in Greece*, session 1843–4. Both cited in Ashton, *Economic and Social Investigations*, Appendix C.
87 The Act established a system of local and superintendent registrars, though the local administrative structure was based initially on the poor law. Registrars were to make quarterly returns on the number of births, deaths and marriages to the Registrar-General, who was responsible for the compilation of an annual population abstract to be laid before Parliament. See John MacCulloch, *A Statistical Account of the British Empire*, London, Charles Knight and Co, 1839, vol. 1, pp. 407–12.
88 William Farr, 'Lecture Introductory to a Course on Hygiene', *Lancet*, 14 November 1835, vol. 1, p. 241. See also Farr's 'Lecture on the History of Hygiene', *Lancet*, 13 February 1836, vol. 1, pp. 773–80.
89 William Farr, Letter to the Registrar-General, *Appendix to the Fourth Annual Report of the Registrar-General of Births, Deaths and Marriages*, 1842, GBPP 1842, XIX, p. 525.
90 *Appendix to the Fifth Annual Report of the Registrar-General of Births, Deaths and Marriages*, 1843, GBPP 1843, XXI, pp. 574–5.
91 Parliamentary divorces, introduced in the 1660s, had always been concerned with the correct transmission of aristocratic inheritance in the male line. The extension of divorce facilities to the middle class via the recommendations of the *Report of the Commissioners on the Law of Divorce, and on the Mode of Obtaining Divorces à Vinculo Matrimonii*, 1853, GBPP 1852–3, XL, and the Divorce and Matrimonial Causes Act, 1857, 20 and 21 Vict., ch. 85, preserved that concern with property transmission. The 1857 Act emphasised that one of the principal reasons for divorce by the husband was the danger of an adulterous

wife palming spurious offspring on to the husband. The *Report of the Royal Commission on the Laws of Marriage*, 1868, GBPP 1867–8, XXXII, addressed itself to working-class immorality, recommending a tightening of the regulations governing the solemnisation and registration of marriage to promote sound moral principles among the poor. See: Oliver MacGregor, *Divorce in England: A Centenary Study*, London, Heinmann, 1957; Rachel Harrison and Frank Mort, 'Patriarchal Aspects of Nineteenth Century State Formation: Property Relations, Marriage and Divorce, and Sexuality', in Philip Corrigan (ed.), *Capitalism, State Formation and Marxist Theory: Historical Investigations*, London, Quartet, 1980, pp. 79–109.

92 Foucault, *The History of Sexuality*, pp. 122–7.

93 Evidence of Mr George Armitage, Children's Employment Commission, *First Report. Mines*, GBPP 1842, XV, p. 43. See also the evidence of John Cawthra, p. 44. For a study of women in the mining industry see Angela John, *By The Sweat of their Brow: Women Workers at Victorian Coal Mines*, London, Routledge & Kegan Paul, 1984.

94 Children's Employment Commission, *First Report. Mines*, p. 268.

95 Autobiographical Memoirs by Chadwick, Papers of Sir Edwin Chadwick, Personal and Family Papers, The Library, University College, London.

96 ibid.

97 Report by Jelinger Symons, Yorkshire Coalfield, Children's Employment Commission, *First Report. Mines*, GBPP 1842, XVI, p. 189. Symons' evidence is discussed by Jane Humphries in 'Protective Legislation, the Capitalist State and Working Class Men: The Case of the 1842 Mines Regulation Act', *Feminist Review*, 1981, no. 7, pp. 1–33.

98 Children's Employment Commission, *First Report. Mines*, GBPP 1842, XVI, p. 189.

99 ibid.

100 ibid.

101 Evidence of Edward Newman, Children's Employment Commission, *First Report. Mines*, GBPP 1842, XVI, p. 258.

102 Instructions to Subcommissioners, Children's Employment Commission, *First Report. Mines*, GBPP 1842, XV, p. 278.

103 Evidence of J. Leifchild, Children's Employment Commission, *First Report. Mines*, GBPP 1842, XVI, pp. 747–8.

104 Girdlestone, *Farewell Sermons*, p. 54.

105 Samuel Finer, *The Life and Times of Sir Edwin Chadwick*, London, Methuen, 1952, p. 5.

106 ibid., p. 4. All of the standard biographies of these civil servants reproduce traditional distinctions between the public and the private spheres, refusing to examine the interrelationship between the two domains.

107 See John Simon, *Personal Recollections*, London, Spottiswoode, 1894, p. 13. See also Lambert, *Sir John Simon*, pp. 27–9, 485–7.

108 Before and after the marriage Jane Simon mixed freely in artistic and scientific circles and later became a close friend of John Ruskin. See Lambert, *Sir John Simon*, pp. 27–9, 489–90.

109 James Kay-Shuttleworth to Lady Janet Kay-Shuttleworth, Stockbridge, 9 February 1851, Kay-Shuttleworth Papers, John Ryelands University Library, Manchester.

110 Lady Kay-Shuttleworth, Capesthorne, 7 December 1841, Kay-Shuttleworth Papers.

111 James Kay-Shuttleworth to his children, Fleetwood, 28 April 1858,

Kay-Shuttleworth Papers. A number of the Kay-Shuttleworth papers remain closed, especially those relating to the couple's estrangement. See Barry Bloomfield, *A Handlist of Papers in the Deed Box of Sir J.P. Kay-Shuttleworth*, College of St Mark and St John, occasional paper no. 2, Manchester, Manchester University Library, 1961.

112 See Catherine Hall, 'The Early Formation of Victorian Domestic Ideology', in Sandra Burman (ed.), *Fit Work for Women*, Oxford, Croom Helm, 1979, pp. 15–32.

113 For a study of the role of women in philanthropic charities see: Frank Prochaska, *Women and Philanthropy in Nineteenth-Century England*, Oxford, Clarendon Press, 1980; Anne Summers, 'A Home from Home: Women's Philanthropic Work in the Nineteenth Century', in Burman (ed.), *Fit Work for Women*, pp. 33–63; John Pringle, *Social Work of the London Churches. Being Some Account of the Metropolitan Visiting and Relief Association 1843–1937*, London, Oxford University Press, 1937, pp. 116–208.

114 Farr, *Appendix to the Fifth Annual Report of the Registrar-General*, p. 575.

115 Edward Sieveking, 'On Dispensaries and Allied Institutions', in F.D. Maurice (ed.), *Lectures to Ladies, On Practical Subjects*, Cambridge, Macmillan, 1855, p. 92.

116 ibid., p. 106.

117 F.D. Maurice, 'The College and the Hospital', in Maurice (ed.), *Lectures to Ladies*, p. 47.

118 ibid., p. 13.

119 ibid.

120 Judith Walkowitz notes how many of the leaders of the Ladies' National Association had a history of involvement in charity and philanthropic work: *Prostitution and Victorian Society: Women, Class and the State*, Cambridge, Cambridge University Press, 1980, pp. 126–7.

121 See: Elspeth Platt, *The Story of the Ranyard Mission 1857–1937*, London, Hodder and Stoughton, 1937; Kathleen Heasman, *Evangelicals in Action: An Appraisal of Their Social Work in the Victorian Era*, London, Geoffrey Bles, 1962, p. 36. For Ranyard's own account of her work see *London and Ten Years Work in It*, London, James Nisbet and Co, 1868. The St Giles' Rookery in Holborn was an early target for sanitary clearance schemes, under the direction of the local medical officer of health.

122 Ellen Ranyard, *Life Work; or, the Link and the Rivet*, London, James Nisbet and Co, 1861, p. 158.

123 ibid., p. 9.

124 ibid., p. 269.

125 Ranyard, *London*, p. 7. Ranyard's journal of the London Bible and Domestic Mission was aptly called *The Missing Link*.

126 Ranyard, *Life Work*, p. 40.

127 ibid., p. 141.

128 ibid., pp. 117–18.

PART TWO THE SANITARY PRINCIPLE IN DOMINANCE: MEDICAL HEGEMONY AND FEMINIST RESPONSE 1860–1880

1 The life of the General Board of Health was not extended by Parliament in 1854. Instead a new, drastically curtailed board was set up, prompting Chadwick's resignation. John Simon entered this second General Board of Health in 1855 as Medical Officer. The board lasted until 1859, when it was replaced

under the terms of the Public Health Act of that year by the Medical Office within the Privy Council, with Simon again holding the medical officership.

2 *The Times*, 1 August 1854.

3 Simon's research team at the Medical Office was part of the system of rudimentary public health administration. The results of his work, which focused on many of the most pressing and unresolved medical issues of the day, and in particular on the problems of contagious and infectious diseases, were attached to Simon's annual reports to the Privy Council and the Local Government Board between 1859 and 1877. See: 'Dr Buchanan on the Distribution of Phthisis as Affected by the Dampness of Soil', *Tenth Annual Report of the Medical Officer of the Privy Council*, 1867, GBPP 1867–8, XXXVI, p. 471; 'Dr Sanderson on the Communicability of the Tubercule by Innoculation', *Tenth Annual Report*, p. 525; 'Dr Thudichum on Researches Intended to Promote an Improved Chemical Identification of Diseases', *Tenth Annual Report*, p. 568.

4 See *Thirteenth Annual Report of the Medical Officer of the Privy Council*, 1870, GBPP 1871, XXI, p. 771.

5 For the impact of technological changes on medical science in the mid-Victorian period see: Savile Bradbury and G. L'E. Turner, *Historical Aspects of Microscopy: Papers Read at a One-Day Conference Held by the Royal Microscopical Society at Oxford*, Cambridge, Heffer for the Royal Microscopical Society, 1967; Harold Malies, *A Short History of the English Microscope: The XIX Century Instrument*, Chicago, Microscope Publications, 1981. Both accounts adopt a technical and evolutionist reading of the new technology.

6 *Tenth Annual Report of the Medical Officer of the Privy Council*, p. 434.

7 See: Public Health Act, 1848, 11 and 12 Vict., ch. 63; Nuisance Removal Act, 1855, 18 and 19 Vict., ch. 121; Sanitary Act, 1866, 20 and 21 Vict., ch. 41; Public Health Act, 1875, 38 and 39 Vict., ch. 55.

8 The effect of these negative street clearance schemes intensified the housing crisis in central London in the late 1860s and 1870s. See Gareth Stedman Jones, *Outcast London: A Study in the Relationship Between Classes in Victorian Society*, Harmondsworth, Penguin, 1984, chs 9, 10.

9 *Thirteenth Annual Report of the Medical Officer of the Privy Council*, p. 771.

10 An Act for the Prevention of Contagious Diseases at Certain Naval and Military Stations, 1864, 27 and 28 Vict., ch. 85; An Act for the Better Prevention of Contagious Diseases at Certain Naval and Military Stations, 1866, 29 and 30 Vict., ch. 96; An Act to Amend the Contagious Diseases Act 1866, 1869, 32 and 33 Vict., ch. 86.

11 Since 1823 military returns had reported a steady increase in venereal diseases. By 1864 one out of every three sick cases was venereal in origin, while admission to hospitals for gonorrhoea and syphilis had reached 290.7 per 1,000 of total troop strength. In the navy one out of eleven hospital patients was suffering from venereal diseases, and these patients comprised 125 admissions per 1,000 troops. See W. Sloggett, *History and Operation of the Contagious Diseases Acts in the Home Ports*, 10 April 1873, PRO ADM1/6418, p. 2.

12 See *Report of the Royal Commission on the Health of the Army*, 1857, GBPP 1857, XVIII, p. xv.

13 There is an expanding body of research on the Contagious Diseases Acts and on nineteenth-century prostitution, especially from feminist historians. This section utilises the history by Judith Walkowitz in *Prostitution and Victorian Society. Women, Class and the State*, Cambridge, Cambridge University Press, 1980. But see also: Paul McHugh, *Prostitution and Victorian Social Reform*, London,

Croom Helm, 1980; E. Sigsworth and T. Wyke, 'A Study of Victorian Prostitution and Venereal Disease', in Martha Vicinus (ed.), *Suffer and Be Still: Women in the Victorian Age*, Bloomington and London, Indiana University Press, 1972, pp. 77–99; Jean L'Esperance, 'The Work of the Ladies' National Association for the Repeal of the Contagious Diseases Acts', *Bulletin of the Society for the Study of Labour History*, 1973, no. 26, pp. 13–15; Keith Nield (ed.), *Prostitution in the Victorian Age: Debates on the Issues from Nineteenth Century Critical Journals*, Farnborough, Gregg International, 1973; Judith Walkowitz and Daniel Walkowitz, ' "We are Not Beasts of the Field": Prostitution and the Poor in Plymouth and Southampton Under the Contagious Diseases Acts', *Feminist Studies*, 1973, no. 1, pp. 73–106; Nancy Wood, 'Prostitution and Feminism in Nineteenth-Century Britain', *m/f*, 1982, no. 7, pp. 61–77.

14 'The Contagious Diseases Act', *Lancet*, 29 July 1871, vol. 2, pp. 166–7. For similar appeals to the sanitary principle see 'Venereal Disease in the Army and Navy', *Lancet*, 19 March 1864, vol. 1, p. 329.

15 *Westminster Review*, 1850, vol. 53, p. 502.

16 See *Report of the Committee to Inquire into the Prevalence of Venereal Disease in the Army and Navy*, 1862, PRO WO 33/12.

17 See especially Alexandre Parent-Duchâtelet, *De la prostitution dans la Ville de Paris. Considerée sous le Rapport de l'Hygiène Publique, de la Morale et de l'Administration*, Paris, J.B. Ballière, 1836, 2 vols. Paris had a comparatively extensive network of public health regulation, controlled by the Prefect of the Seine and established under the First Empire.

18 Harveian Medical Society of London, *Report of the Committee for the Prevention of Venereal Diseases*, 1867. For medical campaigns to extend the acts to the civilian population see: 'The Contagious Diseases Act', *Lancet*, 26 January 1867, vol. 1, p. 127; 'The Contagious Diseases Act', *Lancet*, 15 February 1868, vol. 1, pp. 232–4.

19 'Theology and Therapeutics', *Lancet*, 3 March 1860, vol. 1, p. 226.

20 William Acton, *Prostitution Considered in Its Moral, Social and Sanitary Aspects in London and Other Large Cities; with Proposals for the Mitigation and Prevention of Its Attendant Evils*, London, John Churchill, 1857, p. viii.

21 'Out-Patient Administrative Reform', *Lancet*, 6 May 1871, vol. 1, p. 619.

22 'Theology and Therapeutics', *Lancet*. See also 'Public Immoralities', *Lancet*, 16 July 1864, vol. 2, pp. 75–6.

23 *Report from the Royal Commission on the Administration and Operation of the Contagious Diseases Acts 1866–69*, 1871, GBPP 1871, XIX, p. 11.

24 See Victor Plarr, *Plarr's Lives of the Fellows of the Royal College of Surgeons of England*, revised by Sir D'Arcy Power, London, Simpkin Marshall Ltd, 1930, vol. 1, pp. 537–8. See also Deborah Gorham, 'Victorian Reform as a Family Business: The Hill Family', in Anthony Wohl (ed.), *The Victorian Family: Structures and Stresses*, London, Croom Helm, 1978, pp. 119–47.

25 For changing mid-century attitudes to the problem of poverty see Stedman Jones, *Outcast London*, pp. 179–96. For an account of the pathologisation of criminals and the insane see John Tagg, 'Power and Photography: Part One. A Means of Surveillance: The Photograph as Evidence in Law', *Screen Education*, 1980, no. 36, pp. 17–55.

26 See *Report on the Organization of the Permanent Civil Service*, 1854, GBPP 1854, XXVII. Recommendations included the introduction of a system of open competitive examination and the abolition of political jobbery and aristocratic influence. The aim was to create a new cadre of intellectuals within the state, backed by an ideology of neutral administrative expertise. See George Kitson

Clark, ' "Statesmen in Disguise": Reflections on the History of the Neutrality of the Civil Service', *The Historical Journal*, 1959, vol. II, no. 1, pp. 19–39.

27 See Philip Abrams, *The Origins of British Sociology 1834–1914: An Essay with Selected Papers*, Chicago, University of Chicago Press, 1968, pp. 42, 47–8.

28 *Report of the Royal Commission on the Health of the Army.*

29 Evidence of William Hickman, *Report of the House of Commons Select Committee to Inquire into the Pathology and Treatment of the Venereal Disease, with a View to Diminish its Injurious Effects on the Men of the Army and Navy*, 1868, GBPP 1867–8, XXXVII, p. 1058.

30 Evidence of Dr Barclay, ibid., p. 707. The *Report from the Royal Commission on the Contagious Diseases Acts* dismissed appeals for the periodic examination of the lower ranks of the army and navy, insisting that there was no comparison between the 'irregular indulgence' of the men and the 'crime' committed by the prostitute, p. 17.

31 John Curgenven, *The Contagious Diseases Act of 1866, and its Extension to the Civil Population of the United Kingdom*, London, W.W. Head, 1868.

32 'Extension of the Contagious Diseases Act', *BMJ*, 16 May 1868, vol. 1, p. 489. See also the evidence of William Sloggett, *Report from the Select Committee on the Contagious Diseases Act (1866)*, 1869, GBPP 1868–9, VII, p. 23.

33 Many local acts and by-laws contained clauses designed to regulate sexual immorality among the urban poor. The Metropolitan Police Acts, 1829 and 1839, were frequently used against prostitutes, as were the Manchester Police Act, 1844, and the Town Police Clauses Act, 1847. See Walkowitz, *Prostitution and Victorian Society*, ch. 10.

34 Walkowitz, *Prostitution and Victorian Society*, pp. 197–201.

35 See: William Tait, *Magdalenism: An Inquiry into the Extent, Causes and Consequences of Prostitution in Edinburgh*, Edinburgh, P. Rickard, 1840, pp. 4–33; Ralph Wardlaw, *Lectures on Female Prostitution*, Glasgow, James Maclehose, 1842, pp. 8–9.

36 William Acton, *The Functions and Disorders of the Reproductive Organs in Childhood, Youth, Adult Age and Advanced Life Considered in Their Physiological, Social and Moral Relations*, London, John Churchill, 1857, p. 142.

37 ibid., p. 74.

38 ibid., p. 189.

39 See Peter Cominos, 'Late-Victorian Sexual Respectability and the Social System', *International Review of Social History*, 1963, vol. VIII, pp. 18–48, 216–50.

40 *Report from the Royal Commission on the Contagious Diseases Acts*, p. 17.

41 Acton, *The Functions*, p. 184.

42 ibid., p. 183.

43 See especially Abraham Solomon's *Drowned! Drowned!*, 1860. Other paintings, like Alfred Elmore's *On the Brink*, 1865, and William Frith's *At Homburg*, 1869, emphasised that it was only when women left the protection of the home that they put themselves at risk: see Lynda Nead, 'Seduction, Prostitution, Suicide: *On the Brink* by Alfred Elmore', *Art History*, 1982, vol. 5, no. 3, pp. 310–22.

44 See: Wardlaw, *Lectures on Female Prostitution*; Michael Ryan, *Lectures on Population, Marriage and Divorce*, London, Renshaw and Rush, 1831; Michael Ryan, *The Philosophy of Marriage, in Its Social, Moral and Physical Relations; with an Account of the Diseases of the Genito-Urinary Organs*, London, John Churchill, 1837.

45 Wardlaw, *Lectures on Female Prostitution*, pp. 68–9.

46 Ryan, *Lectures on Population*, p. 54. See also Alexander Walker, *Women*

Physiologically Considered as to Mind, Morals, Marriage, Matrimonial Slavery, Infidelity and Divorce, London, A.H. Baily and Co, 1839, p. 91.

47 Acton, *The Functions*, p. 112.
48 For partisan accounts of the improving effects of lock hospitals see: William Acton, *The Contagious Diseases Act, Shall the Contagious Diseases Act be Applied to the Civil Population?*, London, J. & A. Churchill, 1870, pp. 17, 24; 'Contagious Diseases Acts', *Lancet*, 29 July 1871, vol. 2, p. 166.
49 See Stedman Jones, *Outcast London*, ch. 9.
50 'Association of Medical Officers of Health', *BMJ*, 8 January 1870, vol. 1, p. 35.
51 Acton, *The Functions*, p. 142.
52 Speech by Mr Osborne Morgan, Women's Disabilities Removal Bill, Commons, *Hansard's Parliamentary Debates*, 1 May 1872, third series, vol. 211, col. 55.
53 'A Lady Among the Students', *Lancet*, 6 July 1861, vol. 2, p. 16. See also: 'Female Obstetricians', *Lancet*, 23 January 1875, vol. 1, p. 139; 'Female Graduates at the University of London', *Lancet*, 22 January 1876, vol. 1, p. 147.
54 See Joseph and Olive Banks, *Feminism and Family Planning in Victorian England*, Liverpool, Liverpool University Press, 1964, pp. 95–6.
55 Annie Besant, *An Autobiography*, London, T. Fisher Unwin, 1893, pp. 207–8.
56 *Lancet*, 22 January 1859, vol. 1, p. 89.
57 'Walter', *My Secret Life*, quoted in Steven Marcus, *The Other Victorians: A Study of Sexuality and Pornography in Mid-Nineteenth Century England*, London, Weidenfeld & Nicolson, 1966, pp. 91–2.
58 ibid., pp. 122–3.
59 Flora Tristan, *Flora Tristan's London Journal*, trans. Dennis Palmer and Giselle Pincetl, London, George Prior, 1980, pp. 75–6.
60 Quoted in Derek Hudson, *Munby: Man of Two Worlds: The Life and Diaries of Arthur J. Munby, 1828–1910*, London, Abacus, 1974, p. 195. For discussion of the dynamics of the Munby–Cullwick relationship see Leonore Davidoff, 'Class and Gender in Victorian Britain: Arthur J. Munby and Hannah Cullwick', *Feminist Studies*, 1979, vol. 5, no. 1, pp. 89–113.
61 Brian Harrison identified the repeal campaign as a key mid-Victorian pressure group in *Drink and the Victorians: The Temperance Question in England, 1815–1872*, London, Faber, 1971, pp. 174–5, 224, 381, and more especially in his 'State Intervention and Moral Reform', in Patricia Hollis (ed.), *Pressure from Without in Early Victorian England*, London, Edward Arnold, 1974, pp. 319, 321. But see the feminist response to this approach in Walkowitz, *Prostitution and Victorian Society*, p. 6.
62 See George Johnson and Lucy Johnson (eds), *Josephine E. Butler. An Autobiographical Memoir*, London, J.W. Arrowsmith, 1928, pp. 65–72.
63 ibid., p. 72.
64 Speech by Mr Divett, Divorce Bills, Commons, *Hansard's Parliamentary Debates*, 22 April 1836, third series, vol. 33, col. 116.
65 Speech by Mr W. Fowler, Contagious Diseases Acts (1866–9) Repeal Bill, Commons, *Hansard's Parliamentary Debates*, 21 May 1873, third series, vol. 216, col. 218.
66 See Geoffrey Finlayson, *The Seventh Earl of Shaftesbury, 1801–1885*, London, Eyre Methuen, 1981, pp. 43–4. The court of the young Queen Victoria, dominated by Lord Melbourne and the Whig faction, was renowned for its moral laxity. When Robert Peel tried unsuccessfully to form a government in 1839, he insisted on appointing his own nominees to the royal household, in an effort to improve the moral culture of the court.
67 Thomas Biggs, *The Proposed Extension of the Contagious Diseases Act in Its*

Moral and Economical Aspects Read Before the Economy and Trade Section of the National Association for the Promotion of Social Science, London, William Tweedie, 1870, p. 11.

68 See for example: James Wilkinson, *The Forcible Introspection of Women for the Army and Navy by the Oligarchy, Considered Physically*, London, F. Pitman, 1870; Ladies' National Association, *Report for the Year Ending November 1871*, 1871; Charles Taylor, *The Statistical Results of the Contagious Diseases Acts .... Shewing their Total Failure from a Sanitary Point of View*, Nottingham, Stevenson, Bailey and Smith, 1872.

69 James Stansfeld, *Substance of the Speeches of the Rt. Hon. J. Stansfeld M.P., on the Contagious Diseases Acts*, London, National Association for the Repeal of the Contagious Diseases Acts, 1875, p. 11.

70 ibid., p. 2.

71 Josephine Butler, *Personal Reminiscences of a Great Crusade*, London, H. Marshall & Sons, 1896, p. 294.

72 Stansfeld, *Substance of Speeches*, p. 12.

73 *Eleventh Annual Report of the Medical Officer of the Privy Council*, 1868, GBPP 1868–9, XXXII, pp. 3–13.

74 George Butler to Josephine Butler, 13 July 1856, quoted in George Johnson and Lucy Johnson, *Josephine E. Butler*, p. 29.

75 See William Fowler, *A Study in Radicalism and Dissent: The Life and Times of Henry Joseph Wilson 1833–1914*, London, Epworth Press, 1961, pp. 25–7.

76 Butler to Joseph Edmondson, 28 April 1872, Josephine Butler Collection, Fawcett Library, London, no. 3136.

77 Butler, *Personal Reminiscences*, p. 73.

78 Barbara Taylor, *Eve and the New Jerusalem: Socialism and Feminism in the Nineteenth Century*, London, Virago, 1983, ch. V.

79 Butler, *Personal Reminiscences*, p. 319.

80 Josephine Butler, *Social Purity. An Address Given at Cambridge*, London, Morgan & Scott, 1879, p. 5.

81 Josephine Butler, *A Letter to the Members of the Ladies' National Association*, Liverpool, T. Brakell, 1875, p. 5.

82 Mary Hume-Rothery, *A Letter Addressed to the Right Hon. W.E. Gladstone M.P. and Other Members of Her Majesty's Government Touching the Contagious Diseases Acts of 1866 and 1869*, London, Simpkin, Marshall and Co, 1870.

83 Wilkinson, *The Forcible Introspection*, p. 15.

84 See Kell's evidence in the *Report of the Royal Commission on the Contagious Diseases Acts*, pp. 690–7.

85 George Johnson and Lucy Johnson, *Josephine E. Butler*, pp. 44–5.

86 Josephine Butler, 'Introduction', in Josephine Butler (ed.), *Women's Work and Women's Culture*, London, Macmillan, 1869, pp. xxv–xxxvii.

87 Hume-Rothery, *A Letter*, pp. 8–9.

88 *Report of the Royal Commission on the Contagious Diseases Acts*, pp. 690–3.

89 'Crowded Meetings at Plymouth', *Shield*, 21 October 1876, pp. 313–14.

90 'Rescue and Defence Work – Plymouth and Devonport District', *Shield*, 20 January 1877, pp. 9–10. For similar accounts see *National League Journal*, August 1883, pp. 1, 4.

91 See 'The "On Dits" in the Subjected Districts', *Shield*, 25 February 1882, p. 39. For similar misgivings from Mrs Hampson see 'Extract of Letters from Mrs Hampson' *Shield*, 1 October 1870, p. 240.

92 See *National League Journal*, 1 January 1881, pp. 12–13.

93 *Report from the Royal Commission on the Contagious Diseases Acts*, pp. 691–2.

Butler herself tended to stress the penitence shown by reformed prostitutes. As she put it in her letter to James Wilkinson: 'I believe at this moment that there is a general feeling of penitence on the part of the women', quoted in Wilkinson, *The Forcible Introspection*, p. 25.

94 Butler, *Women's Work*, p. xxxvii.
95 ibid.

PART THREE FROM STATE MEDICINE TO CRIMINAL LAW: PURITY, FEMINISM AND THE STATE 1880–1914

1 *The Times*, 31 July 1885, p. 11.
2 'The Maiden Tribute of Modern Babylon', *Pall Mall Gazette*, 6, 7, 8, 10 July 1885.
3 *Pall Mall Gazette*, Special Morning Edition, 22 August 1885.
4 NVA, *Objects, Constitution and Rules of the National Vigilance Association*, 1885, p. 3. See also NVA, Minutes, Fawcett Library, London.
5 William Coote, 'Law and Morality', in James Marchant (ed.), *Public Morals*, London, Morgan and Scott, 1902, p. 45. See also Alfred Barry, 'The Duty of the Church of Christ Against Impurity', in Marchant (ed.), *Public Morals*, pp. 26–7.
6 Coote, 'Law and Morality', p. 69.
7 Legislation included: Indecent Advertisements Act, 1889, 52 and 53 Vict., ch. 18; Vagrancy Act, 1898, 61 and 62 Vict., ch. 39, criminalising male pimping and importuning; Incest Act, 1908, 8 Ed. 7, ch. 45; Criminal Law Amendment Act, 1912, 2 and 3, Geo. 5, ch. 20, increasing penalties and police powers against procurers and brothel keepers and clarifying the scope of the 1898 act to include male homosexuals; Criminal Law Amendment Act, 1922, 12 and 13, Geo. 5, ch. 56, abolishing the 'reasonable cause to believe' clause in cases of indecent assault on girls under sixteen and again increasing penalties for brothel keeping.
8 See Gareth Stedman Jones, *Outcast London: A Study in the Relationship Between Classes in Victorian Society*, Penguin, Harmondsworth, 1984, chs. 9–13.
9 See especially the following fictional and journalistic accounts: James Greenwood, *The Wilds of London*, London, Chatto & Windus, 1874; *Low Life Deeps: An Account of the Strange Fish to Be Found There*, London, Chatto & Windus, 1876; George Sims, *How the Poor Live in Horrible London*, London, Chatto & Windus, 1883; Jack London, *The People of the Abyss*, London, Isbister and Co, 1903.
10 Andrew Mearns, *The Bitter Cry of Outcast London*, London, James Clarke and Co, 1883.
11 Evidence of Rev R.C. Billing, Royal Commission on the Housing of the Working Classes, *First Report of the Commissioners, England*, 1884, GBPP 1884–5, XXX, p. 254. For opposing arguments, which ascribed incest primarily to drunkenness, see Rev A.T. Fryer, curate of St Philip's, Clerkenwell, *First Report of the Commissioners*, p. 169.
12 Mearns, *The Bitter Cry*, p. 268.
13 See: 'Agitation Against the Contagious Diseases Acts', *Lancet*, 17 March 1883, vol. 1, p. 486; 'The Contagious Diseases Acts', *Lancet*, 4 August 1883, vol. 2, p. 192.
14 The Royal Commission on the Sanitary Laws, 1869, recommended the creation of one responsible administrative body for public health. Under the Local Government Act, 1871, the staff at the Poor Law Board, the General Register Office, the Local Government Office and, subsequent to a limitation, the staff of the

Privy Council Medical Department, were amalgamated to form the new Local Government Board. But the new act did not define the character, internal structure and professional relations of the new board. The direction of central health administration was left to the discretion of ministers and permanent officials. See John Simon, *Sanitary Institutions Reviewed in the Course of Their Development and in Some of their Political and Social Relations*, London, Cassell, 1890, pp. 348–9.

15 Jeanne Brand, *The British Medical Profession and State Intervention in Public Health, 1870–1911*, unpublished Ph.D. dissertation, London University, 1953, p. 86. See also John Hammond and Barbara Hammond, *James Stansfeld: A Victorian Champion of Sex Equality*, London, Longman, 1932, pp. 108–11.

16 For Lambert's work at the Local Government Board see Herbert Thomas, *Work and Play of a Government Inspector*, London and Edinburgh, William Blackwood & Sons, 1909. See also Miscellaneous Correspondence, 1876, PRO LGB58096/76, and Government Office Correspondence, 1873, PRO LGB78178/73.

17 For the *Lancet's* support for Simon's embattled position see: 'Mr Simon's Annual Report', *Lancet*, 25 July 1874, vol. 2, pp. 134–5; 'Mr Simon's Latest Reports', *Lancet*, 15 April 1876, vol. 1, pp. 576–7.

18 'Mr John Simon', *Lancet*, 27 May 1876, vol. 1, pp. 782–3.

19 Administrative historians have tended to explain the eclipse of state medicine in terms of the personality clash between Simon and Lambert, and more broadly via the idea that the movement for public health reform had run out of steam. See especially Royston Lambert, *Sir John Simon, 1816–1904, and English Social Administration*, London, MacGibbon & Kee, 1963, ch. XXIII, and Brand, *The British Medical Profession*.

20 Ralph Lingen, Treasury Minute, 1 June 1871, PRO T1/18, 953.

21 The secretariat at the board conformed to the new civil service model and worked to circumscribe medical authority. The majority were Oxbridge graduates, recruited by public examination, whose subsequent experience was primarily 'paper experience', acquired by minutes, correspondence and occasional conferences.

22 George Buchanan to Arthur Newsholme, quoted in Arthur Newsholme, *The Last Thirty Years in Public Health. Recollections and Reflections on My Official and Post-Official Life*, London, Allen & Unwin, 1936, p. 34.

23 Ellice Hopkins, *Work in Brighton*, London, Hatchards, 1877, p. 49.

24 Elizabeth Blackwell, *How to Keep a Household in Health. An Address*, London, Ladies' Sanitary Association, 1870; *The Religion of Health*, London, Moral Reform Union, 1889. See also Rachel Baker, *The First Woman Doctor: The Story of Elizabeth Blackwell M.D.*, London, Harrap & Co, 1946.

25 Elizabeth Blackwell, *The Human Element in Sex: Being a Medical Enquiry in the Relation of Sexual Physiology to Christian Morality*, London, J. and A. Churchill, 1884, pp. 11–12, 57.

26 For the impact of Darwinism on the mid-Victorian Church see: Owen Chadwick, *The Victorian Church*, London, A. & C. Black, 1966, vol. 1, pp. 527–72; Thomas Heyck, *The Transformation of Intellectual Life in Victorian England*, London, Croom Helm, 1982.

27 'Archbishop Manning on Evolution', *BMJ*, 12 October 1872, vol. 2, p. 416. Many scientists were arguing for a similar compromise in the 1870s. At the annual meeting of the British Association in 1871, Sir William Thompson, the President, affirmed that God's divine plan was manifest in the formal beauty of creation: 'The British Association', *BMJ*, 12 August 1871, vol. 2, p. 187.

28 Charles Darwin, *The Descent of Man. Selection in Relation to Sex*, London, John Murray, 1871, vol. 1, chs III and IV.

29 Social Purity Alliance, *Schoolboy Morality: An Address to Mothers*, London, Social Purity Alliance, 1884, pp. 8–9.

30 Blackwell, *The Human Element in Sex*, p. 17.

31 ibid.

32 Ellice Hopkins, *Village Morality: A Letter to Clergymen's Wives and Christian Workers*, London, Hatchards, 1882, pp. 18–19. See also Frances Power Cobbe, 'The Causes of Evil', in Marchant, *Public Morals*, p. 25. Stedman Jones has argued strongly that renewed anxiety over the urban poor in the 1880s ruptured moral and environmental explanations of poverty and prepared the ground for new theories of urban degeneracy, based on the hereditary transmission of characteristics. Yet the move away from traditional explanations was extremely uneven. In many areas of social reform a modified version of moral environmentalism remained dominant. Purists' practical religion of rescue and reclamation militated against any wholesale adoption of social Darwinism.

33 See for example: 'Cases of Conversion', *Quarterly Record of the Tower Hamlets Mission*, 1881, no. 1, p. 5, and 'Cases of Conversion', 1881, no. 2, p. 6. The mission was founded by Frederick Charrington, from the prominent brewing family.

34 Alfred Dyer, *Facts for Men on Moral Purity and Health*, London, Dyer Brothers, 1884, p. 6.

35 Other similar groups included the Metropolitan Association for Befriending Young Servants, 1877, and the Travellers' Aid Society, 1885. See Edward Bristow, *Vice and Vigilance: Purity Movements in Britain since 1700*, Dublin, Gill and Macmillan, 1977, ch. 5.

36 See Hopkins, *Village Morality*, pp. 9–10, and her *The Early Training of Girls and Boys. An Appeal to Working Women*, London, P.S. King and Son, 1902, pp. 18, 22–3. Purists were also encouraged to cooperate with the new elementary schoolteachers provided under the Education Act, 1870. See Ellice Hopkins, *The Girls' Friendly Society – An Appeal to the Mistresses of Elementary Schools*, London, Hatchards, 1882, pp. 9–10.

37 Purity campaigns against the London music halls consistently attacked the perceived immoral alliance between the aristocracy, big business and the urban working class. The most famous campaign was against the Empire Theatre in 1894. See Laura Ormiston Chant, *Why We Attacked the Empire*, London, Marshall and Son, 1895.

38 See NVA, *Pernicious Literature: Debate in the House of Commons: Trial and Convictions for Sale of Zola's Novels with Opinions of the Press*, London, National Vigilance Association, 1889.

39 'Allegation Libel on Mr Oscar Wilde', *Daily Telegraph*, 6 April 1895, and 'Editorial', *Daily Telegraph*, 27 May 1895.

40 'Retribution', *Evening News*, 27 May 1895.

41 Speech by the Lord Chancellor, the Earl of Halsbury, Incest Bill, Lords, *Parliamentary Debates*, 16 July 1903, fourth series, vol. 125, col. 822. See also speech by Mr Rawlinson, Incest Bill, Commons, *Parliamentary Debates*, 26 June 1908, fourth series, vol. 191, cols 278–9.

42 Ellice Hopkins, *The White Cross Army. A Statement of the Bishop of Durham's Movement*, London, Hatchards, 1883, p. 3. See also Blackwell, *The Human Element in Sex*, p. 32.

43 James Wilson, *Sins of the Flesh. A Sermon Preached in Clifton College Chapel*, London, Macmillan, 1883, p. 5. See also Wilson, *An Address*, London, Hatchards, 1884, p. 12.

44 Dyer, *Facts for Men*, p. 12.

45 See Rosa Barrett, *Ellice Hopkins: A Memoir*, London, Wells Gardiner & Co, 1907, p. 157.

46 Darwin was ambiguous about the evolutionary potential of women. While acknowledging that women's maternal instincts gave them a greater capacity for tenderness and selflessness, he insisted that men had attained a higher stage of evolution. Yet Darwin was aware that women were more advanced on moral issues: Darwin, *The Descent of Man*, vol. 2, ch. XIX.

47 Blackwell, *The Human Element in Sex*, p. 22.

48 ibid., p. 46.

49 See: Judith Walkowitz, 'Science, Feminism and Romance: The Men and Women's Club 1885–1889', *History Workshop Journal*, 1986, no. 21, pp. 36–59; Lucy Bland, 'Marriage Laid Bare: Middle-Class Women and Marital Sex c. 1880–1914', in Jane Lewis (ed.), *Labour and Love: Women's Experience of Home and Family, 1850–1940*, Oxford, Basil Blackwell, 1986, pp. 123–46.

50 In the 1890s Butler expressed her strong opposition to the new purity campaigns which were: 'ready to accept and endorse any amount of coercive and degrading treatment of their fellow creatures in the fatuous belief that you can oblige human beings to be moral by force.' Josephine Butler, quoted in Jessie Higson, *The Story of a Beginning: An Account of Pioneer Work for Moral Welfare*, London, SPCK, 1955, pp. 35–6.

51 Jeffrey Weeks, *Sex, Politics and Society: The Regulation of Sexuality since 1800*, London, Longman, 1981, ch. 5.

52 Judith Walkowitz, 'Male Vice and Feminist Virtue: Feminism and the Politics of Prostitution in Nineteenth-Century Britain', *History Workshop Journal*, 1982, no. 13, p. 89.

53 Sheila Jeffreys, 'The Spinster and her Enemies: Sexuality and the Last Wave of Feminism', *Scarlet Woman*, 1981, no. 13, pp. 22–7.

54 Barrett, *Ellice Hopkins*, p. 157.

55 Ellice Hopkins, *An Englishwoman's Work Among Workingmen*, London, New Britain, 1875, pp. 4–5.

56 ibid., p. 5.

57 Hopkins, *Work in Brighton*, p. 16.

58 Barrett, *Ellice Hopkins*, p. 254.

59 Hopkins, *Village Morality*, p. 13.

60 Barrett, *Ellice Hopkins*, pp. 173–4.

61 Ellice Hopkins, *The Power of Womanhood: or, Mothers and Sons*, London, Wells Gardner & Co, 1899, p. 2.

62 ibid., p. 19.

63 Hopkins, *Work in Brighton*, p. 60.

64 Hopkins, *The Power of Womanhood*, p. 160.

65 See: Thomas Green, *Lectures on the Principles of Political Obligation and Freedom of Contract*, London, Longman, 1885; Leonard Hobhouse, *Mind in Evolution*, London, Macmillan & Co, 1901, and *Democracy and Reaction*, London, T. Fisher Unwin, 1904. New liberal philosophies of the organic state are discussed in Michael Freeden, *The New Liberalism: An Ideology of Social Reform*, Oxford, Clarendon Press, 1978.

66 Hopkins, *The Early Training*, pp. 5–6.

67 Hopkins, *Work in Brighton*, p. 86.

68 Hopkins, *The Power of Womanhood*, pp. 46, 127.

69 *Journal of the Vigilance Association for the Defence of Personal Rights*, 15 November 1882, no. 11, p. 90.

70 Minutes of the National Association for the Repeal of the Contagious Diseases Acts, 15 December 1879, no. 2184, Fawcett Library, London. See also Minutes, 12 January 1880, no. 2201.

71 Mrs Jerome Mercier, 'The Bonds of Union between Women of Different Ranks', in Girls' Friendly Society, *A Special Report*, London, Hatchards, 1879, p. 29.

72 Hopkins, *Work in Brighton*, p. 23.

73 For a retrospective account of the Brussels scandal see the *Shield*, January 1909, p. 52.

74 ibid.

75 *Second Report from the Select Committee [HL] on the State of the Law relating to the Protection of Young Girls*, 1882, GBPP 1882, XIII, p. 841.

76 *Report from the Select Committee [HL] on the State of the Law Relating to the Protection of Young Girls*, 1881, GBPP 1881, IX, pp. 436–47.

77 Bath Preventive Mission and Ladies' Association for the Care of Friendless Girls to Sir Vernon Harcourt, 23 February 1884, PRO HO45/59343 G.

78 London Women's Christian Association to William Gladstone, 22 February 1884, PRO HO45/59343 G.

79 Lord Hartington to Lord Rosebery, 30 May 1883, PRO HO45/ 59343 G.

80 Town Clerk of Hereford to Sir R. Cross, Under Secretary of State, Home Office, 29 September 1885, PRO HO45/A40683.

81 See H. Broadhurst's speech in the debate on the Criminal Law Amendment Bill, Commons, *Hansard's Parliamentary Debates*, 9 July 1885, third series, vol. 299, cols 203–4. See also similar opposition from the radical liberal C. Hopwood in the same debate, cols 199–202.

82 James Stuart to Samuel Smith, 8 July 1884, PRO HO45/59343 I. For similar protests by the Vigilance Association see H. Beaumont, 'The Criminal Law Amendment Bill', *Journal of the Vigilance Association for the Defence of Personal Rights*, 15 June 1885, no. 51, p. 493.

83 *Pall Mall Gazette, The Maiden Tribute of Modern Babylon. The Report of the 'Pall Mall Gazette's' Secret Commission*, London, Pall Mall Gazette, 1885, pp. 13–14.

84 Evidence of Mrs Anna Wilkes, *Second Report from the Select Committee on the Protection of Young Girls*, 1882, pp. 872–4.

85 Criminal Law Amendment Act, 1885, 48 and 49 Vict., ch. 69, section 11. The legislation criminalised all acts of gross indecency between males, with a penalty of up to two years' imprisonment. See: H. Montgomery Hyde, *The Other Love: An Historical and Contemporary Survey of Homosexuality in Britain*, London, Mayflower, 1972, p. 325; Jeffrey Weeks, *Coming Out: Homosexual Politics in Britain from the Nineteenth Century to the Present*, London, Quartet, 1977, pp. 14–16.

86 *The Times*, 11 June 1885.

87 *The Times*, 18 August 1885.

88 Wiliam Coote, *A Romance of Philanthropy: A Record of Thirty Years Work of the National Vigilance Association*, London, National Vigilance Association, 1916, p. 27.

89 Clapham Vigilance Association to the Under Secretary of State, Home Office, 4 December 1886, PRO HO45/A45364.

90 Assistant Metropolitan Commissioner of Police to the Under Secretary of State, Home Office, 19 December and 27 December 1886, PRO HO45/A45364.

91 Metropolitan Police to the Under Secretary of State, Home Office, 18 February 1889, PRO HO45/X15663.

92 Alfred Gardiner, *The Life of Sir William Harcourt*, London, Constable, 1923, vol. 1, pp. 607–8.

93 H.J. Wilson to Robert Eadon Leader, 13 December 1882, quoted in Paul McHugh, *Prostitution and Victorian Social Reform*, London, Croom Helm, 1980, p. 239. For evangelical influence on the Liberal Party in the 1880s see D. A. Hamer, *Liberal Politics in the Age of Gladstone and Rosebery: A Study in Leadership and Policy*, Oxford, Clarendon Press, 1972, pp. 5–9.

94 Coote, *A Romance of Philanthropy*, pp. 156–60.

95 Report on Application from St George's Vigilance Association for the appropriation of fines imposed on brothel keepers, 9 July 1887, PRO HO45/X14891. For purists' reactions see Coote, *A Romance of Philanthropy*, p. 27.

96 Coote, *A Romance of Philanthropy*, p. 95.

97 NVA annual reports noted with satisfaction the growing help and encouragement received from the police and the watch committees of local councils. See NVA, *Eleventh Annual Report*, 1896, p. 33.

98 NVA, *Sixteenth Annual Report*, 1901, p. 27. For Home Office responses to mounting pressure for law reform see PRO HO45/A57406/1. See also Victor Bailey and Sheila Blackburn, 'The Punishment of Incest Act 1908: A Case Study of Criminal Law Creation', *Criminal Law Review*, November 1979, pp. 708–18.

99 See NUWW, *Handbook and Report*, 1909–10, pp. 60–1, 125.

100 Until the creation of the new tier of borough councils in 1889, responsibility for legal action lay with the old parish vestries who displayed a reluctance to prosecute. See Bristow, *Vice and Vigilance*, p. 163.

101 See *Report of the Royal Commission upon the Duties of the Metropolitan Police*, 1908, GBPP 1908, L, p. 478.

102 ibid., p. 94.

103 ibid., p. 135.

104 ibid.

105 ibid., p. 686.

106 Between 1895 and 1912 the NUWW passed a series of annual conference resolutions calling for criminal law amendments to protect women and children. See: NUWW, *Handbook and Report*, 1909–10, pp. 60–1; NUWW, *Occasional Paper*, September 1910, special issue no., p. 37.

107 'Resolutions, 30th Congress of the International Federation for the Abolition of the State Regulation of Vice', *Shield*, November 1903, pp. 59–60.

108 'To Suppress the White Slave Traffic', *Suffragette*, 11 July 1913, p. 660. See also 'The Lessons of the Great Crusade', *Common Cause*, 11 May 1910.

109 See Sheila Jeffreys, 'Free From All Uninvited Touch of Man: Women's Campaigns Around Sexuality, 1880–1914', *Women's Studies International Forum*, 1982, vol. 5, no. 6, p. 641.

110 See especially W.C.D. and C.D. Whetham, 'Decadence and Civilisation', *The Hibbert Journal*, October 1911, vol. X, no. 1, pp. 179–200.

111 Lucy Re-Bartlett, *Sex and Sanctity*, London, Longman, Green & Co, 1912, p. 26.

112 Cicely Hamilton, *Marriage as a Trade*, London, Chapman and Hall, 1909, pp. 37–8.

113 Medics, psychiatrists and criminologists frequently explained the physical and mental diseases of women in terms of excessive sexuality or a malfunctioning of the reproductive system. See: Henry Maudsley, *Body and Mind: An Inquiry into Their Connection and Mutual Influence, Specially in Reference to Mental Disorders*, London, Macmillan, 1870; Daniel Tuke (ed.), *Dictionary of Physiological Medicine*, London, J. & A. Churchill, 1892, 2 vols; Caesare Lombroso and William Ferrero, *The Female Offender*, London, Fisher Unwin, 1895. Havelock Ellis and Edward Carpenter worked with the understanding that

women's sexuality was repressed and needed to be liberated by the care and skill of men. See: Henry Havelock Ellis, *Studies in the Psychology of Sex*, vol. III, *Analysis of the Sexual Impulse Love and Pain. The Sexual Impulse in Women*, Philadelphia, F.A. Davis and Co, 1903; Edward Carpenter, *Love's Coming-of-Age. A Series of Papers on the Relations of the Sexes*, Manchester, Labour Press, 1896.

114 Christabel Pankhurst, *The Great Scourge, and How to End It*, London, E. Pankhurst, 1913, p. 20. See also Hamilton, *Marriage as a Trade*, p. 183.

115 Frances Swiney, *The Bar of Isis; or the Law of the Mother*, London, Open Road Publishing Co, 1907, pp. 48, 51. For a contemporary account of Swiney's work see *Suffragette Annual and Women's Who's Who*, London, Stanley Paul and Co, 1913, p. 372.

116 Frances Swiney, *The Mystery of the Circle and the Cross; or, the Interpretation of Sex*, London, Open Road Publishing Co, 1908, p. 64.

117 Lucy Re-Bartlett, *The Coming Order*, London, Longman, Green & Co, 1911, p. 33.

118 Pankurst, *The Great Scourge*, p. viii.

119 Re-Bartlett, *Sex and Sanctity*, p. 28.

120 Hamilton, *Marriage as a Trade*, p. 135.

121 Pankhurst, *The Great Scourge*, pp. 118–19. See also Hamilton, *Marriage as a Trade*, p. 135.

122 'A Case of Child Assault', *Vote*, 28 October 1911, p. 27; 'How Men Protect Women', *Vote*, 23 March 1912, p. 26.

123 'A Wronged Woman', *Common Cause*, 9 November 1911, p. 530.

124 'Scapegoats of Our Respectability', *Vote*, 20 March 1912, p. 276.

125 Home Office Memorandum on the White Slave Traffic Bill, 24 May 1911, PRO HO45/178486.

126 Home Office Memorandum in response to parliamentary question from Mr France on the Criminal Law Amendment Bill, 8 May 1912, PRO HO45/178486.

127 NUWW, *Occasional Paper*, no. 54. The demands debated at this meeting were incorporated into the NUWW annual conference resolutions in October 1911: see NUWW, *Handbook and Report*, 1911–12, p. 165.

128 'The Criminal Law Amendment (White Slave Traffic) Bill', *Shield*, June 1912, p. 121. See also: 'White Slave Traffic Bill', *Shield*, November–December 1911, pp. 78–9; Wolverhampton Suffrage Societies to G. Thomas MP, 20 May 1912, PRO HO45/178486.

129 NUWW, *Handbook and Report*, 1912–13, p. 173.

130 'White Slave Traffic Bill', *Common Cause*, 13 June 1912, p. 150.

131 'The Next Step', *Shield*, January 1913, pp. 14–15.

132 'The War Against White Slavery', *Suffragette*, 11 April 1913, p. 426.

133 Teresa Billington-Greig, 'The Truth About White Slavery', *English Review*, June 1913, vol. 14, p. 445.

134 ibid.

135 'Protecting Women', *Women's Dreadnought*, 19 December 1914, p. 159.

136 The *Freewoman* was established in November 1911, edited by Dora Marsden and Mary Gawthorpe. It was dedicated to developing the 'subjectivist side of feminist politics'. Discussion of sexuality was high on the agenda because the readjustment of relations between men and women was seen as central to women's freedom and to the evolution of a higher stage of civilisation. See Jane Lidderdale and Mary Nicholson, *Dear Miss Weaver: Harriet Shaw Weaver, 1875–1961*, London, Faber, 1970.

137 See for example: Gertrude Slater, 'Champions of Morality', *Freewoman*, 13 June 1912, p. 79; Katherine Vulliamy, 'Pass the Bill', *Freewoman*, 20 June 1912, p. 96. For attacks on the purity position see C.H. Norman, 'Champions of Morality', *Freewoman*, 6 June 1912, pp. 45–6.

138 See: Legitimation League, *Aims and Objects* (undated), p. 3; G. Moore, 'The Logic of Free-Love', *Adult*, September 1898, vol. 2, no. 8, p. 240: 'GDL', 'Free Love and Sexual Relations', *Adult*, December 1898, vol. 2, no. 11, pp. 293–4.

139 Orford Northcote, 'The Mutability of Sex Love', *Adult*, September 1897, vol. 1, no. 2, p. 24.

140 'Eve and her Eden', *Adult*, March 1898, vol. 2, no. 2, p. 30.

141 *Adult*, January 1898, vol. 1, no. 6, p. 138.

142 Lillian Harman, 'Some Problems of Social Freedom', *Adult*, 1898, extra issue, no. 2, p. 7.

143 See especially: Stella Browne, *Sexual Variety and Variability Among Women and Their Bearing Upon Social Reconstruction*, London, British Society for the Study of Sex Psychology, 1917; Sheila Rowbotham, *A New World for Women: Stella Browne, Socialist Feminist*, London, Pluto Press, 1977, section 1.

144 'A New Subscriber', *Freewoman*, 22 February 1912, p. 270.

145 See for example: Winifred Carey, 'The Idealism of Sex Relations', *Freewoman*, 22 February 1912, pp. 273–4; Kathryn Oliver, 'Chastity and Normality', *Freewoman*, 29 February 1912, p. 290.

146 See Mary and Stanley Randolph, 'Free Unions', *Freewoman*, 13 January 1912, p. 79.

147 The point is made by Athar Hussain in his critique of Foucault's distinction between juridical and discursive forms of power: 'Foucault's History of Sexuality', *m/f*, 1981, nos 5 and 6, pp. 169–91.

PART FOUR FROM PURITY TO SOCIAL HYGIENE: EARLY TWENTIETH-CENTURY CAMPAIGNS FOR SEX EDUCATION

1 The whole account of the Dronfield sex education case is preserved in the Public Record Office at PRO ED50/185.

2 ibid.

3 Deposition of Doris Harrison, pupil at Dronfield School, taken by the School Managers and sent to the Board of Education on 6 March 1914, as evidence against Miss Outram, PRO ED50/185.

4 Evidence of Mrs S. Milnes, Dronfield School Managers' meeting, 27 January 1914, PRO ED50/185.

5 Evidence of Mr Bradwell, Dronfield School Managers' meeting, 14 January 1914, PRO ED50/185.

6 Speech by Miss Outram, Dronfield School Managers' meeting, 14 January 1914.

7 Dronfield School Managers' meeting, 14 January 1914.

8 ibid.

9 Derbyshire Education Committee to Rt Hon Joseph Pease, MP, President of the Board of Education, 6 March 1914, PRO ED50/185.

10 Evidence of Mrs Milnes, Dronfield School Managers' meeting, 14 January 1914.

11 Evidence given at Dronfield School Managers' meeting, 27 January 1914.

12 'Teacher and the Girls She Told', *Weekly Dispatch*, 7 February 1914. See also 'Should Eugenics Be Taught in Elementary Schools', *Derbyshire Times*, 7 February 1914.

13 F. Oakes, Private Secretary to the President, to Pease, 23 March 1914, and Oakes to H. Lucas, Clerk to Dronfield School Managers, 26 March 1914, PRO ED50/185.

14 'Dronfield Scholars on Strike', *Derbyshire Times*, 25 April 1914.

15 National Council of Public Morals, *Manifesto*, 1910, pp. 3–4.

16 The most notable of the auxiliary studies sponsored by the board were the series undertaken by Dr L. Thudichum on the chemistry of the brain. The main research was disease-orientated, carried out under the direction of Sir J. Burdon Sanderson. See Jeanne Brand, *Doctors and the State: The British Medical Profession and Government Action in Public Health, 1870–1912*, Baltimore, Johns Hopkins University Press, 1965.

17 'Past and Present: The Expansion of Medicine', *BMJ* (Queen's Commemoration Number), 19 June 1897, vol. 1, p. 1521.

18 Between 1870 and 1905 many of the bacilli of the major infectious and contagious diseases were isolated, including: leprosy, typhoid, tuberculosis, cholera, diphtheria and tetanus. This scientific process was accompanied by the development of vaccines and anti-toxins. See Sir George Newman, *An Outline of the Practice of Preventive Medicine*, 1919, GBPP 1919, XXXIX, p. 681.

19 ibid., p. 695. See also 'Pathology', *BMJ*, 19 June 1897, vol. 1, pp. 1547–50.

20 Newman, *An Outline*, pp. 682, 735–6. See also: J. Burns, 'An Address on the Relationship Between Medicine and Health', *Lancet*, 16 August 1913, vol. 2, pp. 455–61; Sir Clifford Allbutt, 'The New Birth of Medicine', *BMJ*, 12 April 1919, vol. 1, pp. 433–8.

21 See for example: Sale of Food and Drugs Acts, 1879, 1899; Housing of the Working Classes Acts, 1900, 1903; Factory and Workshops Acts, 1901, 1907; National Insurance Acts, 1911, 1917, 1918.

22 Brand, in *Doctors and the State*, loosely ascribes this medical resurgence to the growing trend towards collectivism, while Anna Davin explains it directly in terms of the political and military exigencies of the immediate situation, in 'Imperialism and Motherhood', *History Workshop Journal*, 1978, no. 5, pp. 9–12.

23 See especially: *Annual Reports of the Inspector-General of Recruiting*, 1900–3, GBPP 1901, IX, 1902, X, 1903 XXXVIII; *Report of the Interdepartmental Committee on Physical Deterioration*, 1904, GBPP 1904, XXXII; Arnold White, *Efficiency and Empire*, London, Methuen and Co, 1901. For discussion see Anne Summers, 'Militarism in Britain Before the Great War', *History Workshop Journal*, 1976, no. 2, pp. 104–23.

24 See: Major General Sir Frederick Maurice, 'National Health: A Soldier's Study', *Contemporary Review*, January 1903, pp. 41–55; 'Pretorious', 'The Army and the Empire', *Empire Review*, March 1901, pp. 189–94; T.J. Macnamara, 'In Corpore Sano', *Contemporary Review*, February 1905, pp. 239–48; C.T. Ewart, 'National Health', *Empire Review*, May 1910, pp. 255–63.

25 'The Medical Service of the Army', *BMJ*, 20 February 1904, vol. 1, pp. 445–6. Medics had first expressed these anxieties during the Boer War campaign, see: 'Enteric Fever and the South Africa Campaign', *Lancet*, 28 April 1900, vol. 1, pp. 1218–19.

26 'The Physique of the Japanese', *BMJ*, 12 March 1904, vol. 1, pp. 622–3.

27 The 1902 syllabus was closely based on military drill which had first been introduced for army recruits in the 1860s. Subsequent revisions between 1904 and 1909 moved to a broader conception of physical training. See: Board of Education, *Syllabus of Physical Exercises for Use in Public Elementary Schools*, London, HMSO, 1904, and the *Report of the Interdepartmental Committee on*

Physical Exercises, 1904, GBPP 1904, XIX, p. 411; W. David Smith, *Stretching Their Bodies: The History of Physical Education*, Newton Abbott, David & Charles, 1974, chs 5 and 6.

28 *Annual Report for 1909 of the Chief Medical Officer of the Board of Education*, 1910, GBPP 1910, XXIII, pp. 359–61.

29 Board of Education, *Syllabus of Physical Exercises for Use in Public Elementary Schools*, London, HMSO, 1909, p. vii.

30 Despite a decline in the general death rate for England and Wales between 1851 and 1901, infant mortality had increased. By 1900 it was almost as high as it had been fifty years earlier. Coupled with this problem was the rapid decline in Britain's birth rate over the same period. In an extensive statistical study, Arthur Newsholme, Medical Officer to the Local Government Board, drew on the recent annual reports of the Registrar-General to compare the average rate of population increase of 11.2 per cent for England and Wales, with 14.8 per cent for the German Empire: Arthur Newsolme, *The Declining Birth-Rate. Its National and International Significance*, London, Cassell and Co, 1911, p. 10. But as Newsholme noted, the birth rate was not declining uniformly. It was most marked among the upper classes, who had more than halved their fertility rate in fifty years. In the face of both sets of problems, the call was for a greater focus on the health of the mother and child, in the interests of qualitative and quantitative population increase. See: Davin, 'Imperialism and Motherhood'; Carol Dyhouse, 'Working-Class Mothers and Infant Mortality in England 1895–1914', *Journal of Social History*, 1978, vol. 12, no. 2, pp. 248–67; Jane Lewis, *The Politics of Motherhood: Child and Maternal Welfare in England 1900–1939*, London, Croom Helm, 1980.

31 See especially: John Ballantyne, *Manual of Ante-Natal Pathology and Hygiene. The Embryo*, Edinburgh, W. Green, 1904; Arthur Newsholme, 'Infantile Mortality: A Statistical Study from the Public Health Standpoint', *Practitioner*, October 1905, pp. 489–500.

32 Newsholme, *The Declining Birth-Rate*, p. 57.

33 Quoted in Karl Pearson, *Darwinism, Medical Progress and Eugenics. The Cavendish Lecture. An Address to the Medical Profession*, London, Dulau and Co, 1912, pp. 4–5. For an account of the take-up of eugenics in Britain see Geoffrey Searle, *Eugenics and Politics in Britain 1900–1914*, Leyden, Noordhoff International, 1976.

34 The most sustained attack on medical environmentalism came from Pearson. See: Karl Pearson, *Eugenics and Public Health. An Address to Public Health Officers*, London, Dulau and Co, 1912, pp. 32–4, and his *The Problem of Practical Eugenics*, London, Dulau and Co, 1909, p. 31; Ethel Elderton, *The Relative Strength of Nurture and Nature*, London, Dulau and Co, 1909, pp. 32–3.

35 Henry Havelock Ellis, *The Task of Social Hygiene*, London, Constable, 1912, p. 15.

36. Caleb Saleeby, *The Methods of Race-Regeneration*, London, Cassell and Co, 1911, p. 63.

37 Karl Pearson, *The Scope and Importance to the State of the Science of National Eugenics*, London, Dulau and Co, 1909, pp. 16, 43. The new statistical approach to theories of probability and error was also registered by the statistical societies. See H. Macrosty and J. Bonar, *Annals of the Royal Statistical Society, 1834–1934*, London, Royal Statistical Society, 1934, pp. 177–83. The whole debate is discussed in Nikolas Rose, *The Psychological Complex: Psychology, Politics and Society in England 1869–1939*, London, Routledge & Kegan Paul, 1985.

38 In the 1880s the German biologist Weismann had argued that there was a clear

distinction between the germ cells and the somatic cells. The germ plasm could not be affected by any modification of the bodily organs. Acceptance of this logically entailed a rejection of Lamarck's belief that acquired characteristics could be inherited, see Searle, *Eugenics and Politics*, p. 6.

39 Pearson, *Eugenics and Public Health*, pp. 32–4.

40 Robert Rentoul, *Race Culture: or, Race Suicide? A Plea for the Unborn*, London, Walter Scott Publishing Co, 1906. For medical attacks on Rentoul's proposals see 'A Short Way with Degenerates', *BMJ*, 12 March 1904, vol. 1, pp. 625–6.

41 Edgar Schuster, 'The Scope and the Science of Eugenics', *BMJ*, 2 August 1913, vol. 2, pp. 223–4; Henry Cambell, 'Eugenics from the Physical Standpoint', *BMJ*, 2 August 1913, vol. 2, pp. 225–7.

42 'Eugenics', *BMJ*, 23 August 1913, vol. 2, pp. 508–9.

43 For the influence of eugenic thinking on these major social inquiries see: *Report of the Interdepartmental Committee on Physical Deterioration*, pp. 44–5; *Report of the Royal Commission on the Care and Control of the Feeble-Minded*, 1908, GBPP 1908, XXXIX, pp. 363–86; *Report of the Royal Commission on Divorce and Matrimonial Causes*, 1912, GBPP 1912–13, XVIII, p. 313; Royal Commission on Venereal Diseases, *Final Report of the Commissioners*, 1916, GBPP 1916, XVI, pp. 49–56.

44 Newman, *An Outline*, p. 682.

45 James Marchant, *The Master Problem*, London, Stanley Paul, 1917, pp. 128–9. See also his *Aids to Purity: Seven Personal Letters*, London, Health and Strength Ltd., 1909, pp. 36, 44.

46 NCPM, *The Nation's Morals*, London, Cassell and Co, 1910, pp. 3–4.

47 Geoffrey Searle, *The Quest for National Efficiency: A Study in British Politics and Political Thought, 1899–1914*, Oxford, Blackwell, 1971, p. 97.

48 William Inge, 'Some Moral Aspects of Eugenics', *Eugenics Review*, April 1909–January 1910, vol. 1, no. 1, pp. 30–1. For similar arguments see 'Racial Responsibility', *BMJ*, 8 March 1913, vol. 1, pp. 521–2.

49 See: Sidney Dark, *Five Deans*, London, Jonathan Cape, 1928, pp. 223; William Inge, *Diary of a Dean. St Pauls 1911–1934*, London, Hutchinson, 1949.

50 Newman, *An Outline*, p. 692.

51 See especially: George Newman, *The Place of Public Opinion in Preventive Medicine*, London, Ministry of Health, 1920; Christopher Addison, *Politics from Within, 1911–1918*, London, Herbert Jenkins, 1924, vol. 1, pp. 221–2. For health education programmes in the inter-war period see the work of the Central Council for Health Education, Minute Book, 1935–9, PRO MH82/1. The council was established in 1927 to coordinate national campaigns and propaganda for health improvement.

52 People's League of Health, *Second General Report for the Years 1922–5*.

53 ibid., p. 3.

54 George Newman, *Infant Mortality. A Social Problem*, London, Methuen and Co, 1906, p. v.

55 For moralists' continuing suspicion of the medical profession over venereal diseases see: Blanche Leppinton, 'Neo-Regulationism – Its Principles, Its Practice and Its Prospects', *Shield*, November–December 1904, p. 72; 'The Need for Watchfulness', *Shield*, October 1909, p. 1.

56 'Newly Issued Regulation in India and Hong-Kong', *Shield*, April 1899, pp. 17–18; 'New Developments of Regulation in the Crown Colonies', *Shield*, November 1899, pp. 56–7. For an account of regulationism in India see Kenneth Ballhatchet, *Race, Sex and Class Under the Raj: Imperial Attitudes and Policies and their Critics, 1793–1905*, London, Weidenfeld & Nicolson, 1980.

57 For changing medical conceptions of the regulation of venereal diseases see: Local Government Board, *Report on Venereal Diseases by Dr R.W. Johnstone with an Introduction by the Medical Officer of the Local Government Board*, 1913, GBPP 1913, XXXII, p. 423; Sir Malcolm Morris, 'A Plea for the Appointment of a Royal Commission', *Lancet*, 28 June 1913, vol. 1, pp. 1817–19. For analysis of the changes see Lucy Bland, ' "Cleansing the Portals of Life": The Venereal Disease Campaign in the Early Twentieth Century', in Mary Langan and Bill Schwarz (eds), *Crises in the British State 1880–1930*, London, Hutchinson, 1985, pp. 192–208. The general call was for the confidential notification of syphilis, together with systematic diagnosis and treatment. Medical pressure led to the setting up of a royal commission in October 1913.

58 Blanche Leppington, 'Public Morals and the Public Health', in James Marchant (ed.), *Public Morals*, London, Morgan and Scott, 1902, p. 229. For the gradual shift in the position of the British Branch of the International Abolitionist Federation and the LNA on science and scientific research see: Eduard Rest, 'Concerning Infection as an Offence', *Shield*, November–December 1904, p. 74; 'Prevention of Venereal Disease: Recent Medical Utterances', *Shield*, January 1910, p. 1; International Abolitionist Federation, *Morals and the Public Health: Report of the Portsmouth Conference*, June 1914.

59 'The Federation and Hygiene', *Shield*, January 1906, p. 5.

60 *Shield*, October 1913, p. 69.

61 'Moral Hygiene', *Shield*, October 1915, p. 63.

62 ibid.

63 F. J. Gould, 'Some Vital Principles of Moral Education', *Shield*, June 1917, p. 292. See also: NUWW, *Handbook and Report*, 1909–10, pp. 106–8; Elizabeth Gaskell, 'The Unspeakable', *Freewoman*, 18 January 1912, p. 176.

64 See: Mary Scharlieb, *Womanhood and Race Regeneration*, London, Cassell and Co, 1912, p. 7, and her *The Seven Ages of Woman: A Consideration of the Successive Phases of Woman's Life*, London, Cassell, 1915, p. 76.

65 Alice Ravenhill, 'Eugenic Ideals for Womanhood', *Eugenics Review*, April 1909–January 1910, vol. 1, no. 4, pp. 267–73.

66 Christabel Pankhurst, *The Great Scourge, and How to End It*, London, E. Pankhurst, 1913, p. vi.

67 Frances Swiney, *Women and Natural Law*, second edition, London, C.W. Daniel, 1912, p. 12.

68 Frances Swiney, *The Mystery of the Circle and the Cross; or, the Interpretation of Sex*, London, Open Road Publishing Co, 1908, p. 27. For Geddes' and Thomson's original theories see Patrick Geddes and John Thomson, *Sex*, London, Home University Library, 1914.

69 Frances Swiney, *The Bar of Isis; or, the Law of the Mother*, London, Open Road Publishing Co, 1907, p. 38. Swiney claimed that under favourable environmental conditions mothers only produced daughters. Self-fertilisation, using modern science, would be a real possibility for women as the race developed: Swiney, *The Mystery of the Circle*, p. 55.

70 'Sexual Hygiene', *Lancet*, 4 January 1913, vol. 1, p. 5.

71 Gould, 'Some Vital Principles of Moral Education', pp. 292–3. See also Norah March, 'Education of the Young in the Morals of Sex', *Shield*, July 1916, pp. 79–80.

72 Henry Havelock Ellis, *Studies in the Psychology of Sex*, vol. III, *Analysis of the Sexual Impulse Love and Pain. The Sexual Impulse in Women*, Philadelphia, F.A. Davis and Co, 1903, pp. 16–17. By the early twentieth century many of these debates were registering the impact of research into hormonal theory. See

especially Blair Bell, *The Sex Complex: A Study of the Relationships of the Internal Secretions to the Female Characteristics and Functions in Health and Disease*, London, Ballière and Co, 1916. For a summary of this research see Edwin Seligman (ed.), *Encyclopedia of the Social Sciences*, London, Macmillan, 1930–5, vol. 8, pp. 81–3.

73 Havelock Ellis, *Analysis of the Sexual Impulse*, pp. 3, 58. See also 'Chastity and Sexual Discipline', *Lancet*, 22 December 1900, vol. 2, pp. 1819–20.

74 See especially: NCPM, *Manifesto*, pp. 6–7; National Birth-Rate Commission, *Youth and the Race: The Development and Education of Young Citizens for Worthy Parenthood. Being the Fourth Report of the Commission 1920–1923*, London, Kegan Paul, Trench, Trubner and Co, 1923, pp. 3–7.

75 Alfred Schofield, *Continence*, 1909, p. 11.

76 Helen Wilson, 'Ideals of Parenthood', *Shield*, July 1916, p. 83. See also Frederick Gould, *On the Threshold of Sex: A Book for Readers Aged 14 to 21*, London, C.W. Daniel, 1909, p. 7.

77 Elizabeth Sloan Chesser, *From Girlhood to Womanhood*, London, Cassell, 1913, p. x.

78 National Birth-Rate Commission, *Youth and the Race*, pp. 10–11.

79 For details of the NCCVD's educational and propaganda work see: NCCVD, *Fifth Annual Report*, 1920, pp. 34, 145; NCCVD, *Sixth Annual Report*, 1921, p. 134.

80 Geddes and Thomson, *Sex*, pp. 16, 20. See also Henry Havelock Ellis, *Little Essays of Love and Virtue*, London, A. and C. Black, 1922, p. 61.

81 See: Henry Havelock Ellis, *The Criminal*, London, Walter Scott, 1890; Caesare Lombroso and William Ferrero, *The Female Offender*, London, Fisher Unwin, 1895.

82 William McDougall, *An Introduction to Social Psychology*, London, Macmillan, 1908, p. vi.

83 ibid., pp. 150, 359. See also William McDougall, *An Outline of Abnormal Psychology*, New York and Boston, C. Scribner and Sons, 1926.

84 Scharlieb, *The Seven Ages of Women*, p. 25. For early medical responses to Freud's work see: 'Freud's Theory of Hysteria', *Lancet*, 21 May 1909, vol. 1, pp. 1424–5; 'Freud's Theory Criticised', *Lancet*, 4 May 1912, vol. 1, p. 1238.

85 See especially the work of the Institute for the Scientific Treatment of Delinquency in Edward Glover, *The Diagnosis and Treatment of Delinquency*, London, Institute for the Study and Treatment of Delinquency, 1944, also the National Council for Mental Hygiene, *Eleventh Annual Report*, 1934.

86 Scharlieb, *The Seven Ages of Women*, p. 25.

87 Evidence of Mrs M. McMillan, Headmistress, Moberly Elementary School, Paddington, London County Council, *Report of the Education Committee on the Teaching of Sex Hygiene*, 1914, LCC no. 176, p. 15. For discreet warnings about lesbianism see Mary Scharlieb, 'Adolescent Girlhood under Modern Conditions', *Eugenics Review*, April 1909–January 1910, vol. 1, no. 2, p. 174.

88 Evidence of Mr W. Nicholls, late Head, Boys' Department, Ruby Street School, Peckham, London County Council, *Report of the Education Committee*, p. 21.

89 Lucy Bland, ' "Guardians of the Race" or "Vampires Upon the Nation's Health?": Female Sexuality and its Regulation in Early Twentieth-Century Britain', in Elizabeth Whitelegg *et al.* (eds), *The Changing Experience of Women*, Oxford, Martin Robertson, 1982, pp. 373–88. For contemporary panics over 'the amateur' see: evidence of Sir Ernley Blackwell, Under Secretary of State for the Home Office, and J. Dickenson, Chief Magistrate, *Report of the Joint Select Committee on the Criminal Law Amendment Bill and Sexual Offences Bill [HL]*,

1918, GBPP 1918, III, pp. 331–3. For feminist responses see Alison Neilans, 'Disorderly Women', *Shield*, February 1915, pp. 20–1.

90 Mary Douie, *How Girls Can Help Towards Social Hygiene*, London, National Council for Combating Venereal Disease, 1924, pp. 16–17. See also Louise Creighton, *Successful and Unsuccessful Marriages*, London, Longman, Green & Co, 1916, p. 29.

91 Evidence of McMillan, London County Council, *Report of the Education Committee*, p. 26.

92 Chesser, *From Girlhood to Womanhood*, p. 23.

93 Havelock Ellis, *Analysis of the Sexual Impulse*, pp. 229, 241.

94 ibid., p. 18.

95 Marie Stopes, *Married Love: A New Contribution to the Solution of Sex Difficulties*, London, A.C. Fifield, 1918, p. 21. See also Stopes, *Contraception: Its Theory, History and Practice*, London, J. Bale and Co, 1923.

96 See Edward Lyttleton's evidence to the Royal Commission on Venereal Diseases, *Final Report of the Commissioners*, 1916, GBPP 1916, XVI, p. 359. For older style prohibitions see Mary Scharlieb and Frederic Sibly, *Youth and Sex: Dangers and Safeguards for Girls and Boys*, London, T.C. & E.C. Jack, 1912, pp. 59–60.

97 Schofield, *Continence*, p. 3.

98 Evidence of Sir Robert Baden-Powell, National Birth-Rate Commission, *Youth and the Race*, p. 206.

99 Schofield, *Continence*, p. 3.

100 ibid.

101 See A.G.Tansley's evidence, National Birth-Rate Commission, *Youth and the Race*, p. 78.

102 Evidence of Lyttleton, Royal Commission on Venereal Diseases, *Final Report*, p. 353.

103 Scharlieb and Sibly, *Youth and Sex*, p. 109.

104 See E.M. Hughes, 'Sex Teaching in Girls' Schools', *Eugenics Review*, April 1910–January 1911, vol. II, no. 1, pp. 144–6.

105 London County Council, *Report of the Education Committee*, pp. 9–12.

106 ibid., p. 15.

107 Mary Scharlieb, *Womanhood and Race-Regeneration*, London, Cassell and Co, 1912, p. 21.

108 See Helen Wilson's evidence to the Royal Commission on Venereal Diseases, *First Report of the Commissioners*, 1914, GBPP 1914, XLIX, pp. 295–6.

109 London County Council, *Report of the Education Committee*, pp. 4–5.

110 Royal Commission on Venereal Diseases, *Final Report*, pp. 82–3.

111 ibid. See also *Forty-Sixth Annual Report of the Local Government Board for 1916–1917, Supplement Containing the Report of the Medical Officer*, 1917, GBPP 1917–18, XVI, pp. 220–1.

112 NCCVD, *Fifth Annual Report*, 1920, p. 10. The Royal Commission on Venereal Diseases recommended that the NCCVD should be recognised as an authoritative body for the purpose of spreading knowledge and giving advice on venereal diseases. During 1918 grants totalling £13,000 were made to the council by the Local Government Board. These funds were continued by the Ministry of Health throughout the 1920s.

113 See British Social Hygiene Council, *Empire and Social Hygiene Yearbook*, London, Allen & Unwin, 1934, p. 97.

114 In 1924 the Ministry of Health upheld the dismissal of Nurse E.S. Daniels, a health worker in Edmonton, London, for giving contraceptive advice to local

maternity clinics. See Sheila Rowbotham, *A New World for Women: Stella Browne, Socialist Feminist*, London, Pluto Press, 1977. Under a memorandum of July 1930, 153/MCW, the Minister of Health allowed maternity centres to give contraceptive advice to married women 'in cases where further pregnancy would be detrimental to health'. For politicians' ambiguity over the issue, see Mr F.A. Broad to Neville Chamberlain, Minister of Health, Birth Control (Information), Commons, *Parliamentary Debates*, 25 July 1923, fifth series, vol. 167, col. 480.

115 See Bill Schwarz, 'The Language of Constitutionalism: Baldwinite Conservatism', in *Formations of Nation and People*, London, Routledge & Kegan Paul, 1984, pp. 1–18.

116 National Birth-Rate Commission, *Youth and the Race*, p. v.

117 Jeffrey Weeks discusses the relationship between the new patterns of consumption and changes in sexual and marital behaviour in *Sex, Politics and Society: The Regulation of Sexuality since 1800*, London, Longman, 1981, ch. 11. For the impact of the new consumerism on women's lives see Catherine Hall, 'Married Women at Home in Birmingham in the 1920s and 1930s', *Oral History*, 1977, vol. 5, no. 2, pp. 62–83. For women's magazines see Cynthia White, *Women's Magazines 1693–1968*, London, Joseph, 1970.

118 See Frances Stevenson to Marie Stopes, 3 March 1921, quoted in Ruth Hall (ed.), *Dear Dr Stopes: Sex in the 1920s*, London, Deutsch, 1978, p. 202.

119 Speech by Viscountess Astor, Supply Committee: Ministry of Health, Commons, *Parliamentary Debates*, 17 July 1935, fifth series, vol. 304, col. 1135.

120 See especially: 'Birmingham Cinema Enquiry Committee', NVA, Executive Committee Minutes, 26 April 1932, Fawcett Library, London, p. 127; 'Mother's Union, Cinema Films', NVA, Executive Committee Minutes, 27 June 1933, p. 175.

121 NVA, Executive Committee Minutes, 25 March 1919.

122 Dame Katherine Furse, Biological Education Congress, 1928, preserved in NVA, *Papers*, box 98, 10A, Fawcett Library, London.

123 Sex Education, NVA, Minutes, 23 February 1932, Fawcett Library, London, pp. 115–16.

124 Sir W. Arbuthnot Lane, 'What are the Disabilities and the Compensations Entailed by the Reproductive Function of the Female?', *Lancet*, 9 November 1918, vol. 2, p. 622.

125 'Married Love', *Lancet*, 28 December 1918, vol. 2, p. 886; *BMJ*, 26 November 1921, vol. 2, p. 903.

126 'Current Sexual Decorum', *Lancet*, 6 September 1919, vol. 2, p. 463.

127 The focus for the modernist challenge was the Churchman's Union, with its journal the *Modern Churchman*. See also: Michael Glazebrook, *Faith of a Modern Churchman*, second edition, London, John Murray, 1925; William Pyke, *Modernism as a Working Faith*, Cambridge, W. Heffer and Sons, 1925; Percy Gardner, *Modernism in the English Church*, London, Methuen, 1926.

128 Conference of Bishops of the Anglican Communion, *The Lambeth Conference 1930. Encyclical Letter from the Bishops with Resolutions and Reports*, London, SPCK, 1930, pp. 66–7.

129 ibid., p. 85. For similar statements see Travers Rogers, *The Church and the People*, London, Sampson Low, 1930, pp. 139–43.

130 Theodoor van de Velde, *Ideal Marriage: Its Physiology and Technique*, London, Heinemann, 1928, p. 111. See also: Benjamin Lindsey and Wainwright Evans, *The Companionate Marriage*, London, Brentano's, 1928; Max Exner, *The Sexual Side of Marriage*, London, Allen & Unwin, 1932, pp. 98–9;

Helena Wright, *The Sex Factor in Marriage. A Book for Those Who Are or Are About the be Married*, London, Noel Douglas, 1930. For discussion of women's changing experience of sexuality within marriage see Ellen Holtman, 'The Pursuit of Married Love: Women's Attitudes Towards Sexuality and Marriage in Great Britain, 1918–1939', *Journal of Social History*, 1982, vol. 16, no. 2, pp. 39–51.

131 'The Next Step', *Shield*, January 1913, p. 15.

132 In February 1917 the Home Office introduced a new Criminal Law Amendment Bill. Its clauses included a stipulation that sexual intercourse, or its solicitation or invitation, was a criminal offence for any person suffering from communicable venereal disease, together with measures empowering magistrates to order the detention of young women under eighteen who had been convicted of soliciting. A variant of the bill was reintroduced in 1918, along with the Sexual Offences Bill [HL], which addressed many of the same concerns, with similar measures being proposed again in 1920 and 1921. Feminists were divided over the question of the criminalisation of the transmission of venereal disease though most women's organisations were nervous about further use of the criminal law. In 1922 Parliament finally passed the Criminal Law Amendment Act, 12 and 13 Geo. 5, ch. 56. The act dropped the contentious clauses on the transmission of venereal disease and the detention of young girls, while including provisions for the abolition of the 'reasonable cause to believe' clause, in cases of indecent assault on young persons under sixteen, and increasing penalties for brothel keeping.

133 *Vote*, 20 April 1917, p. 189. For the shift in feminist strategy away from the criminal law and towards sex education see: Neilans, 'Disorderly Women'; 'Criminal Law Amendment Bill', *Vote*, 9 March 1917, p.137; 'The Programme of the NUWSS', *Common Cause*, 11 October 1918, p. 294.

134 'The Programme of the NUWSS', *Common Cause*.

EPILOGUE

1 'Rock "Gave AIDS to His Gay Lovers" ', *Sun*, 4 October 1985. See also 'The Hunk Who Lived a Lie', *Sun*, 3 October 1985.

2 'The Hunk Who Lived a Lie'.

3 For reportage which defined gay men as part of the socially undesirable see the coverage of the 1983 Brighton boy sex case: 'A Town Without Innocence', *Daily Express*, 22 August 1983; 'Gays in Revenge Terror', *Sun*, 20 August 1983.

4 For the targeting of high risk groups see: Ministry of Health, *On the State of the Public Health, Being the Annual Report of the Chief Medical Officer for 1961*, GBPP 1962–3, XIX, p. 52.

5 R. Wilcox, 'Society and High Risk Groups', in R. Catterall and C. Nicol (eds), *Sexually Transmitted Diseases: Proceedings of a Conference Sponsored Jointly by the Royal Society of Medicine and the Royal Society of Medical Foundations Inc*, London, Academic Press, 1975, p. 32.

6 See for example: W.L. Drew *et al.*, 'Cytomegalovirus and Kaposi's Sarcoma in Young Homosexual Men', *Lancet*, 17 July 1982, vol. 2, pp. 125–7; Michael Ross, 'Social Factors in Homosexually Acquired vd', *British Journal of Venereal Diseases*, August 1982, vol. 58, no. 4, p. 263.

7 A.J. Pinching *et al.*, 'Studies of Cellular Immunity in Male Homosexuals in London', *Lancet*, 16 July 1983, vol. 2, pp. 126–9. See also 'The Cause of AIDS?', *Lancet*, 12 May 1984, vol. 1, pp. 1053–4.

8 Department of Health and Social Security, *On the State of the Public Health: The Annual Report of the Chief Medical Officer of the DHSS for the Year 1982*, London, HMSO, 1983, p. 53.

9 The Department of Health and Social Security's 'Don't Aid AIDS' campaign was launched with full-page advertisements in the national press on 16 and 17 March 1986.

10 For voices within the gay community which called for a return to monogamy see, in the USA, Larry Kramer, '1, 112 AND COUNTING', *New York Native*, 14–27 March 1983, no. 59, p. 1, and in Britain, N. Smith, 'I Have Stopped Being Promiscuous', *Capital Gay*, 3 February 1984.

11 The most coherent statement of radical pluralism is in Jeffrey Weeks, *Sexuality and Its Discontents: Meaning, Myths and Modern Sexualities*, London, Routledge & Kegan Paul, 1985, chs 9 and 10.

SELECTED BIBLIOGRAPHY

Primary sources

I   Unpublished manuscripts and collections
II Official publications
III Rules, reports and proceedings
IV Newspapers, periodicals and dictionaries
V   Other primary sources

Secondary sources

I   Unpublished works
II Published books and articles

Primary sources

I Unpublished manuscripts and collections

Josephine Butler Collection, Fawcett Library, London.
Papers of Sir Edwin Chadwick, The Library, University College, London.
Kay-Shuttleworth Papers, John Ryelands University Library, Manchester.
Minutes of the National Association for the Repeal of the Contagious Diseases Acts, Fawcett Library, London.
National Vigilance Association Collection, Fawcett Library, London.
Public Record Office, Kew:

Admiralty Papers

History and Operation of the Contagious Diseases Acts in the Home Ports, 1873, ADM/6418.

Board of Education Papers

Dronfield Case, ED50/185.

Home Office Papers

Criminal Law Amendment Bill, 1884–5, HO45/59343G.
Correspondence, Criminal Law Amendment Bill, 1885, HO45/A40683.
Police Powers under Criminal Law Amendment Act, 1886–7, HO45/A45364.
St George's Vigilance Society for Payments, 1887, HO45/X14891.
Difficulties of Police on Convictions, 1887–9, HO45/X15663.
Criminal Law Amendment Bill, 1910, HO45/175440.
Criminal Law Amendment Bills, 1908–13, HO45/178486.

Local Government Board Papers

Government Office Correspondence, 1873, LGB78178/73.
Miscellaneous Correspondence, 1876, LGB58096/76.

Ministry of Health Papers

Central Council for Health Education, Minute Book, 1935–9, MH82/1.

Privy Council Papers

Central Board of Health, Minutes, 1831, PC1/101.
Central Board of Health, Minutes, 1831–2, PC1/105.
Papers Relating to Cholera, 1831–2, PC1/105.
Central Board of Health, Extract from Proceedings, 1831, PC1/2662.
Central Board of Health, Daily Report of Cholera Cases, 1831–2, PC1/4395.

Treasury Papers

Treasury Minutes, 1871, T1/18953.

War Office Papers

Venereal Disease, Army and Navy, 1862, WO33/12.
Shaftesbury Manuscript, National Register of Archives, London.

II Official publications
Civil Service

Report on the Organization of the Permanent Civil Service, GBPP 1854, XXVII.

Criminal Law

Report from the Select Committee [HL] on the State of the Law Relating to the Protection of Young Girls, GBPP 1881, IX.
Second Report, GBPP 1882, XIII.
Report of the Joint Select Committee on the Criminal Law Amendment Bill and Sexual Offences Bill [HL], GBPP 1918, III.

Health

Copies of Certain Papers Relating to Cholera Together with the Report of the Central Board of Health Thereupon, GBPP 1831–2, XXVI.

Report from the Poor Law Commissioners into the Sanitary Condition of the Labouring Population of Great Britain, HL 1842, XXVI–XXVIII.

Report of the Royal Commission on the Health of the Army, GBPP 1857, XVIII.

Tenth Annual Report of the Medical Officer of the Privy Council, GBPP 1867–8, XXXVI.

Eleventh Annual Report, GBPP 1868–9, XXXII.

Thirteenth Annual Report, GBPP 1871, XXI.

Annual Reports of the Inspector-General of Recruiting, GBPP 1901, IX; 1902, X; 1903, XXXVIII.

Report of the Interdepartmental Committee on Physical Deterioration, GBPP 1904, XXXII.

Report of the Interdepartmental Committee on Physical Exercises, GBPP 1904, XIX.

Report of the Royal Commission on the Care and Control of the Feeble-Minded, GBPP 1908, XXXV–XXXIX.

Annual Report for 1909 of the Chief Medical Officer of the Board of Education, GBPP 1910, XXIII.

Forty-Sixth Annual Report of the Local Government Board for 1916–1917, Supplement Containing the Report of the Medical Officer, GBPP 1917–18, XVI.

Sir George Newman, An Outline of the Practice of Preventive Medicine, GBPP 1919, XXXIX.

First Annual Report of the Ministry of Health for 1919–1920, GBPP 1920, XVII.

Ministry of Health, On the State of the Public Health, Being the Annual Report of the Chief Medical Officer for 1961, GBPP, 1962–3, XIX.

Department of Health and Social Security, On the State of the Public Health: The Annual Report of the Chief Medical Officer of the DHSS for the Year 1982, London, HMSO, 1983.

Housing

Royal Commission on the Housing of the Working Classes, First Report of the Commissioners, England, GBPP 1884–5, XXX.

Industrial conditions

Children's Employment Commission, First Report. Mines, GBPP 1842, XV–XVII.

Marriage and divorce

Report of the Commissioners on the Law of Divorce, and on the Mode of Obtaining Divorce a Vinculo Matrimonii, GBPP 1852–3, XL.

Report of the Royal Commission on the Laws of Marriage, GBPP 1867–8, XXXII.

Report of the Royal Commission on Divorce and Matrimonial Causes, GBPP 1912–13, XVIII–XX.

Police

Report of the Royal Commission upon the Duties of the Metropolitan Police, GBPP 1908, L.

Population

Fourth Annual Report of the Registrar-General of Births, Deaths and Marriages, GBPP 1842, XIX.
Fifth Annual Report, GBPP 1843, XXI.

Venereal disease

Report of the House of Commons Select Committee to Inquire into the Pathology and Treatment of the Venereal Disease, with a View to Diminish its Injurious Effects on the Men of the Army and Navy, GBPP 1867–8, XXXVII.
Report from the Select Committee on the Contagious Diseases Act (1866), GBPP 1868–9, VII.
Report from the Royal Commission on the Administration and Operation of the Contagious Diseases Acts 1866–69, GBPP 1871, XIX.
Local Government Board, Report on Venereal Diseases by Dr. R.W. Johnstone with an Introduction by the Medical Officer of the Local Government Board, GBPP 1913, XXXII.
Royal Commission on Venereal Diseases, First Report of the Commissioners, GBPP 1914, XLIX.
Royal Commission on Venereal Diseases, Final Report of the Commissioners, GBPP 1916, XVI.

III Rules, reports and proceedings

British Social Hygiene Council, Empire and Social Hygiene Year Book, London, Allen & Unwin, 1934.
Conference of Bishops of the Anglican Communion, The Lambeth Conference 1930. Encyclical Letter from the Bishops with Resolutions and Reports, London, SPCK, 1930.
Girls' Friendly Society, A Special Report, London, Hatchards, 1879.
Harveian Medical Society of London, Report of the Committee for the Prevention of Venereal Disease, 1867.
International Abolitionist Federation, Morals and Public Health: Report of the Portsmouth Conference, June 1914.
Ladies' National Association, Report for the Year Ending November 1871.
Legitimation League, Aims and Objects, undated.
London County Council, Report of the Education Committee on the Teaching of Sex Hygiene, 1914, LCC no. 176.
National Birth-Rate Commission, Youth and the Race: The Development and Education of Young Citizens for Worthy Parenthood. Being the Fourth Report of the Commission 1920–1923, London, Kegan, Paul, Trench, Trubner and Co, 1923.

National Council for Combating Venereal Disease, *Annual Reports*, 1916–23.
National Council for Mental Hygiene, *Eleventh Annual Report*, 1934.
National Council of Public Morals, *Manifesto*, 1910.
National Union of Women Workers, *Handbooks and Reports*, 1909–13.
National Vigilance Association, *Objects, Constitution and Rules*, 1885.
National Vigilance Association, *Annual Reports*, 1894–1908.
People's League of Health, *Second General Report for the Years 1922–5*.

IV Newspapers, periodicals and dictionaries

Adult
British Medical Journal
Common Cause
Derbyshire Times
Eugenics Review
Freewoman
Journal of the Vigilance Association for the Defence of Personal Rights
Lancet
London Medical Directory and General Medical Register
National League Journal
Practitioner
Quarterly Record of the Tower Hamlets Mission
Shield
Suffrage Annual and Woman's Who's Who
Suffragette
The Times
Vote
Weekly Dispatch
Westminster Review
Women's Dreadnought

V Other Primary Sources

Abraham, James, *Lettsom: His Life, Times, Friends and Descendants*, London, William Heinemann, 1933.

Acton, William, *The Functions and Disorders of the Reproductive Organs in Childhood, Youth, Adult Age and Advanced Life Considered in Their Physiological, Social and Moral Relations*, London, John Churchill, 1857.

Acton, William, *Prostitution Considered in Its Moral, Social and Sanitary Aspects in London and Other Large Cities; with Proposals for the Mitigation and Prevention of Its Attendant Evils*, London, John Churchill, 1857.

Acton, William, *The Contagious Diseases Act, Shall the Contagious Diseases Act be Applied to the Civil Population?*, London, J. and A. Churchill, 1870.

Addison, Christopher, *Politics from Within, 1911–1918*, London, Herbert Jenkins, 1924, 2 vols.

Anon., *Tabes Dorsalis or, the Causes of Consumption in Young Men and Women*, London, J. Bailey, 1818.

Anon., *Twenty Minutes Advice on Diet, Regimen and All Other Matters Connected with Health*, undated.

Appleyard, Rollo, *A Tribute to Michael Faraday*, London, Constable and Co, 1931.

Armstrong, Richard, *Our Duty in the Matter of Social Purity, An Address to Young Men*, London, Social Purity Alliance, 1885.

Ashley, Lord, *Moral and Religious Education of the Working Classes, The Speech of Lord Ashley M.P. in the House of Commons, February 28, 1843*, London, John Ollivier, 1843.

Ayre, Joseph, *A Report on the Methods and Results of the Treatment for the Malignant Cholera*, London, Longman and Co, 1833.

Ballantyne, John, *Manual of Ante-Natal Pathology and Hygiene. The Embryo*, Edinburgh, W. Green, 1904.

Banks, Abraham, *Medical Etiquette; or, an Essay upon the Laws and Regulations which Ought to Govern the Conduct of Members of the Medical Profession in Their Relation to Each Other*, London, Charles Fox, 1839.

Barber, Geoffrey, *School Education in Hygiene and Sex. Lectures Given at Feldsted School*, Cambridge, W. Heffer and Sons, 1936.

Barrett, Rosa, *Ellice Hopkins: A Memoir*, London, Wells Gardiner & Co, 1907.

Bell, Blair, *The Sex Complex: A Study of the Relationships of the Internal Secretions to the Female Characteristics and Functions in Health and Disease*, London, Ballière and Co, 1916.

Besant, Annie, *An Autobiography*, London, T. Fisher Unwin, 1893.

Biggs, Thomas, *The Proposed Extension of the Contagious Diseases Act in Its Moral and Economical Aspects Read Before the Economy and Trade Section of the National Association for the Promotion of Social Science*, London, William Tweedie, 1870.

Billington-Greig, Teresa, 'The Truth About White Slavery', *English Review*, June 1913, vol. 14, pp. 428–46.

Blackwell, Elizabeth, *How to Keep a Household in Health. An Address*, London, Ladies' Sanitary Association, 1870.

Blackwell, Elizabeth, *The Human Element in Sex: Being a Medical Enquiry in the Relation of Sexual Physiology to Christian Morality*, London, J. and A. Churchill, 1884.

Blackwell, Elizabeth, *The Religion of Health*, London, Moral Reform Union, 1889.

Blackwell, Elizabeth, *Christian Duty in Regard to Vice*, London, Moral Reform Union, 1891.

Board of Education, *Syllabus of Physical Exercises for Use in Public Elementary Schools*, London, HMSO, 1904 and 1909.

Booth, Charles, *Life and Labour of the People of London*, second edition, London, Macmillan, 1902, 17 vols.

Brougham, Henry, *Paley's Natural Theology with Illustrative Notes*, London, Charles Knight, 1826.

Brougham, Henry, *A Discourse of the Objects, Advantages and Pleasures of Science*, London, Society for the Diffusion of Useful Knowledge, 1827.

Browne, Stella, *Sexual Variety and Variability Among Women and Their Bearing Upon Social Reconstruction*, London, British Society for the Study of Sex Psychology, 1917.

Bullen, Robert, *Our Duty as Teachers, with Reference to Social Purity Work. An Address*, London, J. and F. Wood, 1884.

Burnell, George, *Letter to the Rt. Hon. Viscount Palmerston, M.P. in Reply to the Report of the Public Health Act*, London, J. Davy & Sons, 1854.

Butler, Josephine (ed.), *Women's Work and Women's Culture*, London, Macmillan, 1869.

Butler, Josephine, *Sursum Corda; Annual Address to the Ladies' National Association*, Liverpool, T. Brakell, 1871.

Butler, Josephine, *Speech Delivered . . . at the Fourth Annual Meeting of the Vigilance Association for the Defence of Personal Rights*, London, Vigilance Association for the Defence of Personal Rights, 1874.

Butler, Josephine, *A Letter to the Members of the Ladies' National Association*, Liverpool, T. Brakell, 1875.

Butler, Josephine, *Social Purity. An Address Given at Cambridge*, London, Morgan & Scott, 1879.

Butler, Josephine, *Personal Reminiscences of a Great Crusade*, London, H. Marshall & Sons, 1896.

Butter, Henry, *Marriage for the Million: For the Lads and Lassies of the Working Classes*, London, W.H. Guest, 1875.

Butter, Henry, *What's the Harm? A Young Man's Questions, Answered*, London, W.H. Guest, 1880.

Carpenter, Edward, *England's Ideal, and Other Papers on Social Subjects*, London, Swan Sonnenschen & Co, 1887.

Carpenter, Edward, *Love's Coming-of-Age. A Series of Papers on the Relations of the Sexes*, Manchester, Labour Press, 1896.

Carpenter, Edward, *Prisons, Police and Punishment. An Inquiry into the Causes and Treatment of Crime and Criminals*, London, A.C. Fifield, 1905.

Carpenter, Edward, *My Days and Dreams, Being Autobiographical Notes*, London, Allen & Unwin, 1916.

Chalmers, Thomas, *The Christian and Civic Economy of Large Towns*, Glasgow, William Collins, 1821–6, 3 vols.

Chant, Laura Ormiston, *Why We Attacked the Empire*, London, Marshall and Son, 1895.

Charrington, Frederick, *An Oasis in the Desert*, London, Morgan & Scott, 1886.

Chesser, Elizabeth Sloan, *From Girlhood to Womanhood*, London, Cassell, 1913.

Chesser, Elizabeth Sloan, *Physiology and Hygiene for Girls' Schools and Colleges*, London, G. Bell & Sons, 1914.

Chesser, Elizabeth Sloan, *The Woman Who Knows Herself*, London, William Heinemann, 1926.

Chesser, Elizabeth Sloan, *Five Phases of Love*, London, Herbert Jenkins, 1939.

Cooke, William, *An Address to British Females on the Moral Management of Pregnancy and Labour*, London, E. Cox & Co, 1817.

Cooke, William, *Mind and the Emotions Considered in Relation to Health and Disease*, London, Longman & Co, 1839.

Coote, William, *A Vision and Its Fulfilment*, London, National Vigilance Association, 1910.

Coote, William, *A Romance of Philanthropy. A Record of Thirty Years Work of the National Vigilance Association*, London, National Vigilance Association, 1916.

Creighton, Louise, *Successful and Unsuccessful Marriages*, London, Longman, Green & Co, 1916.

Curgenven, John, *The Contagious Diseases Act of 1866, and Its Extension to the Civil Population of the United Kingdom*, London, W.W. Head, 1868.

Dark, Sidney, *Five Deans*, London, Jonathan Cape, 1928.

Darwin, Charles, *The Descent of Man. Selection in Relation to Sex*, London, John Murray, 1871, 2 vols.

Dicey, Albert Venn, *The Law and Public Opinion in England During the Nineteenth Century*, London, Macmillan, 1905.

Douie, Mary, *How Girls Can Help Towards Social Hygiene*, London, National Council for Combating Venereal Disease, 1924.

Douie, Mary, *England's Girls and England's Future*, revised edition, London, British Social Hygiene Council, 1927.

Dyer, Alfred, *Facts for Men on Purity and Health*, London, Dyer Brothers, 1884.

Elderton, Ethel, *The Relative Strength of Nurture and Nature*, London, Dulau and Co, 1909.

Ellis, Henry Havelock, *The Criminal*, London, Walter Scott, 1890.

Ellis, Henry Havelock, *Studies in the Psychology of Sex*, vol. I, *Sexual Inversion*, London, University Press, 1897.

Ellis, Henry Havelock, *Studies in the Psychology of Sex*, vol. III, *Analysis of the Sexual Impulse Love and Pain. The Sexual Impulse in Women*, Philadelphia, F.A. Davis and Co, 1903.

Ellis, Henry Havelock, *The Problem of Race-Regeneration*, London, Cassell and Co, 1911.

Ellis, Henry Havelock, *The Task of Social Hygiene*, London, Constable, 1912.

Ellis, Henry Havelock, *Little Essays of Love and Virtue*, London, A. and C. Black, 1922.

Ellis, Henry Havelock, *The Play Function of Sex*, London, British Society for the Study of Sex Psychology, 1923.

Ellis, Henry Havelock, *Morals, Manners and Men*, London, Watts & Co, 1939.

Ellis, Henry Havelock, *My Life*, London and Toronto, William Heinemann, 1940.

Elmy, Elizabeth Wolstenholme, *The Human Flower*, third edition, Congleton, Mrs W. Elmy, 1895.

Elmy, Elizabeth Wolstenholme, *Phases of Love*, Congleton, Mrs W. Elmy, 1897.

Engström, Charles, *Purity Treated Purely. A Sermon*, London, Rivingtons, 1885.

Exner, Max, *The Sexual Side of Marriage*, London, Allen & Unwin, 1932.

Forel, Auguste, *Sexual Ethics*, London, New Age Press, 1908.

Gallichan, Walter, *The Great Unmarried*, London, T. Werner Laurie, 1916.

Gardiner, Alfred, *The Life of Sir William Harcourt*, London, Constable, 1923, 2 vols.

Gardner, Percy, *Modernism in the English Church*, London, Methuen, 1926.

Garle, Henry, *Legislative Theories Underlying Social Hygiene*, London, British Social Hygiene Council, 1933.

Gaulter, Henry, *The Origin and Progress of the Malignant Cholera in Manchester, Considered Chiefly in Their Bearing on Contagiousness and the Secondary Causes of the Disease*, London, Longman, 1833.

Geddes, Patrick and Thomson, John, *The Evolution of Sex*, London, Walter Scott, 1890.

Geddes, Patrick and Thomson, John, *Sex*, London, Home University Library, 1914.

Girdlestone, Charles, *Seven Sermons Preached During the Prevalence of Cholera in the Parish of Sedgley*, London, J.G. and F. Rivington, 1833.

Girdlestone, Charles, *Farewell Sermons: Preached in the Parish Church of Sedgley*, London, J.G. and F. Rivington, 1837.

Girdlestone, Charles, *Letters on the Unhealthy Condition of the Lower Class of Dwellings Especially in Large Towns. Founded on the First Report of the Health of Towns Commission*, London, Longman, 1845.

Girls' Friendly Society, *An Appeal to the Mistresses of Elementary Schools from the Girls' Friendly Society*, London, Hatchards, 1892.

Glazebrook, Michael, *Faith of a Modern Churchman*, second edition, London, John Murray, 1925.

Glover, Edward, *The Diagnosis and Treatment of Delinquency*, London, Institute for the Study and Treatment of Delinquency, 1944.

Gould, Frederick, *On the Threshold of Sex: A Book for Readers Aged 14 to 21*, London, C.W. Daniel, 1909.

Gray, Arthur, *Sex Teaching*, London, National Sunday School Union, 1929.

Green, Thomas, *Lectures on the Principles of Political Obligation and Freedom of Contract*, London, Longman, 1885.

Greenwood, James, *A Night in a Workhouse*, London, Pall Mall Gazette, 1866.

Greenwood, James, *The Wilds of London*, London, Chatto & Windus, 1874.

Greenwood, James, *Low Life Deeps: An Account of the Strange Fish to Be Found There*, London, Chatto & Windus, 1876.

Greg, Robert, *The Factory Question, Considered in Relation to Its Effects on the Health and Morals of Those Employed in Factories*, London, James Ridgway, 1837.

Greg, William, *The Great Sin of Great Cities*, London, John Chapman, 1853.

Griffith, Edward, *Modern Marriage and Birth Control*, London, Victor Gollancz, 1935.

Guy, William, *Unhealthiness of Towns, Its Causes and Remedies Being a Lecture Delivered at Crosby Hall, Bishopsgate Street*, London, Charles Knight & Co, 1845.

Halford, Henry, *On the Education and Conduct of a Physician*, London, John Murray, 1834.

Hamilton, Cicely, *Marriage as a Trade*, London, Chapman and Hall, 1909.

Hammond, John and Hammond, Barbara, *James Stansfeld. A Victorian Champion of Sex Equality*, London, Longman, 1932.

Hartley, David, *Observations on Man, his Frame, his Duty, and his Expectations*, London, James Leake and William Frederick, 1749.

Hawksley, T., *A Letter to the Most Hon. The Marquis of Chandos, M.P. in Relation to the Extraordinary Powers Assumed by the General Board of Health*, London, Saunders and Stanford, 1853.

Hazelwood, J., 'The Knight of Purity': Some Thoughts for Schoolboys*, Leeds, Inchbold & Beck, 1884.

Health of Towns Association, *Address from the Committee of the Health of Towns Association to the Bishop of London and the Rev. the Clergy*, London, Richard Barrett, 1848.

Hicks, William Joynson, *Do We Need a Censor?*, London, Faber & Faber, 1929.

Hobhouse, Leonard, *Mind in Evolution*, London, Macmillan & Co, 1901.

Hobhouse, Leonard, *Democracy and Reaction*, London, T. Fisher Unwin, 1904.

Hodder, Edwin, *The Life and Work of the Seventh Earl of Shaftesbury*, London, Cassell and Co, 1887, 3 vols.

Hopkins, Ellice, *An Englishwoman's Work Among Workingmen*, London, New Britain, 1875.

Hopkins, Ellice, *Work in Brighton*, London, Hatchards, 1877.

Hopkins, Ellice, *Grave Moral Questions Addressed to the Men and Women of England*, London, Hatchards, 1882.

Hopkins, Ellice, *The Girls' Friendly Society – An Appeal to the Mistresses of Elementary Schools*, London, Hatchards, 1882.

Hopkins, Ellice, *Village Morality: A Letter Addressed to Clergymen's Wives and Christian Workers*, London, Hatchards, 1882.

Hopkins, Ellice, *The White Cross Army. A Statement of the Bishop of Durham's Movement*, London, Hatchards, 1883.

Hopkins, Ellice, *The Power of Womanhood; or, Mothers and Sons*, London, Wells Gardner & Co, 1899.

Hopkins, Ellice, *The Early Training of Girls and Boys. An Appeal to Working Women*, London, P.S. King and Son, 1902.

Horner, Leonard, *On the Employment of Children, in Factories and Other Works in the United Kingdom, and in Some Foreign Countries*, London, Longman, 1840.

Hume-Rothery, Mary, *A Letter Addressed to the Right Hon. W.E. Gladstone M.P. and Other Members of Her Majesty's Government Touching the Contagious Diseases Acts of 1866 and 1869*, London, Simpkin, Marshall and Co, 1870.

Humphreys, Noel (ed.), *Vital Statistics. A Memorial Volume of Selections from the Reports and Writings of William Farr*, London, Sanitary Institute, 1885.

Inge, William, *Diary of a Dean. St Pauls 1911–1934*, London, Hutchinson, 1949.

Inskip, Thomas, *Sunday a National Heritage. A Broadcast Talk*, London, Imperial Alliance for the Defence of Sunday, 1939.

Johnson, George and Johnson, Lucy (eds), *Josephine E. Butler. An Autobiographical Memoir*, London, J.W. Arrowsmith, 1928.

Jones, William, *Practical Observations on Diseases of Women*, London and Paris, H. Ballière, 1839.

Kay, James, *A Letter to the People of Lancashire, Concerning the Future Representation of the Commercial Interest, by the Return of Members of Its New Boroughs to the Reformed Parliament*, London, James Ridgway, 1831.

Kay, James, *The Moral and Physical Condition of the Working Classes Employed in the Cotton Manufacture in Manchester*, second edition, London, James Ridgway, 1832.

Kingsley, Charles, *His Letters and Memories of his Life, Edited by his Wife*, Leipzig, Bernhard Tauchnitz, 1881, 2 vols.

Krafft-Ebing, Richard von, *Psychopathia Sexualis. Eine Klinische-Forensische Studie*, Stuttgart, Ferdinand Enke, 1887.

Ladies' National Association, *The Contagious Diseases Acts and the Royal Commission by a Necessarian*, Manchester, A. Ireland & Co, 1871.

Layard, Daniel, *Directions to Prevent the Contagion of the Jail-Distemper, Commonly Called Jail-Fever*, London, James Robson, 1772.

Lazarsfeld, Sophie, *Rhythm of Life. A Guide to Sexual Harmony for Women*, trans. Karsten and E. Pelham Stapelfeldt, London, G. Routledge and Sons, 1934.

Leader, Robert (ed.), *Life and Letters of John Arthur Roebuck*, London, E. Arnold, 1897.

Leigh, John and Gardiner, Ner, *History of Cholera in Manchester in 1849*, London, Simpkin, Marshall and Co, 1850.

Leigh, William, *An Authentic Narrative of the Melancholy Occurrence at Bilston .... During the Awful Visitation ... by Cholera ... in 1832*, Wolverhampton, William Parke, 1833.

Lettsom, John Coakley, *Hints Respecting the Prison of Newgate*, London, 1794.

Lettsom, John Coakley, *Hints Designed to Promote Beneficence, Temperance and Medical Science*, London, J. Manman, 1801, 3 vols.

Lewes, Gertrude, *Dr Southwood Smith: A Retrospect*, Edinburgh, W. Blackwood & Sons, 1898.

Liddle, John, *On the Moral and Physical Evils Resulting from the Neglect of Sanitary Measures. A Lecture*, London, Health of Towns Association, 1847.

Lind, James, *An Essay on the Most Effectual Means of Preserving the Health of Seamen in the Royal Navy*, London, D. Wilson, 1762.

Lindsey, Benjamin and Evans, Wainwright, *The Companionate Marriage*, London, Brentano's, 1928.

Lois, *Pleas for Those Who Greatly Need Them. Three Letters on Helping and Visiting the Poor. Addressed to a Lady*, London, W. Mackintosh, 1869.

Lombroso, Caesare and Ferrero, William, *The Female Offender*, London, Fisher Unwin, 1895.

London, Jack, *The People of the Abyss*, London, Isbister and Co, 1903.

Lyttleton, Edward, *The Causes and Prevention of Immorality in Schools*, London, Social Purity Alliance, 1883.

McCleary, George, *The Maternity and Child Welfare Movement*, London, P.S. King and Son, 1935.

MacCulloch, John, *A Statistical Account of the British Empire*, second edition, London, Charles Knight and Co, 1839, 2 vols.

MacDougall, William, *An Introduction to Social Psychology*, London, Macmillan, 1908.

MacDougall, William, *An Outline of Abnormal Psychology*, New York and Boston, C. Scribner and Sons, 1926.

Macrosty, H. and Bonar, J., *Annals of the Royal Statistical Society 1834–1934*, London, Royal Statistical Society, 1934.

Marchant, James (ed.), *Public Morals*, London, Morgan and Scott, 1902.

Marchant, James, *Aids to Purity: Seven Personal Letters*, London, Health and Strength Ltd, 1909.

Marchant, James, *Birth Rate and Empire*, London, Williams & Norgate, 1917.

Marchant, James, *The Master Problem*, London, Stanley Paul, 1917.

Marchant, James (ed.), *The Control of Parenthood*, London and New York, G.P. Putnam's Sons, 1920.

Martindale, Louisa, *Under the Surface*, Brighton, Southern Publishing Co, 1908.

Maudsley, Henry, *Body and Mind: An Inquiry into Their Connection and Mutual Influence, Specially in Reference to Mental Disorders*, London, Macmillan, 1870.

Maurice, F.D. (ed.), *Lectures to Ladies, On Practical Subjects*, Cambridge, Macmillan, 1855.

Mearns, Andrew, *The Bitter Cry of Outcast London*, London, James Clarke and Co, 1883.

Miller, Edward, *Counsel to the Young. The Substance of a Sermon Preached at Putney Chapel*, London, Roake and Varty, 1833.

More, Hannah, *Strictures on the Modern System of Female Education*, London, T. Cadell and W. Davies, 1799.

National Council of Public Morals, *The Nation's Morals*, London, Cassell and Co, 1910.

National Vigilance Association, *Pernicious Literature: Debate in the House of Commons: Trial and Convictions for Sale of Zola's Novels with Opinions of the Press*, London, National Vigilance Association, 1889.

National Vigilance Association, *Work Accomplished by the Association*, London, National Vigilance Association, 1907.

Neville-Rolfe, Sybil, *The Changing Moral Standard*, London, National Council for Combating Venereal Disease, 1918.

Neville-Rolfe, Sybil, *Modern Marriage and Monogamy*, London, British Social Hygiene Council, 1930.

Neville-Rolfe, Sybil, *Why Marry?* London, Faber & Faber, 1935.

Newman, George, *Infant Mortality. A Social Problem*, London, Methuen and Co, 1906.

Newman, George, *The Place of Public Opinion in Preventive Medicine*, London, Ministry of Health, 1920.

Newman, George, *Recent Advances in Medical Education in England. A Memorandum Addressed to the Minister of Health*, London, Ministry of Health, 1923.

Newman, George, *Public Education in Health. A Memorandum Addressed to the Minister of Health*, London, Ministry of Health, 1924.

Newman, George, *Citizenship and the Survival of Civilization*, New Haven, Yale University Press, 1928.

Newsholme, Arthur, 'Infantile Mortality: A Statistical Study from the Public Health Standpoint', *Practitioner*, October 1905, pp. 489–500.

Newsholme, Arthur, *The Declining Birth-Rate. Its National and International Significance*, London, Cassell and Co, 1911.

Newsholme, Arthur, *The Moral Aspects of Social Hygiene*, London, National Council for Combating Venereal Disease, 1924.

Newsholme, Arthur, *The Evolution of Preventive Medicine*, London, Ballière, 1927.

Newsholme, Arthur, *Medicine and the State. The Relation Between the Private and Official Practice of Medicine with Special Reference to Public Health*, London, Allen & Unwin, 1932.

Newsholme, Arthur, *Fifty Years in Public Health. A Personal Narrative with Comments*, London, Allen & Unwin, 1935.

Newsholme, Arthur, *The Last Thirty Years in Public Health. Recollections and Reflections on My Official and Post-Official Life*, London, Allen & Unwin, 1936.

Paley, William, *The Principles of Moral and Political Philosophy*, second edition, London, J. Davis, 1786.

Pall Mall Gazette, *The Maiden Tribute of Modern Babylon. The Report of the 'Pall Mall Gazette's' Secret Commission*, London, Pall Mall Gazette, 1885.

Pankhurst, Christabel, *The Great Scourge, and How to End It*, London, E. Pankhurst, 1913.

Parent-Duchâtelet, Alexandre, *De la Prostitution dans la Ville de Paris, Considérée sous le Rapport de l'Hygiène Publique, de la Morale et de l'Administration*, Paris, J.B. Ballière, 1836, 2 vols.

Paul, Maurice Eden, *Socialism and Eugenics*, Manchester, National Labour Press, 1911.

Pearson, Karl, *The Groundwork of Eugenics*, London, Dulau and Co, 1909.

Pearson, Karl, *The Problem of Practical Eugenics*, London, Dulau and Co, 1909.

Pearson, Karl, *The Scope and Importance to the State of the Science of National Eugenics*, London, Dulau and Co, 1909.

Pearson, Karl, *Darwinism, Medical Progress and Eugenics. The Cavendish Lecture. An Address to the Medical Profession*, London, Dulau and Co, 1912.

Pearson, Karl, *Eugenics and Public Health. An Address to Public Health Officers*, London, Dulau and Co, 1912.

Percival, Thomas, *Medical Ethics, or a Code of Institutes and Precepts Adapted to the Professional Conduct of Physicians and Surgeons*, Manchester, J. Johnson, 1803.

Plarr, Victor, *Plarr's Lives of the Fellows of the Royal College of Surgeons of England*, revised by Sir D'Arcy Power, London, Simpkin, Marshall Ltd, 1930, 2 vols.

Platt, Elspeth, *The Story of the Ranyard Mission 1857–1937*, London, Hodder and Stoughton, 1937.

Pringle, John, *Social Work of the London Churches. Being Some Account of the Metropolitan Visiting and Relief Association*, London, Oxford University Press, 1937.

Pyke, William, *Modernism as a Working Faith*, Cambridge, W. Heffer and Sons, 1925.

Ranyard, Ellen, *Life Work; or, the Link and the Rivet*, London, James Nisbet and Co, 1861.

Ranyard, Ellen, *London, and Ten Years Work in It*, London, James Nisbet and Co, 1868.

Re-Bartlett, Lucy, *The Coming Order*, Longman, Green & Co, 1911.

Re-Bartlett, Lucy, *Sex and Sanctity*, London, Longman, Green & Co, 1912.

Rentoul, Robert, *Proposed Sterilization of Certain Mental and Physical Degenerates. An Appeal to Asylum Managers and Others*, London, Walter Scott Publishing Co, 1903.

Rentoul, Robert, *Race Culture: or, Race Suicide? A Plea for the Unborn*, London, Walter Scott Publishing Co, 1906.

Rogers, Travers, *The Church and the People*, London, Sampson Low, 1930.

Rout, Ettie, *Sex and Exercise: A Study of the Sex Function in Women and Its Relation to Exercise*, London, William Heinemann, 1925.

Royden, Maud, *Sex and Common-Sense*, London, Hurst and Blackett, 1922.

Royden, Maud, *The Moral Standards of the Rising Generation*, London, League of the Church Militant, 1922.

Royden, Maud, *Beauty in Religion*, London, G.P. Putnam's Sons, 1923.

Russell, Bertrand, *Marriage and Morals*, London, Allen & Unwin, 1929.

Russell, Dora, *The Right to be Happy*, London, G. Routledge & Sons, 1927.

Ryan, Michael, *Lectures on Population, Marriage and Divorce*, London, Renshaw and Rush, 1831.

Ryan, Michael, *The Philosophy of Marriage, in Its Social, Moral and Physical*

Relations; with an Account of the Diseases of the Genito-Urinary Organs, London, John Churchill, 1837.

Ryan, Michael, *Prostitution in London*, London, H. Ballière, 1839.

Saleeby, Caleb, *The Methods of Race-Regeneration*, London, Cassell and Co, 1911.

Saleeby, Caleb, *The Eugenic Prospect: National and Racial*, London, T. Fisher Unwin, 1921.

Scharlieb, Mary, *Womanhood and Race-Regeneration*, London, Cassell and Co, 1912.

Scharlieb, Mary, *The Seven Ages of Women: A Consideration of the Successive Phases of Woman's Life*, London, Cassell, 1915.

Scharlieb, Mary, *What Mothers Must Tell Their Children*, third edition, London, National Council for Combating Venereal Disease, 1920.

Scharlieb, Mary, *Reminiscences*, London, Williams & Norgate, 1924.

Scharlieb, Mary, *The Bachelor Woman and her Problems*, London, Williams & Norgate, 1929.

Scharlieb, Mary and Sibly, Frederic, *Youth and Sex. Dangers and Safeguards for Girls and Boys*, London, T.C. and E.C. Jack, 1912.

Schofield, Alfred, *Continence*, 1909.

Seccombe, Charles, *The Basis of Christian Marriage*, London, Student Christian Movement Press, 1933.

Seligman, Edwin (ed.), *Encyclopedia of the Social Sciences*, London, Macmillan, 1930–5, 15 vols.

Shaw, Charles, *Manufacturing Districts. Replies of Sir Charles Shaw to Lord Ashley MP Regarding the Moral and Physical Condition of the Labouring Classes*, London, John Ollivier, 1843.

Simon, John, *English Sanitary Institutions Reviewed in the Course of Their Development and in Some of Their Political and Social Relations*, London, Cassell, 1890.

Simon, John, *Personal Recollections*, London, Spottiswoode, 1894.

Sims, George, *How the Poor Live in Horrible London*, London, Chatto & Windus, 1883.

Smith, Frank, *The Life and Times of Sir James Kay-Shuttleworth*, London, John Murray, 1923.

Smith, Joshua Toulmin, *Centralization or Representation? A Letter to the Metropolitan Sanatory Commissioners*, second edition, London, S. Sweet, 1848.

Smith, Kingsley, *A Hundred Years of English Government*, London, Duckworth, 1937.

Smith, Thomas Southwood, *A Treatise on Fever*, London, Longman, 1830.

Social Purity Alliance, *Schoolboy Morality. An Address to Mothers*, London, Social Purity Alliance, 1884.

Sprigge, Samuel Squire, *The Life and Times of Thomas Wakley MD*, London, Longman, 1897.

Stansfeld, James, *Substance of the Speeches of the Rt. Hon. J. Stansfeld, M.P., on the Contagious Diseases Acts*, London, National Association for the Repeal of the Contagious Diseases Acts, 1875.

Stead, Estelle, *My Father. Personal and Spiritual Reminiscences*, London, William Heinemann, 1913.

Stopes, Marie, *Married Love: A New Contribution to the Solution of Sex Difficulties*, London, A.C. Fifield, 1918.

Stopes, Marie, *Radiant Motherhood*, London, G.P. Putnam's Sons, 1920.

Stopes, Marie, *Contraception: Its Theory, History and Practice*, London, J. Bale and Co, 1923.

Stopes, Marie, *Sex and the Young*, London, Gill Publishing Co, 1926.

Stopes, Marie, *Enduring Passion. Further New Contributions to the Solution of Sex Difficulties. Being the Continuation of Married Love*, London, G.P. Putnam's Sons, 1928.

Sutherland, John, *Report on the Epidemic of Cholera of 1848–49*, London, General Board of Health, 1850.

Swiney, Frances, *The Awakening of Women; or, Women's Part in Evolution*, London, William Reeves, 1905.

Swiney, Frances, *The Bar of Isis; or, the Law of the Mother*, London, Open Road Publishing Co, 1907.

Swiney, Frances, *The Mystery of the Circle and the Cross; or, the Interpretation of Sex*, London, Open Road Publishing Co, 1908.

Swiney, Frances, *Women and Natural Law*, second edition, London, C.W. Daniel, 1912.

Tait, William, *Magdalenism. An Inquiry into the Extent, Causes and Consequences of Prostitution in Edinburgh*, Edinburgh, P. Rickard, 1840.

Talbot, Charles, *Meliora: or, Better Times to Come: Being the Contribution of Many Men Touching the Present State and Prospects of Society*, London, John Parker, 1852.

Talbot, James, *The Miseries of Prostitution*, London, J. Madden and Co, 1844.

Taylor, Charles, *The Statistical Results of the Contagious Diseases Acts . . . . Shewing Their Total Failure from a Sanitary Point of View*, Nottingham, Stevenson, Bailey and Smith, 1872.

Thomas, Herbert, *Work and Play of a Government Inspector*, London and Edinburgh, William Blackwood & Sons, 1909.

Thomson, John and Geddes, Patrick, *Problems of Sex*, London, Cassell and Co, 1912.

Tilt, Edward, *The Serpentine 'As it is' and 'As it ought to be'. And the Board of Health 'As it is' and 'As it ought to be'*, London, John Churchill, 1848.

Tristan, Flora, *Flora Tristan's London Journal* [1840], trans. Dennis Palmer and Giselle Pincetl, London, George Prior, 1980.

Tuke, Daniel (ed.), *Dictionary of Physiological Medicine*, London, J. and A. Churchill, 1892, 2 vols.

Twining, Louisa, *Recollections of Life and Work*, London, E. Arnold, 1893.

Twining, William, *A Practical Account of the Epidemic Cholera, and of the Treatment Requisite in the Various Modifications of that Disease*, London, Parbury, Allen and Co, 1833.

Velde, Theodoor van de, *Ideal Marriage: Its Physiology and Technique*, London, Heinemann, 1928.

Walker, Alexander, *Women Physiologically Considered as to Mind, Morals, Marriage, Matrimonial Slavery, Infidelity and Divorce*, London, A.H. Baily and Co, 1839.

Wardlaw, Ralph, *Lectures on Female Prostitution*, second edition, Glasgow, James Maclehose, 1843.

Wathen, Jonathan, *Practical Observations Concerning the Cure of Venereal Disease by Mercurials*, London, J. Rivington, 1765.

White, Arnold, *The Problems of a Great City*, London, Remington and Co, 1886.
White, Arnold, *Efficiency and Empire*, London, Methuen and Co, 1901.
Wilkinson, James, *The Forcible Introspection of Women for the Army and Navy by the Oligarchy, Considered Physically*, London, F. Pitman, 1870.
Wilson, James, *Sins of the Flesh. A Sermon Preached in Clifton College Chapel*, London, Macmillan, 1883.
Wilson, James, *An Address*, London, Hatchards, 1884.
Wright, Helena, *The Sex Factor in Marriage. A Book for Those Who Are or Are About to be Married*, London, Noel Douglas, 1930.

Secondary sources

I *Unpublished works*

Brand, Jeanne, *The British Medical Profession and State Intervention in Public Health, 1870–1911*, unpublished Ph.D. dissertation, London University, 1953.
Hodgkinson, Ruth, *The Medical Services of the New Poor Law 1834–71*, unpublished Ph.D. dissertation, London University, 1950, 2 vols.

II *Published books and articles*

Abrams, Philip, *The Origins of British Sociology 1834–1914: An Essay with Selected Papers*, Chicago, University of Chicago Press, 1968.
Anderson, C. Digby (ed.), *Health Education in Practice*, London, Croom Helm, 1979.
Anderson, Mosa, *Henry Joseph Wilson: Fighter for Freedom, 1833–1914*, London, James Clarke, 1953.
Ashton, Thomas, *Economic and Social Investigations in Manchester, 1833–1933: A Centenary History of the Manchester Statistical Society*, Hassocks, Harvester, 1977.
Bailey, Victor and Blackburn, Sheila, 'The Punishment of Incest Act 1908: A Case Study of Criminal Law Creation', *Criminal Law Review*, November 1979, pp. 708–18.
Baker, Rachel, *The First Woman Doctor: The Story of Elizabeth Blackwell M.D.*, London, Harrap & Co, 1946.
Ballhatchet, Kenneth, *Race, Sex and Class Under the Raj: Imperial Attitudes and Policies and their Critics, 1793–1905*, London, Weidenfeld & Nicolson, 1980.
Banks, Joseph and Banks, Olive, *Feminism and Family Planning in Victorian England*, Liverpool, Liverpool University Press, 1964.
Bland, Lucy, ' "Guardians of the Race" or "Vampires Upon the Nation's Health?": Female Sexuality and its Regulation in Early Twentieth-Century Britain', in Elizabeth Whitelegg *et al.* (eds), *The Changing Experience of Women*, Oxford, Martin Robertson, 1982, pp. 373–88.
Bland, Lucy, ' "Cleansing the Portals of Life": The Venereal Disease Campaign in the Early Twentieth Century', in Mary Langan and Bill Schwarz (eds), *Crises in the British State 1880–1930*, London, Hutchinson, 1985, pp. 192–208.
Bland, Lucy, 'Marriage Laid Bare: Middle-Class Women and Marital Sex c. 1880–1914', in Jane Lewis (ed.), *Labour and Love: Women's Experience of Home and Family, 1850–1940*, Oxford, Basil Blackwell, 1986, pp. 123–46.

Bland, Lucy and Mort, Frank, 'Look Out for the "Good Time" Girl: Dangerous Sexualities as a Threat to National Health', in *Formations of Nation and People*, London, Routledge & Kegan Paul, 1984, pp. 131–51.

Bloomfield, Barry, *A Handlist of Papers in the Deed Box of Sir J.P. Kay-Shuttleworth*, College of St Mark and St John, occasional paper no. 2, Manchester, Manchester University Library, 1961.

Bloomfield, Barry (ed.), *The Autobiography of Sir James Kay-Shuttleworth*, Education Libraries Bulletin, supplement 7, 1964.

Bradbury, Savile and Turner, G.L'E., *Historical Aspects of Microscopy: Papers Read at a One-Day Conference Held by the Royal Microscopical Society at Oxford*, Cambridge, Heffer for the Royal Microscopical Society, 1967.

Brand, Jeanne, *Doctors and the State: The British Medical Profession and Government Action in Public Health, 1870–1912*, Baltimore, Johns Hopkins University Press, 1965.

Briggs, Asa, 'Cholera and Society in the Nineteenth Century', *Past and Present*, 1961, no. 19, pp. 76–96.

Bristow, Edward, *Vice and Vigilance: Purity Movements in Britain since 1700*, Dublin, Gill and Macmillan, 1977.

Brockington, C. Fraser, *A Short History of Public Health*, London, J. and A. Churchill, 1956.

Catterall, R. and Nicol, C. (eds), *Sexually Transmitted Diseases: Proceedings of a Conference Sponsored Jointly by the Royal Society of Medicine and the Royal Society of Medical Foundations Inc.*, London, Academic Press, 1975.

Chadwick, Owen, *The Victorian Church*, London, A. & C. Black, 1966, 2 vols.

Cominos, Peter, 'Late-Victorian Sexual Respectability and the Social System', *International Review of Social History*, 1963, vol. VIII, pp. 18–48, 216–50.

Cullen, Michael, *The Statistical Movement in Early Victorian Britain: The Foundations of Empirical Social Research*, Hassocks, Harvester, 1975.

Davidoff, Leonore, 'Class and Gender in Victorian Britain: Arthur J. Munby and Hannah Cullwick', *Feminist Studies*, 1979, vol. 5, no. 1, pp. 89–113.

Davin, Anna, 'Imperialism and Motherhood', *History Workshop Journal*, 1978, no. 5, pp. 9–65.

Dyhouse, Carol, 'Working-Class Mothers and Infant Mortality in England 1895–1914', *Journal of Social History*, 1978, vol. 12, no. 2, pp. 248–67.

Dyos, Harold and Woolf, Michael (eds), *The Victorian City: Images and Realities*, London, Routledge & Kegan Paul, 1973, 2 vols.

Eyler, John, *Victorian Social Medicine: The Ideas and Methods of William Farr*, Baltimore, Johns Hopkins University Press, 1979.

Finer, Samuel, *The Life and Times of Sir Edwin Chadwick*, London, Methuen, 1952.

Finlayson, Geoffrey, *The Seventh Earl of Shaftesbury, 1801–1885*, London, Eyre Methuen, 1981.

Finnegan, Frances, *Poverty and Prostitution: A Study of Victorian Prostitutes in York*, Cambridge, Cambridge University Press, 1979.

Foucault, Michel, *Madness and Civilization: A History of Insanity in the Age of Reason*, trans Richard Howard, London, Tavistock, 1971.

Foucault, Michel, *The Archaeology of Knowledge*, trans. A. Sheridan Smith, London, Tavistock, 1972.

Foucault, Michel, *The Birth of the Clinic: An Archaeology of Medical Perception*, trans. A.M. Sheridan Smith, London, Tavistock, 1973.

Foucault, Michel, *Discipline and Punish: The Birth of the Prison*, trans. Alan Sheridan, London, Allen Lane, 1977.

Foucault, Michel, *The History of Sexuality*, vol. 1, *An Introduction*, trans. Robert Hurley, New York, Pantheon Books, 1978.

Foucault, Michel, 'On Governmentality', *I & C*, 1979, no. 6, pp. 5–21.

Fowler, William, *A Study in Radicalism and Dissent: The Life and Times of Henry Joseph Wilson 1833–1914*, London, Epworth Press, 1961.

Freeden, Michael, *The New Liberalism: An Ideology of Social Reform*, Oxford, Clarendon Press, 1978.

Gorham, Deborah, 'The "Maiden Tribute of Modern Babylon" Re-Examined: Child Prostitution and the Idea of Childhood in Late-Victorian England', *Victorian Studies*, 1978, vol. 21, no. 3, pp. 353–74.

Gorham, Deborah, 'Victorian Reform as a Family Business: The Hill Family', in Anthony Wohl (ed.), *The Victorian Family: Structures and Stresses*, London, Croom Helm, 1978, pp. 119–47.

Gray, Robert, 'Bourgeois Hegemony in Victorian Britain', in Jon Bloomfield (ed.), *The Communist University of London: Papers on Class, Hegemony and Party*, London, Lawrence & Wishart, 1977, pp. 73–93.

Green, Nicholas and Mort, Frank, 'Visual Representation and Cultural Politics', *Block*, 1982, no. 7, pp. 59–68.

Hall, Catherine, 'Married Women at Home in Birmingham in the 1920s and 1930s', *Oral History*, 1977, vol. 5, no. 2, pp. 62–83.

Hall, Catherine, 'The Early Formation of Victorian Domestic Ideology', in Sandra Burman (ed.), *Fit Work for Women*, London, Croom Helm, 1979, pp. 15–32.

Hall, Catherine, 'Gender Divisions and Class Formation in the Birmingham Middle Class', in Raphael Samuel (ed.), *People's History and Socialist Theory*, London, Routledge & Kegan Paul, 1981, pp. 164–75.

Hall, Ruth (ed.), *Dear Dr Stopes: Sex in the 1920's*, London, Deutsch, 1978.

Hamer, D. A., *Liberal Politics in the Age of Gladstone and Rosebery: A Study in Leadership and Policy*, Oxford, Clarendon Press, 1972.

Harrison, Brian, *Drink and the Victorians: The Temperance Question in England, 1815–1872*, London, Faber, 1971.

Harrison, Brian, 'State Intervention and Moral Reform', in Patricia Hollis (ed.), *Pressure from Without in Early Victorian England*, London, Edward Arnold, 1974, pp. 289–322.

Harrison, Rachel and Mort, Frank, 'Patriarchal Aspects of Nineteenth Century State Formation: Property Relations, Marriage and Divorce, and Sexuality', in Philip Corrigan (ed.), *Capitalism, State Formation and Marxist Theory: Historical Investigations*, London, Quartet, 1980, pp. 79–109.

Hay, Douglas, Linebaugh, Peter, Rule, John, Thompson, E. P. and Winslow, Carl, *Albion's Fatal Tree: Crime and Society in Eighteenth-Century England*, Harmondsworth, Penguin, 1977.

Heasman, Kathleen, *Evangelicals in Action: An Appraisal of Their Social Work in the Victorian Era*, London, Geoffrey Bles, 1962.

Heyck, Thomas, *The Transformation of Intellectual Life in Victorian England*, London, Croom Helm, 1982.

Higson, Jessie, *The Story of a Beginning: An Account of Pioneer Work for Moral Welfare*, London, SPCK, 1955.

Hirst, Paul and Woolley, Penny, *Social Relations and Human Attributes*, London, Tavistock, 1982.

Hoare, Quintin and Nowell-Smith, Geoffrey (eds), *Selections from the Prison Notebooks of Antonio Gramsci*, London, Lawrence & Wishart, 1976.

Hodgkinson, Ruth, 'The Poor Law Medical Officers of England 1843–1871', *Journal of the History of Medicine*, 1956, vol. xi, pp. 299–338.

Holtman, Ellen, 'The Pursuit of Married Love: Women's Attitudes Towards Sexuality and Marriage in Great Britain, 1918–1939', *Journal of Social History*, 1982, vol. 16, no. 2, pp. 39–51.

Hudson, Derek, *Munby: Man of Two Worlds: The Life and Work of Arthur J. Munby, 1828–1910*, London, Abacus, 1974.

Humphries, Jane, 'Protective Legislation, the Capitalist State and Working Class Men: The Case of the 1842 Mines Regulation Act', *Feminist Review*, 1981, no. 7, pp. 1–33.

Hussain, Athar, 'Foucault's History of Sexuality', *m/f*, 1981, nos 5 and 6, pp. 169–91.

Hutchins, John, *Jonas Hanway, 1712–1786*, London, SPCK, 1940.

Hyde, H. Montgomery, *The Other Love: An Historical and Contemporary Survey of Homosexuality in Britain*, London, Mayflower, 1972.

Ignatieff, Michael, *A Just Measure of Pain: The Penitentiary in the Industrial Revolution, 1750–1850*, London, Macmillan, 1978.

Jeffreys, Sheila, 'The Spinster and her Enemies: Sexuality and the Last Wave of Feminism', *Scarlet Woman*, 1981, no. 13, pp. 22–7.

Jeffreys, Sheila, 'Free From All Uninvited Touch of Man: Women's Campaigns Around Sexuality, 1880–1914', *Women's Studies International Forum*, 1982, vol. 5, no. 6, pp. 629–45.

John, Angela, *By the Sweat of their Brow: Women Workers at Victorian Coal Mines*, London, Routledge & Kegan Paul, 1984.

Johnson, Richard, 'Educational Policy and Social Control in Early Victorian England', *Past and Present*, 1970, no. 49, pp. 96–119.

Johnson, Richard, 'Educating the Educators: "Experts" and the State 1833–1839', in A.P. Donajgrodzki (ed.), *Social Control in Nineteenth Century Britain*, London, Croom Helm, 1977, pp. 77–107.

Johnson, Richard, McLennan, Gregor, Schwarz, Bill and Sutton, David (eds), *Making Histories: Studies in History-Writing and Politics*, London, Hutchinson, 1982.

Keating, Peter (ed.), *Into Unknown England 1866–1913: Selections from the Social Explorers*, London, Fontana, 1976.

Kitson Clark, George, ' "Statesmen in Disguise": Reflections on the History of the Neutrality of the Civil Service', *The Historical Journal*, 1959, vol. II, no. 1, pp. 19–39.

Kitson Clark, George, *Churchmen and the Condition of England, 1832–1885: A Study in the Development of Social Ideas and Practice from the Old Regime to the Modern State*, London, Methuen, 1973.

Lambert, Royston, *Sir John Simon, 1816–1904, and English Social Administration*, London, MacGibbon & Kee, 1963.

Layton, Thomas, *Sir William Arbuthnot Lane, Bt.: An Enquiry into the Mind and Influence of a Surgeon*, Edinburgh and London, E. & S. Livingstone, 1956.

Lee, Alan, *The Origins of the Popular Press in England, 1855–1914*, London, Croom Helm, 1976.

L'Esperance, Jean, 'The Work of the Ladies' National Association for the Repeal of the Contagious Diseases Acts', *Bulletin of the Society for the Study of Labour History*, 1973, no. 26 , pp. 13–15.

Lewis, Jane, *The Politics of Motherhood: Child and Maternal Welfare in England 1900–1939*, London, Croom Helm, 1980.

Lidderdale, Jane and Nicholson, Mary, *Dear Miss Weaver: Harriet Shaw Weaver, 1875–1961*, London, Faber, 1970.

Longmate, Norman, *King Cholera: The Biography of a Disease*, London, Hamish Hamilton, 1966.

MacDonagh, Oliver, 'The Nineteenth-Century Revolution in Government: A Reappraisal', *The Historical Journal*, 1958, vol. I, no. 1, pp. 52–67.

MacGregor, Oliver, *Divorce in England: A Centenary Study*, London, Heinemann, 1957.

McHugh, Paul, *Prostitution and Victorian Social Reform*, London, Croom Helm, 1980.

Malies, Harold, *A Short History of the English Microscope: The XIX Century Instrument*, Chicago, Microscope Publications, 1981.

Marcus, Steven, *The Other Victorians: A Study of Sexuality and Pornography in Mid-Nineteenth Century England*, London, Weidenfeld & Nicolson, 1966.

Marsh, Peter (ed.), *The Conscience of the Victorian State*, Hassocks, Harvester, 1979.

Middlemas, Keith, *Politics in Industrial Society: The Experience of the British System since 1911*, London, Deutsch, 1979.

Morris, R.J., *Cholera 1832: The Social Response to an Epidemic*, London, Croom Helm, 1976.

Mort, Frank, 'The Domain of the Sexual', *Screen Education*, 1980, no. 36, pp. 69–84.

Mort, Frank, 'Purity, Feminism and the State: Sexuality and Moral Politics, 1880–1914', in Mary Langan and Bill Schwarz (eds), *Crises in the British State 1880–1930*, London, Hutchinson, 1985, pp. 209–25.

Morton, Robert, *Sexual Freedom and Venereal Disease*, London, Peter Owen, 1971.

Morton, Robert, *V.D. and Diseases Transmitted Sexually*, London, Corgi, 1971.

Nead, Lynda, 'Seduction, Prostitution, Suicide: *On the Brink* by Alfred Elmore', *Art History*, 1982, vol. 5, no. 3, pp. 310–22.

Nield, Keith (ed.), *Prostitution in the Victorian Age: Debates on the Issues from Nineteenth Century Critical Journals*, Farnborough, Gregg International, 1973.

Pelling, Margaret, *Cholera, Fever and English Medicine, 1825–1865*, Oxford, Oxford University Press, 1978.

Peterson, M. Jeanne, *The Medical Profession in Mid-Victorian London*, Berkeley, University of California Press, 1978.

Prochaska, Frank, *Women and Philanthropy in Nineteenth-Century England*, Oxford, Clarendon Press, 1980.

Richards, Paul, 'State Formation and Class Struggle, 1832–48', in Philip Corrigan (ed.), *Capitalism, State Formation and Marxist Theory: Historical Investigations*, London, Quartet, 1980, pp. 49–78.

Rose, Nikolas, 'The Psychological Complex: Mental Measurement and Social Administration', *Ideology and Consciousness*, 1979, no. 5, pp. 5–68.

Rose, Nikolas, *The Psychological Complex: Psychology, Politics and Society in England 1869–1939*, London, Routledge & Kegan Paul, 1985.

Rowbotham, Sheila, *A New World for Women: Stella Browne, Socialist Feminist*, London, Pluto Press, 1977.

Sayers, Janet, *Biological Politics: Feminist and Anti-Feminist Perspectives*, London, Tavistock, 1982.

Schofield, Michael, *The Sexual Behaviour of Young People*, London, Longman, 1965.

Schwarz, Bill, 'The Language of Constitutionalism: Baldwinite Conservatism', in *Formations of Nation and People*, London, Routledge & Kegan Paul, 1984, pp. 1–18.

Searle, Geoffrey, *The Quest for National Efficiency: A Study in British Politics and Political Thought, 1899–1914*, Oxford, Blackwell, 1971.

Searle, Geoffrey, *Eugenics and Politics in Britain, 1900–1914*, Leyden, Noordhoff International, 1976.

Shorter, Edward, *The Making of the Modern Family*, London, Fontana, 1977.

Sigsworth, E. and Wyke, T., 'A Study of Victorian Prostitution and Venereal Disease', in Martha Vicinus (ed.), *Suffer and Be Still: Women in the Victorian Age*, Bloomington and London, Indiana University Press, 1972, pp. 77–99.

Smith, W. David, *Stretching Their Bodies: The History of Physical Education*, Newton Abbot, David & Charles, 1974.

Stedman Jones, Gareth, *Outcast London: A Study in the Relationship Between Classes in Victorian Society*, Harmondsworth, Penguin, 1984.

Stone, Lawrence, *The Family, Sex and Marriage in England, 1500–1800*, London, Weidenfeld & Nicolson, 1977.

Summers, Anne, 'Militarism in Britain Before the Great War', *History Workshop Journal*, 1976, no. 2, pp. 104–23.

Summers, Anne, 'A Home from Home: Women's Philanthropic Work in the Nineteenth Century', in Sandra Burman (ed.), *Fit Work for Women*, Oxford, Croom Helm, 1979, pp. 33–63.

Tagg, John, 'Power and Photography: Part One. A Means of Surveillance: The Photograph as Evidence in Law', *Screen Education*, 1980, no. 36, pp. 17–55.

Taylor, Barbara, *Eve and the New Jerusalem: Socialism and Feminism in the Nineteenth Century*, London, Virago, 1983.

Thomas, Keith, 'The Double Standard', *Journal of the History of Ideas*, 1959, vol. XX, pp. 195–216.

Trudgill, Eric, *Madonnas and Magdalens: The Origins and Development of Victorian Sexual Attitudes*, London, Heinemann, 1976.

Vaughan, Paul, *Doctor's Commons: A Short History of the British Medical Association*, London, Heinemann, 1959.

Vincent, John, *The Formation of the Liberal Party, 1857–68*, London, Constable, 1966.

Walkowitz, Judith, *Prostitution and Victorian Society: Women, Class and the State*, Cambridge, Cambridge University Press, 1980.

Walkowitz, Judith, 'Male Vice and Feminist Virtue: Feminism and the Politics of

Prostitution in Nineteenth-Century Britain', *History Workshop Journal*, 1982, no. 13, pp. 79–93.

Walkowitz, Judith, 'Science, Feminism and Romance: The Men and Women's Club 1885–1889', *History Workshop Journal*, 1986, no. 21, pp. 36–59.

Walkowitz, Judith and Walkowitz, Daniel, ' "We Are Not Beasts of the Field": Prostitution and the Poor in Plymouth and Southampton Under the Contagious Diseases Acts', *Feminist Studies*, 1973, no. 1, pp. 73–106.

Weeks, Jeffrey, *Coming Out: Homosexual Politics in Britain from the Nineteenth Century to the Present*, London, Quartet, 1977.

Weeks, Jeffrey, *Sex, Politics and Society: The Regulation of Sexuality since 1800*, London, Longman, 1981.

Weeks, Jeffrey, *Sexuality and Its Discontents: Meaning, Myths and Modern Sexualities*, London, Routledge & Kegan Paul, 1985.

White, Cynthia, *Women's Magazines 1693–1968*, London, Michael Joseph, 1970.

Wilson, Dorothy, *Lone Woman: The Story of Elizabeth Blackwell, the First Woman Doctor*, London, Hodder & Stoughton, 1970.

Wohl, Anthony (ed.), *The Victorian Family: Structures and Stresses*, London, Croom Helm, 1978.

Wood, Nancy, 'Prostitution and Feminism in Nineteenth-Century Britain', *m/f*, 1982, no. 7, pp. 61–77.

Woodward, John and Richards, David (eds), *Health Care and Popular Medicine in Nineteenth Century England: Essays in the Social History of Medicine*, London, Croom Helm, 1977.

ADDITIONAL BIBLIOGRAPHY

Since the first edition of *Dangerous Sexualities* was published there has been an ever-expanding literature on the histories of sexuality. This bibliographical essay is selective, providing the reader with a guide to this proliferating field of research and scholarship. The bibliography is structured around the major themes covered in the first edition and follows the sections of the book. Suggestions for further reading are generally confined to works focused on Britain and its imperial relations, except in the case of sources for AIDS and the HIV virus where the coverage is more international.

Introduction: Narratives of sex

Michel Foucault's later volumes of *The History of Sexuality*, vol. 2, *The Use of Pleasure*, trans. Robert Hurley, Harmondsworth, Viking, 1986, and vol. 3, *The Care of the Self*, trans. Robert Hurley, Harmondsworth, Allen Lane, 1988, extend and develop his analysis of sexuality, especially in relation to Greco-Roman society. Feminist assessments of Foucault are contained in: Biddy Martin, 'Feminism, Criticism, and Foucault', *New German Critique*, 1982, no. 27, pp. 3–30; Naomi Schor, 'Dreaming Dyssymetry: Barthes, Foucault, and Sexual Difference', in Alice Jardine and Paul Smith (eds), *Men in Feminism*, New York, Methuen, 1987, pp. 98–110; Irene Diamond and Lee Quinby (eds), *Feminism and Foucault: Reflections on Resistance*, Boston, Northeastern University Press, 1988; Jana Sawicki, *Disciplining Foucault: Feminism, Power and the Body*, London and New York, Routledge, 1991; Carol Ramazanoğlu (ed.), *Up Against Foucault: Explorations of Some Tensions between Foucault and Feminism*, London and New York, Routledge, 1993; Lois McNay, *Foucault: A Critical Introduction*, New York, The Continuum Publishing Co, 1994. For an assessment of Foucault's impact on medical history see: Colin Jones and Roy Porter (eds), *Reassessing Foucault: Power, Medicine and the Body*, London, Routledge, 1994; Alan Petersen and Robin Bunton (eds), *Foucault, Health and Medicine*, London, Routledge, 1997.

On broader histories of sexuality and sexual regulation see: Thomas Laqueur, *Making Sex: Body and Gender from the Greeks to Freud*, Cambridge, MA., Harvard University Press, 1990; Jonathan Dollimore, *Sexual Dissidence: Augustine to Wilde, Freud to Foucault*, Oxford, Clarendon Press, 1991; Peter Gay, *The Bourgeois Experience: Victoria to Freud*, vol. 1, *Education of the Senses*, Oxford and New

231

York, Oxford University Press, 1984; vol. 2, *The Tender Passion*, Oxford and New York, Oxford University Press, 1986, and vol. 5, *The Pleasure Wars*, New York and London, W.W. Norton, 1998.

There has been a sustained engagement by feminist historians with the issues raised by post-structuralist theory. For some of the most significant works in this area see: Jane Flax, 'Postmodernism and Gender Relations in Feminist Theory', *Signs*, 1987, vol. 12, no. 4, pp. 621–43; Denise Riley, *'Am I That Name'? Feminism and the Category of Women in History*, Basingstoke, Macmillan, 1988; Joan Scott, *Gender and the Politics of History*, New York, Columbia University Press, 1988; Judith Butler, *Gender Trouble: Feminism and the Subversion of Identity*, London and New York, Routledge, 1990. For more specific analyses of the relationship between gender and science see: Ludmilla Jordanova (ed.), *Languages of Nature: Critical Essays on Science and Literature*, London, Free Association Books, 1986, and her *Sexual Visions: Images of Gender in Science and Medicine Between the Eighteenth and Twentieth Centuries*, London, Harvester Wheatsheaf, 1989. On masculinity as a methodological problem for historians see: Frank Mort, 'Crisis Points: Masculinities in History and Social Theory', *Gender and History*, 1994, vol. 6, no. 1, pp. 124–30; John Tosh, 'What Should Historians do with Masculinity? Reflections on Nineteenth-Century Britain', *History Workshop Journal*, 1994, no. 38, pp. 179–202.

The colonial and imperial dimensions of sexuality have been a burgeoning field of research. The important study by George Mosse, *Nationalism and Sexuality: Respectability and Abnormal Sexuality in Modern Europe*, New York, Howard Fertig, 1985, explores this area, as does the collection by Andrew Parker, Mary Russo, Doris Sommer and Patricia Yaeger, *Nationalisms and Sexualities*, New York, Routledge, 1992. The 'Introduction' by Catherine Hall, Jane Lewis, Keith McClelland and Jane Rendall to *Gender and History*, 1993, vol. 5, no. 2, pp. 159–64 (special issue on gender, nationalisms and national identities), also contains some discussion of sexuality.

Part One Moral environmentalism 1830–1860

The first part of *Dangerous Sexualities* addresses the particular formation of medico-moral discourse in the mid-nineteenth century. However, developments in eighteenth-century social and sexual medicine are also briefly discussed. Works centred on those earlier forms of knowledge include: Paul-Gabriel Boucé (ed.), *Sexuality in Eighteenth-Century Britain*, Manchester, Manchester University Press, 1982; Robert Baker, Dorothy Porter and Roy Porter (eds), *The Codification of Historical and Philosophical Studies of the Formalization of Western Medical Morality in the Eighteenth and Nineteenth Centuries*, vol. 1, *Medical Ethics and Etiquette in the Eighteenth Century*, Dordrecht and London, Kluwer Academic Publications, 1993. Discussions of the intellectual forces shaping attitudes towards sexuality in the Victorian period can be found in Michael Mason's *The Making of Victorian Sexual Attitudes*, Oxford, Oxford University Press, 1994, as well as in Roy Porter and Mikulas Teich (eds), *Sexual Knowledge, Sexual Science: The History of Attitudes to Sexuality*, Cambridge, Cambridge University Press, 1994. For a broader overview see Roy Porter and Lesley Hall, *The Facts of Life: The Creation of Sexual Knowledge in Britain, 1650–1950*, New Haven and London, Yale University Press, 1995. On birth control see Angus McLaren, *Birth Control in Nineteenth-Century England: A Social and Intellectual History*, London, Croom Helm, 1978, and his *A History of Contraception, from Antiquity to the Present*, Oxford, Blackwell, 1990. The gendered dynamics of gynaecology are the subject of Ornella Moscucci's *The Science of Women: Gynaecology and Gender in England, 1800–1929*, Cambridge, MA., and London, Cambridge University Press, 1990, while for analysis of the construction of femininity in nineteenth-century science see Cynthia Eagle Russett, *Sexual Science: The Victorian Construction of Womanhood*, London, Harvard University Press, 1989. For an overview of recent historiographical debates on nineteenth-century sexuality see Carol Stearns and Peter Stearns, 'Victorian Sexuality: Can Historians Do It Better?' *Journal of Social History*, 1985, vol. 18, no. 4, pp. 625–34.

On public health and sanitary reform Anthony Wohl's *Endangered Lives: Public Health in Victorian Britain*, London, Dent, 1983, remains a useful discussion. Mary Poovey in *Making a Social Body: British Cultural Formation, 1830–1864*, Chicago and London, University of Chicago Press, 1995, explores the cultural and political anxieties about anatomy and contagion, arguing that these concerns generated a distinct domain of 'the social'. For more specific studies of the discourses of sanitary reform see also Poovey's 'Domesticity and Class Formation: Chadwick's 1842 Sanitary Report', in David Simpson (ed.), *Subject to History: Ideology, Class, Gender*, Ithaca and London, Cornell University Press, 1991, pp. 63–83, and her 'Curing the "Social Body" in 1832: James Phillips Kay and the Irish in Manchester', *Gender and History*, 1993, vol. 5, no. 2, pp. 196–211. Jill Matus considers mid-Victorian bio-medical discourses in her Foucauldian *Unstable Bodies: Victorian Representations of Sexuality and Maternity*, Manchester, Manchester University Press, 1995. The cultural dimensions of nineteenth-century sanitary politics are addressed by Peter Stallybrass and Allon White in *The Politics and Poetics of Transgression*, London, Methuen, 1986. Eileen Yeo analyses British social science and its growing pre-eminence in *The Contest for Social Science: Relations and Representations of Gender and Class*, London, Rivers Oram Press, 1996. Assessments of pre-Darwinian anthropology are contained in George Stocking's *Victorian Anthropology*, New York, Free Press, 1987.

The dynamics of the bourgeois family and its relation to the formation of middle-class gendered identities are extensively discussed in major works by: Catherine Hall and Leonore Davidoff, *Family Fortunes: Men and Women of the English Middle Class, 1780–1850*, London, Hutchinson, 1987, and Mary Poovey, *Uneven Developments: The Ideological Work of Gender in Mid-Victorian England*, London, Virago, 1988. Nineteenth-century marital relations are addressed by Gertrude Himmelfarb in *Marriage and Morals Among the Victorians: Essays*, London and Boston, Faber, 1986, and by Lawrence Stone in *Road to Divorce: England 1530–1987*, Oxford, Clarendon Press, 1990, and in his *Uncertain Unions, and Broken Lives: Marriage and Divorce in England, 1660–1857*, Oxford, Oxford University Press, 1995. A number of the essays in Catherine Gallagher and Thomas Laqueur (eds), *The Making of the Modern Body: Sexuality and Society in the Nineteenth Century*, Berkeley and London, University of California Press, 1987, address the construction of female sexuality in this period. The question of the sexual representation of femininity in artistic and related cultural practices is the subject of Lynda Nead's *Myths of Sexuality: Representations of Women in Victorian Britain*, Oxford,

Blackwell, 1988. In this context see also Joanna de Groot, ' "Sex" and "Race": The Construction of Language and Image in the Nineteenth Century', in Susan Mendus and Jane Rendall (eds), *Sexuality and Subordination: Interdisciplinary Studies of Gender in the Nineteenth Century*, London and New York, Routledge, 1989, pp. 89–128. For a specific study of prostitution see Linda Mahood, *The Madgalenes: Prostitution in the Nineteenth Century*, London and New York, Routledge, 1990.

For analysis of the formation of middle-class masculinity see: Catherine Hall, *White, Male and Middle-Class: Explorations in Feminism and History*, Cambridge, Polity, 1992; Leonore Davidoff, *Worlds Between: Historical Perspectives on Gender and Class*, Cambridge, Polity, 1995; Robert Gray, *The Factory Question and Industrial England, 1830–1860*, Cambridge, Cambridge University Press, 1996; John Tosh, *A Man's Place: Masculinity and the Middle-Class Home in Victorian England*, New Haven and London, Yale University Press, 1999. The collection by Michael Roper and John Tosh (eds), *Manful Assertions: Masculinities in Britain since 1800*, London, Routledge 1991, also contains a number of valuable studies on men during this period.

For recent work on class and government, Peter Mandler's study *Aristocratic Government in the Age of Reform: Whigs and Liberals 1830–1852*, Oxford, Clarendon Press, 1990, is a significant re-assessment of the politics of mid-century reform. Patrick Joyce, *Visions of the People: Industrial England and the Question of Class 1848–1914*, Cambridge, Cambridge University Press, 1991, and his *Democratic Subjects: The Self and the Social in Nineteenth-Century England*, Cambridge, Cambridge University Press, 1994, are important studies in the cultural and linguistic resources of class formation. Raphael Samuel addresses the impact of evangelical morality in 'The Discovery of Puritanism, 1820–1914: A Preliminary Sketch', in Jane Garnett and Colin Matthew (eds), *Revival and Religion since 1700: Essays for John Walsh*, London, Hambledon, 1993, pp. 201–47.

Part Two The sanitary principle in dominance: medical hegemony and feminist response 1860–1880

Susan Kingsley Kent's *Sex and Suffrage in Britain, 1860–1914*, London, Routledge, 1990, contains significant material on feminist campaigns for the repeal of the contagious diseases legislation. Philippa Levine's 'Consistent Contradictions: Prostitution and Protective Legislation in Nineteenth-Century England', *Social History*, 1994, vol. 19, no. 1, pp. 17–35, is a reassessment of the legislative traditions defining female sexuality during this period. The relationship of feminism to medical professionalism is addressed by Regina Markell Morantz in 'Feminism, Professionalism, and Germs: The Thought of Mary Putnam Jacobi and Elizabeth Blackwell', *American Quarterly*, 1982, vol. 34, no 5, pp. 459–78. On William Acton's sexual theories see M. Jeanne Peterson, 'Dr Acton's Enemy: Medicine, Sex, and Society in Victorian England', *Victorian Studies*, 1986, vol. 29, no. 4, pp. 569–90. The construction of femininity by medical discourse and popular culture is the subject of Sally Shuttleworth's 'Female Circulation: Medical Discourse and Popular Advertising in the Mid-Victorian Era', in Mary Jacobus, Evelyn Fox Keller and Sally Shuttleworth (eds), *Body/Politics: Women and the Discourse of Science*, London and New York, Routledge, 1990, pp. 47–68. For the impact of venereal disease on marriage see Gail

Savage, '"The Wilful Communication of a Loathsome Sore": Marital Conflict and Venereal Disease in Victorian England', *Victorian Studies*, 1990, vol. 34. no. 1, pp. 35–54. Women's relationship to the public, political sphere of local government is covered by Patricia Hollis, *Ladies Elect: Women in English Local Government 1865–1914*, Oxford, Clarendon, 1987. For discussion of the role of female philanthropy see: Frank Prochaska, *The Voluntary Impulse: Philanthropy in Modern Britain*, London, Faber, 1988; Anne Summers, *Angels and Citizens: British Women as Military Nurses, 1854–1914*, London, Routledge & Kegan Paul, 1988.

Further specific material on the relationship between Hannah Cullwick and Arthur Munby is provided in Liz Stanley (ed.), *The Diaries of Hannah Cullwick*, London, Virago, 1984. Analysis of mid-Victorian masculinities is contained in: Alex Tuss, *The Inward Revolution: Troubled Young Men in Victorian Fiction 1850–1880*, New York, P. Lang, 1992; Donald Hall (ed.), *Muscular Christianity: Embodying the Victorian Age*, Cambridge, Cambridge University Press, 1994; Joseph Kestner, *Masculinities in Victorian Painting*, Aldershot, Scolar Press, 1995.

For exploration of the more general themes touched on in this section, Anna Clark's *The Struggle for the Breeches: Gender and the Making of the British Working-Class*, Berkeley, University of California Press, 1995, examines contests over birth-control, the bastardy clauses in the New Poor Law, and the Chartist demand for the enfranchisement of women. A number of the essays in the collection by Carol Smart (ed.), *Regulating Womanhood: Historical Essays on Marriage, Motherhood, and Sexuality*, London and New York, Routledge, 1992, are relevant to the mid-nineteenth-century period. For the experience of marriage see James Hammerton, *Cruelty and Companionship: Conflict in Nineteenth-Century Married Life*, London and New York, Routledge, 1992.

Part Three From state medicine to criminal law: purity, feminism and the state 1880–1914

A major expansion of work on the history of sexuality has occurred around the late Victorian period. Judith Walkowitz, *City of Dreadful Delight: Narratives of Sexual Danger in Late-Victorian London*, London, Virago, 1992, is not only a study of nineteenth-century dangerous sexualities and related feminist responses, but also a major contribution to the methodologies of cultural history. In this context see also Elaine Showalter's *fin de siècle* studies: *Sexual Anarchy: Gender and Culture at the Fin de Siècle*, London, Bloomsbury, 1991, and 'Syphilis, Sexuality and the Fiction of the *Fin de Siècle*', in Ruth Yeazell (ed.), *Sex, Politics, and Science in the Nineteenth-Century Novel*, Baltimore and London, Johns Hopkins University Press, 1986, pp. 88–115. Kali Israel explores the narration and interpretations of a late Victorian sex scandal in her 'French Vices and British Liberties: Gender, Class and Narrative Competition in a Late-Victorian Sex Scandal', *Social History*, 1997, vol. 22, no. 1, pp. 1–26, and in her larger study *Names and Stories: Emilia Dilke and Victorian Culture*, New York, Oxford University Press, 1999. Earlier coverage of the Dilke affair is contained in Roy Jenkins, *Dilke: A Victorian Tragedy*, London and Basingstoke, Papermac, 1996, while accounts of other scandals in the same period are the subject of: H. Montgomery Hyde, *The Cleveland Street Scandal*, London, W.H. Allen, 1976; G. H. Fleming, *Victorian 'Sex Goddess': Lady Colin Campbell and the Sensational*

Divorce Case of 1886, Oxford, Oxford University Press, 1990. On the cultural legacy of the Oscar Wilde trial see: Ed Cohen, *Talk on the Wilde Side: Towards a Genealogy of a Discourse on Male Sexualities*, New York and London, Routledge, 1993; Alan Sinfield, *The Wilde Century: Effeminacy, Oscar Wilde and the Queer Moment*, London, Cassell, 1994; Martin Duberman, Martha Vicinus and George Chauncey (eds), *Hidden from History: Reclaiming the Gay and Lesbian Past*, London, Penguin, 1991. For a biographical study of Wilde see Richard Ellman, *Oscar Wilde*, London, Hamish Hamilton, 1987.

Eve Kosofsky Sedgwick analyses the cultural significance of male homosexual relations in literary discourse in *Between Men: English Literature and Male Homosexual Desire*, New York, Columbia University Press, 1985, and in *Epistemology of the Closet*, Berkeley, University of California Press, 1990. Historical studies of same-sex relations between women during this period include: Lillian Faderman, *Surpassing the Love of Men: Romantic Friendship and Love Between Women from the Renaissance to the Present*, London, Women's Press, 1985; Martha Vicinus, *Independent Women: Work and Community for Single Women 1850–1920*, London, Virago, 1985, and her 'Distance and Desire: English Boarding School Friendships, 1870–1920', in Duberman *et al.* (eds), *Hidden from History*, pp. 212–29; Deborah Epstein Nord, ' "Neither Pairs nor Odd": Female Community in Late-Nineteenth Century London', *Signs*, 1990, vol. 15, no. 4, pp. 733–54.

For broader discussion of the formation and regulation of class-specific femininities see: Carol Dyhouse, *Girls Growing Up in Late Victorian and Edwardian England*, London, Routledge & Kegan Paul, 1981; Susan Edwards, *Female Sexuality and the Law: A Study of Constructs of Female Sexuality as They Inform Statute and Legal Procedure*, Oxford, Martin Robertson, 1981; Deborah Gorham, *The Victorian Girl and the Feminine Ideal*, London, Croom Helm, 1982; Anna Davin, *Growing up Poor: Home, School and Street in London 1870–1914*, London, Rivers Oram Press, 1996. Peter Bailey investigates the resonances of female sexuality within late nineteenth-century popular culture in 'Parasexuality and Glamour: The Victorian Barmaid as Cultural Prototype', *Gender and History*, 1990, vol. 2, no. 2, pp. 148–72, while his edited collection, *Music Hall: The Business of Pleasure*, Milton Keynes, Open University Press, 1986, contains studies of this aspect of popular culture. See also in this context Bailey's major series of essays, *Popular Culture and Performance in the Victorian City*, Cambridge, Cambridge University Press, 1998. Penny Boumelha's *Thomas Hardy and Women: Sexual Ideology and Narrative Form*, Brighton, Harvester Press, 1982, contains useful analysis of literary representations of femininity. The relationship between contemporary theories of sexuality and an emergent consumer culture is the subject of Lawrence Birken's *Consuming Desire: Sexual Science and the Emergence of a Culture of Abundance 1871–1914*, Ithaca and London, Cornell University Press, 1988.

The development of a feminist politics of sexuality is the subject of Lucy Bland's important study, *Banishing the Beast: English Feminism and Sexual Morality 1885–1914*, London, Penguin, 1995. In this context see also: Linda Gordon and Ellen DuBois, 'Seeking Ecstasy on the Battlefield: Danger and Pleasure in Nineteenth Century Feminist Sexual Thought', *Feminist Review*, 1983, no. 13, pp. 42–54; Diana Burfield, 'Theosophy and Feminism: Some Explorations in Nineteenth-Century Biography', in Pat Holden (ed.), *Women's Religious Experience*, London, Croom Helm, 1983, pp. 27–56; Pat Jalland, *Women, Marriage and Politics, 1860–1914*,

Oxford, Clarendon Press, 1986; Carol Dyhouse, *Feminism and the Family in England, 1880–1939*, Oxford, Blackwell, 1989; Philippa Levine, ' "So Few Prizes and So Many Blanks": Marriage and Feminism in Late Nineteenth-Century England', *Journal of British Studies*, 1989, vol. 28, pp. 150–74; Mary Lyndon Shanley, *Feminism, Marriage and the Law in Victorian England 1850–1895*, London, I. B.Tauris, 1989; Laura Chrisman, 'Allegory, Feminist Thought and the Dreams of Olive Schreiner', *Prose Studies*, 1990, vol. 13, no. 1, pp. 126–50. On the new woman see Ruth Brandon, *The New Women and the Old Men: Love, Sex and the Woman Question*, London and New York, Secker & Warburg, 1990. Anti-feminist perspectives are addressed in Dorchen Leidholt and Janice Raymond (eds), *The Sexual Liberals and the Attack on Feminism*, Oxford, Pergamon Press, 1990.

The racial dimensions of the representation of female sexuality are the concern of Sander Gilman, 'Black Bodies, White Bodies: Toward an Iconography of Female Sexuality in Late Nineteenth Century Art, Medicine and Literature', *Critical Inquiry*, 1985, no. 12, pp. 204–42, while the impact of racial discourses on early twentieth-century feminism are confronted by: Antoinette Burton, 'The Feminist Quest for Identity: British Imperialist Suffragism and "Global Sisterhood", 1900–1915', *Journal of Women's History*, 1991, vol. 3, no. 2, pp. 46–81, and Mariana Valverde, ' "When the Mother of the Race is Free": Race, Reproduction, and Sexuality in First-Wave Feminism', in Franca Iacovetta and Mariana Valverde (eds), *Gender Conflicts: New Essays in Women's History*, Toronto and London, University of Toronto Press, 1992, pp. 3–27.

For shifting conceptions of the public sphere in the late nineteenth century see Stephan Collini, *Public Moralists: Political Thought and Intellectual Life in Britain, 1850–1930*, Oxford, Clarendon Press, 1991. Feminist understandings of the public domain are the subject of Lucy Bland's 'Purifying the Public World: Feminist Vigilantes in Late Victorian England', *Women's History Review*, 1992, vol. 1, no. 3, pp. 397–412. For feminist uses of strategies of public representation see Lisa Tickner, *The Spectacle of Women: Imagery and the Suffrage Campaign 1907–1914*, London, Chatto & Windus, 1987. On the policing of public space see Philippa Levine, ' "Walking the Streets in a Way No Decent Woman Should": Women Police in World War 1', *Journal of Modern History*, 1994, vol. 66, no.1, pp. 34–78. The new forms of sexual knowledge generated in the period are the subject of Lucy Bland and Laura Doan (eds), *Sexology in Culture: Labelling Bodies and Desires*, Cambridge, Polity Press, 1998.

On male sexuality see Leslie Hall, *Hidden Anxieties: Male Sexuality 1900–1950*, Cambridge, Polity Press, 1991. From a very different perspective see Margaret Jackson, 'Sexology and the Social Construction of Male Sexuality (Havelock Ellis)', in Lal Coveney, M. Jackson, S. Jeffreys, L. Kaye and P. Mahony (eds), *The Sexuality Papers: Male Sexuality and the Social Control of Women*, London, Hutchinson, 1984, pp. 45–68. See also Martha Vicinus' very suggestive piece, 'The Adolescent Boy: Fin de Siècle Femme Fatale?' *Journal of the History of Sexuality*, 1994, vol. 5, no. 1, pp. 90–114.

Part Four From purity to social hygiene: early twentieth-century campaigns for sex education

There is a burgeoning literature addressing the impact of imperialism on gender relations and sexual politics in the early twentieth century. For the relationship to femininity and feminism see: Antoinette Burton, 'The White Woman's Burden: British Feminists and the Indian Woman, 1865–1915', *Women's Studies International Forum*, 1990, vol. 13, no. 4, pp. 295–308; Leonore Manderson, *Sickness and the State: Health and Illness in Colonial Malaya, 1870–1940*, Cambridge, Cambridge University Press, 1996, and her 'Colonial Desires: Sexuality, Race, and Gender in British Malaya', *Journal of the History of Sexuality*, 1997, vol. 7, no. 3, pp. 372–88. For masculinity and empire see Graham Dawson's important study, *Soldier Heroes: British Adventure, Empire, and the Imagining of Masculinities*, London, Routledge, 1994. Other works in this area include: Joseph Bristow, *Empire Boys: Adventures in a Man's World*, London, Unwin Hyman, 1991; Robert MacDonald, *Sons of Empire: The Frontier and the Boy Scout Movement, 1890–1918*, Toronto and London, University of Toronto Press, 1993; Christopher Lane, *The Ruling Passion: British Colonial Allegory and the Paradox of Homosexual Desire*, Durham and London, Duke University Press, 1995; Mrinalini Sinha, *Colonial Masculinity: The 'Manly Englishman' and the 'Effeminate Bengali' in the Late Nineteenth Century*, Manchester, Manchester University Press, 1995; Richard Phillips, *Mapping Men and Empire: A Geography of Adventure*, London, Routledge, 1997. Angus McLaren's *The Trials of Masculinity: Policing Sexual Boundaries 1870–1930*, Chicago and London, University of Chicago Press, 1997, is a broader survey of masculinities during the period.

For studies of the impact of venereal disease see Philippa Levine, 'Venereal Disease, Prostitution, and the Politics of Empire: The Case of British India', *Journal of the History of Sexuality*, 1994, vol. 4, no. 4, pp. 579–602. See also an overview of the venereal disease campaigns in Richard Davenport-Hines' *Sex, Death and Punishment: Attitudes to Sex and Sexuality in Britain since the Renaissance*, London, Collins, 1990. For the eugenic movement see Lyndsay Farrall, *The Origins and Growth of the English Eugenics Movement 1865–1925*, New York and London, Garland, 1985. On populationism see: Allan Soloway, *Birth Control and the Population Question in England, 1877–1930*, Chapel Hill, University of North Carolina Press, 1982; Maria Quine, *Population Politics in Twentieth Century Europe*, London, Routledge, 1996.

For general discussions of the structuring of sex and desire in the twentieth century see Cate Haste, *Rules of Desire: Sex in Britain: World War I to the Present*, London, Chatto & Windus, 1992. On the construction of femininity see Sally Alexander's *Becoming a Woman, and Other Essays in 19th and 20th Century Feminist History*, London, Virago, 1994, and on lesbianism see: Emily Hamer, *Britannia's Glory: A History of Twentieth-Century Lesbians*, London and New York, Cassell, 1996. Susan Kingsley Kent's continuation of her earlier project is *Making Peace: The Reconstruction of Gender in Interwar Britain*, Princeton, Princeton University Press, 1993, while Susan Pedersen examines the role of gender in framing early twentieth-century welfare policy in 'Gender, Welfare and Citizenship in Great Britain during the Great War', *American Historical Review*, 1990, vol. 95, no. 4, pp. 983–1006. On the feminisation of politics in inter-war Britain see Alison Light's highly original study, *Forever England: Femininity, Literature and Conservatism Between the Wars*, London, Routledge, 1991.

On the specific issues of birth-control and sex education see June Rose, *Marie Stopes and the Sexual Revolution*, London, Faber, 1992. For the complexities of Stopes' conception of pleasurable marital intercourse for women, especially working-class women, see Deborah Cohen, 'Private Lives in Public Spaces: Marie Stopes, the Mothers' Clinics and the Practice of Contraception', *History Workshop Journal*, 1993, no. 35, pp. 95–116, and for how some men felt about Stopes' advice see Lesley Hall, 'Impotent Ghosts from No Man's Land, Flappers' Boyfriends, or Crypto-Patriarchs? Men, Sex and Social Change in 1920s Britain', *Social History*, 1996, vol. 21, no. 1, pp. 54–70. On the more informal practices of sex education for women see Sally Alexander, 'The Mysteries and Secrets of Women's Bodies: Sexual Knowledge in the First Half of the Twentieth Century', in Mica Nava and Alan O'Shea (eds), *Modern Times: Reflections on a Century of English Modernity*, London and New York, Routledge, 1996, pp. 161–75.

There is also a growing literature which assesses the impact of late nineteenth- and early twentieth-century forms of consumerism on sexuality and gender relations. For work in this area see: Mica Nava, 'Modernity's Disavowal: Women, the City and the Department Store', in Mica Nava and Alan O'Shea (eds), *Modern Times*, pp. 38–76, and Nava's 'The Cosmopolitanism of Commerce and the Allure of Difference: Selfridges, the Russian Ballet and the Tango 1911–1914', *International Journal of Cultural Studies*, 1998, vol. 1, no. 2, pp. 163–96; Christopher Breward, *The Hidden Consumer*, Manchester, Manchester University Press, 1999. On the cinema and sexuality see Annette Kuhn, *Cinema, Censorship and Sexuality 1909–1925*, London, Routledge, 1988.

Epilogue

On the AIDS crisis there are now numerous social and cultural accounts of the infection and its impact in Britain, the USA and worldwide. Prominent among these are: Simon Watney, *Policing Desire: Pornography, AIDS and the Media*, London, Methuen, 1987; Douglas Crimp (ed.), *AIDS: Cultural Analysis, Cultural Activism*, Cambridge, MA, and London, MIT Press, 1988; Cindy Patton, *Inventing AIDS*, New York and London, Routledge, 1990; Kenneth MacKinnon, *The Politics of Popular Representation: Reagan, Thatcher, AIDS, and the Movies*, London and Toronto, Associated University Presses, 1992; Steven Kruger, *AIDS Narratives: Gender and Sexuality, Fiction and Science*, New York and London, Garland, 1996. For historical studies of the epidemic see: Elizabeth Fee and Daniel Fox (eds), *AIDS: The Burdens of History*, Berkeley and London, University of California Press, 1988; Virginia Berridge and Philip Strong (eds), *AIDS and Contemporary History*, Cambridge, Cambridge University Press, 1993. The relationship of AIDS to broader questions of health policy is dealt with by Virginia Berridge, *AIDS in the UK: The Making of a Policy, 1981–1994*, Oxford, Oxford University Press, 1996. In this context see also: Peter Aggleton and Hilary Homans (eds), *Social Aspects of AIDS*, London, Falmer, 1988; Peter Aggleton, Graham Hart and Peter Davies (eds), *AIDS: Social Representations, Social Practices*, New York and London, Falmer, 1989; Peter Aggleton, Peter Davies and Graham Hart (eds), *AIDS: Individual, Cultural and*

Policy Dimensions, London, Falmer, 1990; Peter Aggleton, Peter Davies and Graham Hart (eds), *AIDS: Foundations for the Future*, London, Taylor & Francis; 1994; Christine Overall, with William Zion (eds), *Perspectives on AIDS: Ethical and Social Issues*, Toronto and Oxford, Oxford University Press, 1991. Political appraisals are contained in: Dennis Altman, *AIDS and the New Puritanism*, London, Pluto, 1986, and in his *Power and Community: Organizational and Cultural Responses to AIDS*, London, Taylor & Francis, 1994; Erica Carter and Simon Watney (eds), *Taking Liberties: AIDS and Cultural Politics*, London, Serpent's Tail in association with the ICA, 1989; Simon Watney, *Practices of Freedom: Selected Writings on HIV/AIDS*, London, Rivers Oram Press, 1994.

The effect of the HIV virus on contemporary sexual practices is the subject of: William Masters, Virginia Johnson and Robert Kolodny, *Crisis: Heterosexual Behaviour in the Age of AIDS*, London, Weidenfeld & Nicolson, 1988; E. Knox, C. MacArthur and K. Simons, *Sexual Behaviour and AIDS in Britain*, London, HMSO, 1993; Gary Dowsett, *Practicing Desire: Homosexual Sex in the Era of AIDS*, Stanford, Stanford University Press, 1996. More popular, and controversial, accounts are provided in Randy Shilts, *And the Band Played On: Politics, People and the AIDS Epidemic*, London, Penguin, 1988; Michael Fumento, *The Myth of Heterosexual AIDS*, New York, Basic Books, 1990; Larry Kramer, *Reports from the Holocaust: The Making of AIDS Activist, Larry Kramer*, Harmondsworth, Penguin, 1990. The issue of sexual representation is addressed in the following texts: Sander Gilman, *Disease and Representation: Images of Illness from Madness to AIDS*, Ithaca and London, Cornell University Press, 1988; Susan Sontag, *AIDS and its Metaphors*, London, Allen Lane, 1989; Tessa Boffin and Sunil Gupta (eds), *Ecstatic Antibodies: Resisting the AIDS Mythology*, London, Rivers Oram Press, 1990; Richard Dellamora, *Apocalyptic Overtures: Sexual Politics and the Sense of an Ending*, New Brunswick, Rutgers University Press, 1994. Women's relationship to the virus is the subject of: Diane Richardson, *Women and the AIDS Crisis*, London, Pandora, 1987; Nicola Swords, '*I Never Promised You a Rose Garden': Female Sexuality , Disease and AIDS*, Department of Sociology, University of Manchester, Manchester Sociology Occasional Papers, no. 26, 1990; Marge Berer, with Sunandra Ray (eds), *Women and HIV/AIDS*, London, Pandora, 1993; Lesley Doyal, Jenny Naido and Tamsin Wilton (eds), *AIDS: Setting a Feminist Agenda*, London, Taylor & Francis, 1994; Cindy Patton, *Last Served? Gendering the HIV Pandemic*, London, Taylor & Francis, 1994.

On the broader dimensions of contemporary sexual politics see: Martin Durham, *Sex and Politics: The Family and Morality in the Thatcher Years*, Basingstoke, Macmillan, 1991; Lynne Segal (ed.), *New Sexual Agendas*, Basingstoke, Macmillan, 1997. On the specific agenda of a radical pluralist sexual politics see: Jeffrey Weeks, *Invented Moralities: Sexual Values in an Age of Uncertainty*, Cambridge, Polity Press, 1995; Kenneth Plummer, *Telling Sexual Stories: Power, Change, and Social Worlds*, London and New York, Routledge, 1994. The wider political and cultural debates about the nature of pluralist democracy are analysed in: Ernesto Laclau and Chantal Mouffe, *Hegemony and Socialist Strategy: Towards a Radical Democratic Politics*, trans. Winston Moore and Paul Cammack, London, Verso, 1985; Richard Rorty, *Contingency, Irony, and Solidarity*, Cambridge, Cambridge University Press, 1989.

The past decade has witnessed a rapid expansion of studies of contemporary masculinities. For historically informed perspectives see: Lynne Segal, *Slow Motion: Changing Masculinities, Changing Men*, London, Virago, 1990; Michael Roper, *Masculinity and the British Organization Man Since 1945*, Oxford, Oxford University Press, 1994; George Mosse and George Lachmann, *The Image of Man: The Creation of Modern Masculinity*, Oxford and New York, Oxford University Press, 1996. For cultural, autobiographical and psychoanalytic analyses see: Andrew Tolson, *The Limits of Masculinity*, London, Tavistock, 1977; Victor Seidler, *Rediscovering Masculinity: Reason, Language and Sexuality*, London, Routledge, 1989; David Gilmore, *Manhood in the Making: Cultural Concepts of Masculinity*, New Haven and London, Yale University Press, 1990; David Jackson, *Unmasking Masculinity: A Critical Autobiography*, London, Unwin Hyman, 1990; Jonathan Rutherford, *Men's Silences: Predicaments in Masculinity*, London, Routledge, 1992; Laurence Goldstein (ed.), *The Male Body: Features, Destinies, Exposures*, Ann Arbor, University of Michigan Press, 1994. For sociological studies see: Arthur Brittan, *Masculinity and Power*, Oxford, Blackwell, 1989; Jeff Hearn and David Morgan (eds), *Men, Masculinities and Social Theory*, London, Unwin Hyman, 1990; David Morgan, *Discovering Men*, London, Routledge, 1992; Victor Seidler, *Unreasonable Men: Masculinity and Social Theory*, London and New York, Routledge, 1994; Robert Connell, *Masculinities*, Cambridge, Polity Press, 1995. For works which foreground the men's movement see: Harry Brod (ed.), *The Making of Masculinities: The New Men's Studies*, Boston and London, Allen & Unwin, 1987; Victor Seidler (ed.), *The Achilles Heel Reader: Men, Sexual Politics and Socialism*, London, Routledge, 1991. For studies of masculinity and contemporary popular culture see: Anthony Easthope, *What a Man's Gotta Do: The Masculine Myth in Popular Culture*, London, Paladin, 1986; Rowena Chapman and Jonathan Rutherford (eds), *Male Order: Unwrapping Masculinity*, London, Lawrence & Wishart, 1988; Frank Mort, *Cultures of Consumption: Masculinities and Social Space in Late Twentieth-Century Britain*, London, Routledge, 1996; Sean Nixon, *Hard Looks: Masculinities, Spectatorship and Contemporary Consumption*, London, UCL Press, 1996.

INDEX